Advance Praise for *Head First iPhone a* ... *ment*

"Rather than textbook-style learning, *Head First iPhone and iPad Development* brings a
and even enjoyable approach to learning iOS development. With coverage of key te...
Core Data and even crucial aspects such as interface design, the content is aptly chosen and ...
Where else could you witness a fireside chat between a UIWebView and UITextField?"

— Sean Murphy, iOS designer and developer

"*Head First iPhone and iPad Development* explains iOS application development from the ground up. Major
enhancements to the first edition cover the changes associated with iOS 4, Xcode 4, and (re-)writing
apps for use on the iPad. The step-by-step approach with an emphasis on the visual makes this a great
way to learn iPhone and iPad app development, from the basics to advanced features."

— Rich Rosen, software developer and co-author of *Mac OS X for Unix Geeks*

"The great thing about this book is its simple, step-by-step approach. It doesn't try to teach everything—it
just launches you right into building iOS applications in a friendly, conversational way. It's a fantastic
book for people who already know how to write code and just want to get straight into the meat of
building iOS applications."

— Eric Shephard, owner of Syndicomm

"*Head First iPhone and iPad Development* was clearly crafted to get you easily creating, using, and learning
iOS technologies without needing a lot of background with Macintosh development tools."

— Joe Heck, Seattle Xcoders founder

"This book is infuriating! Some of us had to suffer and learn iOS development 'the hard way,' and we're
bitter that the jig is up."

— Mike Morrison, Stalefish Labs founder

"*Head First iPhone and iPad Development* continues the growing tradition of taking complex technical subjects
and increasing their accessibility without reducing the depth and scope of the content. iOS development
is a steep learning curve to climb by any measure, but with *Head First iPhone and iPad Development*, that
curve is accompanied with pre-rigged ropes, a harness, and an experienced guide! I recommend this
book for anyone who needs to rapidly improve their understanding of developing for this challenging
and exciting platform."

— Chris Pelsor, snogboggin.com

Praise for other *Head First* books

"*Head First Object-Oriented Analysis and Design* is a refreshing look at subject of OOAD. What sets this book apart is its focus on learning. The authors have made the content of OOAD accessible, usable for the practitioner."

— Ivar Jacobson, Ivar Jacobson Consulting

"I just finished reading HF OOA&D and I loved it! The thing I liked most about this book was its focus on why we do OOA&D—to write great software!"

— Kyle Brown, Distinguished Engineer, IBM

"Hidden behind the funny pictures and crazy fonts is a serious, intelligent, extremely well-crafted presentation of OO Analysis and Design. As I read the book, I felt like I was looking over the shoulder of an expert designer who was explaining to me what issues were important at each step, and why."

— Edward Sciore, Associate Professor, Computer Science Department, Boston College

"All in all, *Head First Software Development* is a great resource for anyone wanting to formalise their programming skills in a way that constantly engages the reader on many different levels."

— Andy Hudson, Linux Format

"If you're a new software developer, *Head First Software Development* will get you started off on the right foot. And if you're an experienced (read: long-time) developer, don't be so quick to dismiss this..."

— Thomas Duff, Duffbert's Random Musings

"There's something in *Head First Java* for everyone. Visual learners, kinesthetic learners, everyone can learn from this book. Visual aids make things easier to remember, and the book is written in a very accessible style—very different from most Java manuals...*Head First Java* is a valuable book. I can see the *Head First* books used in the classroom, whether in high schools or adult ed classes. And I will definitely be referring back to this book, and referring others to it as well."

— Warren Kelly, Blogcritics.org, March 2006

"Another nice thing about *Head First Java, 2nd Edition* is that it whets the appetite for more. With later coverage of more advanced topics such as Swing and RMI, you just can't wait to dive into those APIs and code that flawless, 100000-line program on java.net that will bring you fame and venture-capital fortune. There's also a great deal of material, and even some best practices, on networking and threads—my own weak spot. In this case, I couldn't help but crack up a little when the authors use a 1950s telephone operator—yeah, you got it, that lady with a beehive hairdo that manually hooks in patch lines—as an analogy for TCP/IP ports...you really should go to the bookstore and thumb through *Head First Java, 2nd Edition*. Even if you already know Java, you may pick up a thing or two. And if not, just thumbing through the pages is a great deal of fun."

> **— Robert Eckstein, Java.sun.com, April 2005**

"Of course it's not the range of material that makes *Head First Java* stand out, it's the style and approach. This book is about as far removed from a computer science textbook or technical manual as you can get. The use of cartoons, quizzes, fridge magnets (yep, fridge magnets…). And, in place of the usual kind of reader exercises, you are asked to pretend to be the compiler and compile the code, or perhaps to piece some code together by filling in the blanks or…you get the picture. The first edition of this book was one of our recommended titles for those new to Java and objects. This new edition doesn't disappoint and rightfully steps into the shoes of its predecessor. If you are one of those people who falls asleep with a traditional computer book then this one is likely to keep you awake and learning."

> **— TechBookReport.com, June 2005**

"*Head First Web Design* is your ticket to mastering all of these complex topics, and understanding what's really going on in the world of web design...If you have not been baptized by fire in using something as involved as Dreamweaver, then this book will be a great way to learn good web design. "

> **— Robert Pritchett, MacCompanion, April 2009 Issue**

"Is it possible to learn real web design from a book format? *Head First Web Design* is the key to designing user-friendly sites, from customer requirements to hand-drawn storyboards to online sites that work well. What sets this apart from other 'how to build a web site' books is that it uses the latest research in cognitive science and learning to provide a visual learning experience rich in images and designed for how the brain works and learns best. The result is a powerful tribute to web design basics that any general-interest computer library will find an important key to success."

> **— Diane C. Donovan, California Bookwatch: The Computer Shelf**

"I definitely recommend *Head First Web Design* to all of my fellow programmers who want to get a grip on the more artistic side of the business. "

> **— Claron Twitchell, UJUG**

Other related books from O'Reilly

iOS 4 Programming Cookbook

Programming iOS 4

Augmented Reality in iOS

Graphics and Animation in iOS

iOS 4 Sensor Programming

Writing Game Center Apps in iOS

App Savvy

Other books in O'Reilly's *Head First* series

Head First C#

Head First Java

Head First Object-Oriented Analysis and Design (OOA&D)

Head First HTML with CSS and XHTML

Head First Design Patterns

Head First Servlets and JSP

Head First EJB

Head First SQL

Head First Software Development

Head First JavaScript

Head First Physics

Head First Statistics

Head First Ajax

Head First Rails

Head First Algebra

Head First PHP & MySQL

Head First PMP

Head First Web Design

Head First Networking

Head First iPhone and iPad Development

Second Edition

> Wouldn't it be dreamy if there was a book to help me learn how to develop iOS apps that was more fun than going to the dentist? It's probably nothing but a fantasy...

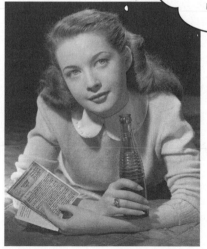

Dan Pilone
Tracey Pilone

O'REILLY®

Beijing • Cambridge • Farnham • Köln • Sebastopol • Tokyo

Head First iPhone and iPad Development

by Dan Pilone and Tracey Pilone

Copyright © 2011 Dan Pilone and Tracey Pilone. All rights reserved.

Printed in the United States of America.

Published by O'Reilly Media, Inc., 1005 Gravenstein Highway North, Sebastopol, CA 95472.

O'Reilly Media books may be purchased for educational, business, or sales promotional use. Online editions are also available for most titles (*http://my.safaribooksonline.com*). For more information, contact our corporate/institutional sales department: (800) 998-9938 or *corporate@oreilly.com*.

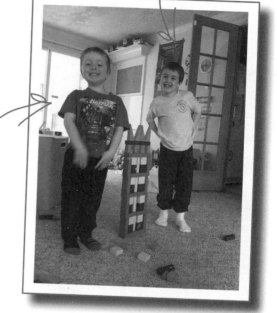

Vinny

Nick

Series Creators:	Kathy Sierra, Bert Bates
Editor:	Courtney Nash
Cover Designer:	Karen Montgomery
Production Editor:	Holly Bauer
Indexer:	Julie Hawks
Proofreader:	Nancy Reinhardt
Page Viewers:	Vinny and Nick

Printing History:

October 2009: First Edition.

June 2011: Second Edition.

ISBN: 978-1-449-38782-2

[M]

To Dan, my best friend, husband, and now business partner; and Vinny and Nick, the best boys a mother could ask for.

—Tracey

This book is dedicated to my family: my parents who made all of this possible, my brothers who keep challenging me, and my wife and sons, who don't just put up with it—they help make it happen.

—Dan

Dan

Tracey

Dan Pilone is the founder and Managing Partner of Element 84, a consulting and mobile software development company. He has designed and implemented systems for NASA, Hughes, ARINC, UPS, and the Naval Research Laboratory. Dan has taught a number of iPhone and iPad development courses for O'Reilly, iPhone Bootcamp, and private development teams. He has taught project management, software design, and software engineering at The Catholic University in Washington, DC.

Dan's previous Head First books are *Head First Software Development* and *Head First Algebra*, so he's used to them being a little out of the ordinary, but this is the first book to involve bounty hunters.

Dan's degree is in computer science with a minor in mathematics from Virginia Tech and he is one of the instructors for the O'Reilly iPhone Development Workshop.

Tracey Pilone is a project manager with Element 84, a startup in the DC area that offers mobile, Web, and backend development services. Recent projects she has worked on include writing for Naval Research Labs and Academic Business Consultants, as well as contributing to other Head First titles and keeping involved with the software development projects at Element 84.

Before working as a writer, she spent several years working in and around the Washington, DC, area for two of ENR's (Engineering News Record) top 20 contractors as a construction manager in commercial construction. She is also the co-author of *Head First Algebra*.

Tracey has a civil engineering degree from Virginia Tech and a masters of education from the University of Virginia, and holds a Professional Engineer's License in Virginia.

Table of Contents (Summary)

Table of Contents (the real thing)

Intro

Your brain on iOS Development. Here *you* are trying to *learn* something, while here your *brain* is doing you a favor by making sure the learning doesn't *stick*. Your brain's thinking, "Better leave room for more important things, like which wild animals to avoid and whether naked snowboarding is a bad idea." So how *do* you trick your brain into thinking that your life depends on knowing enough to develop your own iPhone and iPad apps?

1

getting started

Going Mobile with iOS

The iPhone changed everything.

The iPhone 4 "changed everything, again." And now you've got the iPad to contend with, too. iOS devices are now capable word processors, e-readers, and video cameras. They are being used in business and medicine as enterprise devices and the App Store is a platform for every developer to use, from one-man shows to big name companies. Apple provides the software and we'll help you with the knowledge; we're sure you've got the enthusiasm covered.

iOS app patterns

2

Hello, Renee!

Apps have a lot of moving parts.

OK, actually, they don't have any real moving parts, but they do have lots of **UI controls**. A typical iPhone app has more going on than just a button, and now it's time to build one. Working with some of the **more complicated widgets** means you'll need to pay more attention than ever to how you **design** your app as well. In this chapter, you'll learn how to put together a bigger application and some of the **fundamental design patterns** used in the iOS SDK.

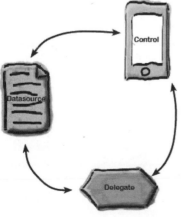

objective-c for iOS

Email needs variety

3

We did a lot in Chapter 2, but what language was that?

Parts of the code you've been writing might look familiar, but it's time you got a sense of what's really going on under the hood. The iOS SDK comes with great tools that mean you don't need to write code for everything, but you can't really write apps without learning something about the underlying language, including properties, message passing, and memory management. Unless you work that out, all your apps will be just default widgets! And you want more than just widgets, right?

Messages going here between textField and the controller.

multiple views

A table with a view

Most iOS apps have more than one View.

4

We've written a cool app with one view, but anyone who's used a smartphone knows that most apps aren't like that. Some of the more impressive iOS apps out there do a great job of working with complex information by using multiple views. We're going to start with navigation controllers and table views, like the kind you see in your Mail and Contact apps. Only we're going to do it with a twist...

plists and modal views
Refining your app

5

So you have this almost-working app...

That's the story of every app! You get some functionality working, decide to add something else, need to do some refactoring, and respond to some feedback from the App Store. Developing an app isn't ~~always~~ ever a linear process, but there's a lot to be learned along the way.

Anatomy of a crash

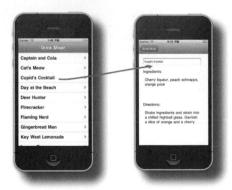

6

saving, editing, and sorting data

Everyone's an editor...

Displaying data is nice, but adding and editing information is what makes an app really hum.

DrinkMixer is great—it uses some cell customization, and works with plist dictionaries to display data. It's a handy reference application, and you've got a good start on adding new drinks. Now, it's time to give the user the ability to modify the data—saving, editing, and sorting—to make it more useful for everyone. In this chapter, we'll take a look at editing patterns in iOS apps and how to guide users with the Nav Controller.

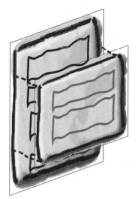

NSNotification object

Red-Headed School Girl

Canadian Whiskey

Cream Soda

Add the whiskey, then the cream soda to a shot glass and drink.

7

migrating to iPad

We need more room

iPhones are great, but a bigger screen can be better.

When the iPad first launched, some panned it by saying that it was "just a big iPhone" (but uh, without the phone). In many ways it is, but that screen opens up many opportunities for better user interaction. More screen real estate means that reading is comfortable, web pages are easily viewed, and the device can act more like a book. Or a calendar. Or many other things that you already know how to use, like a menu...

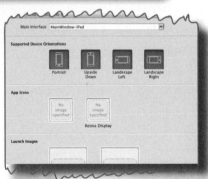

Fireside Chats

Tonight's talk: **Universal App Distribution or not?**

tab bars and core data
Enterprise apps

8

Enterprise apps mean managing more data in different ways.

Companies large and small are a significant market for iPhone and iPad apps. A small handheld device with a custom app can be huge for companies that have staff on the go. Most of these apps are going to manage lots of data, and since iOS 3.0, there has been built-in Core Data support. Working with that and another new controller, the tab bar controller, we're going to build an app for justice!

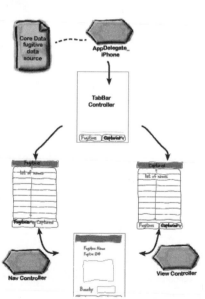

migrating and optimizing with core data

Things are changing

We have a great app in the works.

iBountyHunter successfully loads the data Bob needs and lets him view the fugitives easily. But what about when the data has to change? Bob wants some new functionality, and what does that do to the data model? In this chapter, you'll learn how to handle changes to your data model and how to take advantage of more Core Data features.

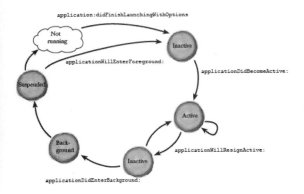

camera, map kit, and core location

10
Proof in the real world
iOS devices know where they are and what they see.

As any iPhone, iPod Touch, or iPad user knows, these devices go way beyond just managing data: they can also take pictures, figure out your location, and put that information together for use in your app. The beauty about incorporating these features is that just by tapping into the tools that iOS gives you, suddenly you can import pictures, locations, and maps without much coding at all.

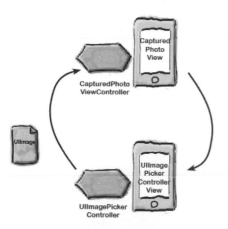

11

iPad UI

Natural interfaces

The iPad is all about existing in the real world.

We've built a basic iPad port of an existing app for DrinkMixer a few chapters back, but now it's time to build an interface that works with some real-world knowledge. By mimicking things that people use in the real world, users know what to do with an interface just by opening the app. We're going to use some real-world elements to help Bob catch the bad guys…

Fugitive.css

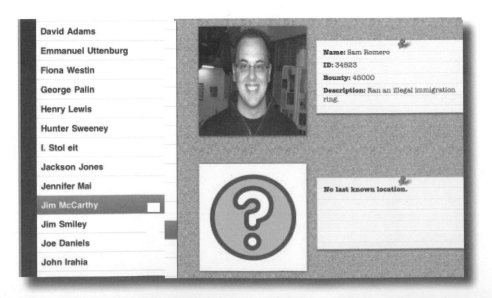

appendix i, leftovers

The top 4 things (we didn't cover)

Ever feel like something's missing? We know what you mean...

Just when you thought you were done, there's more. We couldn't leave you without a few extra details, things we just couldn't fit into the rest of the book. At least, not if you want to be able to carry this book around without a metallic case with castor wheels on the bottom. So take a peek and see what you (still) might be missing out on.

appendix ii, preparing an app for distribution

Get ready for the App Store

You want to get your app in the App Store, right?

So far, we've basically worked with apps in the simulator, which is fine. But to get things to the next level, you'll need to install an app on an actual iPhone, iPad, or iPod Touch before applying to get it in the App Store. And the only way to do that is to register with Apple as a developer. Even then, it's not just a matter of clicking a button in Xcode to get an app you wrote on your personal device. To do that, it's time to talk with Apple.

how to use this book

Intro

In this section, we answer the burning question:
"So why <u>DID</u> they put that in an iOS development book?"

Who is this book for?

If you can answer "yes" to all of these:

① Do you have previous development experience?

② Do you want to **learn**, **understand**, **remember**, and *apply* important iOS design and development concepts so that you can write your own iPhone and iPad apps and start selling them in the App Store?

③ Do you prefer **stimulating dinner party conversation** to **dry**, **dull**, **academic lectures**?

this book is for you.

It definitely helps if you've already got some object-oriented chops, too. Experience with Mac development is helpful, but definitely not required.

Who should probably back away from this book?

If you can answer "yes" to any of these:

① Are you **completely new** to software development?

② Are you already developing iOS apps and looking for a *reference* book on Objective-C?

③ Are you **afraid to try something different**? Would you rather have a root canal than mix stripes with plaid? Do you believe that a technical book can't be serious if there's a bounty hunter in it?

this book is not for you.

Check out Head First Java for an excellent introduction to object-oriented development, and then come back and join us in iPhoneville.

[Note from marketing: this book is for anyone with a credit card. Or cash. Cash is nice, too. — Ed]

We know what you're thinking.

"How can *this* be a serious iOS development book?"

"What's with all the graphics?"

"Can I actually *learn* it this way?"

And we know what your *brain* is thinking.

Your brain craves novelty. It's always searching, scanning, *waiting* for something unusual. It was built that way, and it helps you stay alive.

So what does your brain do with all the routine, ordinary, normal things you encounter? Everything it *can* to stop them from interfering with the brain's *real* job—recording things that *matter*. It doesn't bother saving the boring things; they never make it past the "this is obviously not important" filter.

How does your brain *know* what's important? Suppose you're out for a day hike and a tiger jumps in front of you. What happens inside your head and body?

Neurons fire. Emotions crank up. *Chemicals surge.*

And that's how your brain knows...

This must be important! Don't forget it!

But imagine you're at home, or in a library. It's a safe, warm, tiger-free zone. You're studying. Getting ready for an exam. Or trying to learn some tough technical topic your boss thinks will take a week, 10 days at the most.

Just one problem. Your brain's trying to do you a big favor. It's trying to make sure that this *obviously* non-important content doesn't clutter up scarce resources. Resources that are better spent storing the really *big* things. Like tigers. Like the danger of fire. Like how you should never again snowboard in shorts.

And there's no simple way to tell your brain, "Hey brain, thank you very much, but no matter how dull this book is, and how little I'm registering on the emotional Richter scale right now, I really *do* want you to keep this stuff around."

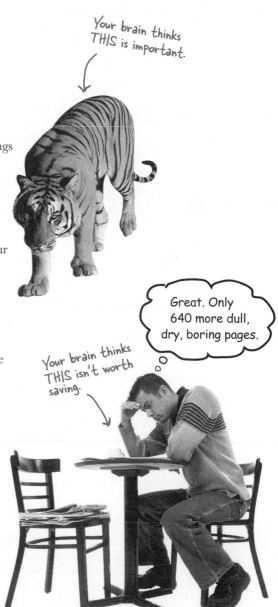

Your brain thinks THIS is important.

Your brain thinks THIS isn't worth saving.

Great. Only 640 more dull, dry, boring pages.

We think of a "Head First" reader as a learner.

So what does it take to *learn* something? First, you have to *get* it, then make sure you don't *forget* it. It's not about pushing facts into your head. Based on the latest research in cognitive science, neurobiology, and educational psychology, *learning* takes a lot more than text on a page. We know what turns your brain on.

Some of the Head First learning principles:

Make it visual. Images are far more memorable than words alone and make learning much more effective (up to 89% improvement in recall and transfer studies). It also makes things more understandable.

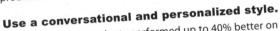

Put the words within or near the graphics they relate to, rather than on the bottom or on another page, and learners will be up to *twice* as likely to solve problems related to the content.

> This sucks. Can't we just import the list from Sam somehow?

Use a conversational and personalized style. In recent studies, students performed up to 40% better on post-learning tests if the content spoke directly to the reader, using a first-person, conversational style rather than taking a formal tone. Tell stories instead of lecturing. Use casual language. Don't take yourself too seriously. Which would *you* pay more attention to: a stimulating dinner party companion, or a lecture?

Get the learner to think more deeply. In other words, unless you actively flex your neurons, nothing much happens in your head. A reader has to be motivated, engaged, curious, and inspired to solve problems, draw conclusions, and generate new knowledge. And for that, you need challenges, exercises, and thought-provoking questions, and activities that involve both sides of the brain and multiple senses.

Get—and keep—the reader's attention. We've all had the "I really want to learn this but I can't stay awake past page one" experience. Your brain pays attention to things that are out of the ordinary, interesting, strange, eye-catching, unexpected. Learning a new, tough, technical topic doesn't have to be boring. Your brain will learn much more quickly if it's not.

> It's so great that Mike and I are communicating now! But I've noticed that Mike's starting to sound like he's in a rut, like saying the same thing over and over again! Is there something we need to talk about?

Touch their emotions. We now know that your ability to remember something is largely dependent on its emotional content. You remember what you care about. You remember when you *feel* something. No, we're not talking heart-wrenching stories about a boy and his dog. We're talking emotions like surprise, curiosity, fun, "what the...?" , and the feeling of "I Rule!" that comes when you solve a puzzle, learn something everybody else thinks is hard, or realize you know something that "I'm more technical than thou" Bob from engineering *doesn't*.

Metacognition: thinking about thinking

If you really want to learn, and you want to learn more quickly and more deeply, pay attention to how you pay attention. Think about how you think. Learn how you learn.

Most of us did not take courses on metacognition or learning theory when we were growing up. We were *expected* to learn, but rarely *taught* to learn.

I wonder how I can trick my brain into remembering this stuff...

But we assume that if you're holding this book, you really want to learn about iOS development. And you probably don't want to spend a lot of time. And since you're going to build more apps in the future, you need to *remember* what you read. And for that, you've got to *understand* it. To get the most from this book, or *any* book or learning experience, take responsibility for your brain. Your brain on *this* content.

The trick is to get your brain to see the new material you're learning as Really Important. Crucial to your well-being. As important as a tiger. Otherwise, you're in for a constant battle, with your brain doing its best to keep the new content from sticking.

So just how *DO* you get your brain to think that iOS development is a hungry tiger?

There's the slow, tedious way, or the faster, more effective way. The slow way is about sheer repetition. You obviously know that you *are* able to learn and remember even the dullest of topics if you keep pounding the same thing into your brain. With enough repetition, your brain says, "This doesn't *feel* important to him, but he keeps looking at the same thing *over* and *over* and *over*, so I suppose it must be."

The faster way is to do **anything that increases brain activity,** especially different *types* of brain activity. The things on the previous page are a big part of the solution, and they're all things that have been proven to help your brain work in your favor. For example, studies show that putting words *within* the pictures they describe (as opposed to somewhere else on the page, like a caption or in the body text) causes your brain to try to makes sense of how the words and picture relate, and this causes more neurons to fire. More neurons firing = more chances for your brain to *get* that this is something worth paying attention to, and possibly recording.

A conversational style helps because people tend to pay more attention when they perceive that they're in a conversation, since they're expected to follow along and hold up their end. The amazing thing is, your brain doesn't necessarily *care* that the "conversation" is between you and a book! On the other hand, if the writing style is formal and dry, your brain perceives it the same way you experience being lectured to while sitting in a roomful of passive attendees. No need to stay awake.

But pictures and conversational style are just the beginning.

Here's what WE did:

We used **pictures**, because your brain is tuned for visuals, not text. As far as your brain's concerned, a picture really *is* worth a thousand words. And where text and pictures work together, we embedded the text *in* the pictures because your brain works more effectively when the text is *within* the thing the text refers to, as opposed to in a caption or buried in the text somewhere.

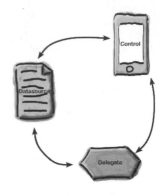

We used **redundancy**, saying the same thing in *different* ways and with different media types, and *multiple senses*, to increase the chance that the content gets coded into more than one area of your brain.

We used concepts and pictures in **unexpected** ways because your brain is tuned for novelty, and we used pictures and ideas with at least *some* **emotional** *content*, because your brain is tuned to pay attention to the biochemistry of emotions. That which causes you to *feel* something is more likely to be remembered, even if that feeling is nothing more than a little **humor**, **surprise**, or **interest**.

We used a personalized, **conversational style**, because your brain is tuned to pay more attention when it believes you're in a conversation than if it thinks you're passively listening to a presentation. Your brain does this even when you're *reading*.

We included loads of **activities**, because your brain is tuned to learn and remember more when you **do** things than when you *read* about things. And we made the exercises challenging-yet-do-able, because that's what most people prefer.

BULLET POINTS

We used **multiple learning styles**, because *you* might prefer step-by-step procedures, while someone else wants to understand the big picture first, and someone else just wants to see an example. But regardless of your own learning preference, *everyone* benefits from seeing the same content represented in multiple ways.

Fireside Chats

We include content for **both sides of your brain**, because the more of your brain you engage, the more likely you are to learn and remember, and the longer you can stay focused. Since working one side of the brain often means giving the other side a chance to rest, you can be more productive at learning for a longer period of time.

And we included **stories** and exercises that present **more than one point of view,** because your brain is tuned to learn more deeply when it's forced to make evaluations and judgments.

We included **challenges**, with exercises, and asked **questions** that don't always have a straight answer, because your brain is tuned to learn and remember when it has to *work* at something. Think about it—you can't get your *body* in shape just by *watching* people at the gym. But we did our best to make sure that when you're working hard, it's on the *right* things. That **you're not spending one extra dendrite** processing a hard-to-understand example, or parsing difficult, jargon-laden, or overly terse text.

We used **people**. In stories, examples, pictures, etc., because, well, *you're* a person. And your brain pays more attention to *people* than it does to *things*.

Here's what YOU can do to bend your brain into submission

So, we did our part. The rest is up to you. These tips are a starting point; listen to your brain and figure out what works for you and what doesn't. Try new things.

Cut this out and stick it on your refrigerator.

----

(1) Slow down. The more you understand, the less you have to memorize.

Don't just *read*. Stop and think. When the book asks you a question, don't just skip to the answer. Imagine that someone really *is* asking the question. The more deeply you force your brain to think, the better chance you have of learning and remembering.

(2) Do the exercises. Write your own notes.

We put them in, but if we did them for you, that would be like having someone else do your workouts for you. And don't just *look* at the exercises. **Use a pencil.** There's plenty of evidence that physical activity *while* learning can increase the learning.

(3) Read the "There Are No Dumb Questions" sections.

That means all of them. They're not optional sidebars—*they're part of the core content!* Don't skip them.

(4) Make this the last thing you read before bed. Or at least the last challenging thing.

Part of the learning (especially the transfer to long-term memory) happens *after* you put the book down. Your brain needs time on its own, to do more processing. If you put in something new during that processing time, some of what you just learned will be lost.

(5) Drink water. Lots of it.

Your brain works best in a nice bath of fluid. Dehydration (which can happen before you ever feel thirsty) decreases cognitive function.

(6) Talk about it. Out loud.

Speaking activates a different part of the brain. If you're trying to understand something, or increase your chance of remembering it later, say it out loud. Better still, try to explain it out loud to someone else. You'll learn more quickly, and you might uncover ideas you didn't know were there when you were reading about it.

(7) Listen to your brain.

Pay attention to whether your brain is getting overloaded. If you find yourself starting to skim the surface or forget what you just read, it's time for a break. Once you go past a certain point, you won't learn faster by trying to shove more in, and you might even hurt the process.

(8) Feel something!

Your brain needs to know that this *matters*. Get involved with the stories. Make up your own captions for the photos. Groaning over a bad joke is *still* better than feeling nothing at all.

(9) Create something!

Apply this to your daily work; use what you're learning to make decisions on your projects. Just do something to get some experience beyond the exercises and activities in this book. All you need is a pencil and a problem to solve…a problem that might benefit from using the tools and techniques you're studying for the exam.

Read me

This is a learning experience, not a reference book. We deliberately stripped out everything that might get in the way of learning whatever it is we're working on at that point in the book. And the first time through, you need to begin at the beginning, because the book makes assumptions about what you've already seen and learned.

We start off by building an app in the very first chapter.

Believe it or not, even if you've never developed for iOS before, you can jump right in and starting building apps. You'll also learn your way around the tools used for iOS development.

We don't worry about preparing your app to submit to the App Store until the end of book.

In this book, you can get on with the business of learning how to create iOS apps without stressing over the packaging and distribution of your app out of the gate. But we know that's what everyone who wants to build an iOS app ultimately wants to do, so we cover that process (and all its glorious gotchas) in an Appendix at the end.

We focus on what you can build and test on the simulator.

The iOS SDK comes with a great (and free!) tool for testing your apps on your computer. The simulator lets you try out your code without having to worry about getting it in the app store or on a real device. But, it also has its limits. There's some cool iOS stuff you just can't test on the simulator, like the accelerometer and compass. So, we don't cover those kinds of things in very much detail in this book since we want to make sure you're creating and testing apps quickly and easily.

The activities are NOT optional.

The exercises and activities are not add-ons—they're part of the core content of the book. Some of them are to help with memory, some are for understanding, and some will help you apply what you've learned. ***Don't skip the exercises.*** Even crossword puzzles are important—they'll help get concepts into your brain so they stay there when you're coding. But more importantly, they're good for giving your brain a chance to think about the words and terms you've been learning in a different context.

The redundancy is intentional and important.

One distinct difference in a Head First book is that we want you to *really* get it. And we want you to finish the book remembering what you've learned. Most reference books don't have retention and recall as a goal, but this book is about *learning*, so you'll see some of the same concepts come up more than once.

The Brain Power exercises don't have answers.

For some of them, there is no right answer, and for others, part of the learning experience of the Brain Power activities is for you to decide if and when your answers are right. In some of the Brain Power exercises, you will find hints to point you in the right direction.

System requirements

To develop for the iPhone and iPad, you need an Intel-based Mac, period. We wrote this book using Snow Leopard and Xcode 4.0. If you're running Leopard with an older version of Xcode, we tried to point out where there were places that would trip you up. For some of the more advanced capabilities, like the accelerometer and the camera, you'll need an actual iPhone, iPod Touch, or iPad and to be a registered developer. In Chapter 1, we tell you where to get the SDK and Apple documentation, so don't worry about that for now.

The technical review team

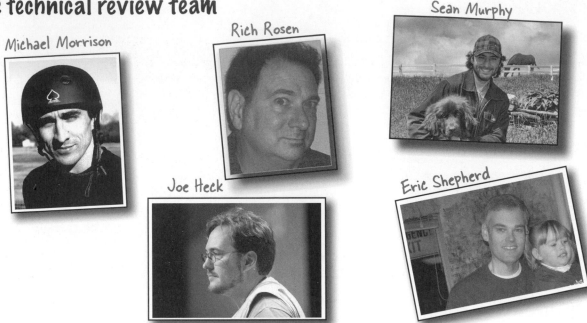

Michael Morrison

Rich Rosen

Sean Murphy

Joe Heck

Eric Shepherd

Rich Rosen is one of the co-authors of *Mac OS X for Unix Geeks*. He also collaborated with Leon Shklar on *Web Application Architecture: Principles, Protocols & Practices*, a textbook on advanced web application development. He began his career eons ago at Bell Labs, where his work with relational databases, Unix, and the Internet prepared him well for the world of web technology. He lives in New Jersey with his wife, Celia, whose singing provides a sweet counterpoint to the cacophony he produces in his Mac-based home recording studio.

Sean Murphy has been a Cocoa aficionado for almost 10 years, contributes to open source projects such as Camino, and works as an independent iOS designer and developer. He lives in Pennsylvania with his best friends—a fiancée, horses, dogs, and cats—and seriously loves hiking, hockey, and nature.

Joe Heck is a software developer, technology manager, author, and instructor who's been involved with computing for 25 years and developing for the iPhone platform since the first beta release. He's the founder of the Seattle Xcoders developer group, which supports Macintosh and iPhone development in the Seattle area, and the author of SeattleBus, an iPhone app that provides real-time arrival and departure times of Seattle public transportation (available on the App Store).

Eric Shepherd got started programming at age nine and never looked back. He's been a technical writer, writing developer documentation since 1997, and is currently the developer documentation lead at Mozilla. In his spare time, he writes software for old Apple II computers—because his day job just isn't geeky enough—and spends time with his daughter. His thorough review means that no one else has to go through the problems he had in actually making the code work.

Michael Morrison is a writer, developer, and author of *Head First JavaScript*, *Head First PHP & MySQL*, and even a few books that don't have squiggly arrows, stick figures, and magnets. Michael is the founder of Stalefish Labs (*www.stalefishlabs.com*), an edutainment company specializing in games, toys, and interactive media, including a few iPhone apps. Michael spends a lot of time wearing helmets, be it for skateboarding, hockey, or iPhone debugging. Since he has iPhone Head First experience, Mike was a great resource to have helping us.

Acknowledgments

Our editors:

Thanks to **Courtney Nash**, who has turned into not just our editor, but general all-around O'Reilly handler. She has listened to lots of rants, spent a week on camera with Dan, and still managed to carry us through two updates to the book, one that didn't get published! She has had her hand in every single one of the over 600 pages in the book and it's better because of her involvement.

Courtney Nash

Brett McLaughlin

And to **Brett McLaughlin**, who kicked off the first edition of this book by responding to an IM that said, "What do you think about Head First iPhone?" and trained us both up in the ways of Head First.

The O'Reilly team:

To **Karen Shaner**, who, as always, kept things running smoothly, which is helpful when we keep changing things. And to **Laurie Petrycki,** who continues to let us write more Head First books, which apparently is habit forming.

Our friends and family:

To all the **Pilones** and **Chadwicks**, who have always been supportive of our efforts and helped us to become grown ups who can write this stuff. To all our friends at **Element 84**, who have made this book part of our company and helped us create a place where we enjoy working. And to **Paul**, who in addition to kicking off this Apple thing by bringing Macs into our house years ago, was employee #1 at Element 84 and a proofreader of this book.

To **Vinny** and **Nick**, who think that everybody's parents work together, thank you for putting up with us constantly talking about iOS development. We're hoping they're going to be ready to intern this summer.

Finally, to **Apple**, as silly as it sounds, because iOS development has been good to us! We thought the iPhone was great, but the iPad has already changed how we read and interact with the Web. We're looking forward to being a part of that change.

Safari® Books Online

 Safari® Books Online is an on-demand digital library that lets you easily search over 7,500 technology and creative reference books and videos to find the answers you need quickly.

With a subscription, you can read any page and watch any video from our library online. Read books on your cell phone and mobile devices. Access new titles before they are available for print, and get exclusive access to manuscripts in development and post feedback for the authors. Copy and paste code samples, organize your favorites, download chapters, bookmark key sections, create notes, print out pages, and benefit from tons of other time-saving features.

O'Reilly Media has uploaded this book to the Safari Books Online service. To have full digital access to this book and others on similar topics from O'Reilly and other publishers, sign up for free at *http://my.safaribooksonline.com*.

1 getting started

Going Mobile with iOS

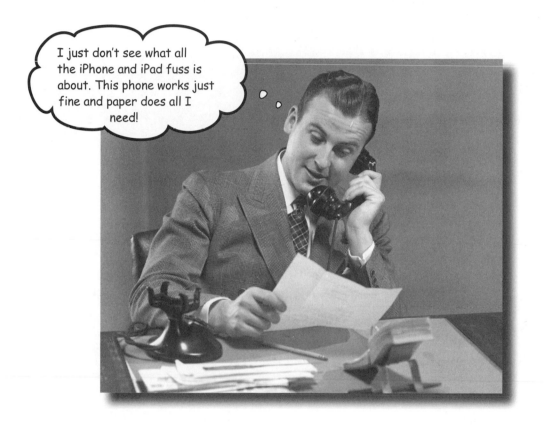

I just don't see what all the iPhone and iPad fuss is about. This phone works just fine and paper does all I need!

The iPhone changed everything.

The iPhone 4 "changed everything, again." And now you've got the iPad to contend with, too. iOS devices are now capable word processors, e-readers, and video cameras. They are being used in business and medicine as enterprise devices, and the App Store is a platform for every developer to use, from one-man shows to big-name companies. Apple provides the software and we'll help you with the knowledge—we're sure you've got the enthusiasm covered.

So, you want to build an iOS app...

Maybe you use an iPhone all the time and wish "it could do that." Maybe you have an app you love that could be **so** much better. You might have a business that wants to leverage computing power that fits in your customers' hands. Or perhaps you have an idea for an app that could start a business. There are a lot of motivations to want to code for iPhone and iPad, and lots of customers, too.

Your App here...

...'cause everyone wants one!

There's a big market out there for iPhone and iPad developers. iOS apps are rapidly becoming advertising tools that non-tech businesses want to use, like websites. Enterprises are starting to use iPhones, iPads, and iPod Touches for employees to perform work that they once did with a clipboard or even a laptop.

But while there's a lot of opportunity, there's also plenty for you to learn, even as an experienced OO developer. Most companies are choosing to outsource iOS development work, making it a great opportunity for freelancers, too.

Just look at the app store

At the time this book went to print, there were over 500,000 different apps available for download from the App Store. More than that, the percentage of apps for sale that are games has held steady, while the gross number of apps continues to rise.

That means that the number of apps for sale that allow users to perform a task is going up; people are integrating mobile computing into their lives for more than just playing.

Let's start with how an app gets from your head to a device...

Apps live in an iTunes universe

To get an app approved, sold, distributed, or installed, you need to work with the Apple iOS SDK before getting your app into the iTunes App Store. Here's a quick picture of the cycle of which you're going to be a part.

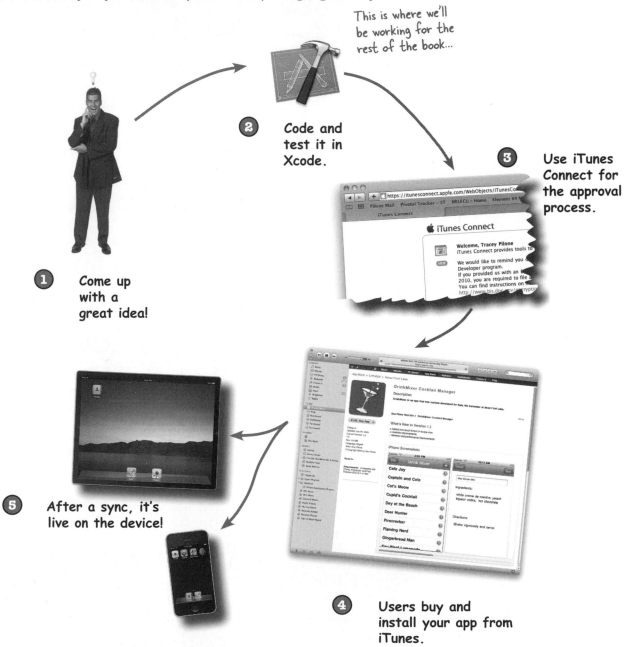

This is where we'll be working for the rest of the book...

2 Code and test it in Xcode.

3 Use iTunes Connect for the approval process.

1 Come up with a great idea!

5 After a sync, it's live on the device!

4 Users buy and install your app from iTunes.

Time to make a decision

You're probably brimming with app ideas, but for this first one, we're going to start simple. Our first application is pretty straightforward: it is going to be a single view with a button that the user can push to make a decision. For now we'll build this just for iPhone; we'll get into iPads a bit later in the book.

When users start up your application, the first thing they see is a **view**. It's essentially the user interface, and it needs to be easy to use and focused on what your application is supposed to do. Throughout this book, whenever we start a new application, we're going to take a little time to sketch up what we want our views to look like.

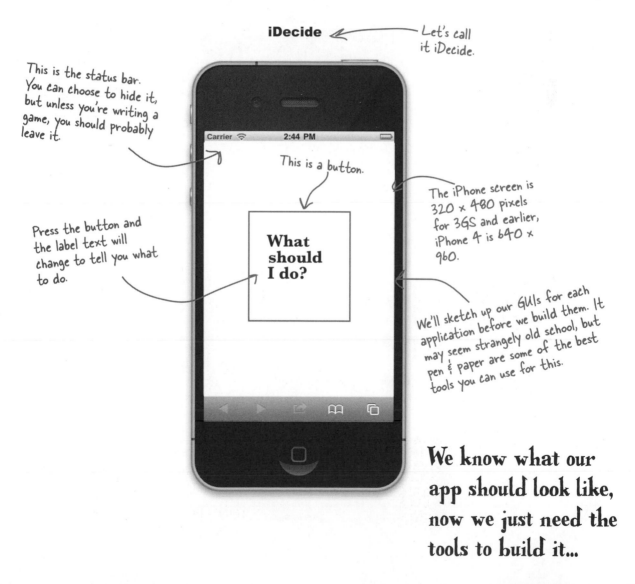

iDecide

Let's call it iDecide.

This is the status bar. You can choose to hide it, but unless you're writing a game, you should probably leave it.

This is a button.

The iPhone screen is 320 x 480 pixels for 3GS and earlier, iPhone 4 is 640 x 960.

Press the button and the label text will change to tell you what to do.

What should I do?

We'll sketch up our GUIs for each application before we build them. It may seem strangely old school, but pen & paper are some of the best tools you can use for this.

We know what our app should look like, now we just need the tools to build it...

It all starts with the iOS SDK

Head over to *http://developer.apple.com/ios*. You can download the SDK (and other useful Apple development resources) for free with the basic registration—but to distribute a completed app in the App Store or install your app on an iPhone, iPod Touch, or iPad for testing, you'll need to become a paid Standard or Enterprise Developer. The basic registration provides the SDK with a simulator for testing directly on your Mac, so you can go the free route for now to get started.

☐ Register as a developer at *http://developer.apple.com/ios*.

☐ Download the latest SDK; this book is based on the 4.3 SDK. Just look for the **Download** button at the top of the page.

☐ Install the SDK. Once the Installation completes, you can find Xcode.app in /Developer/Applications.

You will probably want to drag it onto your Dock—we're going to be using it a lot.

Take a look around

Navigate over to the install directory, which is /Developer/Applications by default. If your installation went right, the install directory should have a few key things.

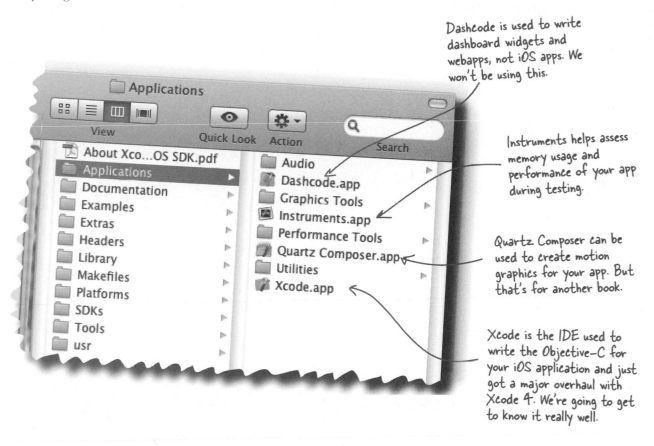

Dashcode is used to write dashboard widgets and webapps, not iOS apps. We won't be using this.

Instruments helps assess memory usage and performance of your app during testing.

Quartz Composer can be used to create motion graphics for your app. But that's for another book.

Xcode is the IDE used to write the Objective-C for your iOS application and just got a major overhaul with Xcode 4. We're going to get to know it really well.

The iPhone Simulator (installed in /Developer/Platforms/ iPhoneSimulator.platform/Developer/Applications/iPhoneSimulator. App) lets you run iOS in a simulated device on your Mac for simplified app testing while you're writing code. We'll be firing this up shortly, too.

Now that you have everything installed, go ahead and double-click on Xcode to get it started.

Xcode includes app templates to help you get started

When you start Xcode, you'll get a welcome screen where you can select **Create a New Project**. Each project is a collection of files (a.k.a. a template) that have some info and code already populated based on the type of project.

These are the basic App templates. Based on your selection, different code and files are set up for you.

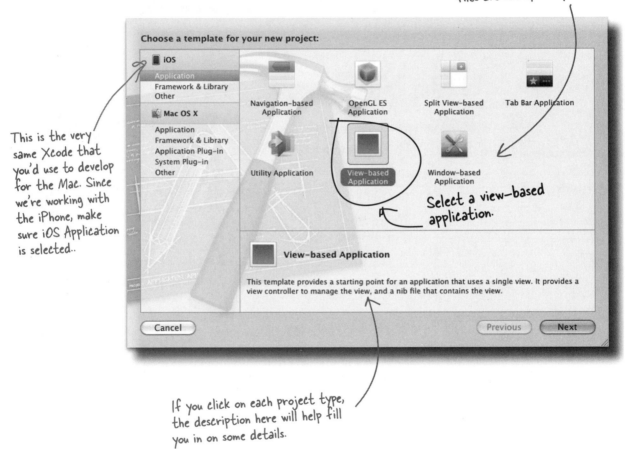

This is the very same Xcode that you'd use to develop for the Mac. Since we're working with the iPhone, make sure iOS Application is selected..

Select a view-based application.

If you click on each project type, the description here will help fill you in on some details.

As we go through the book, we'll use different types of projects and discuss why you'd choose one over another for each app. For iDecide, we have just one screen (or view), so start with the **View-based Application** and give it the **Product Name** iDecide. Leave the **Device Family** as iPhone and uncheck the box for **Include Unit Tests**. In the final dialog box, uncheck the box for **Create Local Git Repository.**

Xcode is a full-featured IDE

Xcode is much more than just a text editor. As you've already seen, Xcode includes templates to get you started developing an application. Depending on your application, you may use all of a template or just parts of it, but you'll almost always start with one of them. Once you get your basic app template in place, you'll use Xcode for a lot more:

Maintaining your project resources

Xcode will create a new directory for your project and sort the various files into subdirectories. You don't have to stick with the default layout, but if you decide to reorganize, do it from within Xcode. Xcode also has built-in support for version control tools like Git and Subversion and can be used to check out and commit your project changes.

Editing your code and resources

You'll use Xcode to edit your application code, and it supports a variety of languages beyond just Objective-C. Xcode also has a number of built-in editors for resource files like plists and xib and nib files (we'll talk more about these later on). For resources Xcode doesn't handle natively, double-clicking on one of those files in Xcode will launch the appropriate editor. Some file types Xcode can only view, like pictures, or it will merely list, like sound files.

Building and testing your application

Xcode comes with all of the compilers necessary to build your code and generate a working application. Once your application is compiled, Xcode can install it on the iOS Simulator or a real device. Xcode includes LLVM and GDB debuggers with both graphical and command-line interfaces to let you debug your application. You can also launch profiling tools like Instruments to check for memory or performance issues.

Prepare your application for sale

Once you get your application thoroughly tested and you're ready to sell it, Xcode manages your provisioning profiles and code signing certificates that let you put your application on real devices or upload it to the iTunes App Store for sale. We've got more info on this process in the Appendix.

⟶ Turn the page to see what Xcode looks like.

Xcode is the hub of your iOS project

When Xcode opens your new View-based project, it is populated with all of the files that you see here, but we've changed the view a bit. By expanding the project and selecting a .xib file (which is your view, more on that in a minute), the GUI editor is open on the left. To open the side-by-side assistant view, click the Assistant Editor button on the upper right of the editor.

Here is where you can configure whether to build your app for the simulator or a real device. We'll stick with the simulator throughout the book.

The iDecide folder has all the Objective-C class files that make up your app, as well as the .xib files that will make up the views for your app.

Every class has a .h (header) and .m (implementation) file to go with it.. They work together to create each class.

Supporting Files include your main function and an application-wide header file, pictures, data, and other data that your app will need to run.

Frameworks shows a list of the libraries you're using.

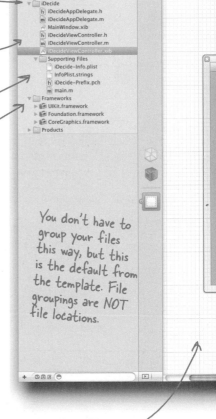

You don't have to group your files this way, but this is the default from the template. File groupings are NOT file locations.

The Editor Pane shows the selected file with the appropriate editor. We've selected the default view for iDecide, so you can see the GUI editor.

The toolbar includes options for setting breakpoints, building and running your application, searching, and showing warnings and file listings.

This button changes your view to show the Assistant Editor.

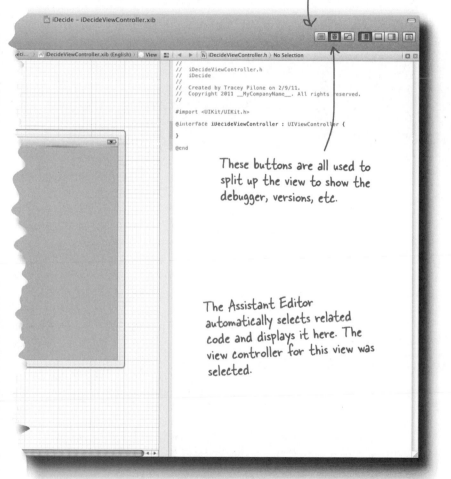

iDecide – iDecideViewController.xib

eci... ⟩ iDecideViewController.xib (English) ⟩ View ⟩ ◀ ▶ ⟩ h iDecideViewController.h ⟩ No Selection

```
//
//  iDecideViewController.h
//  iDecide
//
//  Created by Tracey Pilone on 2/9/11.
//  Copyright 2011 __MyCompanyName__. All rights reserved.
//

#import <UIKit/UIKit.h>

@interface iDecideViewController : UIViewController {

}

@end
```

These buttons are all used to split up the view to show the debugger, versions, etc.

The Assistant Editor automatically selects related code and displays it here. The view controller for this view was selected.

We'll be using some of the other tools that came with the SDK (especially the Simulator), but they are all working with the files that are included here.

The files and frameworks shown were stubbed out based on our selection of a View-based application. As we go forward, we'll use different types of apps, and that will lead to different defaults.

For our app, the template includes iDecideViewController.h and iDecideViewController.m. Every Objective-C class in the template has both a **header** (.h) and an **implementation** (.m) file. When the app is compiled, they work together to create a class. We'll dive into the view controller shortly.

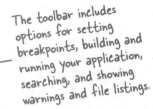

Geek Bits

Frameworks are what libraries are called in Objective-C. UIKit, CoreGraphics, and Foundation are loaded by default, but we'll show you how to add more later.

Xcode Files Up Close

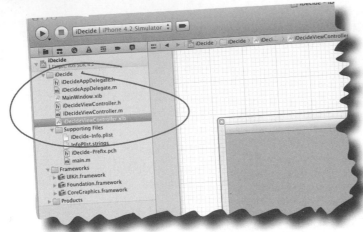

If you take a closer look at the files that were generated by Xcode, you'll see iDecideViewController.h and iDecideViewController.m, as well as iDecideAppDelegate.h and iDecideAppDelegate.m. Those .h and .m pairs work together to create a class.

You'll also see the iDecideViewController.xib file. It creates the first view for the app.

> OK, so I have an idea about how Xcode is organized. But what about the views? What are those .xib files anyway, and do I work with them in XCode, too?

Sort of—the GUI editor in XCode handles .xib files.

Those .xib files (also called "nibs") are XML documents that are loaded by the Cocoa Touch framework when the app starts up. We'll talk a lot more about this in the next chapter, but for now it's just important to understand that the GUI editor in XCode (often also called Interface Builder) is not creating Objective-C code. It's creating an XML description of the GUI you're building, and the Cocoa Touch framework uses that to actually create the buttons and whatnot for your application at runtime. Everything we do in Interface Builder *could* be done in pure Objective-C code, but as you'll see, there are some things that are really just easier to lay out with a GUI builder.

We'll be using "GUI Editor" and "Interface Builder" to mean the same thing.

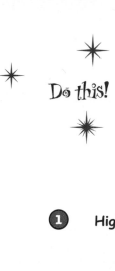

Do this!

To edit the view files in Xcode, you'll need to open up the .xib file and change some settings in the workspace.

1 Highlight the iDecideViewController.xib file.

2 Close the Assistant Editor by clicking this button.

Only necessary if you opened it earlier to see the editor. We'll use it more later, but we're focusing on the GUI for now.

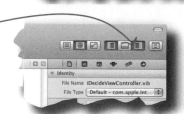

3 Show the library by opening the Utilities Pane, here.

4 Show the Objects Library for the views by clicking on this button.

5 Adjust the size of the library by dragging this bar up.

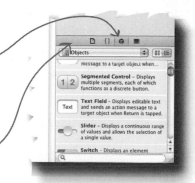

Build your interface within Xcode

When you open up any .xib file in Xcode, the GUI editor will be launched in the main window. With the view tweaking you just finished on the previous page, Xcode will be ready to work with the views. Now it shows an overview of items in your nib, your view, and a library of UI elements (on the right). You can drag and drop any of the basic library elements into your view, edit them, and work with the connections between the code and these elements, using the assistant editor. All of these elements come from the Cocoa Touch framework, a custom UI framework for iOS devices.

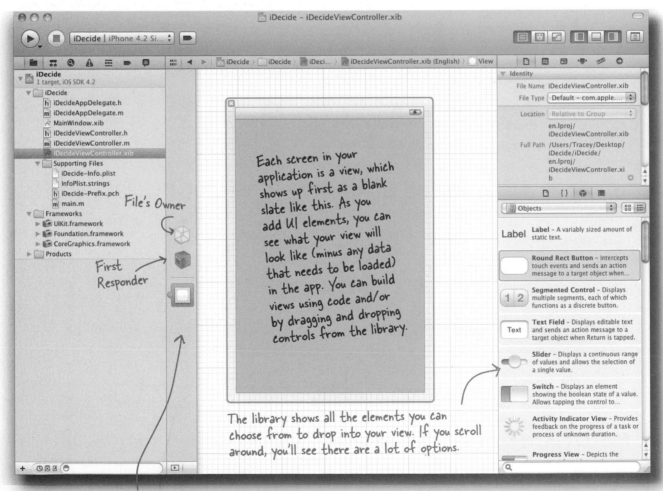

Each screen in your application is a view, which shows up first as a blank slate like this. As you add UI elements, you can see what your view will look like (minus any data that needs to be loaded) in the app. You can build views using code and/or by dragging and dropping controls from the library.

The library shows all the elements you can choose from to drop into your view. If you scroll around, you'll see there are a lot of options.

This section shows the objects and views that are currently created for that particular nib. File's Owner and the First Responder exist for every nib, and the others will vary. We'll talk about both in much greater detail later.

Add the button to your view

To add elements, all you need to do is drag and drop the
elements you want onto your view. For our app, we just need a
button with text that can be changed.

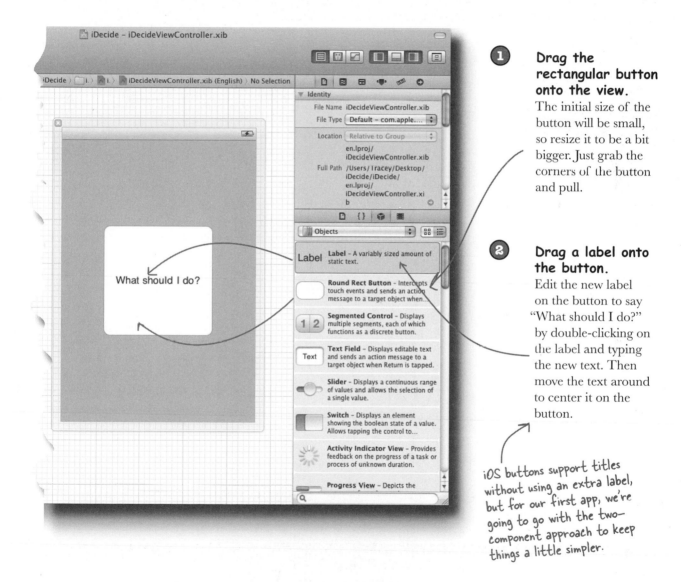

1 Drag the
rectangular button
onto the view.
The initial size of the
button will be small,
so resize it to be a bit
bigger. Just grab the
corners of the button
and pull.

2 Drag a label onto
the button.
Edit the new label
on the button to say
"What should I do?"
by double-clicking on
the label and typing
the new text. Then
move the text around
to center it on the
button.

iOS buttons support titles
without using an extra label,
but for our first app, we're
going to go with the two-
component approach to keep
things a little simpler.

TEST DRIVE

Now, **save** your work. To build the file, make sure that the scheme selected is the "iPhone 4.x Simulator," then press the **Build and Run** button here.

Welcome to the iPhone Simulator!

What should I do?

The iOS simulator lets you test your app on your Mac

The Simulator is a great tool for testing your apps quickly and for free. It doesn't come with all the applications that a real device does, but for the most part, it behaves the same way. When you first start the simulator, you see the **springboard**—just like on a real iPhone (it's the initial screen that shows all your app icons)—with iDecide installed (and a default icon that you can change later). Xcode then opens the app and your code is running.

There are some differences between using the Simulator and your iPhone. For starters, shaking and rotating your Mac won't accomplish anything, so those don't work in the Simulator. To approximate rotation and check landscape and portrait views, there are some commands under the **Hardware** menu. You also have limited gesture support, CPU and memory usage don't represent reality, and hardware capabilities like tilt sensors (or the accelerometer or gyroscope) don't exist at all.

Even with these issues, testing on the simulator is just so much quicker and easier than a real device that you'll find you use it for major portions of your development. You can always start with the Simulator and then move to a real device as your application (or hardware needs) mature.

You don't have to do anything special to launch the Simulator other than build and run your app.

Watch it!

The Simulator has limitations.

*Memory, performance, camera, GPS, and other characteristics **cannot** be reliably tested using the Simulator. We'll talk more about these later, but memory usage and performance are tough to test on the simulator simply because your Mac has so many more resources than the iPhone or iPad. To test these things, you need to install on an actual device (which means joining one of the paid development programs).*

So, you probably want to push this button right now and see what happens, right? Go ahead...

OK, so the button exists, but it doesn't do anything. It needs a little code, right?

UI behavior is implemented in Objective-C.

Interface Builder creates your button, but to make that button actually *do* something, you'll need to write some code that tells the button how to behave.

Controls—which are the UI elements like the button you just added—trigger **events** when things happen to them, like the button being pressed. For events like button presses, Interface Builder can connect the view controls with code in your controller class for action methods, tagged with IBAction (for Interface Builder Action). We'll talk more about the Objective-C syntax for actions a bit later, but for now, you'll need to declare a method in your header (.h) file and implement it in the .m.

iDecide's logic

Any controls you create need a method that Interface Builder can use to connect the control to behaviors specified in the implementation file.

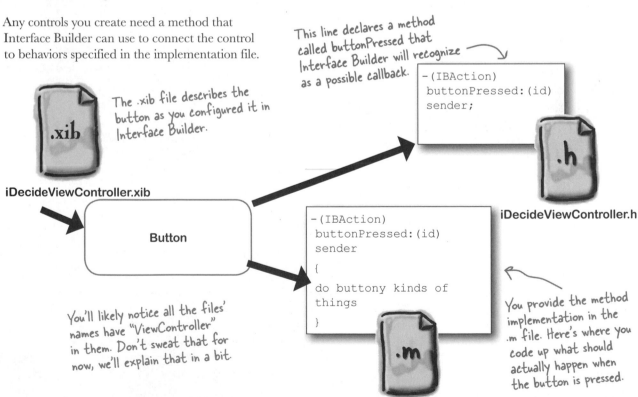

The .xib file describes the button as you configured it in Interface Builder.

iDecideViewController.xib

This line declares a method called buttonPressed that Interface Builder will recognize as a possible callback.

```
-(IBAction)
buttonPressed:(id)
sender;
```

iDecideViewController.h

Button

```
-(IBAction)
buttonPressed:(id)
sender
{

do buttony kinds of
things

}
```

iDecideViewController.m

You'll likely notice all the files' names have "ViewController" in them. Don't sweat that for now, we'll explain that in a bit.

You provide the method implementation in the .m file. Here's where you code up what should actually happen when the button is pressed.

Changing the button text

You know that the button is going to need an IBAction to respond to the button press and that we write up what the button should do in the implementation file. But just what is it that the button should do?

We want to change the text in the button to provide an answer. So that means we need some way to reach back "out" to the interface and change the label text. We'll use an IBOutlet to do that.

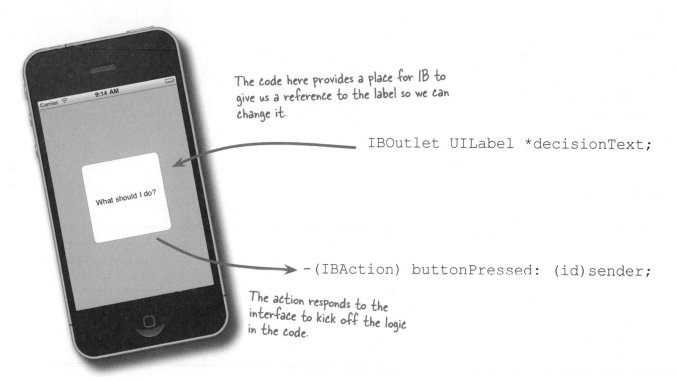

The code here provides a place for IB to give us a reference to the label so we can change it.

```
IBOutlet UILabel *decisionText;
```

```
-(IBAction) buttonPressed: (id)sender;
```

The action responds to the interface to kick off the logic in the code.

We'll get into actions and outlets more later.

IBActions and IBOutlets are both key for understanding how to work with controls, and we'll go into a lot more detail on both in the next chapter. For now, just remember that actions are used to *react to events* in the interface, and outlets are used to reach out from the code to *change the interface*.

there are no
Dumb Questions

Q: What happens if I don't implement everything in the .h file?

A: At compile time, Xcode will complain. It's going to check that you fully implemented the class you declared in the corresponding header file. Since that's not the case, you'll start with a warning telling you that happened. If you need that code to support anything else, then it'll crash at runtime.

Q: What exactly are frameworks? Are they the same thing as libraries?

A: They're really similar. They include shared, compiled code like libraries, but they also can bundle in images, headers, documentation, etc.

Q: Do I have to use Interface Builder to build my views?

A: No. You *can* do everything you can do in Interface Builder in code (and then some). However, using Interface Builder doesn't mean you can't do things in code, too. Since Interface Builder gives you a nice, graphical way of laying out your views, most apps have at least some of their UI built in Interface Builder then tweaked or animated in code.

Q: Do I have to write my application in Objective-C?

A: Earlier releases of the iOS Developer Agreement required the use of Objective-C for any application that will be distributed through the iTunes App Store. Apple later relaxed that requirement, opening up the possibility of using other tools or languages. Having said that, nearly everything you'll find about iOS development will make the assumption you're using Objective-C. All the underlying frameworks are written in Objective-C (or written to work with it), the documentation and sample code uses it, and the tool suite is built around it. Basically, if you're serious about writing native applications, you should learn Objective-C and start writing in that.

Q: Can I give applications I write out to friends?

A: Yes and no. First, if you want to put an application on anyone's actual device (including your own), you'll need to register for the paid Apple iOS Developer program. Once you've done that, you can register up to 100 devices and install your application on them. However, that's not really a great way to get your application out there, since Apple limits how many devices you can register this way. It's great for testing your application, but not how you want to go about passing it around.

A better way is to submit your application to the iTunes App Store. You can choose to distribute your application for free or charge for it, but by distributing it through the iTunes App Store, you make your application available to the world (and maybe make some money, too!). We'll talk more about distributing apps later in the book.

Finally, there's an Enterprise Developer program you can join that lets you distribute applications internally without using the App Store. This works, but is more expensive than the normal program.

Q: Do I have to use an IDE? I'm really a command-line kinda developer.

A: Technically speaking, no, you don't have to use the Xcode IDE for straight development. However, the IDE makes iOS development so much easier that you really should ask yourself if you have a good reason for avoiding it, especially since testing on an actual device or the simulator is so tightly coupled to Xcode. This book uses the Xcode IDE as well as other Apple development tools, and we encourage you to at least try them out before you abandon them. For things like automated builds or automated testing, the SDK comes with a command-line build tool called xcodebuild that can build your application just like Xcode does, but you'll most likely still want to do your actual development in Xcode.

Q: Can I develop an app for the iPhone and then rebuild it for other phones like Windows Mobile or Android phones?

A: In a word, no. When you develop for iPhone, you use Apple's iOS frameworks, like Cocoa Touch, as well as Objective-C. Neither of these are available on other devices.

Sharpen your pencil

Below is the code for when the button gets tapped. Add the bolded code to the iDecideViewController.h and iDecideViewController.m files. We are creating three things: the UILabel property, the IBAction to respond to the button press, and the IBOutlet to change the label when the button is pressed.

```objc
#import <UIKit/UIKit.h>
@interface iDecideViewController :   UIViewController {
     UILabel *decisionText_;
}
@property (retain, nonatomic) IBOutlet UILabel *decisionText;

-(IBAction)buttonPressed:(id)sender;
@end
```

We need to change the label text to provide our answer, so we need an IBOutlet to be able to get to the label control that the framework will build from our nib.

We'll talk more about properties later in the book.

Here's the action that will be called when the button is pressed.

iDecideViewController.h

```objc
#import "iDecideViewController.h"
@implementation iDecideViewController
@synthesize decisionText=decisionText_;

-(IBAction)buttonPressed:(id)sender
{
   decisionText_.text = @"Go for it!";
}

- (void)dealloc {
     [decisionText_ release];
     [super dealloc];
}
```

The @synthesize tells the compiler to create a getter and setter for the property we declared in the header file. We'll get into that more in Chapter 3.

This is the implementation of the method that gets called when the button is pressed.

We'll use our reference to the label to change the text.

The dealloc method is where you clean up your memory usage. We'll talk more about this in Chapter 3, too.

iDecideViewController.m

Sharpen your pencil
Solution

Here's the code from before in the context of the full files for
iDecideViewController.h and iDecideViewController.m.

```objective-c
#import <UIKit/UIKit.h>
@interface iDecideViewController :
UIViewController {
        UILabel *decisionText_;
}
@property (retain, nonatomic)
IBOutlet UILabel *decisionText;
-(IBAction)buttonPressed:(id)
sender;
@end
```

This code is typical of what you'll see in a header file. There's a declaration of the new IBOutlet and IBAction and a property for our UILabel.

The IBOutlet is a reference to the label that we'll change the text on the button, and the IBAction specifies what will actually happen when the button is pressed.

iDecideViewController.h

```objective-c
#import "iDecideViewController.h"
@implementation iDecideViewController

@synthesize
decisionText=decisionText_;
-(IBAction)buttonPressed:(id)
sender
{
decisionText_.text=@"Go for it!";
}
```

This is implementation code. Here, we're defining the method that is called when the button is pressed. We use a constant string to change the text in the label. Remember, decisionText is a reference to the UILabel we created in Interface Builder.

```objective-c
- (void)dealloc {
    [decisionText_ release];
    [super dealloc];
}
```

iDecideViewController.m

The release call is for memory management. Objective-C uses reference counting for memory management (we'll talk more about this in a bit) and needs to be released to free up the memory.

You're using the Model View Controller pattern

Model View Controller (MVC) is a pattern that is discussed at length in *Head First Design Patterns*. You see it used a lot with GUI applications, and it's all over the Cocoa Touch framework. The short version is that as much as possible, you want to separate out your logic from your view and data. It's especially key when you want to write one set of logic to support both iPhone and iPad UIs, which we'll do later in the book.

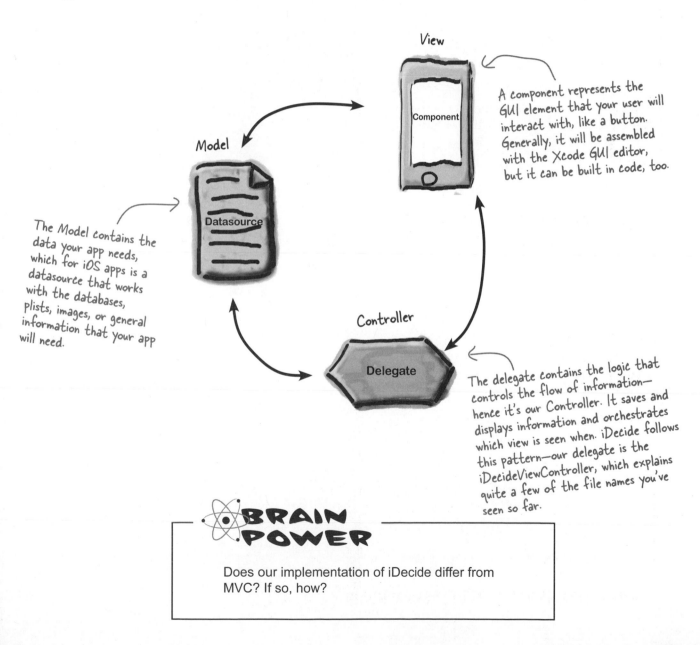

View

A component represents the GUI element that your user will interact with, like a button. Generally, it will be assembled with the Xcode GUI editor, but it can be built in code, too.

Model

Component

The Model contains the data your app needs, which for iOS apps is a datasource that works with the databases, plists, images, or general information that your app will need.

Datasource

Controller

Delegate

The delegate contains the logic that controls the flow of information—hence it's our Controller. It saves and displays information and orchestrates which view is seen when. iDecide follows this pattern—our delegate is the iDecideViewController, which explains quite a few of the file names you've seen so far.

☀ BRAIN POWER

Does our implementation of iDecide differ from MVC? If so, how?

iDecide is actually a little simpler

For iDecide, we don't have a datasource we're dealing with—there's nothing to store since we're just changing the text label and can specify that in one line in iDecideViewController.m. So iDecide is simplified to more of a **View - View Controller** pattern. You can think of it like the MVC pattern without an M—we don't need a model here.

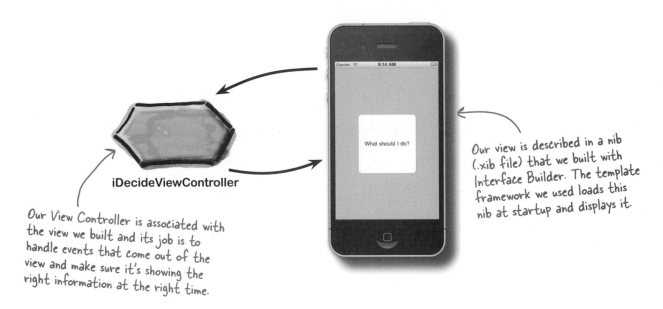

iDecideViewController

What should I do?

Our View Controller is associated with the view we built and its job is to handle events that come out of the view and make sure it's showing the right information at the right time.

Our view is described in a nib (.xib file) that we built with Interface Builder. The template framework we used loads this nib at startup and displays it.

This pattern is the secret to iOS development

If you only have room in your brain for one thing from this chapter, this is what should fill that space: **the Model-View-Controller pattern and the View-ViewController pattern are really just specific examples of a general *Delegation* pattern used everywhere in iOS development**. Something delegates responsibility out to another class that's responsible for actually performing an action as a result. In this case, the view needs to delegate out to the ViewController (through UI events) and let the ViewController know that something happened.

The ViewController (or delegate) then picks up the responsibility of reacting to that event and doing whatever the app has to do next. Sometimes setting up delegates is an explicit thing where you actually tell an object what its delegate is. Sometimes it's a little more indirect and you do it by linking controls up to methods, like Interface Builder does.

TEST DRIVE

You've got your IBAction and IBOutlets set up, so build and run the code again. Try clicking on the button in the simulator and see if it works.

What should I do?

Nothing happens!

BRAIN POWER

Why didn't the button change? Who's not doing their job?

What happened?

The Objective-C that we wrote is all set to handle things when the button is pressed, but the view hasn't been set up to connect the button to that code. We need to use the GUI editor to hook up our button to the buttonPressed method we just wrote. Then when the .xib file is loaded by the framework, it will connect the button object it creates with our code.

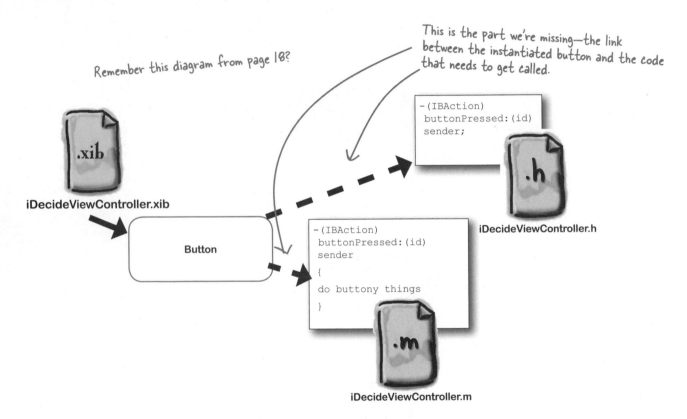

Remember this diagram from page 18?

This is the part we're missing—the link between the instantiated button and the code that needs to get called.

```
-(IBAction)
buttonPressed:(id)
sender;
```

iDecideViewController.xib

Button

iDecideViewController.h

```
-(IBAction)
buttonPressed:(id)
sender

{

do buttony things

}
```

iDecideViewController.m

Unless the UI components are hooked up to the code, nothing is going to happen.

We need to connect the button's "Hey, I just got pressed" event to our buttonPressed action method. That will get our method called when the user taps on the button. We then need to get a reference to the UILabel that the framework is going to create for us when the nib is loaded—that's where the IBOutlet comes in. Let's start with the outlet so we can change the UILabel text when the button is pressed.

Use the GUI editor to connect UI controls to code

Highlight iDecideViewController.xib to bring up the GUI editor, and open the Assistant Editor so you can see iDecideViewController.h alongside. Now let's hook up the button to our new code.

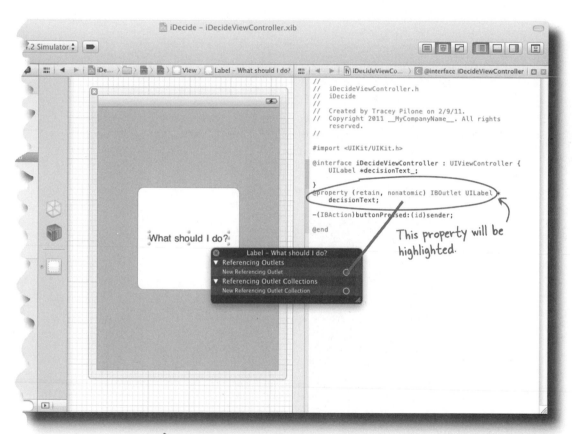

This property will be highlighted.

If you don't have a two-button mouse, just hold CTRL and then click.

1 Right-click on the label you dropped on the button. This will bring up a list of events and references.

2 Click on the circle next to New Referencing Outlet and drag it to the @property statement for the Outlet in the .h file on the right. Now when the decisionText UILabel is generated, our decisionText property will reference the control, through the IBOutlet.

OK—I get how we can now change the label, but how does the GUI know that you pressed a button?

A component can trigger certain events

We need to attach the right component event to our code. Remember that action method you wrote earlier that you can connect the button to?

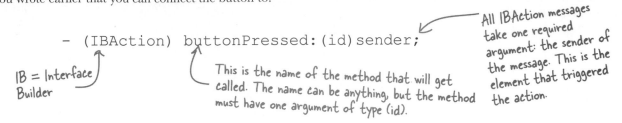

- (IBAction) buttonPressed:(id)sender;

IB = Interface Builder

This is the name of the method that will get called. The name can be anything, but the method must have one argument of type (id).

All IBAction messages take one required argument: the sender of the message. This is the element that triggered the action.

Now we need to pick the event that should trigger this method. If you right-click on the button in the editor, you'll see a list of events it could dispatch. We want the TouchUpInside event.

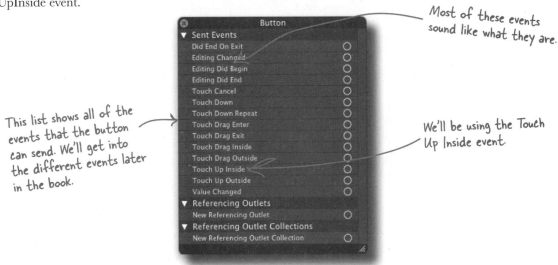

Most of these events sound like what they are.

This list shows all of the events that the button can send. We'll get into the different events later in the book.

We'll be using the Touch Up Inside event.

Components dispatch events when things happen to them

Whenever something happens to a component—for instance, a button gets tapped—the component dispatches one or more events. What we need to do is tell the button to notify us when that event gets raised. We'll be using the TouchUpInside event. If you think about how you click a button on an iPhone or iPad, the actual click inside the button isn't what matters: it's when you remove your finger (or "touch up") that the actual tap occurs. Connecting an event to a method is just like connecting an element to an outlet, which you just did on the previous page.

Connect your events to methods

Just like with outlets, you drag the connection from the button event to the - (IBAction) code in iDecideViewController.h and select the action that should be called.

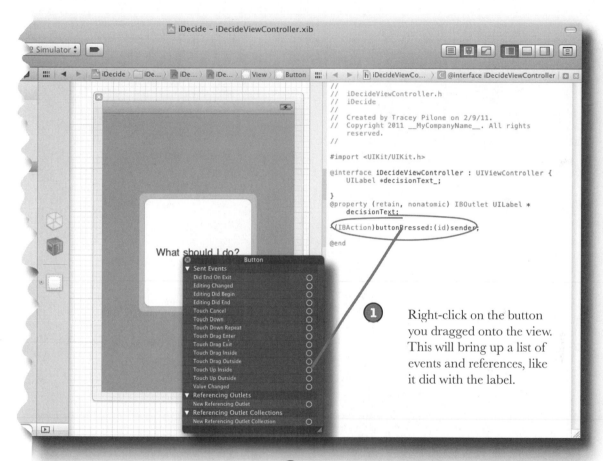

① Right-click on the button you dragged onto the view. This will bring up a list of events and references, like it did with the label.

② Then click on the circle next to Touch Up Inside and drag it to the IBAction in the .h file. Now when the button gets pressed, our buttonPressed method will be called.

Test Drive

Now that everything is hooked up, it's ready to run. Make sure you save everything and then build and run.

Test Drive

Get a message here!

What should I do?

Go for it!

Click here!

It works!

You've built your first iPhone app!

All the pieces are fitting together:

⬤ **The nibs (*.xib) describe the interface.**
iDecide is made up of two nibs: the MainWindow.xib and our iDecideViewController.xib. Together, these describe the UI the user sees.

⬤ **The views are connected to the code in the View Controller.**
Our views are connected to the implementation code through Interface Builder using IBOutlets and IBActions. IBOutlets give us references to UI components, and IBActions are called when events happen.

⬤ **Our application behavior is implemented in our View Controller.**
Following the MVC pattern (or really, just the VC pattern), we have all of our behavior implemented in our View Controller, cleanly separated from the view itself. The View Controller uses IBOutlets to get back to our actual UI controls if it needs to update them.

BULLET POINTS

- Interface Builder creates nib files (with a .xib extension) that describe the GUI in XML.

- Nib files are loaded by the Cocoa Touch framework and are turned into real instances of Cocoa Touch classes at runtime.

- In order to connect the components described in a nib to your code, you use IBOutlets and IBActions.

- Xcode is where your code and files are maintained for your application.

- Xcode is the hub for your project development and offers support for editing your code, building your application, and debugging it once it's running.

- The iPhone Simulator lets you test your application on your Mac without needing a real device.

there are no
Dumb Questions

Q: What is that File's Owner thing?

A: Interface Builder has an expectation of what class will be the nib's File's Owner. You can change what class Interface Builder thinks it will be, but by default, a new project is set up so that the main View Controller created by Xcode is the File's Owner for the main view created by Xcode. That's why we didn't have to change anything. Since the File's Owner is set up to be our iDecideViewController, Interface Builder looks at the iDecideViewController header and sees that we have an IBOutlet named descriptionText and an IBAction named buttonPressed. When you connected the UILabel's referencing outlet to File's Owner descriptionText, Interface Builder saved the information necessary so that when the nib is loaded by the application, the references are set correctly in our iDecideViewController. The same thing happened with the TouchUpInside event, except in this case, instead of hooking up a component to a reference, it hooked up a component's event to a method that should be called.

Beware—Interface Builder's expectation of the class that will load the nib does not mean that other classes can't try—it just might not work well if that class doesn't have the necessary properties and methods.

Q: Why does our new text string have an @ in front of it?

A: The Cocoa Touch framework uses a string class named NSString for its text strings. Since it's so common, Objective-C has built-in support for creating them from constants. You indicate a string constant should be an NSString by putting an @ symbol in front of it. Otherwise, it's just a normal char* like in C or C++.

Q: How much of what we've covered is iPhone-specific? Is developing for the iPod Touch or iPad very different?

A: Not at all! One of the benefits of developing for iOS is that most things built for one iOS device can be used directly on another iOS device. You'll need to be careful about device-specific hardware capabilities (for example, trying to use a camera on an older iPod Touch or iPad won't work), and the screen resolution of your views and images will need to change, but otherwise, developing for different devices is largely hidden from you.

If you keep the MVC pattern in mind and make sure to separate logic from views, it's much easier to add new views for other devices to your app.

Q: How does Xcode actually build an application?

A: We're going to get into this more in the coming pages. The short version is that Xcode can gather up all your resources and code, link them together, and then spit out a nice package at the end that drops into the sandbox available on the iOS device.

Q: Why do I keep hearing about Interface Builder? What is that really?

A: Before, Xcode 4 views were edited in a separate application called Interface Builder. Now it's a part of XCode and isn't really called Interface Builder any more. Since this transition is still new, folks may still be working in and talking about IB.

Q: When the views are compiled, why do they stay .xib files? Shouldn't something change?

A: After compilation, the .xib files are actually .nib files in their binary form.

Q: What exactly are these "undocumented APIs" I keep hearing about?

A: These are private methods that Apple gets to use, but you don't. An example is multitasking. It just became available for developer use with iOS 4, but some of Apple's applications have been able to run in the background from the beginning (for example, the iPod application doesn't stop playing when you switch to another app).

You typically see developers touching undocumented, private methods when trying to customize a standard iOS control or change what a physical button does. Don't do this. Apple will catch it during the approval process and they will reject your application for it. Protecting these APIs is part of Apple protecting the platform, and what is undocumented now may be allowed in the future.

WHO DOES WHAT?

Match each iOS development item to its description.

Item	Description

IBOutlet

The Model View Controller pattern where the view delegates behavior to a controller.

Functions of Xcode

Xcode, Instruments, Interface Builder, and the iOS Simulator.

MVC

Reference from the code to an object in the nib.

IBAction

Images, databases, the icon file, etc.

Components of the SDK

Maintaining and editing code and resources, debugging code, and preparing an app for deployment.

Application resources

Indicates a method that can be called in response to an event.

Match each iPhone development item to its description.

Item	Description

IBOutlet

The Model View Controller pattern where the view delegates behavior to a controller.

Functions of Xcode

Xcode, Instruments, Interface Builder, and the iPhone Simulator.

MVC

Reference from the code to an object in the nib.

IBAction

Images, databases, the icon file, etc.

Components of the SDK

Maintaining and editing code and resources, debugging code, and preparing an app for deployment.

Application resources

Indicates a method that can be called in response to an event.

Pⓞⓞl Puzzle

Your **job** is to take filenames from the pool and place them into the blank lines pointing to the diagram. You may **not** use the same filename more than once, and you won't need to use all the names. Your **goal** is to make a complete diagram that will show the design of iDecide.

If we put together what we learned earlier about how the app works with the diagram about the code for the button press, you get an idea of which files do what.

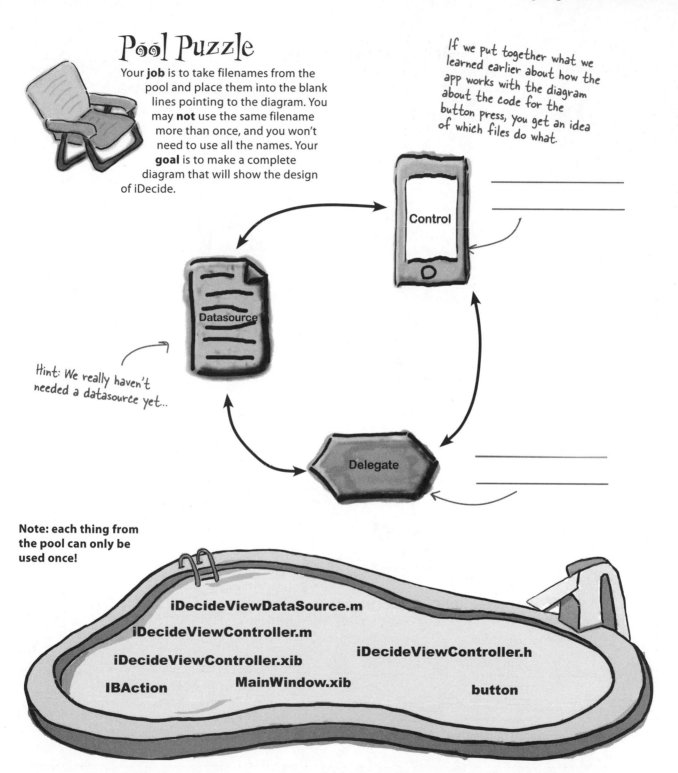

Control

Datasource

Hint: We really haven't needed a datasource yet...

Delegate

Note: each thing from the pool can only be used once!

iDecideViewDataSource.m

iDecideViewController.m

iDecideViewController.xib   iDecideViewController.h

IBAction   MainWindow.xib

button

Pool Puzzle Solution

Your **job** is to take filenames from the pool and place them into the blank lines pointing to the diagram. You may **not** use the same filename more than once, and you won't need to use all the names. Your **goal** is to make a complete diagram that will show the design of iDecide.

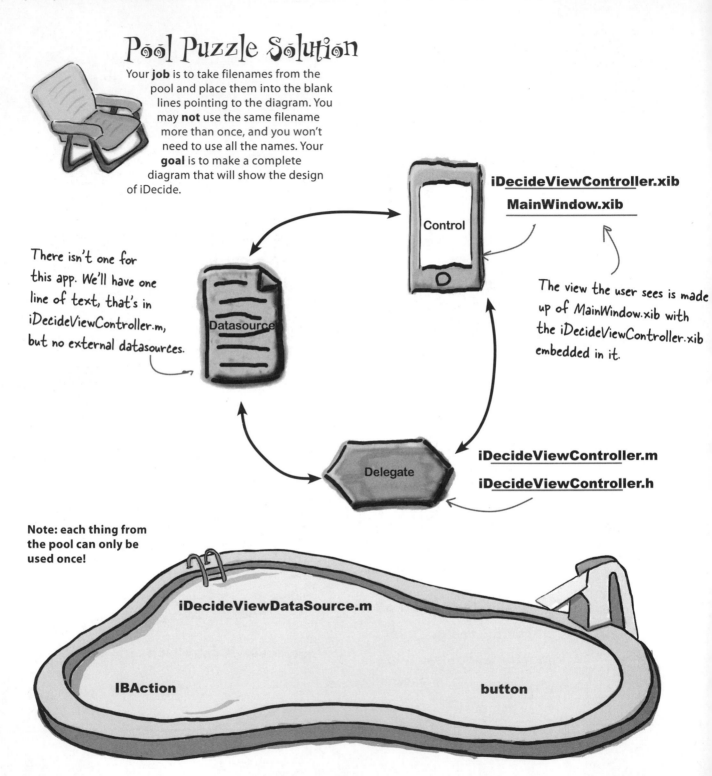

iDecideViewController.xib

MainWindow.xib

Control

There isn't one for this app. We'll have one line of text, that's in iDecideViewController.m, but no external datasources.

Datasource

The view the user sees is made up of MainWindow.xib with the iDecideViewController.xib embedded in it.

iDecideViewController.m

iDecideViewController.h

Delegate

Note: each thing from the pool can only be used once!

iDecideViewDataSource.m

IBAction

button

iOS cross

Bend your brain around some of the new terminology we used in this chapter.

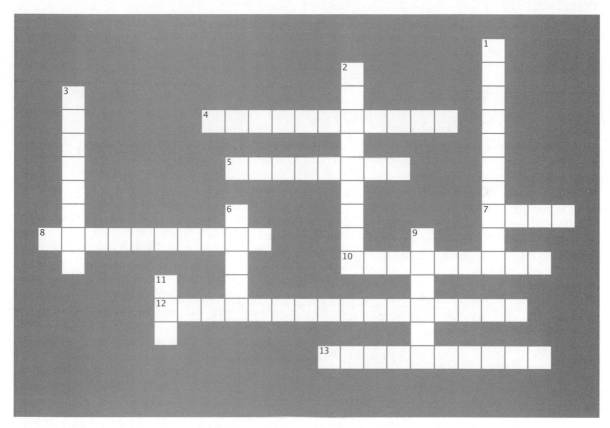

Across

4. Something that the simulator cannot reliably test.
5. This is used to set up an outgoing connection from the implementation code to the view.
7. The term to describe each screen of an iPhone app.
8. The framework used to write iPhone apps.
10. The folder used to organize the images for the app.
12. The name of the IDE for iPhone apps.
13. These are used in Xcode to provide classes to be accessed.

Down

1. The language used to write iPhone apps.
2. This is used on a desktop to test an app.
3. This is used to recieve an event in code and trigger something.
6. This is the name of the editor used for Objective-C.
9. The iPhone is this kind of device.
11. The name of a file used to create a view.

iOS cross Solution

Bend your brain around some of the new terminology we used in this chapter.

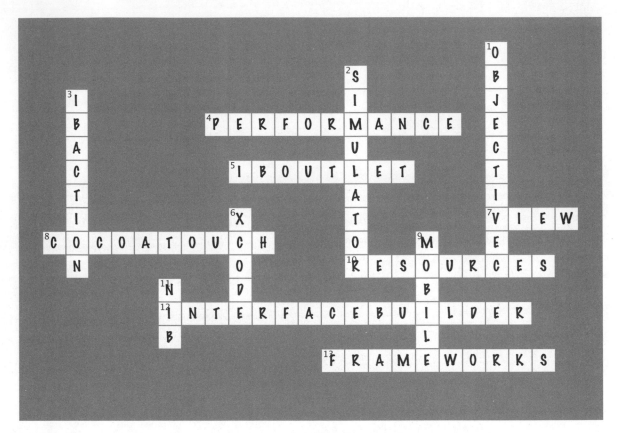

Across

4. Something that the simulator cannot reliably test.
   [PERFORMANCE]
5. This is used to set up an outgoing connection from the implementation code to the view. [IBOUTLET]
7. The term to describe each screen of an iPhone app. [VIEW]
8. The framework used to write iPhone apps. [COCOATOUCH]
10. The folder used to organize the images for the app.
    [RESOURCES]
12. The name of the IDE for iPhone apps.
    [INTERFACEBUILDER]
13. These are used in Xcode to provide classes to be accessed.
    [FRAMEWORKS]

Down

1. The language used to write iPhone apps. [OBJECTIVEC]
2. This is used on a desktop to test an app. [SIMULATOR]
3. This is used to recieve an event in code and trigger something. [IBACTION]
6. This is the name of the editor used for Objective-C.
   [XCODE]
9. The iPhone is this kind of device. [MOBILE]
11. The name of a file used to create a view. [NIB]

Your iOS Toolbox

You've got Chapter 1 under your belt and now you've added basic iOS app interactions to your tool box.

Views are constructed in Interface Builder.

A view is made up of nib (*.xib) files and the GUIs are edited with Interface Builder.

Then, you write the code that makes the views work...

This code is almost always written in Objective-C using Xcode, and includes IBActions and IBOutlets.

...and connect component events to the code.

Back in Interface Builder, you connect your actions and outlets to the components you included in your view.

The Simulator runs your app virtually.

As you build your app, you can run your code in the simulator and test it to see if it works.

2 iOS app patterns

Hello, Renee!

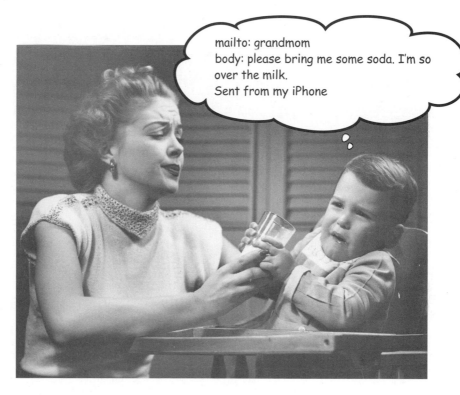

mailto: grandmom
body: please bring me some soda. I'm so over the milk.
Sent from my iPhone

Apps have a lot of moving parts. OK, actually, they don't have any *real* moving parts, but they do have lots of UI controls. A typical iOS app has more going on than just a button, and it's time to build one. Working with some of the more complicated controls means you'll need to pay more attention than ever to how you design your app. In this chapter, you'll learn about some of the fundamental design patterns used in the iOS SDK, and how to put together a bigger application.

Author's note:

Head First does not take any responsibility for Mike's relationship problems.

Mike

You have this friend Mike. He has a great girlfriend, Renee, but they've been having some problems. She thinks that he doesn't talk about his feelings enough.

> I could use my iPhone to send her emails about my feelings, but it's so much work. Can you speed that process up?

There's (about to be) an app for that.

Using some solid design and the basic controls included in the Interface Builder library, you can have Mike sending off emails in no time. The app can handle filling out some basics, setting it up to go straight to Renee, and Mike can just fill in some blanks. But first, what should his messages say?

First, we need to figure out what Mike (really) wants

Mike isn't a complex guy. He wants an easy interface to create his emails and he really doesn't want to have to type much.

Here's what Mike handed you at the end of the night.

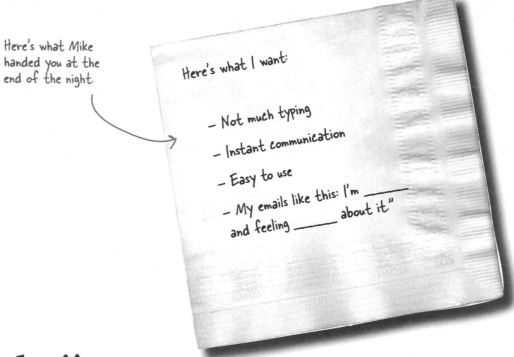

Here's what I want:

- Not much typing

- Instant communication

- Easy to use

- My emails like this: I'm _____ and feeling _____ about it."

App Magnets

Now that we know what Mike wants, what do we need to do? Take the magnets below and put them in order of the steps you'll follow to build his email app.

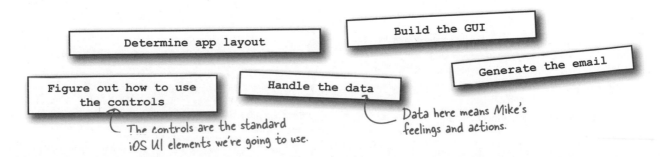

| Determine app layout |

| Build the GUI |

| Generate the email |

| Figure out how to use the controls |

| Handle the data |

The controls are the standard iOS UI elements we're going to use.

Data here means Mike's feelings and actions.

App Magnets Solution

Now that we know what Mike wants, what do we need to do? Take the magnets below and put them in order of the steps you'll follow to build his email app.

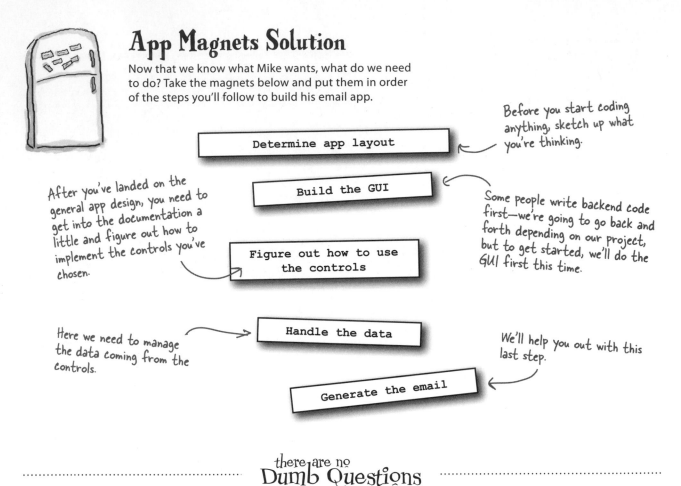

Before you start coding anything, sketch up what you're thinking.

| Determine app layout |

After you've landed on the general app design, you need to get into the documentation a little and figure out how to implement the controls you've chosen.

| Build the GUI |

Some people write backend code first—we're going to go back and forth depending on our project, but to get started, we'll do the GUI first this time.

| Figure out how to use the controls |

| Handle the data |

Here we need to manage the data coming from the controls.

We'll help you out with this last step.

| Generate the email |

there are no Dumb Questions

Q: How do you figure out the app layout?

A: We're going to give you a couple to choose from to get started, but in general, it's important to think about what your app needs to do and focus on those features first.

Q: Are we always going to start with a sketch?

A: Yes! Good software design starts with knowing what you're building and how the user is going to work with the app. Expect to spend about 50 percent of your development time on the UI—it's what separates the great apps from the rest.

Q: How do we talk to the email messaging framework?

A: Don't worry, we'll give you some code to help you to work with that.

Q: Why isn't Mike texting Renee? Why send an email?

A: Simply put, because that won't work in the simulator. Once you have a good handle on creating the email, porting that to texting isn't hard.

Q: Does every control work differently than the others?

A: For the most part, no—once you learn a few basic patterns, you'll be able to find your way through most of the SDK. Some of the controls have a few peculiarities here and there, but for the most part, they should start to look familiar.

APP LAYOUT CONSTRUCTION

Here are two designs to evaluate. Based on aesthetics, usability, and standard iPhone app behavior, which one is better for Mike?

Option #1

Option #2

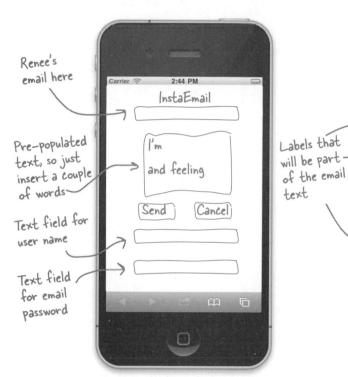

Renee's email here

Pre-populated text, so just insert a couple of words

Text field for user name

Text field for email password

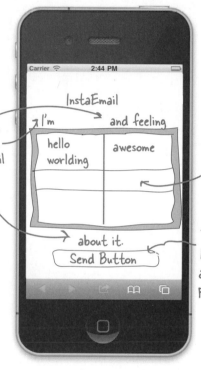

Labels that will be part of the email text

Spinning controller filled in with activities and feelings

The button will have email addresses and passwords preconfigured

Which UI is better? ....

Why? (Be specific.) ....

....

Why not the other? ....

APP LAYOUT CONSTRUCTION — — — — — — — —

Here are two designs to evaluate. Based on aesthetics, usability, and standard iPhone app behavior, which one is better for Mike?

Bad Option #1

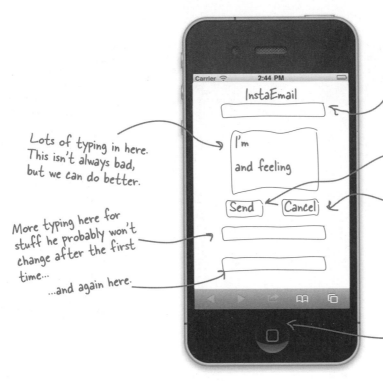

Your user doesn't need to type in the email address again. Since it's always the same, we can take care of this for him.

Lots of typing in here. This isn't always bad, but we can do better.

The send button would be better at the bottom of the page, not stuck between controls like this.

More typing here for stuff he probably won't change after the first time...

...and again here.

Cancel what? iPhone apps almost never have "Quit"-type buttons. If the user changes his mind, he hits the home button and the app is moved to the background.

Which app is better? **#2.**

Why? (Be specific.) **Option #2 has a lot less typing and fewer fields overall.** Since the user doesn't need to change his username or password often, there's no reason to put it on the main view every time he runs the app.

Why not the other? **Option #1 has a lot of typing and settings to remember. The buttons are confusing.**

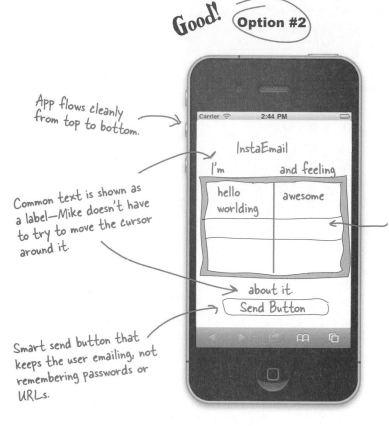

Good! (Option #2)

App flows cleanly from top to bottom.

Common text is shown as a label—Mike doesn't have to try to move the cursor around it.

Smart send button that keeps the user emailing, not remembering passwords or URLs.

InstaEmail

I'm ... and feeling

hello worlding | awesome

about it.

Send Button

Instead of having Mike type in what he's doing and his feelings, we can give him a picker to select from. This means fewer options since they're predetermined, but it's way easier to use. We'd want to double-check this with him, but this seems consistent with what Mike's after.

This is the one you're going to build for Mike.

there are no Dumb Questions

Q: Do I really need to care about usability and aesthetics so much?

A: Usability and aesthetics are what made the iPhone a success, and Apple will defend them to the death. Even more important, you don't get to put anything on the App Store or on anyone else's iPhone without their approval. Apple has sold billions of apps—if yours doesn't fit with the iPhone look and feel or is hard to use, people will find someone else's app and never look back.

Q: We got rid of the username, password, and email fields. The email one I understand, but what about the other two?

A: Anytime your app needs configuration information that the user doesn't need to change frequently, you should keep it out of the main task flow. Apple even provides a special place for these called a Settings bundle that fits in with the standard iPhone settings. We're not going to use that in this chapter (we'll just hard code the values), but later we'll show you how to put stuff in the Settings page. That's usually the right place for things like login details.

Q: How am I supposed to know what Apple thinks is good design or aesthetically pleasing?

A: Funny you should ask...go ahead, turn the page.

App design rules—the iOS HIG

The iOS Human Interface Guide (HIG) is a document that Apple distributes for guidance in developing iOS Apps for sale on the App Store. You can download it at *http://developer.apple.com/ios*. This isn't just something nice they did to help you out; when you submit an app for approval, you agree that your app will conform to the HIG.

We can't overstate this: ***you have to follow the HIG,*** as Apple's review process is thorough and they will reject your application if it doesn't conform. Complain, blog with righteous anger, and then conform. Now let's move on.

Apple also distributes a few other guides and tutorials, including the iPhone Application Programming Guide. This is another great source of information and explains how you should handle different devices, like the iPhone, devices with old versions of iOS, and the iPod Touch. Not paying attention to the iPod Touch is another great way to get your app rejected from the App Store.

Note: While the authors do not suggest testing these methods of being rejected from the App Store, we can say with authority that they work.

Application types

The HIG details three main types of applications that are commonly developed for the iPhone. Each type has a different purpose and therefore offers a different kind of user experience. Figuring out what type of application you're building before you start working on the GUI helps get you started on the road to good interface design.

Immersive Apps

Games are a classic example, but like this simulated level, immersive apps use a very custom interface that allows the user to interact with the device. As a result, HIG guidelines aren't as crucial in this case.

Productivity Apps

Help manage information and complete tasks. Info is hierarchical, and you navigate by drilling down into more levels of detail.

Utility Apps

Get a specific set of info to the user with as little interaction or settings configuration as possible.

Usually have more interface design than a productivity app, and are expected to stay very consistent with the HIG.

WHO DOES WHAT?

Below are a bunch of different application ideas. For each one, think about what kind of app it really is and match it to the app types on the right.

App Description   Type of App

InstaEmail 1.0: Allows you to email
with minimal typing.

News Reader: Gives you a list of
the news categories and you can   Immersive Application
get the details on stories you
choose.

Marble Game: A marble rolling
game that uses the accelerometer   Utility Application
to drive the controls.

Stopwatch Tool: Gives you a
stopwatch that starts and stops by   Productivity Application
touching the screen

Recipe Manager: A meal listing
that allows you to drill down and
look at individual recipes.

WHO DOES WHAT? SOLUTION

Match each app description to its application type.

App Description | Type of App

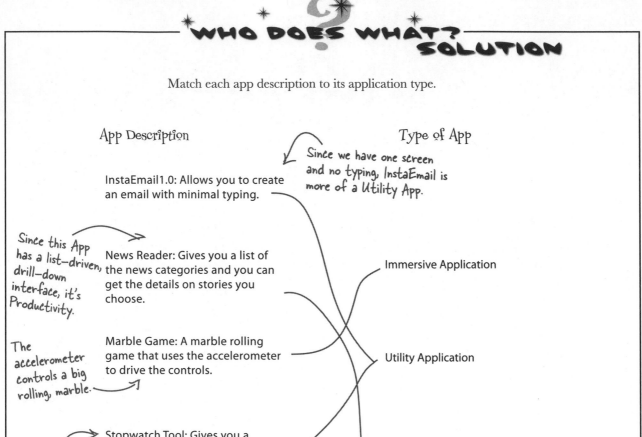

Since we have one screen and no typing, InstaEmail is more of a Utility App.

InstaEmail1.0: Allows you to create an email with minimal typing.

Since this App has a list-driven, drill-down interface, it's Productivity.

News Reader: Gives you a list of the news categories and you can get the details on stories you choose.

The accelerometer controls a big rolling, marble.

Marble Game: A marble rolling game that uses the accelerometer to drive the controls.

We want a very focused stopwatch GUI, no real data to work through.

Stopwatch Tool: Gives you a stopwatch that starts and stops by touching the screen

Recipe Manager: A meal listing that allows you to drill down and look at individual recipes.

Lots of data to work through here: tables, a drill-down to recipes—definitely productivity.

Immersive Application

Utility Application

Productivity Application

We're going to get into more HIG elements later.

This is just the beginning of our relationship with the HIG. As we start designing apps, we're going to be using platform-specific technologies (like cameras) and working with some physical analogs for the iPad.

HIG guidelines for pickers and buttons

The HIG has a section on the proper use of all the standard controls, including the two that we've selected for InstaEmail—a picker and a button. Before you build the view with your controls, it's a good idea to take a quick look at the recommendations from Apple. You'll find this information in the HIG, under iOS UI Element Usage Guidelines.

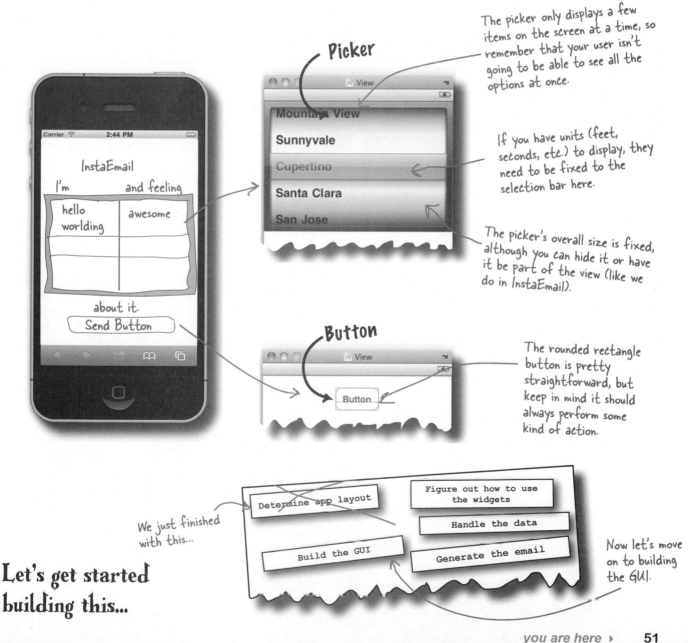

The picker only displays a few items on the screen at a time, so remember that your user isn't going to be able to see all the options at once.

If you have units (feet, seconds, etc.) to display, they need to be fixed to the selection bar here.

The picker's overall size is fixed, although you can hide it or have it be part of the view (like we do in InstaEmail).

The rounded rectangle button is pretty straightforward, but keep in mind it should always perform some kind of action.

We just finished with this...

Determine app layout

Figure out how to use the widgets

Handle the data

Build the GUI

Generate the email

Now let's move on to building the GUI.

Let's get started building this...

Create a new View-based project for InstaEmail

Once you've started Xcode, select **File→New→New Project**. Just like iDecide, for InstaEmail we have one screen and we're not going to be animating it (like the utility app) or starting with a particular navigation for the app, so again choose the **View-based Application** targeted for **iPhone** and name it InstaEmail.

Do this!

This is the project highlighted.

Here are the highlighted targets.

To write an app that can send an email, we'll need to add a new framework. With the project and its targets highlighted, select **Build Phases**, expand the **Link Binary With Libraries** section, and push the + button. Then select MessageUI Framework from the list and click **Add**.

Just to keep things organized, drag the new Framework into the Frameworks folder.

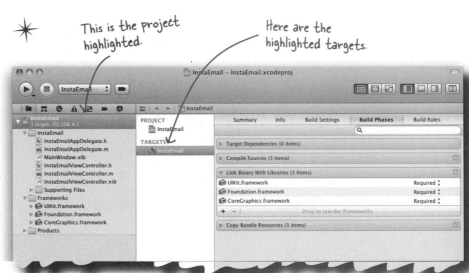

Watch it!

The new project type in Xcode is not necessarily the same as your app type.

For example, a Productivity App can be written as a View-based Application, a Window-based Application, Navigation-based Application, or a Tab Bar Application.

We'll be working with these other project types later in the book.

Alright, wait a minute. I still don't really get this "a .xib file is a nib is a view" thing. I get that I can edit this view in Interface Builder, but how does it all fit in with everything else?

Fair enough.

It can get a little confusing. Let's take a look at how a nib really becomes a view...

The life of a root view

In Chapter 1, we touched on how the Xcode GUI editor creates XML descriptions of your view, called a nib, and that the Cocoa Touch framework turns that into a real view in your application. Let's take a closer look at what's going on under the hood.

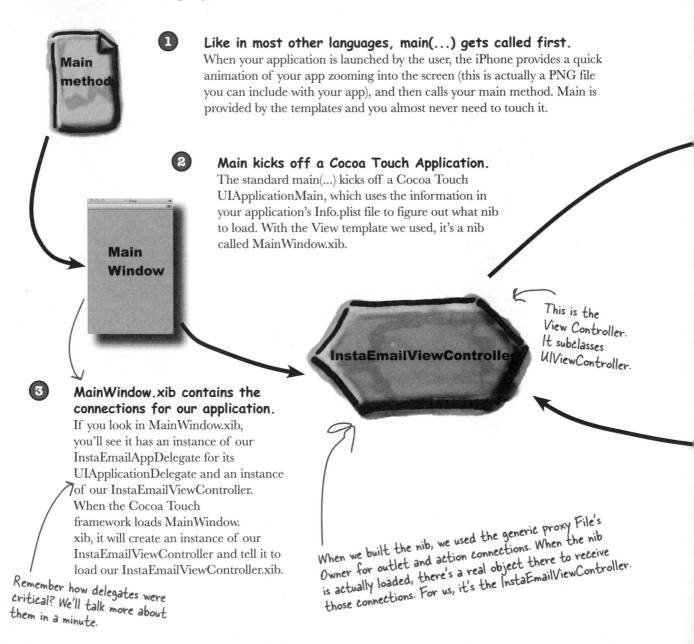

① **Like in most other languages, main(...) gets called first.**
When your application is launched by the user, the iPhone provides a quick animation of your app zooming into the screen (this is actually a PNG file you can include with your app), and then calls your main method. Main is provided by the templates and you almost never need to touch it.

Main method

② **Main kicks off a Cocoa Touch Application.**
The standard main(...) kicks off a Cocoa Touch UIApplicationMain, which uses the information in your application's Info.plist file to figure out what nib to load. With the View template we used, it's a nib called MainWindow.xib.

Main Window

This is the View Controller. It subclasses UIViewController.

InstaEmailViewController

③ **MainWindow.xib contains the connections for our application.**
If you look in MainWindow.xib, you'll see it has an instance of our InstaEmailAppDelegate for its UIApplicationDelegate and an instance of our InstaEmailViewController. When the Cocoa Touch framework loads MainWindow. xib, it will create an instance of our InstaEmailViewController and tell it to load our InstaEmailViewController.xib.

Remember how delegates were critical? We'll talk more about them in a minute.

When we built the nib, we used the generic proxy File's Owner for outlet and action connections. When the nib is actually loaded, there's a real object there to receive those connections. For us, it's the InstaEmailViewController.

④ The Cocoa Touch framework creates our custom view from the InstaEmailViewController.xib.

When we constructed the nib, we used the File's Owner proxy object to stand in for the object that owns the nib contents. At this point, the framework is loading the nib on behalf of our InstaEmailViewController class, so that instance is used for connections. As the framework creates instances of our components, they're connected up to the instance of InstaEmailViewController.

This is our view. It is launched by the framework, on the behalf of our ViewController.

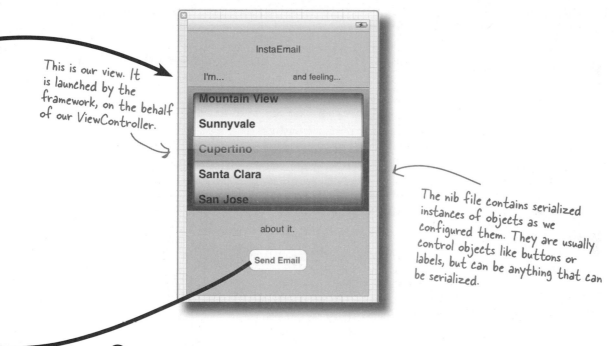

The nib file contains serialized instances of objects as we configured them. They are usually control objects like buttons or labels, but can be anything that can be serialized.

⑤ When events occur with components, methods are invoked on our controller instance.

The actions we associated between the controls and the File's Owner in the nib were translated into connections between the controls and our controller instance (InstaEmailViewController). Now when a control fires off an event (like the Send Email button), the framework calls a method on our InstaEmailViewController instance.

there are no
Dumb Questions

Q: **Isn't good design vs. bad design a little subjective?**

A: Yes and no. Obviously, different people will have differing opinions about what UI looks better. However, Apple has very specific guidelines about how certain controls should be used and best practices that should be followed. In general, if you're using a common iOS control, make sure you're using it in a way that's consistent with existing applications.

Q: **Can I run apps that I build on my own device?**

A: To get an app you write installed on your iPhone, you'll need to sign up for either the Standard or Enterprise Developer programs at *http://developer.apple.com/ios/*. Everything in this book is designed to work with just the **Simulator**, so don't feel like you need to go do that just yet. We'll talk more about putting apps on an actual phone later in the book.

Q: **The InstaEmail icon looks horrible. What can I do?**

A: The icon for an application is just a PNG file in your project. We'll add and configure icons later, but for now, just know that you'll need a .png file in the resources directory for that purpose—we'll hook you up with some cool icons in a bit.

Q: **Do I have to use the GUI builder for the view?**

A: No. Everything you do in the Xcode editor can be done in code. Interface Builder makes it a lot easier to get things started, but sometimes you'll need that code-level control of a view to do what you want. We'll be switching back and forth depending on the project and view.

Q: **I'm still a little fuzzy on this nib thing. Do they hold our UI or regular objects?**

A: They can hold both. When you assemble a view using the Interface Builder GUI editor, it keeps track of the controls you're using and the links to other classes. These controls are serialized into an XML document; when you save it out, this is your nib. Xcode is able to serialize non-control classes, too. That's how it saves out our InstaEmailViewController in MainWindow.xib. When the nib is restored from disk, objects in the nib are reinstantiated and populated with the values you gave them in Interface Builder.

You can think of it like "freeze-drying" the objects and then restoring them at runtime.

Q: **So does the editor save out the File's Owner, too?**

A: No, File's Owner is a proxy. File's Owner represents whatever class is asking to have this nib loaded. So the File's Owner proxy isn't actually stored in the nib, but Interface Builder needs that proxy so you can make association with controls you used in your view. When the nib is restored (and the control objects are instantiated), the nib loading code will make the connections to the real owning object that asked to load the nib.

Exercise

It's time to build the view. Double-click on InstaEmailViewController.xib in the InstaEmail folder, and launch the Interface Builder GUI editor inside of Xcode. Using drag and drop, pull over the elements from the Utilities panel that you need to build the View.

If you don't see this library, check your buttons here and here.

① Find each of the elements (we've given them the proper names for you) in the objects library and drag and drop them into the **View** window.

Labels

Edit label text here.

Picker

Round Rect Button, titled "Send Email"

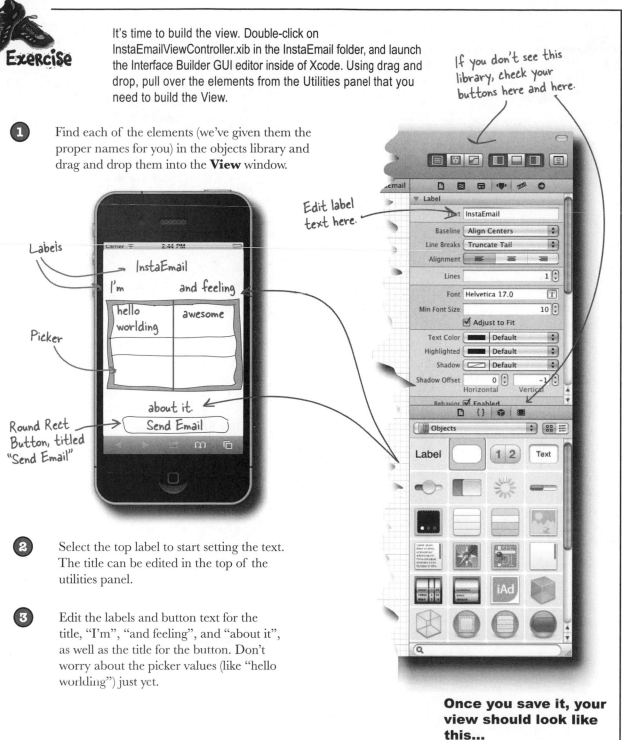

② Select the top label to start setting the text. The title can be edited in the top of the utilities panel.

③ Edit the labels and button text for the title, "I'm", "and feeling", and "about it", as well as the title for the button. Don't worry about the picker values (like "hello worlding") just yet.

Once you save it, your view should look like this...

Exercise Solution

The View is all built and ready to go. Here's what you should have on your screen now. Once you tweak everything to look just how you want it, we'll run InstaEmail in the Simulator.

Your labels may not be this big. By default, the label will not resize to the font, but to fit the space. To make it larger, just resize using the dots at the edges of the label field.

InstaEmail

I'm...   ...and feeling...

Mountain View

Sunnyvale

Cupertino

Santa Clara

San Jose

Filling in the picker data requires some code, and we'll get to that in a minute. What you see here are default values.

...about it.

Send Email

Did you notice the blue guidelines in the simulator? They're in the view when you're laying out elements to help you center things and keep them lined up with each other.

Test Drive

Now it's time to check out InstaEmail in the Simulator. Save in Interface Builder, go back into Xcode, and hit **Run** from the Build menu (or use the keyboard shortcut ⌘+R).

Close, but the picker isn't showing up?!?!

BRAIN POWER

Why do you think the picker isn't showing up?

We need data

For the picker to actually show up, we have to give it data to display. And Mike is just the guy to help. He likes what you have put together for the UI, so now we need a little more information from him to give to the picker.

I like the interface. Here's my list of what I do and how I feel about it so you can fill in the rest. Can't wait until it's done because I'm soooo over talking about it...

Things I do:

sleeping

eating

working

thinking

crying

begging

leaving

shopping

Things I feel:

awesome

sad

happy

ambivalent

nauseous

psyched

confused

hopeful

anxious

Use pickers when you want controlled input

In our case, the picker is the perfect element for our app. No typing at all, but it allows Mike to have control over what gets selected. There's some terminology that you need to know about pickers before we get our data in there.

We want two columns. The picker calls columns components.

The number of rows, or items, comes from Mike's list, so 9 for each component.

A picker is a large element (full screen width) and the overall size cannot be changed.

Remember the screen size issue when building iPhone apps? The longest word needs to fit in a column or it's going to be abbreviated. There's not a lot of space to work with.

OK, so we can just set the picker rows with the values Mike gave us like we did with the button label, right?

The picker is different.

The picker doesn't want to be told what to do, it's going to **ask** when it wants your input. You're going to see this pattern show up with controls that could use a lot of data like pickers, and later we'll see something similar with table views. Let's take a closer look...

Pickers get their data from a datasource...

Many of the elements in the Cocoa Touch framework have the concept of **datasources** along with delegates. Each UI control is responsible for how things look on the screen (the cool spinning dial look, the animation when the user spins a wheel, etc.), but it doesn't know anything about the data it needs to show or what to do when something is selected.

The datasource provides the bridge between the control and the data it needs to display. The control will ask the datasource for what it needs and the datasource is responsible for providing the information in a format the control expects. In our case, the datasource provides the number of components (or columns) for the picker and the total number of rows for the picker. Different controls need different kinds of datasources. For the picker, we need a UIPickerViewDatasource.

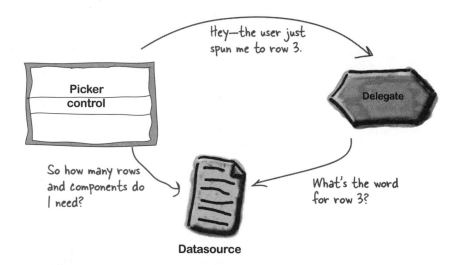

...and tell their delegates when something happens

As we saw in Chapter 1, a **delegate** is responsible for the *behavior* of an element. When someone selects something—or in this case, scrolls the picker to a value—the control tells the delegate what happened and the delegate figures out what to do in response. Just like with datasources, different controls need different kinds of delegates. For the picker, we need a UIPickerViewDelegate.

When in doubt, check out Apple's documentation

You're probably wondering how to use that picker, so don't hesitate to check out the API documentation. In Xcode, go to the **Help** menu and then the **Xcode Help** option.

Search for "UIPickerView" and it will pull up all the information on the class that you need to implement for the picker.

Q: Why is the delegate providing the content? That really seems like data.

A: That's something particular to a picker and it has to do with the fact that the picker delegate can change how the data is shown. In the simplest form, it can just return strings to the picker. If it wants to get fancy, it can return an entire View (yes, just like the View you built with Interface Builder, but smaller) to use images or special fonts, for example.

That pattern is back

You've seen this **Control-Datasource-Delegate** pattern before, when we briefly discussed MVC in Chapter 1. Nearly all the complex controls use it. You'll probably remember that even the **View-View Controller** relationship we've been using follows this pattern (minus the datasource).

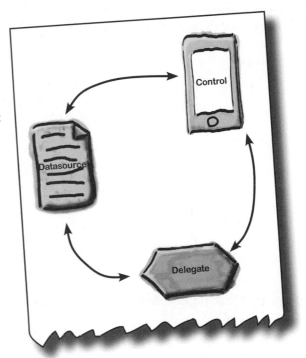

Controls have their own specific datasources and delegates

Each control has specific needs for its datasource and delegate, and we'll talk about how that's handled in Objective-C in a minute. However, it's important to realize that while the responsibilities are split between the datasource and the delegate in the pattern, *they don't necessarily have to be implemented in different classes*. The control wants a delegate and a datasource—it doesn't care whether they're provided by the same object or not: it's going to ask the datasource for datasource-related things and the delegate for delegate-related things.

Let's take a closer look at how the UIPicker uses its datasource and delegate to get an idea of how all of this fits together.

The Picker Exposed

This week's interview:
How to avoid spinning out of control...

Head First: Hello, Picker, thanks for joining us.

Picker: My pleasure. I don't usually get to talk to anyone but my datasource and delegate, so this is a real treat.

Head First: I'm glad you brought those up. So we've worked with controls like buttons and labels, but they just had properties. What's going on with this delegate and datasource business?

Picker: Well, to be clear, I have properties too—there just isn't too much exciting going on there. What makes me different is that I could be working with a lot of data. I might only have one row or I might have a hundred; it just depends on the application.

Head First: Ah, OK. A label only has one string in it, so there can be a property that holds just that string. No problem.

Picker: Exactly! So, instead of trying to cram all of the data into me directly, it's cleaner to just let me ask for what I need when I need it.

Head First: But you need to ask for it in a specific way, right?

Picker: That's the beauty of my setup. I ask for what I need to know in a specific way—that's why there's a UIPickerDatasource—but I don't care where my datasource gets its information. For example, I need to know how many rows I need to show, so I ask my datasource. It could be using an array, a database, a plist, whatever—I don't care. For a picker, I'm not that picky...all I need to know is how many rows.

Head First: That's really nice—so you could be showing data coming from just about anything, and as long as your datasource knows how to answer

your questions, you don't care how it stores the data internally.

Picker: You got it. Now the delegate is a little different. I can draw the wheels and all that, but I don't know what each application wants to do when someone selects a row, so I just pass the buck to my delegate.

Head First: So the delegate is implemented so that when you tell the delegate what happened, it performs the right action. Like saving some value or setting a clock or whatever.

Picker: Exactly, so by using the delegate, you don't have to subclass an object to customize behavior. Now, I have to confess I have one little oddity going on...

Head First: Oh, I was waiting for this. This is where you ask the delegate for the value to show in a row, right?

Picker: Yeah—other controls ask their datasource. I could come up with a lot of excuses, but...well, we all have our little quirks, right?

Head First: I appreciate your honesty. It's not all bad, though; your delegate can do some neat things with each row, can't it?

Picker: Oh yeah! When I ask the delegate for a particular row, it can give me back a full view instead of just a string. Sometimes they have icons in them or pictures—really, anything you can cram in a view, I can display.

Head First: That's great. Well, we're out of time, but thanks again for stopping by.

Picker: My pleasure! Now I'm off to take my new datasource for a spin.

WHO DOES WHAT?

Match each picker characteristic to where it belongs—the delegate or the datasource. You'll need to go digging in the API to figure out where the three methods go.

Picker characteristic (or method)   Delegate or datasource?

Directions for drawing the view
for the items

The number of components   **Delegate**

`pickerView:numberOfRowsInComponent`

`pickerView:titleForRow:forComponent`

                                                                 Datasource

The row values (strings or views)

`numberOfComponentsInPickerView`

Match each picker characteristic to where it belongs—the delegate
or the data source. You'll need to go digging in the API to figure out
where the three methods go.

Picker characteristic (or method)   Delegate or datasource?

Directions for drawing the
view for the items

The number of components   **Delegate**

`pickerView:numberOfRowsInComponent`

A required part of the UIPickerViewDataSource
Protocol that returns the number of rows.

`pickerView:titleForRow:forComponent`

                                                                     Datasource
Part of the UIPickerViewDelegate protocol;
returns a title for one entry in the picker.

The row values (strings or views)

`numberOfComponentsInPickerView`   **Working together, the
                                                    delegate and the datasource
        A required part of the UIPickerViewDataSource provide what is needed to
        Protocol; returns the number of components.   render the picker.**

Hang on—there are protocols in **both** the datasource and the delegate?

Protocols define what messages the datasource and delegates need to respond to.

Pickers (and other controls that use delegates and datasources) have specific **messages** to which their supporting classes need to respond. We'll get into them in more detail in the next chapter, but for now what you need to know is that messages are defined in **protocols**. Protocols are Objective-C's idea of a pure interface. When your class can speak a particular protocol, you're said to *conform* to it.

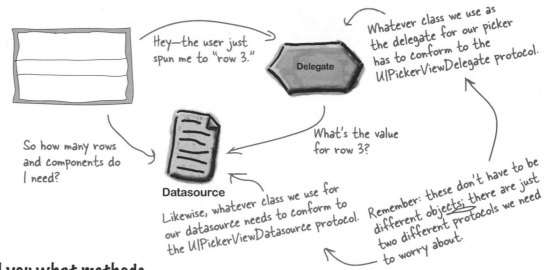

Hey—the user just spun me to "row 3."

Whatever class we use as the delegate for our picker has to conform to the UIPickerViewDelegate protocol.

So how many rows and components do I need?

What's the value for row 3?

Likewise, whatever class we use for our datasource needs to conform to the UIPickerViewDatasource protocol.

Remember: these don't have to be different objects; there are just two different protocols we need to worry about.

Protocols tell you what methods (messages) you need to implement

Protocols typically have some required methods to implement and others that are optional. For example, the UIPickerViewDatasource protocol has a *required* method named pickerView:numberOfRowsInComponent; it has to be in the datasource for the picker to work. However, UIPickerViewDelegate protocol has an *optional* method named pickerView:titleForRow:forComponent, so it doesn't need to be in the delegate unless you want it.

So how do you know what protocols you need to worry about? The documentation for an element will tell you what protocols it needs to talk to. For example, our UIPickerView needs a datasource that speaks the UIPickerViewDataSource protocol and a delegate that speaks the UIPickerViewDelegate protocol. Click on the protocol name and you'll see the documentation for which messages are optional and which are required for a protocol. We'll talk more about how to implement these in the next chapter; for now, we'll provide you the code to get started.

First, declare that the controller conforms to both protocols

Now that you know what you need to make the picker work, namely a delegate and a datasource, let's get back into Xcode and create them. Under **Classes**, you have two files that need to be edited: InstaEmailViewController.h and InstaEmailViewController.m. Both files were created when you started the project.

The .h and .m files work together, with the header file (.h) declaring the class's interface, variable declarations, outlets, and actions, etc.; the implementation file (.m) holds the actual implementation code. We need to update the header file to state that our InstaEmailViewController conforms to both the UIPickerViewDataSource and the UIPickerViewDelegate protocols.

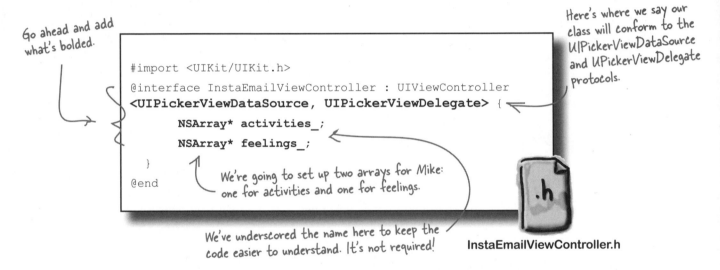

Go ahead and add what's bolded.

Here's where we say our class will conform to the UIPickerViewDataSource and UIPickerViewDelegate protocols.

```
#import <UIKit/UIKit.h>
@interface InstaEmailViewController : UIViewController
<UIPickerViewDataSource, UIPickerViewDelegate> {
    NSArray* activities_;
    NSArray* feelings_;
}
@end
```

We're going to set up two arrays for Mike: one for activities and one for feelings.

We've underscored the name here to keep the code easier to understand. It's not required!

InstaEmailViewController.h

Next, add Mike's activities and feelings to the implementation file

Now we're into InstaEmailViewController.m file, the actual implementation. We'll need to add some methods to implement the required methods from the protocols, but we'll get back to that in a second. First, let's add the list from Mike. We're going to use the two arrays we declared in the header to store the words that Mike gave us.

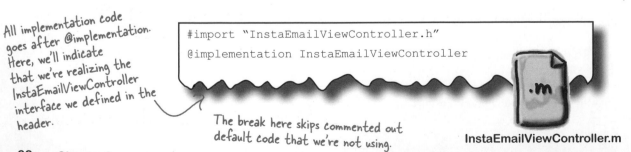

All implementation code goes after @implementation. Here, we'll indicate that we're realizing the InstaEmailViewController interface we defined in the header.

```
#import "InstaEmailViewController.h"
@implementation InstaEmailViewController
```

The break here skips commented out default code that we're not using.

InstaEmailViewController.m

Remove the /* marks that were here and then add the code. Xcode templates come with lots of possible methods stubbed out. For this app, we're using viewDidLoad.

This method gets called on your view controller after the view is loaded from the .xib file. This is where you can do some initialization and setup for the view.

```objc
// Implement viewDidLoad to do additional setup after ...
- (void)viewDidLoad {
    [super viewDidLoad];

    activities_ = [[NSArray alloc] initWithObjects:@"sleeping",
@"eating", @"working", @"thinking", @"crying", @"begging",
@"leaving", @"shopping", @"hello worlding", nil];

    feelings_ = [[NSArray alloc] initWithObjects:@"awesome",
@"sad", @"happy", @"ambivalent", @"nauseous", @"psyched",
@"confused", @"hopeful", @"anxious", nil];

}
```

Here, we establish the arrays with Mike's lists. We'll call them in a bit to fill in the picker.

InstaEmailViewController.m

The "@" before those strings tells the compiler to make them NSStrings instead of char*. NSStrings are real Objective-C objects, as opposed to a simple C-style character pointer. Most Objective-C classes use NSStrings instead of char*'s.

```objc
- (void)dealloc {
    [activities_ release];
    [feelings_ release];
    [super dealloc];
}
```

You need to release all these objects to free up the memory they were using. We'll talk about memory management a lot more in Chapter 3.

InstaEmailViewController.m

Now we just need the protocols...

The datasource protocol has two required methods

Let's focus on the datasource protocol methods first. We said in the header file that InstaEmailViewController conforms to the UIPickerViewDatasource protocol. That protocol has two required methods: numberOfComponentsInPickerView:pickerView and pickerView:numberOfRowsInComponent. Since we know we want two wheels (or components) in our view, we can start by putting that method in our implementation file.

This code can go anywhere in the body of the file. After viewDidLoad works great!

```
#pragma mark -
#pragma mark Picker Datasource Protocol

- (NSInteger)numberOfComponentsInPickerView:(UIPickerView *) pickerView {
    return 2;
}

- (NSInteger)pickerView:(UIPickerView *)pickerView numberOfRowsInComponent
:(NSInteger)component {
    if (component == 0) {
        return [activities_ count];
    }
    else {
        return [feelings_ count];
    }
}
```

The #pragma notation is for Xcode; it helps break up the code, but doesn't provide any logic.

Here are the two required methods for the picker.

How many components?

How many rows in each component? They come from different arrays, so we need to treat them separately.

InstaEmailViewController.m

Our second method needs to return the number of rows for each component. The component argument will tell us which component the picker is asking about, with the first component (the activities) as component 0. The number of rows in each component is the just the number of items in the appropriate array.

Now that we have the methods implemented, let's wire everything up to the picker.

Connect the datasource just like actions and outlets

Now that the datasource protocol is implemented, the data is in place and it's just a matter of linking it to the picker. Hop back into Interface Builder to make that connection:

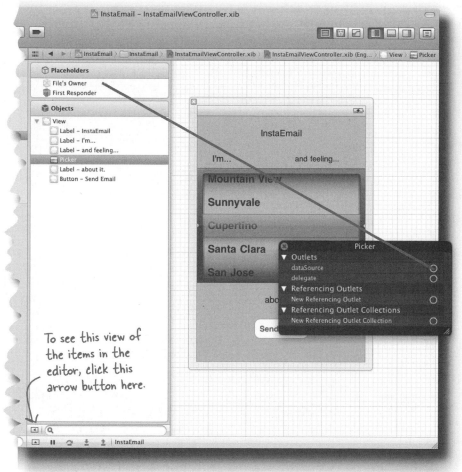

To see this view of the items in the editor, click this arrow button here.

1 Right-click on the **Picker** in the view to bring up the picker connections box.

2 Notice that the **File's Owner** for this view is our InstaEmailViewController, which realizes the datasource and delegate protocols we need. You need to connect the picker's dataSource to our controller, or the **File's Owner.** To do that, click inside the circle next to the dataSource, and drag over the to File's Owner.

There's just one method for the delegate protocol

The UIPickerViewDelegate protocol only has one required method (well, technically there are two optional methods, and you have to implement one of them). We're going to use pickerView:titleForRow: forComponent. This method has to return an NSString with the title for the given row in the given component. Again, both of these values are indexed from 0, so we can use the component value to figure out which array to use, and then use the row value as an index.

```
#pragma mark -
#pragma mark Picker Delegate Protocol
- (NSString *)pickerView:(UIPickerView *)pickerView
titleForRow:(NSInteger)row forComponent:(NSInteger)component {

        if (component == 0) {
                        return [activities_ objectAtIndex:row];
        }
        else {
                return [feelings_ objectAtIndex:row]
        }
        return nil;

}
```

The signature for these messages comes right out of the UIPickerViewDelegate and UIPickerViewDataSource documentation. Just cut and paste it if you want.

Our choice of two methods, one of which needs to be implemented.

Return the string in the array at the appropriate location—row 0 is the first string, row 1 second, etc.

InstaEmailViewController.m

Now back to the view to wire up the delegate...

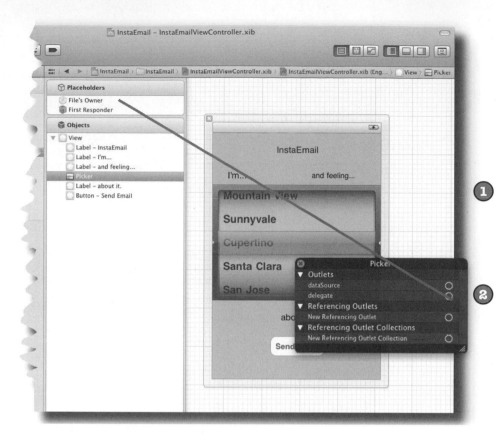

1 Right-click on the picker again and bring up the connections window.

2 The **File's Owner** realizes the delegate protocol as well. Click inside the circle next to the delegate and drag over the to **File's Owner.**

Test Drive

Save your work in and Run (⌘+R) the app. When the Simulator pops up, you should see everything working!

Spin those dials—they're all the things on Mike's list and they work great!

there are no Dumb Questions

Q: **What happens if I don't implement a required method in a protocol?**

A: Your project will compile, but you'll get a warning. If you try to run your application, it will almost certainly crash with an "unrecognized selector" exception when a component tries to send your class the missing required message.

Q: **What if I don't implement an optional method in a protocol?**

A: That's fine. But whatever functionality that it would provide isn't going to be there. You do need to be a little careful in that sometimes Apple marks a couple of methods

as optional but actually, you **have to implement at least one of them.** That's the case with the UIPickerViewDelegate. If you don't implement at least one of the methods specified in the docs, your app will crash with an error when you try to run it.

Q: **Are there limits to the number of protocols a class can realize?**

A: Nope. Now, the more you realize, the more code you're going to need to put in that class, so there's a point where you really need to split things off into different classes to keep the code manageable. But technically speaking, you can conform to as many as you want.

Q: **I'm still a little fuzzy, what's the difference between the interface we put in a header file and a protocol?**

A: An interface in a header file is how Objective-C declares the properties, fields, and messages a class responds to. It's like a header file in C++ or the method declarations in a Java file. However, you have to provide implementation for everything in your class's interface. A protocol, on the other hand, is just a list of messages—there is no implementation. It's the class that realizes the protocol that has to provide implementation. These are equivalent to interfaces in Java and pure virtual methods in C++.

BULLET POINTS

- The picker needs a delegate and a data-source to work.
- In a picker, each dial is a component.
- In a picker, each item is a row.
- Protocols define the messages your class must realize—some of them might be optional.

> OK, that's great and all. It looks really nice. But the "Send Email" button doesn't do anything yet...

Now let's get that button sending emails...

We got the picker working, but if you try out the "Send Email" button, nothing happens when something's selected. We still need to get the button responding to Mike and then get the whole thing to generate and send an email.

BRAIN BARBELL

Think about what we need to do to get the button working. What files will we use? What will the button actually do?

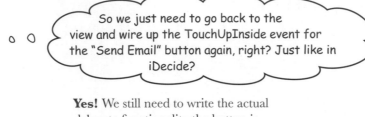

So we just need to go back to the view and wire up the TouchUpInside event for the "Send Email" button again, right? Just like in iDecide?

Yes! We still need to write the actual delegate functionality the button is going to trigger, but that's the idea.

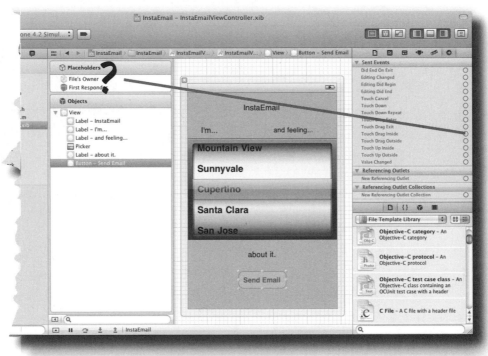

there are no
Dumb Questions

Q: What is an event again?

A: UI controls trigger events when things happen to them. You can "wire" these events to methods so that your method is called when an event is triggered. Most of the time, you can wire events to methods using Interface Builder, but you can also do it in code (we'll do this later in the book).

Q: Why didn't we have to wire up the picker methods? All we did there was set up a delegate and datasource.

A: Great question! Some controls have very fine-grained events that they trigger. Those individual events can be wired to specific methods on other objects (like File's Owner). Other controls want higher-level concepts, like a Datasource or a Delegate. In order to be a Datasource or a Delegate for those controls, you have to provide a set of methods that the control can call. Those methods are defined in a protocol. In the case of the UIPickerView, it doesn't have lots of fine-grained events—instead, it has two key protocols and just wants to know which object(s) will implement them. You can't choose to have half the Datasource methods go to one object and the other half to go somewhere else. You simply give it a datasource and it will call all of the datasource methods on that object as it needs to.

Actions, outlets, and events

Back in iDecide, we used actions and outlets with a button press. Let's go back
for a second to revisit what happened:

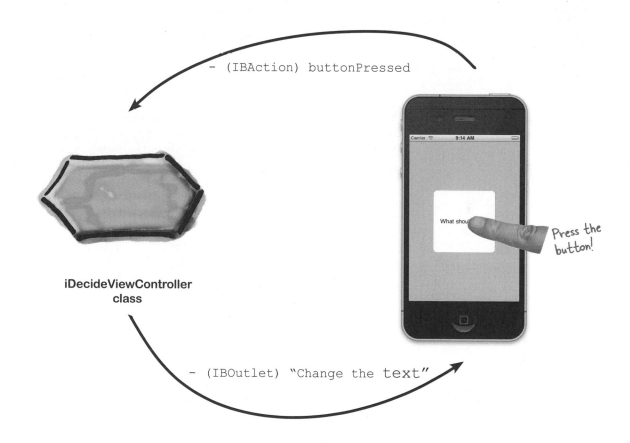

- (IBAction) buttonPressed

**iDecideViewController
class**

- (IBOutlet) "Change the text"

Press the
button!

Here's the action we created for the button press in Chapter 1:

- (IBAction) buttonPressed:(id)sender;

IB = Interface
Builder

This is the name of the method that will get
called. The name can be anything, but the method
must have one argument of type (id).

All IBAction messages
take one argument: the
sender of the message.
This is the element that
triggered the action.

Fireside Chats

Tonight's talk: **IBActions speak louder than...a lot of things**

IBAction:	IBOutlet:
Hi, Outlet. What's it like to only be an enabler?	
	What are you talking about? I do stuff.
Uh—I'm an Action, all about *doing*. My job is to do something when something else happens—an event. That's getting something done. You just sit there and point to stuff going on.	
	Big deal. At least I'm aware of everything going on.
Yeah, but when the user does something, I make it happen! I do the saving, I do the email sending!	
	Listen, it's true that I'm just an instance variable that works with an object in a nib, but that doesn't mean I'm not important.
Really, because the compiler just ignores you!	
	It does, but I tell Interface Builder in Xcode a lot. You're not very tight with IB, are you?
Well, for starters, the "IB" in IBAction stands for Interface Builder!	
	Big deal, I have "IB" in my name, too.
Well, we do have that in common. Anyway, Interface Builder knows when I'm around so that some event in a nib can set me off and keep me informed.	
	Well, I guess that is pretty important.
Thanks. That's nice of you to admit.	

IBAction:

Care to explain?

Oh—I see. You know, there is one thing that you have that I've always wanted.

You can be anything! Stick IBOutlet in front of a UI component's variable name and you're good. I have more complicated syntax, because I need to have the idea of a sender in there.

Me too.

IBOutlet:

But I'm secure in my relationship with Interface Builder. Without me, the code couldn't change anything in the UI.

Sure. An IBOutlet variable can point to a specific object in the nib (like a text field or something), and code (yes, probably *your* code) can use me to change the UI, set a text field's content, change colors, etc.

What's that?

I do like the freedom! Glad we could work things out.

Exercise

Change both the header and implementation files for the InstaEmailViewController to include the IBaction info we need.

① Start with the header and add an IBAction named sendButtonTapped.

② Then provide an implementation for that method in our .m file, and write a message to the log so you know it worked before creating the email and sending it off.

Exercise Solution

Declare your IBAction in the header file and provide the implementation in the .m file.

1

```objc
#import <UIKit/UIKit.h>

@interface InstaEmailViewController : UIViewController
<UIPickerViewDataSource, UIPickerViewDelegate> {

    NSArray* activities_;
    NSArray* feelings_;

}
- (IBAction) sendButtonTapped: (id) sender;


@end
```

The IBAction is what allows the code to respond to a user event, remember...

Declare your IBAction here so we can use it in the .m file and Interface Builder knows we have an action available.

InstaEmailViewController.h

2

Add this bit of code after the picker code.

```objc
#pragma mark -

#pragma mark Actions


 - (IBAction) sendButtonTapped: (id) sender {
    NSLog(@"Email button tapped!");
}
```

Same method declaration as the .h

This will give you the output on the console.

InstaEmailViewController.m

Connect the event to the action

Now that you have an action, you need to wire up the event to the action. Open up InstaEmailViewController.xib in Xcode with the Utilities pane, right-click on the button, and drag the circle for Touch Up Inside to File's Owner. Link it with your new sendButtonTapped method.

Do this!

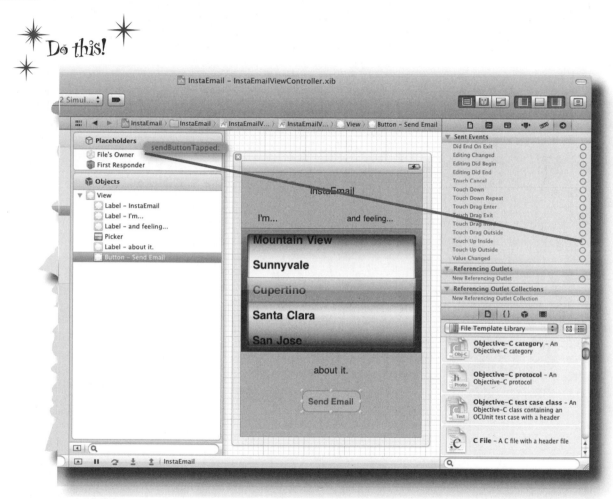

TEST DRIVE

Save, then click Build and Run. You should get the "Email button tapped!" message in the console in Xcode. To see it, you need to enable the debugging pane and select All Output.

Test Drive

Save, then click Build and Run. You should get the "Email button tapped!" message in the console in Xcode. To see it, you need to enable the debugging pane and select All Output.

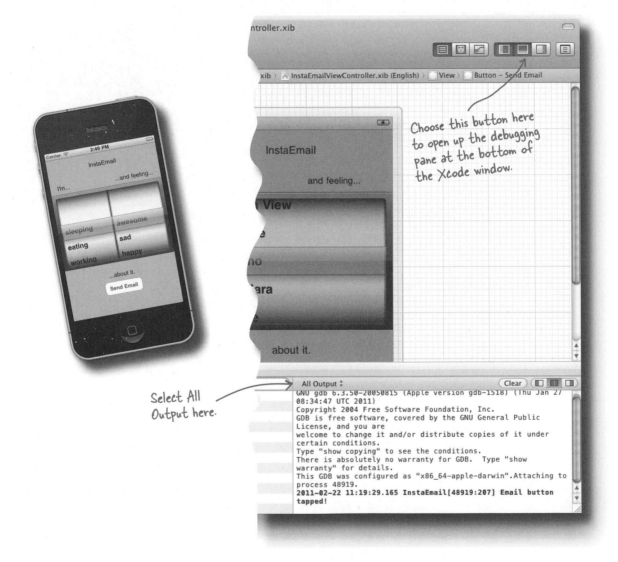

Choose this button here to open up the debugging pane at the bottom of the Xcode window.

Select All Output here.

```
GNU gdb 6.3.50-20050815 (Apple version gdb-1518) (Thu Jan 27
08:34:47 UTC 2011)
Copyright 2004 Free Software Foundation, Inc.
GDB is free software, covered by the GNU General Public
License, and you are
welcome to change it and/or distribute copies of it under
certain conditions.
Type "show copying" to see the conditions.
There is absolutely no warranty for GDB.  Type "show
warranty" for details.
This GDB was configured as "x86_64-apple-darwin".Attaching to
process 48919.
2011-02-22 11:19:29.165 InstaEmail[48919:207] Email button
tapped!
```

So now we need to get the data from that picker for the email, right? Would an IBOutlet be the right thing for that?

Yes! An IBOutlet provides a reference to the picker.

In Chapter 1, we used an outlet to access and change the text field value on the button. Now, to gather up the actual message to create the email, we need to extract the values chosen from the picker, then create a string including the label text.

So far, the picker has been calling us when it needed information; this time, when Mike hits the "Send Email" button, we need to get data out of the picker. We'll use an IBOutlet to do that.

Add the IBOutlet and property to your view controller

We need to declare an IBOutlet property and a class attribute to back it. We'll talk more about properties in the next chapter, but in short, that will get us proper memory management and let the Cocoa Touch framework set our emailPicker property when our nib loads.

Start with the header file by adding the code in bold below:

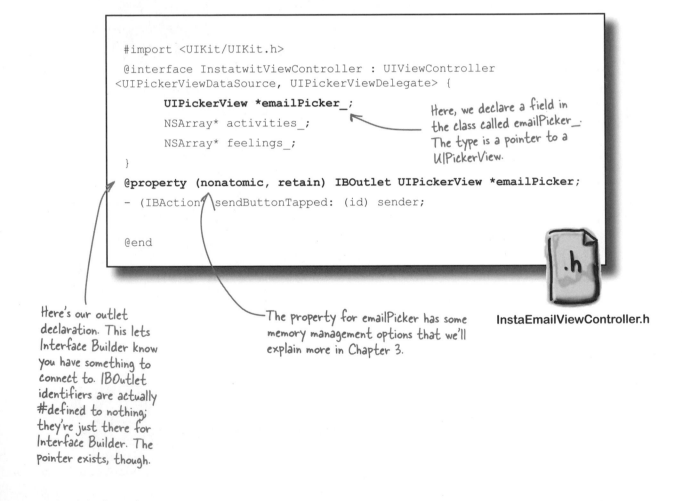

```
#import <UIKit/UIKit.h>
@interface InstatwitViewController : UIViewController
<UIPickerViewDataSource, UIPickerViewDelegate> {

    UIPickerView *emailPicker_;

    NSArray* activities_;

    NSArray* feelings_;

}
@property (nonatomic, retain) IBOutlet UIPickerView *emailPicker;

- (IBAction) sendButtonTapped: (id) sender;


@end
```

Here, we declare a field in the class called emailPicker_. The type is a pointer to a UIPickerView.

Here's our outlet declaration. This lets Interface Builder know you have something to connect to. IBOutlet identifiers are actually #defined to nothing; they're just there for Interface Builder. The pointer exists, though.

The property for emailPicker has some memory management options that we'll explain more in Chapter 3.

InstaEmailViewController.h

Next, synthesize the property...

Once we set up the declarations for the property and instance variable, we need to link them up in the implementation file. We do that with the @ synthesize directive.

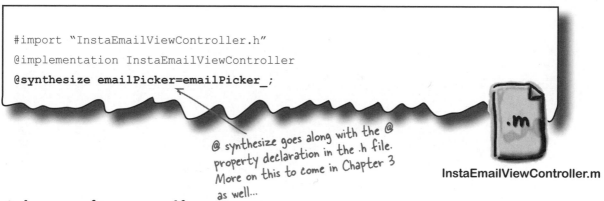

```
#import "InstaEmailViewController.h"
@implementation InstaEmailViewController
@synthesize emailPicker=emailPicker_;
```

@ synthesize goes along with the @ property declaration in the .h file. More on this to come in Chapter 3 as well...

InstaEmailViewController.m

...and clean up after yourself

When our view controller is destroyed, its dealloc method will be called. We need to make sure we release any memory we've allocated. We'll talk a lot more about memory management in Chapter 3, but for now, make sure you release each of your class attributes.

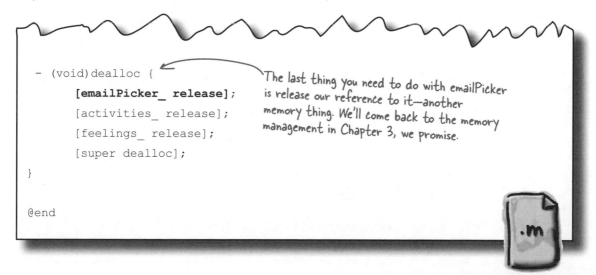

```
- (void)dealloc {
    [emailPicker_ release];
    [activities_ release];
    [feelings_ release];
    [super dealloc];
}

@end
```

The last thing you need to do with emailPicker is release our reference to it—another memory thing. We'll come back to the memory management in Chapter 3, we promise.

InstaEmailViewController.m

What's next?

Connect the picker to our outlet

You're probably expecting this by now! Back into the view to make
the connection from the UIPickerView to the IBOutlet in your view
controller. Right-click on the UIPickerView, grab the circle next to
the "New Referencing Outlet," and drop it on File's Owner—our
InstaEmailViewController sporting its new emailPicker outlet.

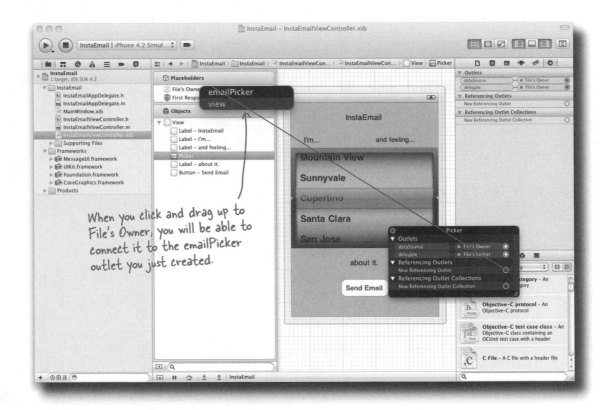

When you click and drag up to
File's Owner, you will be able to
connect it to the emailPicker
outlet you just created.

**BRAIN POWER**

What do you need to do now to get the data out
of the picker and into your email message? Think
about the "Send Email" button action and how that
will need to change...

Use your picker reference to pull the selected values

Now all that's left is to use our reference to the picker to get the actual values Mike selects. We need to change the sendButtonTapped method to pull the values from the picker. Looking at the UIPickerView documentation, the method we need is selectedRowInComponent:. That method returns a row index we can use as an index into our arrays.

Here's the implementation for our callback. We need to create a string and fill in the values from the picker. The "%@" in the string format get replaced with the values we pass in.

To figure out what Mike chose on the picker, we need to ask the picker which row is selected for each component, and get the corresponding string from our arrays.

```objc
- (IBAction) sendButtonTapped: (id) sender {
    NSString* theMessage = [NSString stringWithFormat:@"I'm %@ and feeling %@ about it.",
        [activities_ objectAtIndex:[emailPicker_ selectedRowInComponent:0]],
        [feelings_ objectAtIndex:[emailPicker_ selectedRowInComponent:1]]];
    NSLog(@"%@",theMessage);
    NSLog(@"Email button tapped!");
}
```

We'll pull this log message out and put in the one above to see what the final email message will be.

InstaEmailViewController.m

We want to build a new string with the full email text in it, so we'll use NSString's stringWithFormat method to create a templated string. There are lots of other options you could use with a string format, like characters, integers, etc., but for now we just need to insert the two selected strings, so we'll use %@.

For now we're just going to log this message to the console so we can see the string we're building, and then we'll generate the email to send out in just a minute. Let's make sure we implemented this correctly first before emailing Renee.

Test Drive

OK, try it out. You should get some convincing text in the console.

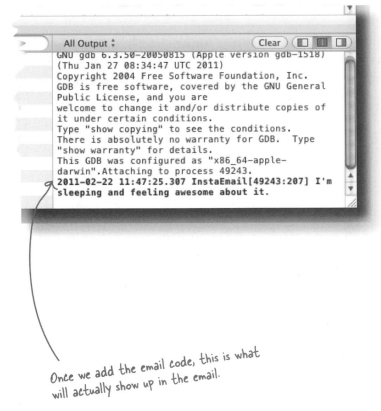

```
GNU gdb 6.3.50-20050815 (Apple version gdb-1518)
(Thu Jan 27 08:34:47 UTC 2011)
Copyright 2004 Free Software Foundation, Inc.
GDB is free software, covered by the GNU General
Public License, and you are
welcome to change it and/or distribute copies of
it under certain conditions.
Type "show copying" to see the conditions.
There is absolutely no warranty for GDB.  Type
"show warranty" for details.
This GDB was configured as "x86_64-apple-
darwin".Attaching to process 49243.
2011-02-22 11:47:25.307 InstaEmail[49243:207] I'm
sleeping and feeling awesome about it.
```

Once we add the email code, this is what will actually show up in the email.

Ready Bake Code

To send the email, we're going to use the messaging API. Rather than go into all the details of the messaging framework right now, we'll give you the code you need. As you get further in the book, this type of framework will become easy to use. Add the bolded code you see below into the appropriate files, and you'll be ready to go.

```objc
#import <UIKit/UIKit.h>

#import <MessageUI/MFMailComposeViewController.h>


@interface InstaEmailViewController : UIViewController <UIPickerViewDataSource,
UIPickerViewDelegate, MFMailComposeViewControllerDelegate> {
    UIPickerView *emailPicker_;
```

InstaEmailViewController.h

```objc
#pragma mark -
#pragma mark Actions
- (IBAction) sendButtonTapped: (id) sender {
    NSString *theMessage = [NSString stringWithFormat:@"I'm %@ and feeling %@
about it.",
            [activities_ objectAtIndex:[emailPicker_ selectedRowInComponent:0]],
            [feelings_ objectAtIndex:[emailPicker_ selectedRowInComponent:1]]];
    NSLog(@"%@", theMessage);


    if ([MFMailComposeViewController canSendMail]) {
        MFMailComposeViewController* mailController =
[[MFMailComposeViewController alloc] init];
        mailController.mailComposeDelegate = self;
        [mailController setSubject:@"Hello Renee!"];
        [mailController setMessageBody:theMessage isHTML:NO];
        [self presentModalViewController:mailController animated:YES];
        [mailController release];
    }
    else {
        NSLog(@"%@", @"Sorry, you need to setup mail first!");
    }
}
```

InstaEmailViewController.m

Ready Bake Code Cont.

```objc
#pragma mark -
#pragma mark Mail composer delegate method


- (void)mailComposeController:(MFMailComposeViewController*)
controller
            didFinishWithResult:(MFMailComposeResult)result
                          error:(NSError*)error;
{

    [self dismissModalViewControllerAnimated:YES];

}
```

InstaEmailViewController.m

Remember when we talked about differences between the simulator and a real device? The simulator can compose an email but won't actually send it to a mail server. So you can see everything work, but can't actually email Renee.

After adding that code, you can just save, build, and go. It will now show up as a preformatted email!

Test Drive

That is great! Now, Renee is happy and feels included and I don't actually have to talk out loud about my feelings. At all. Ever.

iOS cross

Flex your vocab skills with this crossword.

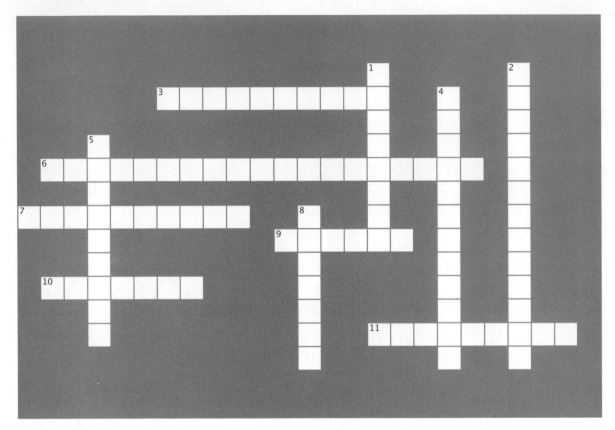

Across

3. This typically handles the information itself in the app.
6. This is the document Apple uses to evaluate apps for the App Store.
7. You see this listed in the view and it controls the view.
9. This component allows for controlled input from several selections.
10. This type of app is typically one screen, and gives you the basics with minimal interaction.
11. These define to which messages the datasource and delegate respond.

Down

1. This typically contains the logic that controls the flow of information in an app.
2. The best way to figure out what protocols you need to worry about is to check the _____.
4. This app type typically involves hierarchical data.
5. This app type is mostly custom controllers and graphics.
8. The other name for an *.xib file.

Exercise

We've listed a couple of descriptions of a some different apps. Using the app description, sketch out a rough view and answer the questions about each one.

① Generic giant button app

There are several of these currently up for sale on the App Store. This app consists of pushing a big button and getting some noise out of your iPhone.

What type of app is this?

....

What are the main concerns in the HIG about this app type?

....

....

....

② Book inventory app

This app's mission is to keep a list of the books in your library, along with a quick blurb of what each is about and the author.

What type of app is this?

....

What are the main concerns in the HIG about this app type?

....

....

....

○ ○ ○   View

○ ○ ○   View

iOS cross Solution

Flex your vocab skills with this crossword.

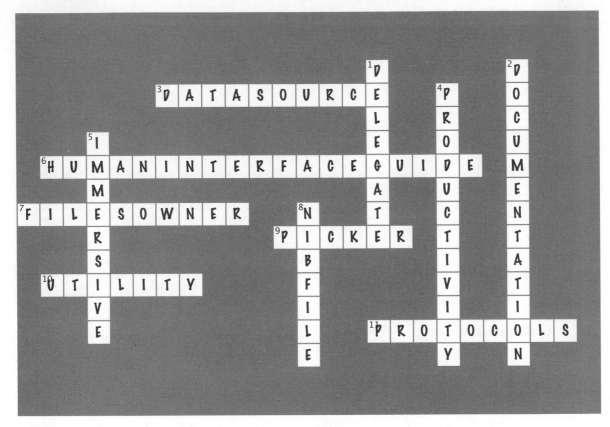

Across

3. This typically handles the information itself in the app. [DATASOURCE]
6. This is the document apple uses to evaluate apps for the App Store. [HUMANINTERFACEGUIDE]
7. You see this listed in the view and it controls the view. [FILESOWNER]
9. This component allows for controlled input from several selections. [PICKER]
10. This type of app is typically one screen, and gives you the basics with minimal interaction. [UTILITY]
11. These define to which messages the datasource and delegate respond. [PROTOCOLS]

Down

1. This typically contains the logic that controls the flow of information in an app. [DELEGATE]
2. The best way to figure out what protocols you need to worry about is to check the _____. [DOCUMENTATION]
4. This app type typically involves hierarchical data. [PRODUCTIVITY]
5. This app type is mostly custom controllers and graphics. [IMMERSIVE]
8. The other name for an *.xib file. [NIBFILE]

Exercise
Solution

We've listed a couple of descriptions of a some different apps.
Using the app description, sketch out a rough view and answer
the questions about each one.

1 **Generic giant button app**
There are several of these currently up for
sale on the App Store. This app consists of
pushing a big button and getting some noise
out of your iPhone.

What type of app is this?

An immersive app

What are the main concerns in the HIG
about this app type?

The big thing Apple cares about is that
controls "provide an internally consistent
experience." So everything can be custom, but
it needs to focused and well organized.

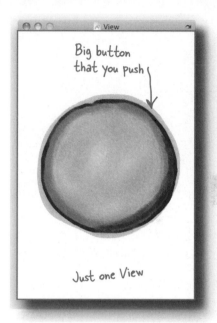

2 **Book inventory app.**
This app's mission is to keep a list of the books
in your library, along with a quick blurb of
what each is about and the author.

What type of app is this?

A productivity app

What are the main concerns in the HIG
about this app type?

The HIG has many more specific rules about
this app type, because you'll be using standard
controls. EACH control needs to be checked
out for proper usage.

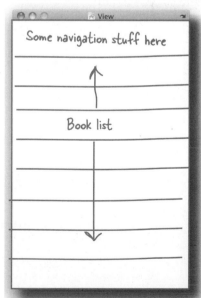

Another View for details, need to figure
out how to get to it...

Your iOS Toolbox

You've got Chapter 2 under your belt and now you've added protocols, delegates, and datasources to your toolbox.

Delegate

Responsible for the behavior of a UI element.

Contains the logic that controls the flow of information, like saving or displaying data, and which view is seen when.

Can be in same object as the datasource, but has its own specific protocols.

Protocols

Define the messages your datasource and delegate must respond to.

Are typically declared in a header (.h) file.

May contain both required and optional methods.

Datasource

Provides the bridge between the control and the data it needs to show.

Works with databases, plists, images, and other general info that your app will need to display.

Can be the same object as a delegate, but has its own specific protocols.

BULLET POINTS

- The picker needs a delegate and data-source to work.

- In a picker, each dial is a component.

- In a picker, each item is a row.

- Protocols define the messages your class must realize—though some of them might be optional.

This is Renee, Mike's girlfriend.

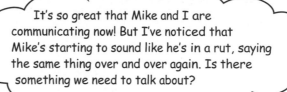

It's so great that Mike and I are communicating now! But I've noticed that Mike's starting to sound like he's in a rut, saying the same thing over and over again. Is there something we need to talk about?

Sounds like Mike is going to need some modifications to InstaEmail to keep his relationship on solid ground...

3 objective-c for iOS

Email needs variety

I know these are letters and all, but I have no idea what you're saying...

We did a lot in Chapter 2, but what language was that?

Parts of the code you've been writing might look familiar, but it's time you got a sense of what's really going on under the hood. The iOS SDK comes with great tools that mean you don't need to write code for everything, but you can't really write apps without learning something about the underlying language, including properties, message passing, and memory management. Unless you work that out, all your apps will be just default widgets! And you want more than just widgets, right?

Renee is catching on....

Mike has been diligently using InstaEmail to communicate his feelings, but his girlfriend is starting to think something weird is going on. Even for Mike, who is a guy who likes his routines, his emails are starting to sound suspicious.

> InstaEmail is working great and is so easy to use! But I think Renee is on to me. She said I sound like I'm in a rut. I need to be able to add some variation to my emails or this isn't going to work much longer.

We need to make some adjustments to our InstaEmail design.

Take a look at the various UI controls available in Interface Builder, and think about what would be a quick and easy way for Mike to add to his emails.

Make room for custom input

It's nothing fancy, but Mike could add a little personal flavor to his emails with a text field at the start. It means he'll need to do some typing, but in the end his emails will be more unique.

Scoot this stuff down a little.

We'll put the text field in here.

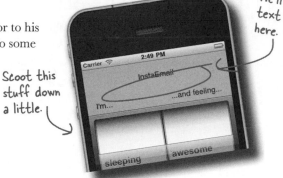

Design Magnets

Using what you know from adding the picker and the button, match the magnet with the method or file that you'll need to edit to add the text field.

1 .... to InstaEmailViewController.h.

2 .... to the top of InstaEmailViewController.m.

3 .... to the dealloc in InstaEmailViewController.m.

4 .... using Interface Builder.

5 .... to the property created in step #1, using Interface Builder.

> Create a delegate and datasource for the notesField

> Add UITextField to the view

> Declare the UITextField and a property that's an IBOutlet

> Add an IBAction for the UITextField

> Add notesField_ to @synthesize

> Add [notesfield_ release]

> Link the UITextField to the IBOutlet

Design Magnets Solution

Using what you know from adding the picker and the button, match the magnet with the method or file that you'll need to edit to add the text field.

1 | Declare the UITextField and a property that's an IBOutlet | to InstaEmailViewController.h.

```
@interface InstaEmailViewController : UIViewController
<UIPickerViewDataSource, UIPickerViewDelegate,
MFMailComposeViewControllerDelegate> {
    UIPickerView *emailPicker_;
    NSArray *activities_;
    NSArray *feelings_;
    UITextField *notesField_;

}


@property (nonatomic, retain) IBOutlet UIPickerView *emailPicker;
@property (nonatomic, retain) IBOutlet UITextField *notesField;
```

What we need is a UITextField. To implement the new field, we need to declare a class member that we'll call notesField_ and add a property marked as an IBOutlet.

InstaEmailViewController.h

> Wait a minute. We keep adding code to this .h file, but I still don't know what a .h file really does! What gives?

A .h file is a header file.

It's where you declare the interface and methods for a class. All of the classes we've used so far, like UITextField, NSString, and NSArray, have header files. Take a minute to look through a couple and start thinking about what is happening in those files.

Header files describe the interface to your class

In Objective-C, classes are defined with interfaces in the header file. It's where you declare whether your class inherits from anything, as well as your class's instance variables, properties, and methods.

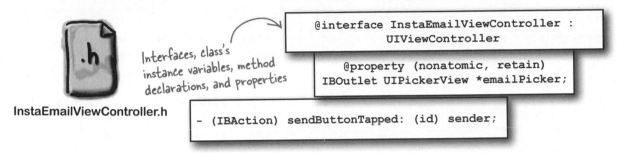

.h

Interfaces, class's instance variables, method declarations, and properties

InstaEmailViewController.h

```
@interface InstaEmailViewController :
        UIViewController
```

```
@property (nonatomic, retain)
IBOutlet UIPickerView *emailPicker;
```

```
- (IBAction) sendButtonTapped: (id) sender;
```

Sharpen your pencil

Here's our current **InstaEmailViewController.h** file. Fill in the blanks and explain what each line does.

```
#import <UIKit/UIKit.h>
```
....
```
#import <MessageUI/MFMailComposeViewController.h>
```
....
....
```
@interface InstaEmailViewController : UIViewController
<UIPickerViewDataSource, UIPickerViewDelegate,
MFMailComposeViewControllerDelegate> {
```
....
```
        UIPickerView *emailPicker_;
```
....
```
        NSArray* activities_;
```
....
....
```
        NSArray* feelings_;
```
....
```
        UITextField *notesField_;
```
....
....
```
}
```
....

....
```
@property (nonatomic, retain) IBOutlet UIPickerView*
emailPicker;
```
....
```
@property (nonatomic, retain) IBOutlet UITextField*
notesField;
```
....

....
```
- (IBAction) sendButtonTapped: (id) sender;
```
```
- (IBAction) textFieldDoneEditing:(id) sender;
```
....
```
@end
```

.h

InstaEmailViewController.h

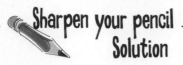

Sharpen your pencil Solution

Here's our current **InstaEmailViewController.h** file. Fill in the blanks and explain what each line does.

```
#import <UIKit/UIKit.h>

#import <MessageUI/
MFMailComposeViewController.h>
```

 # import incorporates another file (almost always a header file) into this file when it's compiled. It's used to pull in classes, constants, etc. from other files.

It's almost identical to C's #include, except that it automatically prevents including the same header multiple times (so no more #ifndef MY_HEADER).

@interface indicates you're going to declare a class.

Next comes the class name and, if it inherits from something, then a colon and the super class's name.

Objective-C doesn't support multiple inheritance...

```
@interface InstaEmailViewController:
UIViewController <UIPickerViewDataSource,
UIPickerViewDelegate,
MFMailComposeViewControllerDelegate>{
```

Here, we specify what we inherit from and what protocols we conform to.

Any protocols you implement go in angle brackets separated by commas. Protocols are like Java interfaces or pure virtual classes in C++, and a class can realize as many as you want.

This is where we can declare instance variables of our class.

```
    UIPickerView *emailPicker_;
    NSArray* activities_;
    NSArray* feelings_;
    UITextField *notesField_;
}
```

The syntax for instance variables is just like in C++: Basic types like int and float are used as-is; pointer types use an asterisk. By default, all fields are given protected access, but you can change that with @private or @public sections similar to C++.

InstaEmailViewController.h

The @property keyword tells the compiler this is a property that will be backed by getter and (maybe) setter methods.

Once you've closed the field section of your interface, you can declare properties. @property tells Objective-C that there will be accessor methods for the given property and let you use the '.' notation to access them.

These are property attributes; we'll talk more about these shortly...

```
@property (nonatomic, retain) IBOutlet UIPickerView* emailPicker;
```

IBOutlet allows Interface Builder to recognize properties that you can attach to controls (like our notes property in InstaEmail).

Here are our type and property name, just like the field in the class.

```
@property (nonatomic, retain) IBOutlet UITextField* notesField;
```

The minus sign means it's an instance method (a + means it's a class method). All methods in Objective-C are public.

These are the method declarations.

```
- (IBAction) sendButtonTapped: (id) sender;
- (IBAction) textFieldDoneEditing:(id) sender;
```

IBAction lets Interface Builder identify methods that can be attached to events.

IBAction method signatures can have no arguments, one argument of type id (which is like an Object reference in Java), or two arguments where one is the id of the sender and one is a UIEvent*.containing the event that triggered the call.

```
@end
```
@end: ends your class interface declaration.

InstaEmailViewController.h

Design Magnets Solution (Continued)

Back in that design we were working on...

Using what you know from adding the picker and the button, match the magnet with the method or file that you'll need to edit to add the text field.

1 .... | Declare the **UITextField** and a property that's an **IBOutlet** | .... to InstaEmailViewController.h.

InstaEmailViewController.h

```
    NSArray *feelings_;
    UITextField *notesField_;
}
@property (nonatomic, retain) IBOutlet UIPickerView *emailPicker;
@property (nonatomic, retain) IBOutlet UITextField *notesField;
```

2 .... | Add notesField to @ synthesize | .... to the top of InstaEmailViewController.m.

```
@synthesize emailPicker=emailPicker_;
@synthesize notesField=notesField_;
```

InstaEmailViewController.m

Here, you synthesize the accessor methods for the property. The equals sign tells the compiler that we're mapping our notesField property to the notesField_ field on the class. It's notesField_ that actually holds our values.

OK, so if we declared a property in the .h file, then adding @synthesize in the .m file must auto-generate some code, right?

Yes! It generates the getter and setter methods.

Using @property lets the compiler know we have a property, but that's not enough. Using the @synthesize keyword in the implementation files, we can have the compiler auto-generate the setter and getter method we talked about earlier. The compiler will generate a getter, and, if it's a readwrite property, a setter and implement it based on the @property attributes declared in the .h file. So what do the different @property attributes do...?

Below is a list of the most commonly used property attributes and definitions. Match each attribute with its definition.

readonly

When you want the property to be modifiable by people. The compiler will generate a getter and a setter for you. This is the default.

retain

When you're dealing with basic types, like ints, floats, etc. The compiler just creates a setter with a simple myField = value statement. This is the default, but not usually what you want.

readWrite

When you're dealing with object values. The compiler will retain the value you pass in (we'll talk more about retaining in a minute) and release the old value when a new one comes in.

copy

When you don't want people modifying the property. You can still change the field value backing the property, but the compiler won't generate a setter.

assign

When you want to hold onto a copy of some value instead of the value itself; for example, if you want to hold onto an array and don't want people to be able to change its contents after they set it. This sends a copy message to the value passed in, then keeps that.

Below is a list of the most commonly used property attributes and definitions. Match each attribute with its definition.

readonly

retain

readWrite

copy

assign

When you want the property to be modifiable by people. The compiler will generate a getter and a setter for you. This is the default.

When you're dealing with basic types, like ints, floats, etc. The compiler just creates a setter with a simple myField = value statement. This is the default, but not usually what you want.

When you're dealing with object values. The compiler will retain the value you pass in (we'll talk more about retaining in a minute) and release the old value when a new one comes in.

When you don't want people modifying the property. You can still change the instance variable value backing the property, but the compiler won't generate a setter.

When you want to hold onto a copy of some value instead of the value itself; for example, if you want to hold onto an array and don't want people to be able to change its contents after they set it. This sends a copy message to the value passed in, then keeps that.

there are no
Dumb Questions

Q: How does the compiler know what field to use to hold the property value?

A: By default, the compiler assumes the property name is the same as the field name, however, it doesn't have to be. We prefer to explicitly name them differently so you know when you're using the property versus the field. You can specify the field to use to back a property when you @synthesize it like this:
@synthesize secretString=superSecretField_;.

Q: What about that nonatomic keyword?

A: By default, generated accessors are multithread safe and use mutexes when changing a property value. These are considered **atomic**. However, if your class isn't being used by multiple threads, that's a waste. You can tell the compiler to skip the whole mutex thing by declaring your property as nonatomic. Note that just making your properties atomic doesn't mean your whole class is thread safe, so be careful here.

Auto-generated accessors also handle memory management

Objective-C under iOS doesn't have a garbage collector and instead uses a mechanism called *reference counting*. That involves keeping up with how many references there are to an object, and only freeing it up when the count drops to zero (it's no longer being used). You can think of this as object-ownership. An object can have more than one owner, and as long as it has at least one, it continues to exist. If an object doesn't have any owners left (its retain count hits 0), it's freed and cleaned up.

When using properties, the compiler handles it for us. The properties we've declared so far have all used the retain attribute. When the compiler generates a setter for that property, it will properly handle memory management for us, like this:

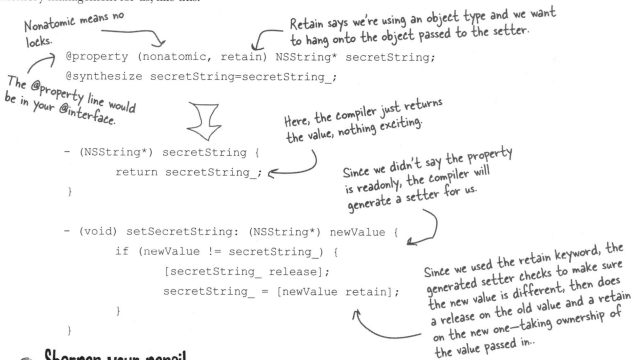

Nonatomic means no locks.

Retain says we're using an object type and we want to hang onto the object passed to the setter.

```objc
@property (nonatomic, retain) NSString* secretString;
@synthesize secretString=secretString_;
```

The @property line would be in your @interface.

Here, the compiler just returns the value, nothing exciting.

```objc
- (NSString*) secretString {
    return secretString_;
}
```

Since we didn't say the property is readonly, the compiler will generate a setter for us.

```objc
- (void) setSecretString: (NSString*) newValue {
    if (newValue != secretString_) {
        [secretString_ release];
        secretString_ = [newValue retain];
    }
}
```

Since we used the retain keyword, the generated setter checks to make sure the new value is different, then does a release on the old value and a retain on the new one—taking ownership of the value passed in.

Sharpen your pencil

Write the code that Objective-C generates for each property declaration below. Assume each one is backed by a field named myField_.

1. `@property (nonatomic, readonly) NSString* myField`

2. `@property (nonatomic, retain) NSString* myField`

3. `@property (nonatomic, assign) NSString* myField`

Sharpen your pencil
Solution

Below is the code that the compiler will generate for each property. Assume each one is backed by a field named myField_.

1. `@property (nonatomic, readonly) NSString* myField`

```
- (NSString*) myField {
  return myField_;
}
```

2. `@property (nonatomic, retain) NSString* myField`

```
- (NSString*) myField {
  return myField_;
}
- (void) setMyField: (NSString*) newValue {
  if (newValue != myField_) {
    [myField_ release];
  myField_ = [newValue retain];
  }
}
```

3. `@property (nonatomic, assign) NSString* myField`

```
- (NSString*) myField {
  return myField_;
}
- (void) setMyField: (NSString*) newValue
{
  myField_ = newValue;
}
```

Be careful with this one...NSStrings are reference-counted objects, so while this will technically work, having an assign property for an NSString is probably a bad idea.

However, for basic types like booleans and floats, you can't do reference counting. Assignment is almost always what you want.

I bet that release just lets go of the memory that your properties use up, right?

Yes, but more importantly, it gives up object ownership.

When you care about an object sticking around, you can take ownership of it by sending it a retain message (and remember, an object can have multiple owners). By sending an object a release message, you relinquish that ownership. If no one else owns the object, it will be cleaned up. Because of this, it's critically important that you don't send release messages to objects you don't own (that is, objects you haven't already sent a retain message to).

There are times when you want to give up ownership of an object, but you need it to stick around long enough for someone else to take it over. In those cases, Objective-C has the concept of an autorelease pool. This is basically an array of objects that the runtime will call release on after it's finished processing the current event. To put something in the autorelease pool, you simply send it the autorelease message (instead of a plain release message):

```
[aString autorelease];
```

It will still have the same retain count and stick around, but after the current event loop finishes, it will be sent a release message on your behalf. You won't want to use this all the time because it's not nearly as efficient and releases objects as soon as you're done with them. It's not a bad thing to use, but it's better to explicitly retain and release when you can.

To keep your memory straight, you need to remember just two things

Memory management can get pretty hairy in larger apps, so Apple has a couple of rules established to keep track of who's in charge of releasing and retaining when.

We'll explain more about retain counts in just a bit—hang on.

① You own objects you create with alloc, new, copy, or mutableCopy.
If you create an object with alloc, new, copy, or mutableCopy, it will have a retain count of 1, and you're responsible for sending a release when you're done with the object. You can also put the object in the autorelease pool if you want the system to handle sending a release later.

② Assume everything else could go away at the end of the event loop unless you take ownership.
If you get an object by any other means (string formatters, array initializers, etc.), you should treat the object as having a retain count of 1 and it will be autoreleased. This means that if you want to hang onto that object outside of the method that got the object, you'll need to take ownership by sending it a retain (and a corresponding release later when you're done with it).

Memory Management Up Close

```
- (void)dealloc {
    [emailPicker_ release];
    [activities_ release];
    [feelings_ release];
    [notesField_ release];
    [super dealloc];
}
```

This is some of the memory management code that YOU have already written!

Memory management is definitely important on iOS, but that doesn't mean it's complicated. Once you get the hang of a few key principles, you'll be able to structure your app so that it doesn't leak memory and get you kicked out of the app store.

When you create an object, it starts with a count of 1, and different things you do can raise and lower the count. When the count reaches 0, the object is released and the memory is made available.

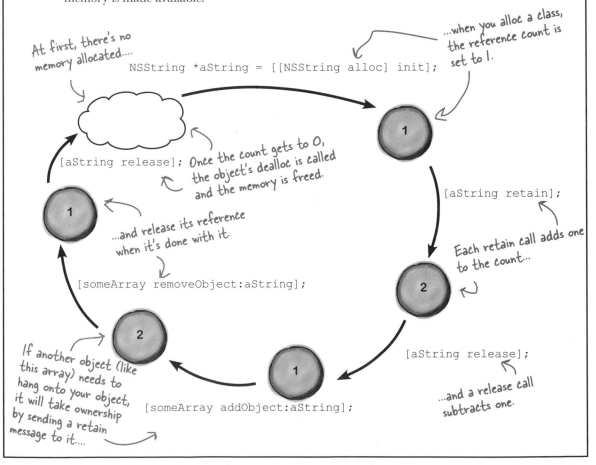

At first, there's no memory allocated....

```
NSString *aString = [[NSString alloc] init];
```

...when you alloc a class, the reference count is set to 1.

`[aString release];`

Once the count gets to 0, the object's dealloc is called and the memory is freed.

...and release its reference when it's done with it.

`[someArray removeObject:aString];`

`[aString retain];`

Each retain call adds one to the count...

`[aString release];`

...and a release call subtracts one.

`[someArray addObject:aString];`

If another object (like this array) needs to hang onto your object, it will take ownership by sending a retain message to it....

Exercise

Determine how many references are left at the end of the chunk of code and whether we have to send it a release for each string.

<u>Final Reference Count</u>

```objectivec
NSString *first = [[NSString alloc] init];
```

```objectivec
NSString *second = [[NSString alloc] init];
[someStringArray addObject:second];
```

```objectivec
NSString *third = [[NSString alloc] init];
[third autorelease];
```

```objectivec
NSString *fourth = [NSString
stringWithFormat:@"Do not read %@", @"Swimming
with your iPhone by TuMuch Monee"];
```

```objectivec
NSMutableArray *newArray = [[NSMutableArray alloc] init];
    NSString *fifth = [[NSString alloc]
initWithFormat:@"Read this instead: %@", "Financing your
iPhone 4G by Cerius Savar"];
    [newArray addObject:fifth];
    [newArray release];
```

```objectivec
NSString *sixth = [NSString stringWithString:@"Toughie"];
    NSArray *anotherArray = [NSArray
arrayWithObjects:sixth count:1];
    NSDictionary *newDictionary = [NSDictionary
dictionaryWithObjects:sixth    forKeys:@"Toughie"
count:1];
    NSString *ignoreMe = [sixth retain];
```

Determine how many references are left at the end of the chunk of code and whether we have to send it a release for each string.

Final Count

```
NSString *first = [[NSString alloc] init];
```

1 — Reference count will be 1 because alloc automatically sets count to 1.

```
NSString *second = [[NSString alloc] init];
[someStringArray addObject:second];
```

2 — "second" will have a retain count of 2 after this block of code: 1 from the alloc, 1 from inserting it into the array. Arrays automatically take ownership of items added to them.

```
NSString *third = [[NSString alloc] init];
[third autorelease];
```

1 — This still has a retain count of 1 because of the alloc, but is now in the autorelease pool, meaning it will be sent a release automatically by the system later.

```
NSString *fourth = [NSString
stringWithFormat:@"Do not read %@", @"Swimming
with your iPhone by TuMuch Monee"];
```

1 — This will have a retain count of 1, but will be in the autorelease pool because we don't own it (we didn't get it via an alloc, new, or some form of a copy).

Determine how many references are left at the end of the chunk of code and if we have to send it a release for each string.

Final Count

"fifth" will have a retain count of 1:

```
NSMutableArray *newArray = [[NSMutableArray
alloc] init];

    NSString *fifth = [[NSString alloc]
initWithFormat:@"Read this instead: %@",
"Financing your iPhone 4G by Cerius Savar"];

    [newArray addObject:fifth];

    [newArray release];
```

1

First, it gets a retain count of 1 from the alloc.

Next, it goes to 2 because "newArray" takes ownership by sending a retain when an object is inserted.

Then it goes back to 1 because an array will send a release to all its items when the array is destroyed.

"sixth" starts out with an autoreleased retain count of 1 from the initial creation (note it wasn't from alloc, so it's autoreleased).

```
NSString *sixth = [NSString
stringWithString:@"Toughie"];

    NSArray *anotherArray = [NSArray
arrayWithObjects:sixth count:1];

    NSDictionary *newDictionary =
[NSDictionary dictionaryWithObjects:sixth
forKeys:@"Toughie" count:1];

    NSString *ignoreMe = [sixth retain];
```

4

Next, another retain from inserting it into the array. Note the array wasn't alloc'ed either, so it will be autoreleased, too.

Then one more retain from the dictionary, also not alloc'ed and will be autoreleased.

Finally, an explicit retain...

So, even though "sixth" has a retain count of 4, we, the developers, only need to send one release to "sixth" and let everything else clean up with the autorelease pool.

Hey, could we get back to my app please?

Design Magnets Solution (Continued)

Using what you know from adding the picker and the button, match the
magnet with the method or file that you'll need to edit to add the text field.

1

> Declare the UITextField and a
> property that's an IBOutlet

.... to InstaEmailViewController.h.

```
    NSArray *feelings_;
    UITextField *notesField_;
}
@property (nonatomic, retain) IBOutlet UIPickerView *emailPicker;
@property (nonatomic, retain) IBOutlet UITextField *notesField;
```

.h

InstaEmailViewController.h

2

> Add notesField to @
> synthesize

to the top of
InstaEmailViewController.m.

```
@synthesize emailPicker=emailPicker_;
@synthesize notesField=notesField_;
```

*Here, you synthesize the accessor methods
from @property. You need to create a
new @synthesize line..*

.m

InstaEmailViewController.m

3

> Add [notesField_ release]

to the dealloc in
InstaEmailViewController.m.

*The property will automatically
retain a reference passed to it—we
need to release that in dealloc.*

```
- (void)dealloc {
    [emailPicker_ release];
    [activities_ release];
    [feelings_ release];
    [notesField_ release];
    [super dealloc];
```

*When we're being freed and our
dealloc is called, we need to release
our reference to the text field.*

*We don't need an
action or a datasource
for the notes field.*

> Add an IBAction for
> the UITextField

> Create a delegate and
> datasource for the notesField

.m

116 Chapter 3   **InstaEmailViewController.m**

**Add UITextField
to the view**

using Interface Builder.

To get into this, you'll need to open up InstaEmailViewController.xib and find the text field in the library. Then drag and drop the text field in between the "InstaEmail" label and the "I'm .... and feeling ..." labels. You'll also need to put a label that says "Notes" in front of the text field.

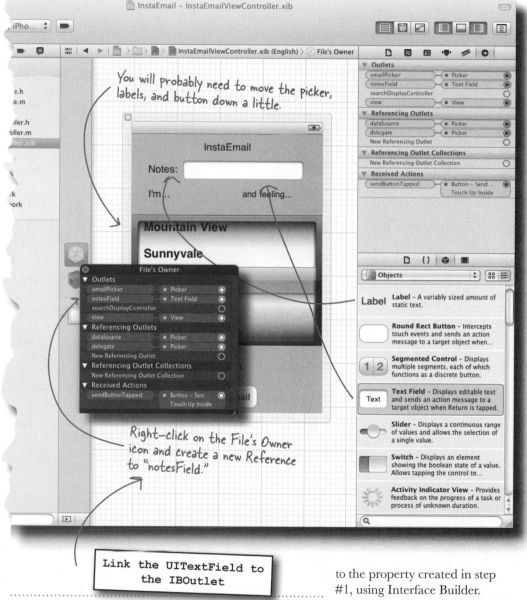

**Link the UITextField to
the IBOutlet**

to the property created in step #1, using Interface Builder.

Save it and then...

TEST DRIVE

Now that everything is saved, go back into Xcode and click Build and Run, and launch the Simulator.

Click here to write a note to customize the email....

The UI works!

Hey, we didn't even have to do anything to make the keyboard show up for the text field. Cool!

Objective-C Exposed

This week's interview:
Who are you anyway?

Head First: Hello Objective-C! Thanks for coming.

Objective-C: Thanks! It's great to be here. I've been getting a lot of attention recently with this whole iPhone thing.

Head First: So you have a pretty strong lineage, right? Why don't you tell us a little about yourself?

Objective-C: Sure. I'm an object-oriented language, so I have classes and objects, but I come from strong C roots. My OO concepts come from Smalltalk. Really, there's not much to me.

Head First: What do you mean you come from C roots?

Objective-C: Well, nearly all of my syntax is just like C syntax. For loops, types, pointers, etc. You can easily use other C libraries like SQLite with me. Things like that.

Head First: But you're more than just that, right?

Objective-C: Oh yeah, definitely. Most obviously, I am an OO language, so classes, abstract interfaces (which I call protocols), inheritance, etc. all work great.

Head First: So what about memory management? Malloc and free like C?

Objective-C: Well, malloc and free work just like they do in C, but I have a really nice memory management model for objects. I use reference counting.

Head First: Ah—so you keep track of who's using what?

Objective-C: Yup. If you want to keep an object around, you just tell me you want to retain a reference to it. Done with it? Just release your reference. When there aren't any references left, I'll clean up the object and free up the memory for you.

Head First: Nice. Any other tricks?

Objective-C: Oh yeah. You know those getter and setter methods you need to write for other OO languages to wrap fields in a class? Not here. I can automatically generate them for you. Not only that, you can tell me how you want to handle the memory associated with them. Oh, and one of my favorites: I can graft new methods onto classes without a problem. They're called categories.

Head First: Oh, that's slick. We're about out of time, so just one more question. What's up with all those "NS"s all over the place, like NSString and NSInteger?

Objective-C: Ah—those are all part of the Cocoa Touch framework. I mentioned my strong lineage earlier; most of the core classes that people use on iOS come from Cocoa Touch, which is a port of Cocoa, which came from OpenStep, which came from NeXTStep, and that's where the NS comes from. The frameworks are written in Objective-C, but they're frameworks, not really language things. When you write for iOS, you'll be using things like that all the time. For example, instead of using char*s for strings, you usually use NSStrings or NSMutableStrings. We all kind of blur together.

Head First: This is great information! Thanks again for coming by, and best of luck with the iPhone!

Objective-C: No problem. Thanks for having me.

Q: **What happens if I don't retain an object I'll need later?**

A: Most likely, the object's retain count will hit 0 and it will be cleaned up before you get to use it. This will crash your application. Now here's the sad part: it might not crash your object on the simulator every time. The simulator has a lot more memory to work with and behaves differently than a real iPhone, iPad, or iPod Touch. Everything might look great until you put it on your device to test it. Then sadness ensues.

Q: **What if I release my object too many times?**

A: Basically the same thing. When the reference count hits 0, the object will be released and memory will be freed. Sending that now-freed memory another release message will almost certainly crash your application.

Q: **What if my project works on the simulator and dies on the real phone? Could that be a memory problem?**

A: Absolutely. Memory on a real device is much tighter than on the simulator. We'll talk more about debugging these and using Instruments to track memory usage and leaks in a later chapter.

Q: **How can I check if I'm managing my memory effectively?**

A: The iOS SDK comes with a great memory tool called Instruments that can show you how your memory is being used, peak memory usage, how fast you're allocating and deallocating it, and possibly most importantly, if you're leaking memory.

Q: **What happens if I set things to nil?**

A: Well, it depends on what you're setting to nil. If it's just a local variable, nothing. The variable is now nil, but the memory for the object it used to point to is still allocated and you've almost certainly leaked something. Now, if it's a property, things are probably a little different. Read on to the next question.

Q: **Do I have to retain things I want to set on my properties?**

A: No. Well, probably not. That's what the "retain" parameter is on the @property declaration. If you put retain there, the property will automatically send values retains and releases when the property is set or cleared. Be careful about clearing properties in your dealloc, though. If you have a property with a retain parameter and it still has a value when your object is released, then whatever that property is set to hasn't been freed. You must send the instance variable an explicit release in your dealloc.

One more quick note: the automatic retain/release ability of properties only works if you use the "." notation or the generated setters and getters. If you explicitly modify the field that backs the property, there's nothing the property can do about it and it can't retain/release correctly.

Q: **Doesn't Objective-C have garbage collection like Java or .NET?**

A: Actually, on the Mac it does. Apple didn't provide garbage collection on iOS, however, so you need to fall back to reference counting with retain and release.

Q: **What about malloc and free? Can I still use them?**

A: Yes, but not for object types. Malloc and free work fine for basic blocks of memory as they do in C, but use alloc to instantiate classes.

Q: **What's with that init call that you always put after the alloc?**

A: Objective-C doesn't have constructors like other object-oriented languages do. Instead, by convention, you can provide one or more init methods. You should always call init on any class you allocate, so you almost always see them together as [[SomeClass alloc] init].

Q: **How do I know if something retains my object, like an array or something?**

A: Basically, you shouldn't care. Follow the memory rules that say if you got it from alloc, new, copy, or mutableCopy, you have to send it a release. Otherwise, retain/release it if you want to use it later. Beyond that, let the other classes handle their own memory management.

But when Mike's finished typing...

> The textField works great, but how do I get the keyboard to go away?

The keyboard is permanent?

Go ahead, play with it and try to get the keyboard to go away. Return won't do it, and neither will clicking anywhere else on the screen. Not so cool.

BE the architect

Your job is to be the architect and plan how the keyboard needs to behave. Fill in the pattern diagram below to explain what needs to happen to make it go away!

View

How should the view communicate what has to happen to the user? What should the user see?

....
....
....
....
....

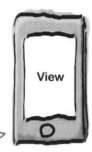

View Controller

What does the View Controller need to do to make these View changes happen?

....
....
....
....
....

BE the architect solution

Your job is to be architect and plan how the keyboard needs to behave. Fill in the pattern diagram below to explain what needs to happen to make it go away!

View

The user needs to understand what to do to make the keyboard go away, so change the "return" button to say "done".

Conventions like using "done" to let the user hide the keyboard are discussed in Apple's HIG. There are lots more; "done" is just one of them.

View Controller

The View Controller needs to receive the "done" message and then make the keyboard go away.

This kind of back and forth between the View and View Controller is common and is going to show up all over the place. Remember, a View Controller provides the behavior for a View.

there are no Dumb Questions

Q: Why didn't we have to do anything to make the keyboard appear in the first place?

A: When the users indicate that they want to interact with a specific control, iOS gives that control focus and sets it to be the "first responder" to events. When certain controls become the first responder, they trigger the keyboard to show automatically.

Let's start with the View.

Customize your UITextField

In InstaEmailViewController.xib, select Mike's custom field and then open up the Attributes Inspector in the Utilities pane. You can specify an initial value of the text in the field (**Text**); text that the field shows in grey if there's no other text to display (**Placeholder**); left, center, or right **Alignment**; different **Borders**, etc. For now, you don't need to add anything for field, so leave these alone.

Change the label on the return key

Changing the name of the button in the keyboard (so it's "done" instead of the "return") is another option in the inspector. The big thing that changing the label on the button brings to the table is that it clearly communicates to the user what to do to make the keyboard go away.

Click on the **Return Key** pop-up menu and pick **Done**.

> Here's the button for the Attributes Inspector.

> There are other options for the "return" button—some of them are obvious (like "Google") and others are little more subtle. Check out Apple's HIG for when to use some of the other ones.

Watch out for the HIG!

Beyond the Text and Placeholder fields, changing some of the other options may hurt your usability and make Apple unhappy, so be careful.

Now, get the keyboard to talk to the View Controller...

Components that use the keyboard ask it to appear...

When users click in the text field, iOS gives that control focus and assigns it as "first responder" for later events. A component can get focus a number of ways: the users explicitly tap on the control, the keyboard is set up so that the Return key moves to the next control they should fill out, the application sets some control to explicitly become first responder because of some event, etc. What a component does when it becomes the first responder varies by component, however; for a UITextField, it asks iOS to display the keyboard. All this chatter between the application and components is fundamental to writing an application, and it all happens through message passing.

...and you ask for things by passing messages to other objects

The idea is that whenever one object (whether that object is your ApplicationDelegate, another component, or the GPS in the iPhone) wants some other object to do something, it sends it a message.

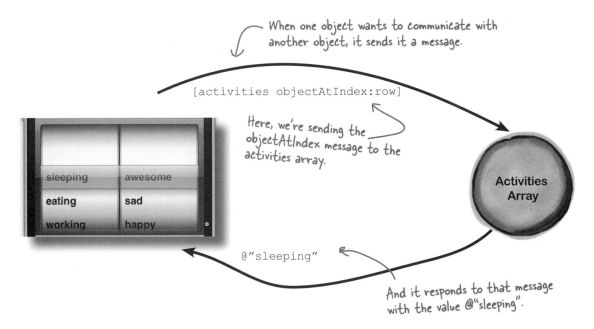

When one object wants to communicate with another object, it sends it a message.

`[activities objectAtIndex:row]`

Here, we're sending the objectAtIndex message to the activities array.

Activities Array

`@"sleeping"`

And it responds to that message with the value @"sleeping".

In Objective-C, you *send a message to an object* and it *responds to that message* (basically returning a value from a method). The Objective-C runtime turns those messages into method calls on objects or classes (in the case of static methods), but get used to thinking about these as messages; you'll see things like "the receiver of this message will..." all over Apple's documentation. Now, let's use message passing to get rid of the keyboard when the user is done with it.

Ask the UITextField to give up focus

In order to get the keyboard to go away, we need to tell the text field that the user is done with it. We do this by asking the UITextField to resign its first responder status.

Sending messages in Objective-C is easy: you list the receiver of the message, the message to send, and any arguments you need to pass along.

This is a statement like any other—don't forget the semicolon.

Surround message passing with square brackets.

```
[notesField resignFirstResponder];
```

This is the receiver for the message, in our case, the notesField.

This is where you put the actual message. In our case, we have no arguments, so this is all we need. See the Apple documentation for details on what messages each component will respond to.

Is that how the View is sending the View Controller information?

Yes! Our View Controller can respond to a number of messages like sendButtonTapped and viewDidLoad.

You've been responding to messages all this time. Now here's the trick: the textField can send a message when the user taps the Done button on they keyboard. We just need to tell it that our ViewController is interested in knowing when that happens.

You can pass messages to nil with no obvious problems.

Objective-C lets you send messages to nil without complaining. If you're used to NullPointerExceptions from other languages, this can make debugging tricky. Be careful of uninitialized variables or nil values coming back as other nil values when you debug.

Watch it!

Handling Messages Up Close

You've been handling messages since Chapter 1, but we really haven't talked about the syntax to make it work. Method declarations go in your header files and the implementation goes in the .m. Here are some snippets from our sendButtonTapped implementation from InstaEmail.

Implementation files (.m) start with @implementation, then the name of the class you're implementing.

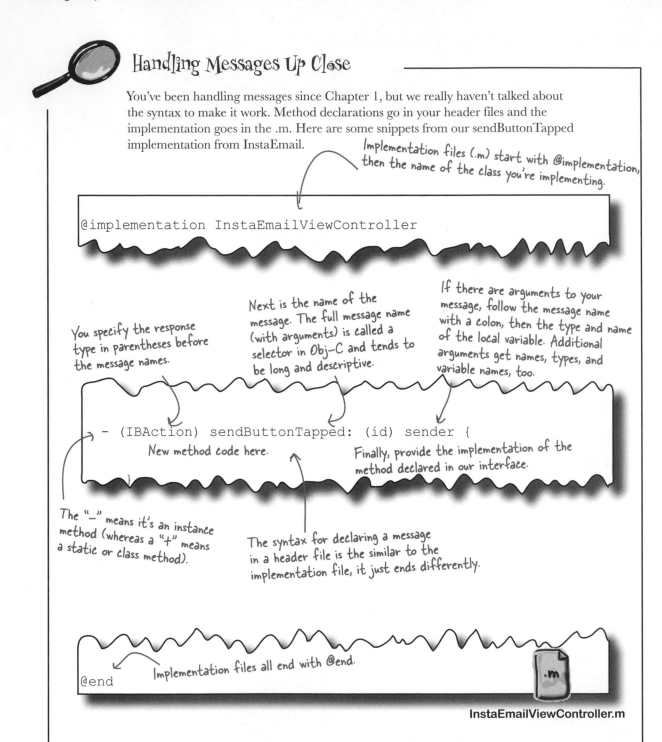

```
@implementation InstaEmailViewController
```

You specify the response type in parentheses before the message names.

Next is the name of the message. The full message name (with arguments) is called a selector in Obj-C and tends to be long and descriptive.

If there are arguments to your message, follow the message name with a colon, then the type and name of the local variable. Additional arguments get names, types, and variable names, too.

```
- (IBAction) sendButtonTapped: (id) sender {
        New method code here.
}
```

Finally, provide the implementation of the method declared in our interface.

The "–" means it's an instance method (whereas a "+" means a static or class method).

The syntax for declaring a message in a header file is the similar to the implementation file, it just ends differently.

```
@end
```

Implementation files all end with @end.

InstaEmailViewController.m

Messages in Objective-C use named arguments

In Objective-C, message names tend to be long and descriptive. This really starts to make sense when you see arguments tacked on. When you send a message with arguments, the message and argument names are all specified. Objective-C messages read more like sentences. Let's look at a method declaration from UIPickerViewDataSource. This method returns the number of rows for a given component in a picker view. It's declared like this:

Return type   Method name   First argument type   Local argument name   Public name of second argument

```
- (NSInteger)pickerView:(UIPickerView *)pickerView numberOfR
owsInComponent:(NSInteger)component;
```

Type of second argument   Local name of second argument

Methods can have internal and external names for arguments; the external name is used when sending the message to the receiver. So when something wants to send this message to our delegate, it creates a call like this:

Receiver   Message name   value   Second argument name   Second argument value

```
[pickerDelegate pickerView:somePicker numberOfRowsInComponent:2];
```

there are no Dumb Questions

Q: You keep switching terms back and forth between methods and messages. Which is it?

A: Both are correct, depending on your context. In Objective-C, you send messages to objects and they respond. The Objective-C runtime turns your message into a method call, which returns a value. So, generally you talk about sending some receiver a message, but if you're implementing what it does in response, you're implementing a method.

Q: So about those arguments to methods...what's the deal with the name before the colon and the one after the type?

A: In Objective-C, you can have a public name and a local name for arguments. The public name becomes part of the selector when someone wants to send that message to your object. That's the name before the colon. The name after the type is the local variable; this is the name of the variable that holds the value. In Objective-C, they don't have to be the same, so you can use a nice friendly public name for people when they use your class and a convenient local name in your code.

More on selectors in a minute.

Use message passing to tell our View Controller when the Done button is pressed

The UITextField can tell our ViewController when the Done button was pressed on the keyboard; we just need to tell it what message to send. We can do this with Interface Builder. You'll need to declare an action in the .h file and implement it in the .m file:

Messages going here between UITextField and the controller.

1 **Add the IBAction to InstaEmailViewController.h.**
Just like we did with the "Send Email" button, go back into Xcode and add this:

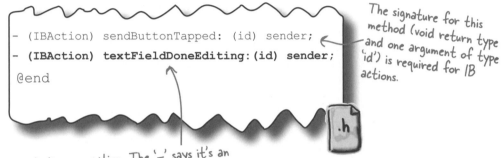

```
- (IBAction) sendButtonTapped: (id) sender;
- (IBAction) textFieldDoneEditing: (id) sender;
@end
```

The signature for this method (void return type and one argument of type 'id') is required for IB actions.

Notice how the IBAction is in parentheses? That's the return type — which is secretly just #defined to void.

Here's the new action. The '–' says it's an instance method, called textFieldDoneEditing, and takes one argument. The sender is of type 'id' (which means a pointer to something).

InstaEmailViewController.h

2 **Add the method implementation in InstaEmailViewController.m.**
Now that we have an action that will be called when the Done button is pressed, we just need to ask the textField to resign its first responder status and it will hide the keyboard.

Implement this just before the dealloc method in your InstaEmailViewController.m.

```
- (IBAction) textFieldDoneEditing: (id) sender
{
    [sender resignFirstResponder];
}
```

Since the sender is the UITextField, we can send the resignFirstResponder right back to it.

The sender argument will be the component that triggered the event. In our case, it will be the UITextField.

InstaEmailViewController.m

Almost there, we just need to wire it up...

3 **Connect the UITextField event in the editor.**

Now that the actions are declared and implemented, go back into
Interface Builder by double-clicking on InstaEmailViewController.xib.
If you right-click on the UITextField, you'll bring up the connections.

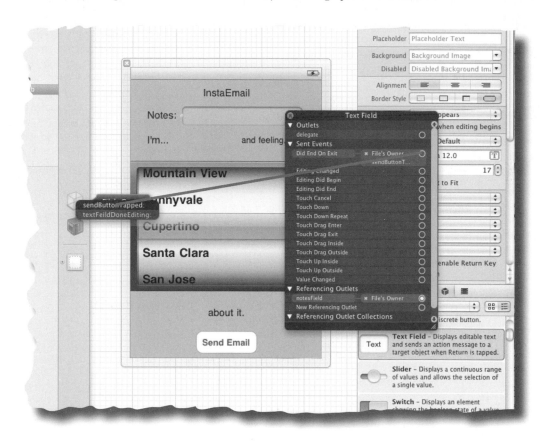

In the list of events that the UITextField can send, choose the
"Did End on Exit" event and connect it to the File's Owner's
"textFieldDoneEditing" action we just created.

Geek Bits

The UITextField has a number of events it can raise, just like the round
rectangular button. Take a second and check out the list that's there.
Along with the customizing you can do in the Inspector with the field, you can
wire up different (or even multiple!) responses to interaction with the field.
Keep it in mind for your own apps.

there are no
Dumb Questions

Q: **Why did we send the message back to the sender in our action and not to our notesField property?**

A: Either one would work fine; they're both references to the same object. We used the sender argument because it would work regardless of whether we had a property that was a reference to our UITextField.

Q: **You mentioned selectors, but I'm still fuzzy on what they are.**

A: Selectors are unique names for methods when Objective-C translates a message into an actual method call. It's basically the method name and the names of the arguments separated by colons. For instance, look at the code using the selector pickerView:numberOfRowsInComponent. You'll see them show up again in later chapters when we do more interface connecting in code. For now, Interface Builder is handling it for us.

Q: **When we send the resignFirstResponder message to sender, the sender type is "id". How does that work?**

A: "id" is an Objective-C type that can point to any Objective-C object. It's like a void* in C++. Since Objective-C is a dynamically typed language, it's perfectly ok with sending messages to an object of type "id". It will figure out at runtime whether or not the object can actually respond to the message.

Q: **What happens if an object can't respond to a message?**

A: You'll get an exception. This is the reason you should use strongly typed variables whenever possible—it will generate warnings at compile time, not just runtime problems. However, there are times when generic typing makes a lot of sense, such as callback methods when the sender could be any number of different objects.

Q: **So seriously, brackets for message passing?**

A: Yes. And indexing arrays. We all just have to deal with it.

Beware of private framework headers

Sometimes you'll come across a really tempting method that's not defined in the Apple Documentation. Using undocumented APIs will get your app rejected from the iTunes store.

BULLET POINTS

- In Objective-C, you send messages to receivers. The runtime maps these to method calls.

- Method declarations go in the header (.h) file after the closing brace of an interface.

- Method implementations go in the implementation (.m) file between the @implementation and the @end.

- Method arguments are usually named, and those names are used when sending a message.

- Arguments can have an internal and external name.

- Use a "-" to indicate an instance method; use "+" to indicate a static method.

TEST DRIVE

Do some typing, go ahead!

Tap the "done" button...

It works! The keyboard goes away and you can play around with the text field and add some notes now.

Where's the custom note?

You're ready to try out the custom field with a demo for Mike, but when he puts
in his custom text and sends his message...

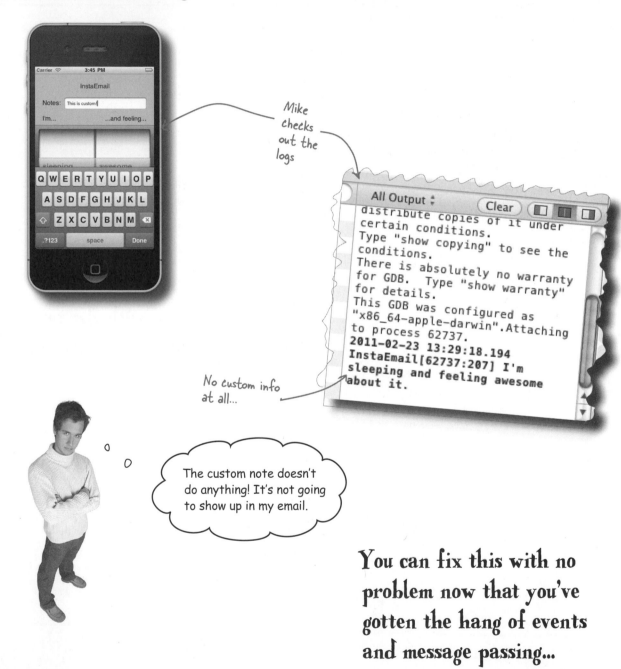

Mike
checks
out the
logs

No custom info
at all...

The custom note doesn't
do anything! It's not going
to show up in my email.

**You can fix this with no
problem now that you've
gotten the hang of events
and message passing...**

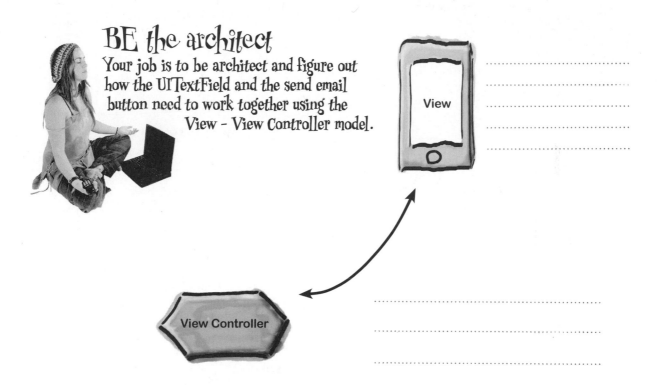

BE the architect

Your job is to be architect and figure out how the UITextField and the send email button need to work together using the View - View Controller model.

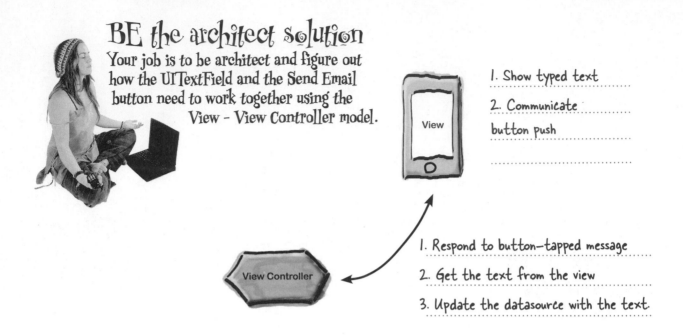

BE the architect solution
Your job is to be architect and figure out how the UITextField and the Send Email button need to work together using the View - View Controller model.

View

1. Show typed text
2. Communicate button push

View Controller

1. Respond to button-tapped message
2. Get the text from the view
3. Update the datasource with the text.

Build the email with strings

We need to incorporate the note text into our email. In order to do that, we're going to do a little string manipulation with the NSString class. You've already built a message to create an email, but this time we have more text to include. Before you refactor the code to send the email with the new text in it, let's take a closer look at what you did in Chapter 2:

This string didn't come from alloc, new, copy, or mutableCopy, so it'll be autoreleased.

This is a static method on NSString that takes a string format and replaces the format placeholders with the values you provide as arguments.

The @ before the quotes means this should be treated as an NSString, not a char*.

```
NSString* theMessage = [NSString stringWithFormat:@"I'm %@ and feeling %@ about it.",
        [activities_ objectAtIndex:[emailPicker_ selectedRowInComponent:0]],
        [feelings_ objectAtIndex:[emailPicker_ selectedRowInComponent:1]]];
NSLog(@"%@", theMessage);
```

NSLog prints out whatever NSString you pass to the console. End users of your app won't see these message.

Here, we use the stringWithFormat to create our message string. Note the %@, which is a placeholder for a string.

Now all you need to do is update this to include the text from the Notes field. Take a look at the magnets on the next page and get it working.

Xcode Magnets

You need to modify InstaEmailViewController.m file to add the custom field to the message. Using the information you just learned and the magnets below, fill in the missing code.

```objc
- (IBAction) sendButtonTapped: (id) sender {
    NSString* theMessage = [NSString stringWithFormat:@"            _____
I'm %@ and feeling %@ about it.",

    _____  ___  _____  _____  ___

    [activities_ objectAtIndex:[emailPicker_ selectedRowInComponent:0]],
    [feelings_ objectAtIndex:[emailPicker_ selectedRowInComponent:1]]];
    NSLog(@"%@", theMessage);
```

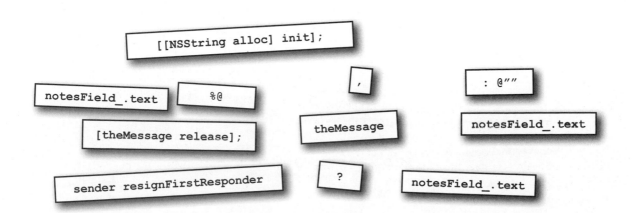

[[NSString alloc] init];

notesField_.text

%@

,

: @""

[theMessage release];

theMessage

notesField_.text

sender resignFirstResponder

?

notesField_.text

Xcode Magnets Solution

You need to modify InstaEmailViewController.m file to add the custom field to the message. Using the information you just learned and the magnets below, fill in the missing code.

InstaEmailViewController.m

Here's our new string placeholder for the notes text.

```
- (IBAction) sendButtonTapped: (id) sender {

    NSString* theMessage = [NSString stringWithFormat:@"
I'm %@ and feeling %@ about it.",
```

| %@ |

| notesField_.text | | ? | | notesField_.text | | : @"" | | , |

```
    [activities_ objectAtIndex:[emailPicker_ selectedRowInComponent:0]],
    [feelings_ objectAtIndex:[emailPicker_ selectedRowInComponent:1]]];
    NSLog(@"%@", theMessage);
```

We have to handle the case where the user didn't enter any text. If the text field is empty, its text property will be nil. Here we use the C style ternary operator. If notesField.text isn't nil, it will use the value in notesField.text.

...and if it is nil, we'll send an empty string. Remember, it has to be an NSString, so we put the @ before the quotes.

The ? is a ternary operator, just like in Java or C++, where if the expression is true it returns the first value; otherwise, it returns the second.

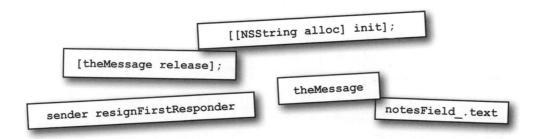

```
[[NSString alloc] init];
```
```
[theMessage release];
```
```
theMessage
```
```
sender resignFirstResponder
```
```
notesField_.text
```

TEST DRIVE

Go ahead and build and run the app with the new text code in it.

Now it has custom text! w00t!

It's so great that we can talk about our feelings...

Objective-C cross

Practice some of your new Objective-C terminology.

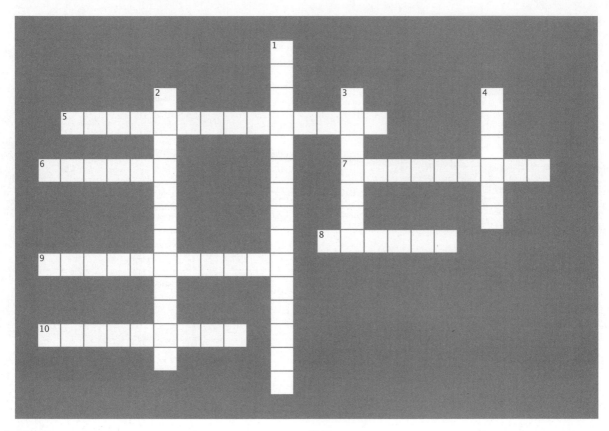

Across

5. The control with focus has _____ status.
6. This incorporates another file.
7. Unique names for methods after Objective-C translation are _____.
8. Signals that the compiler will retain the object.
9. Automatic methods.
10. This tells the compiler to skip mutexes.

Down

1. An array of objects that will be released after the current event.
2. A "+" before a method declaration indicates that it's a _____.
3. This is sent between objects.
4. _____ management is important for iPhone apps.

Your Objective-C Toolbox

You've got Chapter 3 under your belt and now you've added Objective-C to your toolbox.

Attribute	You want it...
readwrite	When you want the property to be modifiable by people. The compiler will generate a getter and a setter for you. This is the default.
readonly	When you don't want people modifying the property. You can still change the field value backing the property, but the compiler won't generate a setter.
assign	When you're dealing with basic types, like ints, floats, etc. The compiler just creates a setter with a simple myField = value statement. This is the default, but not usually what you want.
retain	When you're dealing with object values. The compiler will retain the value you pass in and release the old value when a new one comes in.
copy	When you want to hold onto a copy of some value instead of the value itself. For example, if you want to hold onto an array and don't want people to be able to change its contents after they set it. This sends a copy message to the value passed in, then keeps that.

Objective – C

- Is the language of iOS apps
- Is an object–oriented language
- Uses reference counting for memory management
- Uses message passing and dynamic typing
- Has inheritance and interfaces

Memory Management

You own objects you create through an alloc, new, copy, or mutableCopy.

You need to take ownership of objects you get through other means if you want to stick around by sending them a retain message.

You must release objects you own.

Assume everything else will be cleaned up later (pretend it has a retain count of 1 and is in the autorelease pool).

Objective-C cross Solution

Practice some of your new Objective-C terminology.

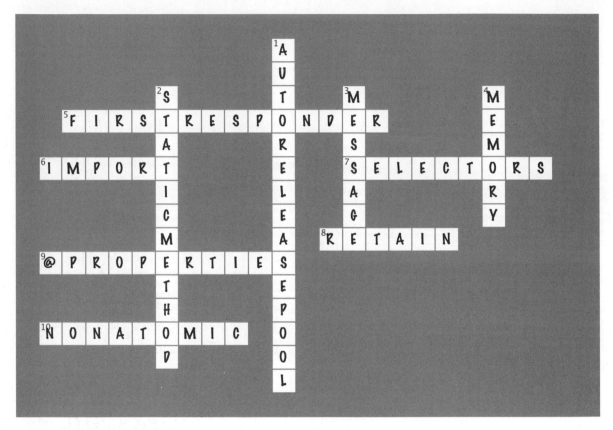

Across

5. The control with focus has _____ status. [FIRSTRESPONDER]
6. This incorporates another file. [IMPORT]
7. Unique names for methods after Objective-C translation are _____. [SELECTORS]
8. Signals that the compiler will retain the object. [RETAIN]
9. Automatic methods. [@PROPERTIES]
10. This tells the compiler to skip mutexes. [NONATOMIC]

Down

1. An array of objects that will be released after the current event. [AUTORELEASEPOOL]
2. A "+" before a method declaration indicates that it's a _____. [STATICMETHOD]
3. This is sent between objects. [MESSAGE]
4. _____ management is important for iPhone apps. [MEMORY]

4 multiple views

A table with a view

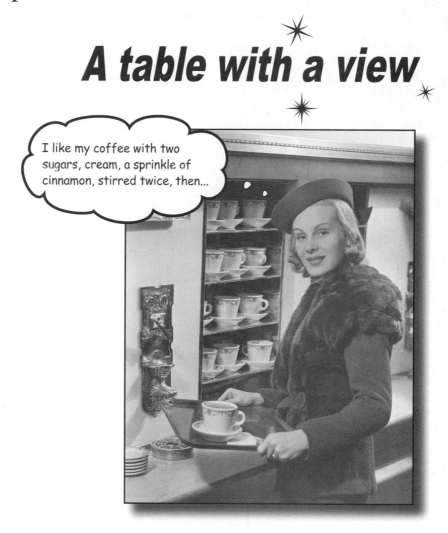

I like my coffee with two sugars, cream, a sprinkle of cinnamon, stirred twice, then...

Most iOS apps have more than one view.

We've written a cool app with one view, but anyone who's used a smartphone knows that most apps aren't like that. Some of the more impressive iOS apps out there do a great job of working with complex information by using multiple views. We're going to start with navigation controllers and table views, like the kind you see in your Mail and Contacts apps. Only we're going to do it with a twist...

Look, I don't have time for talking about my feelings. I need to know a ton of drink recipes every night. Is there an app for that?

Sam, bartender at the HF Lounge

BRAIN BARBELL

This chapter is about apps with more than one view. What views would you need to have for a bartending app?

....

....

....

UI Design Magnets

Using the components shown below, lay out the two views we'll be using for the app.

View #1

View #2

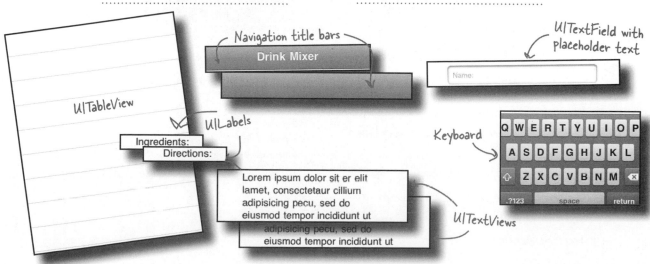

UITableView

Navigation title bars

Drink Mixer

UILabels

Ingredients:

Directions:

Lorem ipsum dolor sit er elit lamet, consectetaur cillium adipisicing pecu, sed do eiusmod tempor incididunt ut

adipisicing pecu, sed do eiusmod tempor incididunt ut

UITextField with placeholder text

Name:

Keyboard

UITextViews

UI Design Magnets Solution

Using the components shown below, lay out the two views we'll be using for the app.

This bar will have buttons, like the back and forward buttons in a web browser.

We'll call it Drink Mixer.

It will also show your app's title.

UITextField with placeholder text

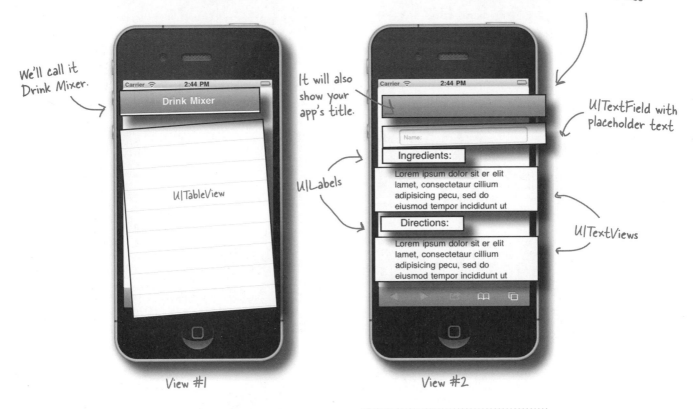

UILabels

UITableView

UITextViews

Drink Mixer

Name:

Ingredients:

Lorem ipsum dolor sit er elit lamet, consectetaur cillium adipisicing pecu, sed do eiusmod tempor incididunt ut

Directions:

Lorem ipsum dolor sit er elit lamet, consectetaur cillium adipisicing pecu, sed do eiusmod tempor incididunt ut

View #1

View #2

Sam needs a list of drink names and to be able to look up what's in them. He'll also want to know how much he needs of each ingredient and any instructions—what's on the rocks, whether to shake or stir, when to light things on fire, etc. So for our two views, we'll put the drinks in a list (View #1), then when Sam taps on one, we'll show the details (View #2).

We're not going to use the keyboard for now—it's a reference app, and Sam just needs to read stuff...

So, how do these views fit together?

Before you pick the template for our bartending app, take a minute to look at how you want the user to interact with the drink information. We're going to have a scrollable list of drink names, and when the user taps on a row, we'll show the detailed drink information using view #2, our detail view. Once our user has seen enough, they're going to want to go back to the drink list.

Once our users are done with the detailed information, the Navigation bar gives them a way to get back to the list.

Tapping on a drink name in the list will bring up the detail view for that drink.

We're going to want some kind of transition between these views...

We need a list of items to work with...

We're going to be coming in and out of this view a lot—each time our user selects a drink.

BRAIN BARBELL

Below are the templates available for an app. Which do you think we should use for DrinkMixer?

☐ Window-based Application   ☐ View-based Application   ☐ Utility Application   ☐ Split view-based Application

☐ Tab Bar Application   ☐ OpenGL ES Application   ☐ Navigation-based Application

The navigation template pulls multiple views together

For this app, we're going to use a Navigation-based project. The navigation template comes with a lot of functionality built in, including a **navigation controller**, which handles transitions between views, and the ability to deal with **hierarchical data**. Hierarchical data means there's layers to it, and each view gives you more detail than the previous one.

Choose a template for your new project:

iOS
Application
Framework & Library
Other

Mac OS X
Application
Framework & Library
Application Plug-in
System Plug-in
Other

Navigation-based Application | OpenGL ES Application | Split View-based Application | Tab Bar Application

Utility Application | View-based Application | Window-based Application

Navigation-based Application

This template provides a starting point for an application that uses a navigation controller. It provides a user interface configured with a navigation controller to display a list of items.

Cancel | Previous | Next

The built-in navigation controller provides back buttons, title bars, and a view history that will keep your user moving through the data without getting lost.

Lemon Drop

Firecracker

Drink

Manhattan
Melon Tree
Mexican Bomb
Miami Vice
Mojito
Music City Sunse
Neapolitan
Neon Geek
Polo Cocktail

Ingredients:
Lorem ipsum lamet, consec adipiscing pe eiusmod temp
Directions:
Lorem ipsum lamet, consec adipiscing pe eiusmod temp

The Navigation Controller provides transitions between views, with really nice animations.

```
Lemon Drop: Citron
vodka, lemon, and
sugar. A
the rim        Firecracker: Wild
pour inc       turkey and hot sauce.
shaker..       Pour ingredients into
               a rocks glass filled
               with ice.
```

The navigation template helps us to move through hierarchical data, starting with a table view that lists all the drinks.

Do this!

To get started, go into Xcode and choose the **File→New Project** option. Choose the Navigation-based application and name it DrinkMixer. Make sure that "Use Core Data" and "Include Unit Tests" are **not** checked.

The table view is built in

The navigation template comes with a navigation controller and a root view that the controller displays on startup. That root view is set up with a table view by default, and that works great for our app, so we'll keep it that way. A table view is typically used for listing items, one of which can then be selected for more details about that item.

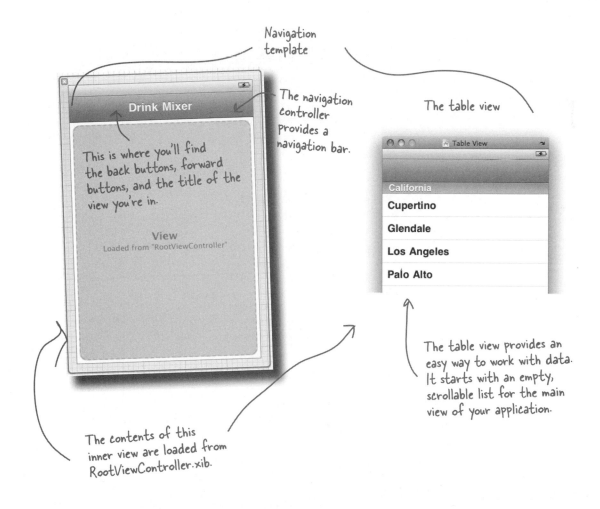

Navigation template

The navigation controller provides a navigation bar.

This is where you'll find the back buttons, forward buttons, and the title of the view you're in.

The contents of this inner view are loaded from RootViewController.xib.

The table view

The table view provides an easy way to work with data. It starts with an empty, scrollable list for the main view of your application.

there are no
Dumb Questions

Q: If the navigation template is about handing lots of views, why does it only come with one?

A: Most navigation-based applications start out with a table view and show detailed views from there. The number of detailed views, what they look like, etc., are very application-specific, so you have to decide which views you want and add those views. The navigation template doesn't assume anything beyond the initial table view.

Q: Which built-in apps on iOS use the Navigation control?

A: Contacts and Mail, which are both core iOS apps, use this design. It's a good idea to spend some time with those apps on your phone to see how the entire template is implemented. For a neat twist, take a look at the Messages (SMS) app. That one uses a Navigation Controller but frequently starts in the "detail" view, showing the last person you sent or received a message from.

On the iPad, Mail uses navigation control, too, but it's part of a split view-based application. We'll get into that more in a couple of chapters.

Q: The UITextField looks editable. Shouldn't we fix that?

A: Maybe. We're going to go on to use that field in a few different ways, so think about it again at the end of the app in a couple of chapters.

To make it look less editable, you can change the font or change the border.

Q: Do I have to use a table view for my root view?

A: No, it's just the most common, since it provides a natural way to show an overview of a lot of data and have the user drill down for more information. Table views are very easily customized, too, so some apps that might not seem like table views really are, like Notes or the iTunes store, for example.

Q: How does the navigation controller relate to view controllers?

A: We'll talk a lot more about this in a minute, but the Navigation Controller coordinates the transition between view controllers. Typically, each top-level view is backed by a View Controller, and as views transition onscreen, the corresponding View Controller starts getting events from its view. There's a whole view lifecycle that we'll work through that lets a View Controller know what's going on with its view.

TEST DRIVE

Add a title to the main view, and take a look at what your empty table view will look like. Open up MainWindow.xib in Interface Builder.

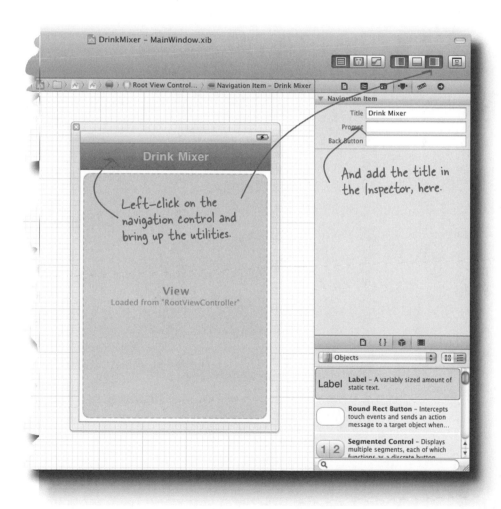

TEST DRIVE

Add a title to the main view right away, and take a look at what your empty
table view will look like. Open up MainWindow.xib in Interface Builder.

Here's the navigation bar—we'll add directional buttons soon.

Carrier 🗢 3:03 PM

Drink Mixer

This is the table view and will hold our drink list.

Each line is an empty table cell.

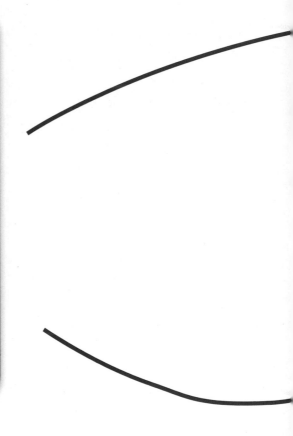

Watch it!

**If you don't add the title here, you won't have a back
button later.**

*The navigation controller uses the title of the current view as the
label in a back button when presenting a second, more detailed view.*

The Table View Up Close

Navigation controllers and table views are almost always used together to work with hierarchical data. When you selected the navigation-based project as your template, Xcode created a different view setup than we've used in the past. The template includes MainWindow.xib, which has a single UINavigationController in it. That controller starts out with a main view, which is a UITableView that is loaded from RootViewController.xib (which is actually a subclass of UITableViewController.xib).

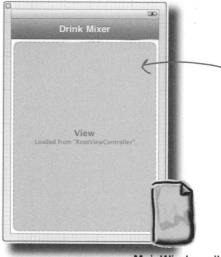

MainWindow.xib

This UINavigationController understands the idea of multiple views, can move between them with nice animations, and has built-in support for buttons on the navigation bar.

RootViewController.xib

This is the UITableView that is loaded from the RootViewController.xib. The UITableViewController provides some basic table behavior, like configuring the datasource and delegate if it's loaded from a nib, and providing editing state controls. We'll talk about these more as we go.

A table is a collection of cells

The UITableView provides a lot of the functionality we need right away, but it still needs to know what data we're actually trying to show and what to do when the user interacts with that data. This is where the datasource and delegate come in. A table view is easy to customize and is set up by the template to talk to the datasource and delegate to see what it needs to show, how many rows, what table cells to use, etc.

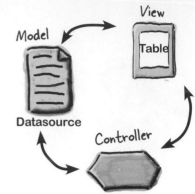

Model
View
Table
Datasource
Controller
Delegate

Remember that MVC pattern from Chapter 1? Now we're adding in the Model piece with a datasource for our drinks list.

The navigation controller, not the table view, provides the navigation bar. Since we're editing the view now, there's no navigation control.

Table views have built-in support for editing their contents, including moving rows around, deleting rows, and adding new ones.

Table views can tell you when your user taps on a cell. It'll tell you the section and row that was tapped.

We're using the default table view cell, but you can create your own and lay them out any way you want.

California
Brea
Burlingame
Canoga Park
Carlsbad
Chula Vista
Corte Madera
Costa Mesa
Emeryville
Escondido
Section Footer

A table view is made up of multiple table cells. The table view will ask how many cells (or rows) are in each section.

A table can have multiple sections, and each section can have a header and a footer. We only have one section, so we don't need either for DrinkMixer.

A table can only have one column, but you can put whatever you want in that column by customizing your table cells.

⚛ BRAIN POWER

Look through some of the apps you have on your device. What are some of the most customized table views you can find? Are they using sections? Are they grouped? How did they lay out their cells?

Table Cell Code Up Close

Below is an excerpt from our updated RootViewController.m file. This is where we create table cells and populate them with the drink list information.

```
- (NSInteger)numberOfSectionsInTableView:(UITableView *)tableView {
    return 1;
}


// Customize the number of rows in the table view.
- (NSInteger)tableView:(UITableView *)tableView numberOfRowsInSection
:(NSInteger)section {
    return [self.drinks count];
}
```

These methods tell the table view how many sections we have and how many rows are in each section.

The indexPath contains a representation of the section and row number for the needed cell.

This method is called when the table view needs a cell.

```
// Customize the appearance of table view cells.
- (UITableViewCell *)tableView:(UITableView *)tableView cellForRowAtIndexPath
:(NSIndexPath *)indexPath {


    static NSString *CellIdentifier = @"Cell";
```

Table cells have identifiers representing a cell type, so when you try to find a cell for reuse, you can be sure you're grabbing the right kind.

```
    UITableViewCell *cell = [tableView dequeueReusableCellWithIdentifier:CellI
dentifier];
    if (cell == nil) {
        cell = [[[UITableViewCell alloc] initWithStyle:UITableViewCellStyleDe
fault reuseIdentifier:CellIdentifier] autorelease];
    }
```

Here, we check with the table view to see if there are any reusable cells with the given cell identifier available.

If there aren't any available for reuse, we'll create a new one.

```
    // Configure the cell.
cell.textLabel.text = [self.drinks objectAtIndex:indexPath.row];
    return cell;
}
```

Here, we customize the text in the cell with the information for the specific drink we need to show.

there are no
Dumb Questions

Q: **How do cells get into that reusable list to begin with?**

A: The table view handles that. When cells scroll off the screen (either the top or the bottom), the table view will queue up cells that are no longer needed. When it asks the datasource for a cell for a particular row, you can check that queue of cells to see if there are any available for use.

Q: **I don't understand the cell identifier...does it have to be "Cell"?**

A: No—that's just the default. When you do more complex table views, you can create custom cell types depending on what data you're trying to display. You use the cell identifier to make sure that when you ask for a reusable cell, the table view gives you back the type you expect. The identifier can be anything you want—just make sure you have a unique name for each unique cell type you use.

Sharpen your pencil

It's time to start displaying some drinks. You'll need to make some modifications to both the RootViewController.h and RootViewController.m files.

1 **Declare the drinks array.**
Using syntax similar to what we used for the picker, declare an array called "drinks" in RootViewController.h with the necessary properties declaration.

2 **Implement and populate the array.**
In RootViewController.m, uncomment and expand the **viewDidLoad** method to create the array with the three drinks from the drink list here.

3 **Tell the table how many rows you have.**
The auto-generated code needs to be modified to tell the table that it will have the same number of rows as there are drinks in the array. Modify the implementation file under this line: // Customize the number of rows in the table view.

4 **Populate the table cells.**
Implement the code that we talked about in "**Table Cell Code Up Close**" so that the table gets populated with the items from the array.

Drink List:

Firecracker

Lemon Drop

Mojito

> Wait, memory in iOS is a big deal, right? Three drinks is no problem, but what happens if we add a whole bunch of drinks?

You're right. Like everything else on iOS, the UITableView does have to worry about memory.

So, how does it balance concerns about memory with an unknown amount of data to display? It breaks things up into cells.

Each drink gets its own temporary cell

The UITableView only has to display enough data to fill an iPhone screen—it doesn't really matter how much data you might have in total. The UITableView does this by reusing cells that scrolled off the screen.

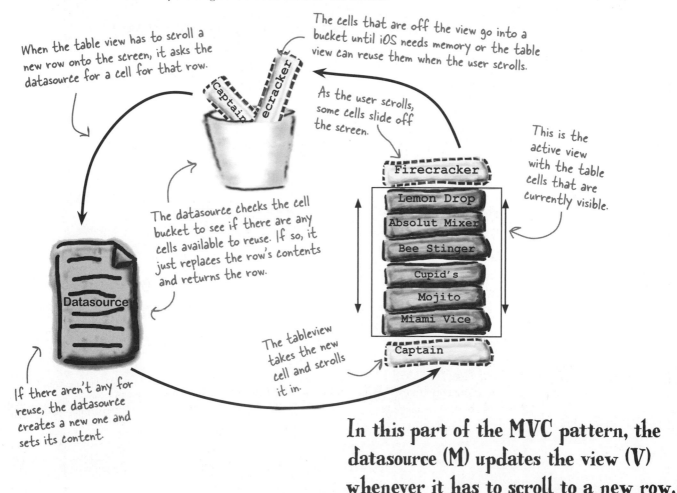

When the table view has to scroll a new row onto the screen, it asks the datasource for a cell for that row.

The cells that are off the view go into a bucket until iOS needs memory or the table view can reuse them when the user scrolls.

As the user scrolls, some cells slide off the screen.

This is the active view with the table cells that are currently visible.

The datasource checks the cell bucket to see if there are any cells available to reuse. If so, it just replaces the row's contents and returns the row.

If there aren't any for reuse, the datasource creates a new one and sets its content.

The tableview takes the new cell and scrolls it in.

Firecracker
Lemon Drop
Absolut Mixer
Bee Stinger
Cupid's
Mojito
Miami Vice
Captain

In this part of the MVC pattern, the datasource (M) updates the view (V) whenever it has to scroll to a new row.

Sharpen your pencil
Solution

It's time to start displaying some drinks. You'll need to make some modifications to both the RootViewController.h and RootViewController.m files.

UITableViewController handles the datasource and delegate protocol for you, so you don't need to declare it here.

1 **Declare the drinks array.**

```
@interface RootViewController : UITableViewController {

        NSMutableArray* drinks_;   Add the new drinks
}                                           array.

@property (nonatomic, retain) NSMutableArray* drinks;
@end
```

Note that we use _' after our instance variable name to differentiate it from our property name—you can't accidentally refer to the wrong one.

Declare the properties for the drinks array.

RootViewController.h

```
@synthesize drinks=drinks_;
```

RootViewController.m

```
-
(void)dealloc {
        [drinks_ release];
        [super dealloc];
}
@end
```

2 **Implement and populate the array.**

In RootViewController.m, uncomment and expand the
ViewDidLoad method.

```
- (void)viewDidLoad {
  [super viewDidLoad];


    drinks_ = [[NSMutableArray alloc]
initWithObjects:@"Firecracker", @"Lemon Drop", @"Mojito",
nil];
```

We're using the
instance variable
directly here since
we already own the
new array.

Here's the three drinks we gave you.

RootViewController.m

3 **Tell the table how many rows you have.**

```
//Customize the number of rows in the table view.
  - (NSInteger)tableView:(UITableView *)tableView numberOfRowsIn
Section:(NSInteger)section {
    return [self.drinks count];
  }
```

This used to say
return: 0.

Now it tells the table view that we
have the same number of rows as the
number of items in the drinks array.

4 **Populate the table cells.**

```
// Configure the cell.
cell.textLabel.text = [self.drinks objectAtIndex:indexPath.row];
    return cell;
}
```

The full method
is shown on page
153.

Here, we customize the text in the cell with the
information for the specific drink we need to show.

TEST DRIVE

Now you're ready to go. Save it and run it, and you'll see the three drinks in your app in the main view.

Try it out—the list will scroll, too!

> Everything looks great. I'll just email over our complete list—it's 40 drinks...

Q: You mentioned the table view's datasource and delegate, but why didn't I have to conform to anything like we did with UIPickerView?

A: Great catch. Normally you would, but the navigation-based template we used has already set this up. To see what's happening, look at the RootViewController.h file. You'll see that it is a subclass of UITableViewController, and that class conforms to the UITableViewDataSourceProtocol and the UITableViewDelegateProtocol. If you look in RootViewController.xib, you'll see that the table view's datasource and delegate are both set to be our RootViewController. If we weren't using a template, you'd have to set these up yourself (we'll revisit this again later in the book).

Q: I noticed we used an NSMutableArray. Is that because we had to initialize it?

A: No—both NSMutableArray and NSArray can be initialized with values when you create them. We're using an NSMutableArray because we're going to manipulate the contents of this array later. We'll get there in a minute.

Q: What's the nil at the end of the drink names when we create the drink array?

A: NSMutableArray's initializer takes a variable number of arguments. It uses nil to know it's reached the end of the arguments. The last element in the array will be the value before the nil—nil won't (and can't) be added to the array.

Q: Tell me again about that @ symbol before our drink names?

A: The @ symbol is shorthand for creating an NSString. NSArrays store arrays of objects, so we need to convert our text names (char*s) to NSStrings. We do that by putting an @ in front of the text constant.

Q: When we customized the table view cells, we used the cell.textLabel. Are there other labels? What's the difference between cell.textLabel and cell.text?

A: Before the iPhone 3.0 SDK, there was just one label and set of disclosure indicators in the default cell, and it was all handled by the cell itself. You just set the text you wanted on the cell.text property. Nearly everyone wanted a little more information on the table cells, so in the iPhone 3.0 SDK, Apple added a few different styles with different label layouts. Once they did that, they introduced specific properties for the different text areas, like textLabel, detailLabel, etc., and deprecated the old cell.text property. You shouldn't use cell.text in your apps—Apple will likely remove it at some point in the future. We'll talk more about the other labels later in the chapter.

Q: You mention that we can use section headers and footers—how do you specify those?

A: The datasource is responsible for that information, too. There are optional methods you can provide that return the title for section headers and the title for section footers based on the section number. They work a lot like our cellForRowAtIndexPath, except they only return strings.

Q: What's the difference between a plain table view and a grouped table view?

A: The only difference is the appearance. In a plain table view, like the one we're using, all the sections touch each other and are separated by the section header and footer if you have them. In a grouped table view, the table view puts space between the sections and shows the section header in bigger letters. Take a look at your contact list, then select a contact. The first view, where all of your contacts are listed together and separated by letters, is a plain table view. The detailed view, where the phone numbers are separated from email addresses, etc., is a grouped table view.

Q: So why are you putting underscores after instance variables again?

A: Remember there are really different things in play when we talk about instance variables and properties. Instance variables are the actual attributes that hold data. We use _'s after those names to help indicate that those are actually internal class information, not really something we want other classes poking around with (we also mark them as private so the compiler enforces that for us).

Next, we have properties. By declaring something as a property, we get the ability to use the dot notation. Accessing a property through the dot notation gets turned into a call to setSomeProperty(...) or getSomeProperty(...). Memory management, copying values we want copied, etc., are all handled in those accessors. To make sure we don't accidentally refer to an instance variable when we really want the functionality of the accessors and vice-versa, we name the instance variable with an '_' and property without.

Just a few more drinks...

The drink menu at Head First Lounge has 40 cocktails.

MENU

Firecracker
Lemon Drop
Mojito
Absolut Mixer
Bee Stinger
Cupid's Cocktail
Strawberry Daquiri
Long Island Ice Tea
Captain and Coke
Miami Vice
Boxcar
Cat's Meow
Apple Martini
Manhattan
After Dinner Mint
Red Rudolph
Day at the Beach
Melon Tree

FREE DELIVERY
FOR RESERVATION
555 0136

Business Hours
Monday thru Friday: 5 p.m.-7 p.m.
Saturday: 5:30 p.m.-3 a.m.

Rum Runner
Blue Dog
Key West Lemonade
Neapolitan
Polo Cocktail
Purple Yummy
Neon Geek
Flaming Nerd
Letter Bomb
Bookmaker's Luck
Baked Apple
Deer Hunter
Mexican Bomb
Aftershock
Black Eyed Susan
Beetle Juice
Terminator
Gingerbread Man
Lost in Space
Music City Sunset
Cafe Joy
Sandbar Sleeper

Get ready to start typing...

This sucks. Can't we just import the list Sam sent us somehow?

We could, but not the way we're set up now.

Since the drinks are populated with an array that's hardcoded into the implementation file, we can't import anything.

What would work well is a standardized way to read and import data; then we would be able to quickly get that drink list loaded.

⚛️BRAIN POWER

There must be a better way to handle this. How can we speed up getting 40 drinks in our list?

Plists are an easy way to save and load data

Plist stands for "property list" and has been around for quite a while with OS X. In fact, there are a number of plists already in use in your application. We've already worked with the most important plist, DrinkMixer-Info.plist. This is created by Xcode when you first create your project, and besides the app icons, it stores things like the main nib file to load when the application starts, the application version, and more. Xcode can create and edit these plists like any other file. Click on DrinkMixer-Info.plist to take a look at what's inside.

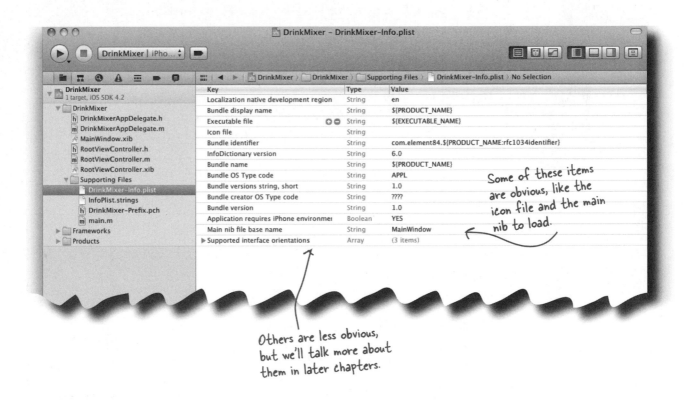

Some of these items are obvious, like the icon file and the main nib to load.

Others are less obvious, but we'll talk more about them in later chapters.

Built-in types can save and load from plists automatically

All of the built-in types we've been using, like NSArray and NSString, can be loaded or saved from plists automatically. They do this through the NSCoding protocol. We can take advantage of this and move our drink list out of our source code and into a plist.

We need to move our drink list out of the source code here and into a plist instead...

```
-  (void) viewDidLoad {
    [super viewDidLoad];


    drinks_ = [[NSMutableArray alloc]
initWithObjects:@"Firecracker", @"Lemon Drop", @"Mojito",
nil];

}
```

RootViewController.m

Exercise

Before you import Sam's list, let's create a sample plist that's the same format. We'll make sure we get that working properly, and then pull in Sam's list.

① **Create the empty plist.**
Go back into Xcode and expand the **Supporting Files** folder. Right-click on **Resources** and select **New file→Mac OS X Resource**, and **Property List**. Call the new list DrinkArray.plist.

Make sure you pick "Resource" under Mac OS X—plists aren't listed under iOS Resources.

② **Format and populate the plist.**
Open up the file using the **Open As→Source Code** and change the <dict/> to <array/> and save. Then right-click and use the **Open As→ASCII Property List** option. Right-click inside the plist editor and click **Add Row**. You will need three string items. Then you can populate the names for the drinks.

Drink List
Firecracker
Lemon Drop
Mojito

Exercise Solution

With the sample list created, we can use it for testing before we get the big list.

① Create the empty plist.
Go back into Xcode and expand the **Supporting Files** folder. Right-click on **Resources** and select **New file→Mac OS X Resource**, and **Property List**. Call the new list DrinkArray.plist.

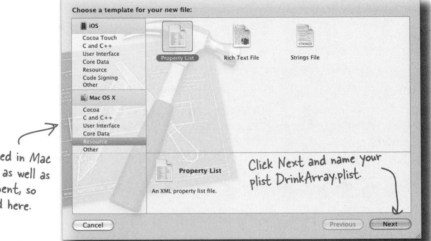

Plists are used in Mac development as well as iOS development, so they're listed here.

Click Next and name your plist DrinkArray.plist.

② Format and populate the plist.
Open up the file using the **Open As→Source Code** and change the <dict/> to <array/> and save. Then right-click and use the **Open As→ASCII Property List** option. Right-click inside the plist editor and click **Add Row**. You will need three string items. Then you can populate the names for the drinks.

When you open it as the ASCII property list...

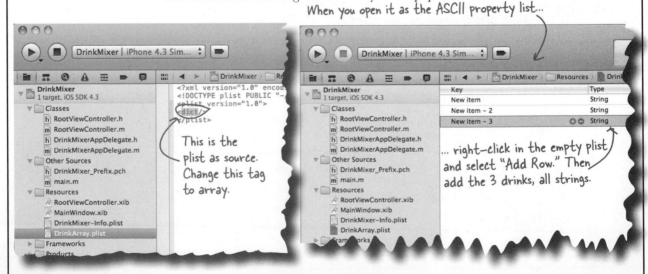

This is the plist as source. Change this tag to array.

... right-click in the empty plist and select "Add Row." Then add the 3 drinks, all strings.

Arrays (and more) have built-in support for plists

Changing the array initialization code to use the plist is remarkably easy. Most Cocoa collection types like NSArray and NSDictionary have built-in support for serializing to and from a plist. As long as you're using built-in types (like other collections, NSStrings, etc.), you can just ask an array to initialize itself from a plist.

The only piece missing is telling the array which plist to use. To do that, we'll use the project's resource bundle, which acts as a handle to application-specific information and files. Add the bolded code below to your RootViewController.m file.

```
- (void) viewDidLoad {
    [super viewDidLoad];
```
Ask the app bundle for a path to our DrinkArray plist.
```
    NSString *path = [[NSBundle mainBundle] pathForResource:@"DrinkArray"
ofType:@"plist"];
```
Initialize the array using the contents of the plist.
```
    drinks_ = [[NSMutableArray alloc] initWithContentsOfFile:path];
    }
```

RootViewController.m

TEST DRIVE

After you've finished up these two things, go ahead and build and run. It should look the same, with just the three drinks.

READY BAKE PLIST

Once this list works, head over to *http://www.headfirstlabs.com/books/hfiphonedev/* and download the DrinkArray.plist file. It has the complete list of the drinks from the Head First Lounge. Drop this in on top of your test plist, rebuild DrinkMixer, and try it out!

Test Drive

The whole
list is in
there now!

By moving the drinks out
of the code and into an
external file, you can
change the drink list
without needing to touch a
line of code.

PLists work great for
built-in types. If you're
going to be using custom
types, you will need to
write some serialization
code. Check out NSCoding
for more information.

PLists are just one way to save
data on the iOS—we'll talk
about others later in the book.

Now we just need to get that detail view all set up, right?

Creating your detail view will complete the app.

The entire list of drinks is great, but Sam still needs to know what goes in those views and how to make them. That information is going to go in the detail view that we sketched up earlier.

BRAIN BARBELL

How are we going to get from the list to the detail view? And how are we going to display the details?

Use a detail view to drill down into data

Earlier, we classified DrinkMixer as a productivity app and we chose a navigation controller because we have hierarchical data. We have a great big list of drinks loaded, but what Sam needs now is the detailed information for each drink: what are the ingredients, how do you mix them, etc. Now we'll use that navigation controller to display a more detailed view of a drink from the list.

The standard pattern for table views is that you show more information about an item when a user taps on a table cell. We'll use that to let the user select a drink and then show our detailed view. The detail view follows the same MVC pattern as our other views.

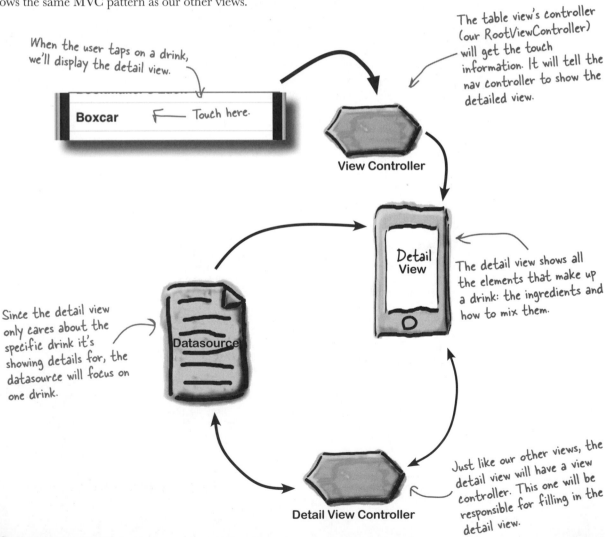

When the user taps on a drink, we'll display the detail view.

Boxcar ← Touch here.

The table view's controller (our RootViewController) will get the touch information. It will tell the nav controller to show the detailed view.

View Controller

Detail View

The detail view shows all the elements that make up a drink: the ingredients and how to mix them.

Since the detail view only cares about the specific drink it's showing details for, the datasource will focus on one drink.

Datasource

Detail View Controller

Just like our other views, the detail view will have a view controller. This one will be responsible for filling in the detail view.

A closer look at the detail view

We sketched out the detail view earlier—but let's look more closely at what we're about to build.

The back button comes with the nav controller.

It will be populated with "Name:" and the drink info, so we don't need a label.

A couple of labels for the bottom two fields

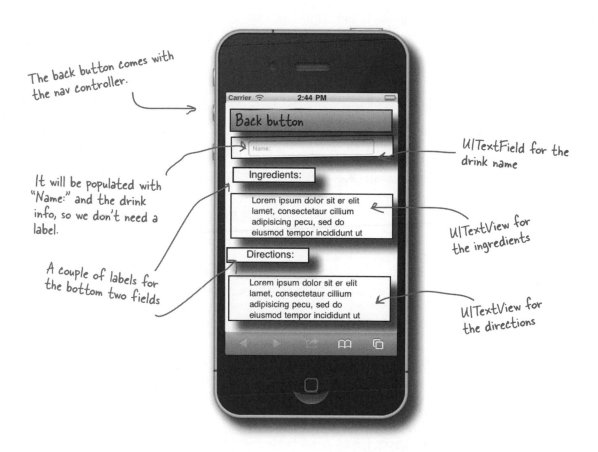

UITextField for the drink name

UITextView for the ingredients

UITextView for the directions

Let's start building...

LONG Exercise

You've got the hang of this now. Start building your detail view by creating the files and code you'll need, then put it together in Interface Builder and wire it up. Get to it!

1 **Create the files you'll need.**
To create the new view, you need a new *.xib file, as well as the supporting header and implementation files. The file type is a Cocoa Touch Class type, and it's a UIViewController subclass.

2 **Lay out the new view in Xcode.**
Use the object library to drag and drop the elements that you need and build the view we sketched out earlier.

Hint: to reserve the space for the navigation controller, just bring up the **Utilities Panel** and choose the **Attributes Inspector.** Under **Simulated Metrics**, **Top Bar**, select **Navigation Controller.** That will make sure that you lay out your view below the navigation bar.

3 **Write the code to handle the declarations and outlets for the new properties.**
You'll need to work in both DetailViewController.h and DetailViewController.m. Call the new properties nameTextField, ingredientsTextView, and directionsTextView. Don't forget to create the instance variables then synthesize and release everything.

4 **Connect the detail view to the new outlets.**
Just like we did for InstaEmail, use Interface Builder to link the controls to the properties.

5 **Make the text fields uneditable.**
Using the inspector, find the checkbox that makes the fields uneditable.

there are no Dumb Questions

Q: We keep drawing the datasource, view, and View Controller as separate things, but then we stick the datasource and controller together into the same class. What's going on?

A: It's all about the pattern. In general, you'll have a view defined in a xib, a View Controller backing it, and a set of data it needs to work on. Whether these are combined into one class or not really depends on the complexity of your application. If you're not using Interface Builder, you can go completely off the deep end and have your single class create the view programmatically. We'll show more of that later in the book. Conceptually, however, you still have a view that's calling into the View Controller when things happen. Likewise, you usually have one or more datasource protocols being realized somewhere that are providing data to your view.

Q: Why do we have to move the *.xib file into the Resources group?

A: You don't *have* to, but we recommend it to help keep your code organized. Different developers use different groups, things like "User Interface," "Business Objects," "Data Objects," etc. Xcode really doesn't care; it's just important that you know how your code is organized and you can find what you're looking for. Reusing a structure that others will recognize is a good practice so people can pick up your code quickly and you can understand their code. We use the templated defaults in this book.

Q: What are other ways to save and load data?

A: There are quite a few of them. We'll cover the more common ones in this book in different projects. The one you're using now, plists, is the simplest, but it does limit what you can save and load. That doesn't make it bad; if it works for what you need, it's a fine solution—it's just too limited for everything. There's a serialization protocol called NSCoding that works well for custom objects, but can make version migration a challenge. iOS supports saving and loading to a database using SQLite. This used to be the preferred way to go if you had a lot of data or needed to search and access it without loading it all into memory. However, with the iPhone 3.0 SDK (now just iOS), Apple introduced Core Data. Core Data is a very powerful framework that provides an OO wrapper on persistence and has nearly all the benefits of using SQLite. It's definitely not trivial to get started, but it's really powerful. We'll build an app on it later.

Q: Why didn't you use a label for the name field?

A: UITextFields allow you to have placeholder text that appears in the field when it's empty. Rather than using up screen space with a Name label, we chose to use the placeholder. If the meaning of the text shown on the screen is obvious to the user, consider using placeholder text.

Q: So why didn't we use it for the ingredients and directions?

A: We could have, but since those contain multiple lines of text, we wanted to break them up with labels clearly showing what they were. Ultimately it's an aesthetic and usability decision, not a technical one.

BULLET POINTS

- Productivity apps work great with hierarchical data.

- Navigation controllers are a good way to manage multiple views.

- Table views usually go with navigation controllers.

- iOS tables only have one column but can render custom cells.

- Tables need a datasource and a delegate.

- Multiple views usually mean multiple *.xib files.

Long Exercise Solution

Here's all the info for the new detail view. After this, you should have a working (but still empty) detail view.

① **Create the files you'll need.**

We need a new .xib for the detail view. To create one from scratch, go back into Xcode and click on the **File→New→New File** menu option.

Make sure that you have the Cocoa Touch Class line selected under iOS.

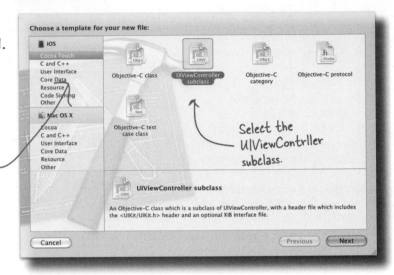

Select the UIViewContrlller subclass.

After clicking **Next**, you can confirm the subclass of UIViewController. In our case, we need both the nib and the supporting files, so leave the "With XIB for user interface" box checked and click **Next.**

One more thing. Xcode will create all your files in the DrinkMixer group, keeping them with the other class files. Name the file "DrinkDetailViewController.m."

② **Lay out the new view in Xcode.**

This came by choosing Navigation Controller from the Simulated Metrics – Top Bar, option in the Attributes Inspector in the utilities panel.

This is the inspector for the first TextField. Put "Name:" in as a placeholder.

This is the same UITextField that we used in InstaEmail. It doesn't scroll.

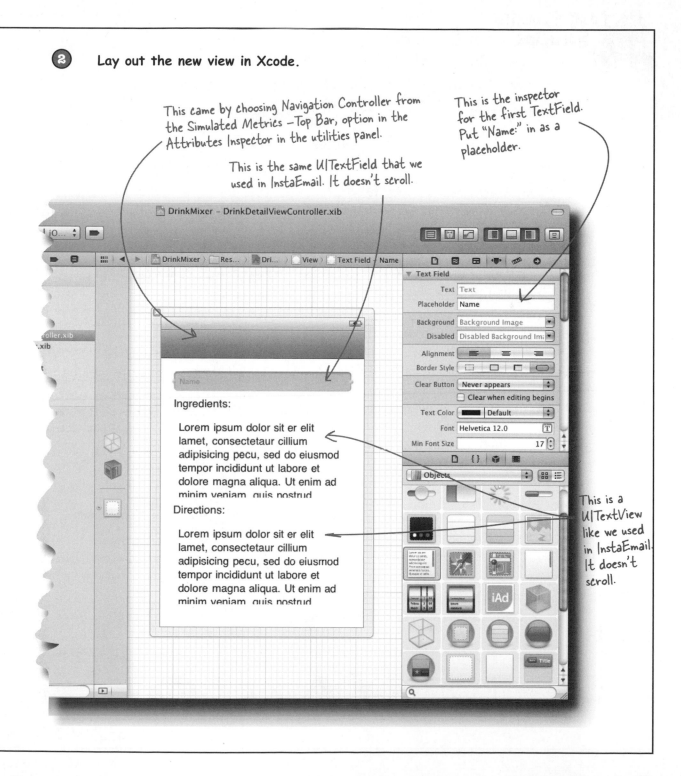

This is a UITextView like we used in InstaEmail. It doesn't scroll.

Long Exercise Solution

Here's all the info for the new detail view. After this, you should have a working (but still empty) detail view.

3 **Write the code to handle the declarations and outlets for the new fields.**

```objc
#import <UIKit/UIKit.h>

@interface DrinkDetailViewController : UIViewController {
@private
    UITextField *nameTextField_;
    UITextView *ingredientsTextView_;
    UITextView *directionsTextView_;
}
@property (nonatomic, retain) IBOutlet UITextField *nameTextField;
@property (nonatomic, retain) IBOutlet UITextView
*ingredientsTextView;
@property (nonatomic, retain) IBOutlet UITextView
*directionsTextView;

@end
```

.h

DrinkDetailViewController.h

```objc
@implementation DrinkDetailViewController
@synthesize nameTextField=nameTextField_, ingredientsTextView=ingre
dientsTextView_, directionsTextView=directionsTextView_;

-(void)dealloc {
    [nameTextField_ release];
    [ingredientsTextView_ release];
    [directionsTextView_ release];
    [super dealloc];
}
```

.m

DrinkDetailViewController.m

④ Connect the detail view to the new outlets.

All three outlets—the directionsTextView, the ingredientsTextView, and the nameTextField—need to be connected to their control on the new view.

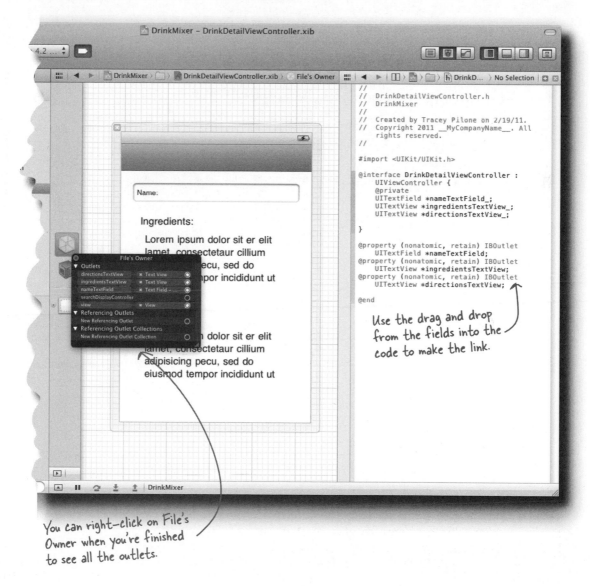

Use the drag and drop from the fields into the code to make the link.

You can right-click on File's Owner when you're finished to see all the outlets.

Long Exercise Solution

5 **Make the text fields un-editable.**

We need to disable both the UITextField and the two UITextViews to prevent the user from making changes. Simply click on each field and toggle the **Enabled** or **Editable** checkboxes to off.

Once those changes are made, the keyboard issue goes away, because there won't be one!

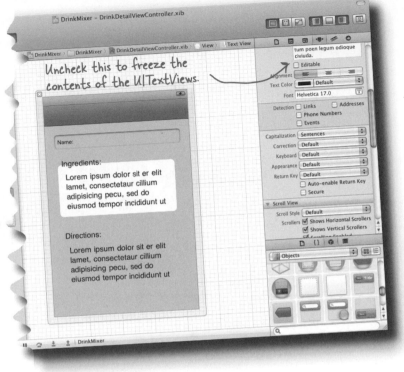

Uncheck this to freeze the contents of the UITextViews.

Test Drive

Build and run your app. You just put in a lot of work, and it's a good time to check for errors. You won't see a difference yet, just the drinks list again...

OK, so I have an order for a Boxcar... but I still don't see the drink details when I click on it.

Boxcar ⊢ Touch here

We still need to get that detail view to load when Sam selects a drink.

Sharpen your pencil

When your users browse through the drink information, they're going to need to switch between the list and detail views. Take a few minutes to think about how to do that while keeping the user from getting lost.

1 How does the user navigate between views?

....

....

2 How can we keep track of what view to show?

....

....

3 How does the detail view know what drink to show?

....

....

4 How do you get the user back to the table view?

....

....

Sharpen your pencil
Solution

When your users browse through the drink information, they're going to need to switch between our list and detail views. Think about how we do that and keep the user from getting lost.

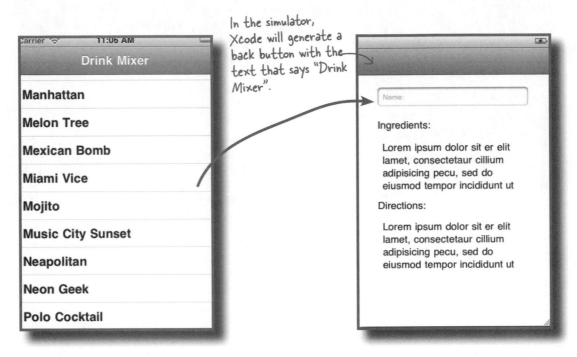

In the simulator, Xcode will generate a back button with the text that says "Drink Mixer".

1 How does the user navigate between views? The user is going to tap on the cell of the drink name that they want to see.

2 How can we keep track of what view to show? The Navigation Controller will keep track with back buttons and the title of the pane.

3 How does the detail view know what drink to show? That's based on the table cell that the user selects.

4 How do you get the user back to the table view? The Navigation Controller can supply a back button that can get us back to the main view.

Use the Navigation Controller to switch between views

Now that we've got the table view populated and the detail view built, it's time to manage moving between the two views. The navigation-based template comes preloaded with the functionality we need:

① **A view stack for moving between views**
As users move back and forth, you can ask the Navigation Controller to display the appropriate view. The Navigation Controller keeps track of where the users are and gives them buttons to go back.

② **A navigation bar for buttons and a title**
The Navigation Controller interacts with the navigation bar to display buttons that interact with the view being shown, along with a title to help the users know where they are.

③ **A navigation toolbar for view-specific buttons**
The Navigation Controller can display a toolbar at the bottom of the screen that shows custom buttons for its current view.

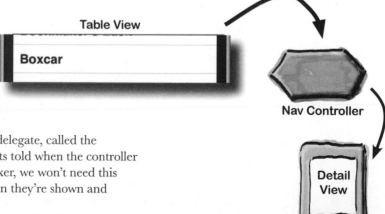

Table View

Boxcar

Nav Controller

Detail View

The UINavigationController supports a delegate, called the UINavigationControllerDelegate, that gets told when the controller is about to switch views, but for DrinkMixer, we won't need this information. Since the views get told when they're shown and hidden, that's all we need for our app.

Now we need to get the Table View and Nav Controller working together to display the detail view.

Navigation Controllers maintain a stack of View Controllers

We've been dragging the Navigation Controller along since the beginning of this project, and now we finally get to put it to use. The Navigation Controller maintains a stack of views and displays the one on top. It will also automatically provide a back button, as well as the cool slide-in and-out animations. We're going to talk more about the whole Navigation Controller stack in the next chapter, but for now, we're just going to push our new view onto the stack and let the controller take care of the rest. We just need to figure out how to get that new view.

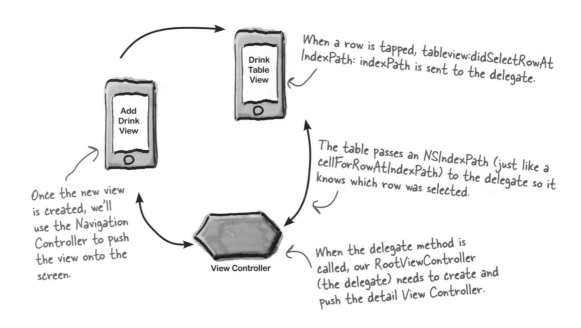

When a row is tapped, tableview:didSelectRowAt IndexPath: indexPath is sent to the delegate.

The table passes an NSIndexPath (just like a cellForRowAtIndexPath) to the delegate so it knows which row was selected.

When the delegate method is called, our RootViewController (the delegate) needs to create and push the detail View Controller.

Once the new view is created, we'll use the Navigation Controller to push the view onto the screen.

Drink Table View

Add Drink View

View Controller

BRAIN POWER

Here's where things get interesting: our RootViewController is our delegate, so it needs to hand off control to a new View Controller to push the detail view onto the screen. How do you think we should handle that?

Instantiate a View Controller like any other class

The only piece left to create is the View Controller for the detail view. Instantiating a View Controller is no different than instantiating any other class, with the exception that you can pass in the nib file it should load its view from:

```
[[DrinkDetailViewController alloc] initWithNibName:@"DrinkDetailView
Controller" bundle:nil];
```

Once we've created the detail View Controller, we'll ask the NavigationController to push the new View Controller onto the view stack. Let's put all of this together by implementing the callback in the delegate and creating the new View Controller to push onto the stack:

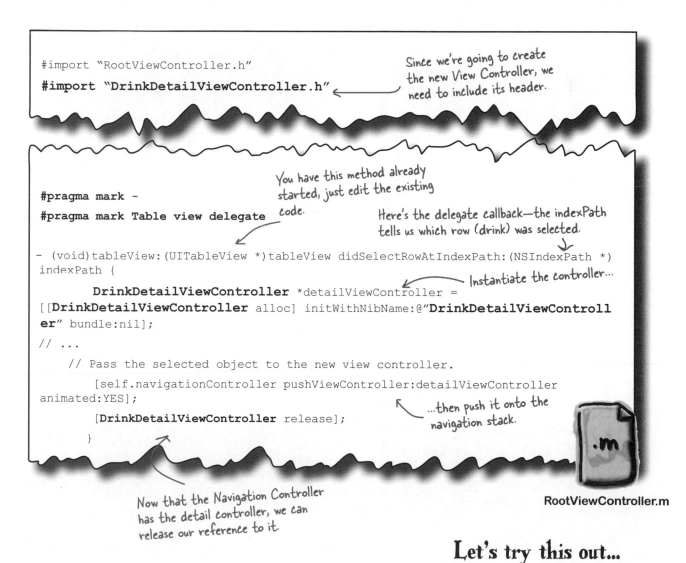

```
#import "RootViewController.h"
#import "DrinkDetailViewController.h"
```

Since we're going to create the new View Controller, we need to include its header.

```
#pragma mark -
#pragma mark Table view delegate
```

You have this method already started, just edit the existing code.

Here's the delegate callback—the indexPath tells us which row (drink) was selected.

```
- (void)tableView:(UITableView *)tableView didSelectRowAtIndexPath:(NSIndexPath *)
indexPath {
    DrinkDetailViewController *detailViewController =
[[DrinkDetailViewController alloc] initWithNibName:@"DrinkDetailViewControll
er" bundle:nil];
// ...
    // Pass the selected object to the new view controller.
    [self.navigationController pushViewController:detailViewController
animated:YES];
    [DrinkDetailViewController release];
}
```

Instantiate the controller...

...then push it onto the navigation stack.

Now that the Navigation Controller has the detail controller, we can release our reference to it.

RootViewController.m

Let's try this out...

TEST DRIVE

Now that both views can talk to each other, go ahead
and build and run.

Tap here to make the
detail view come up.

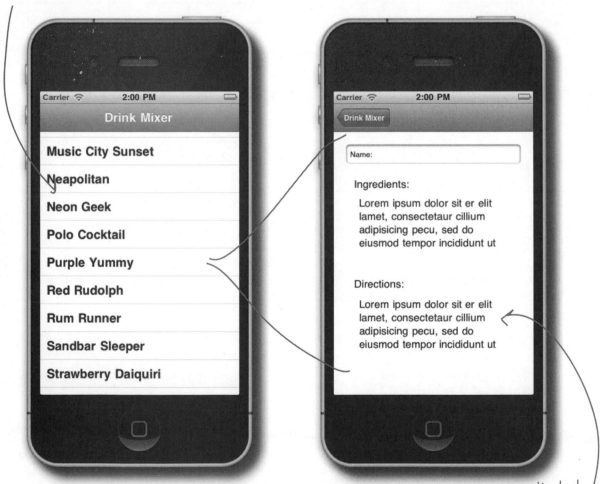

Try clicking in the text
fields—there's no keyboard
because they're not editable!

So, now we can get to the detail view from the drink list, but there aren't any details in there. We don't have that info in our plist, do we?

Yep, we've outgrown our array.

All that's left is to get the ingredients and directions in the detail view, and we'll have a bartender's brain. To save you from having to type in the ingredients and directions, we put together a new file with all the extra information. The problem is we can't just jam that information into an array. To add the drink details to this version, we need a different data model.

Sharpen your pencil

Which options below are possible ways to load the drink data?

☐ Create a database with drink information

☐ Use dictionaries in our plist to hold the drink details

☐ Use an XML file to hold the drink details

☐ Create multiple arrays in our plist

Which of these options is the best for DrinkMixer? Why? ....

....

....

....

Sharpen your pencil Solution

Which options below are possible ways to load the drink data?

We could use a database to store drink information, but since nothing else in this app uses the database, we'd have to do some work to get DB support added...let's keep looking.

☐ Create a database with drink information

We already have a plist of strings—switching over to a plist of dictionaries won't be much work and gives us a data structure that can hold the drink info.

☑ Use dictionaries in our plist to hold the drink details

☐ Use an XML file to hold the drink details

This would work too, but has the same hurdle as using a DB. We're not parsing any XML right now, so we'd have to define the schema, then add parsing code.

☐ Create multiple arrays in our plist

This is basically the worst of all the options— we'd have to make sure multiple arrays line up to keep a single drink straight.

Which of these options is the best for DrinkMixer? Why?

Since we already have code written that uses plists, we can change our plist to have an array of dictionaries instead of an array of strings without a lot of effort. This way we don't have to introduce SQL or XML into our project. However, we do lose out on the strong typing and data checking that both SQL and XML could give us. Since this is a smaller project, we're going to go with dictionaries.

Dictionaries store information as key-value pairs

Our current drink plist is just a single array of drink names. That worked great for populating the table view with just drink names, but doesn't help us at all with drink details. For this plist, instead of an array of strings, we created an array of **dictionaries**. Within each dictionary are three keys: name, ingredients, and directions. Each of these have string values with the corresponding information. Since NSDictionary adopts the NSCoding protocol, it can be saved and loaded in plists just like our basic array from before.

there are no
Dumb Questions

Q: You keep talking about NSCoding. What is that?

A: NSCoding is a protocol that provides an API for encoding and decoding objects. A lot of the basic container types like NSArray NSDictionary conform to this protocol; that's why we can serialize them in and out of a plist. You can conform to this protocol on your own custom objects as well. For more information about NSCoding, see the Apple documentation.

Q: Where did the back button in the detail view come from? We didn't do that...

A: It's automatic functionality that comes with the Navigation Controller. When you added a title for the main view, the Navigation Controller kept track of that name as part of the view stack for navigation, and added a back button with the title in it. So yeah, you did do that!

Ready Bake Code

Go back to *http://www.headfirstlabs.com/books/hfiphonedev/* and download DrinksDirections.plist. It has a different name, so you'll need to make a couple of quick modifications.

1 Open up the new plist in Xcode (again, in the resources directory), and look at what it comes with—all that data is ready to go!

2 Go into the code and change the references from DrinkArray to DrinksDirections.

Test Drive

Build and run the application, but you should pay close attention. (Umm, not that we think anything bad is going to happen, just, well, because...)

TEST DRIVE

It crashed!

Debugging—the dark side of iOS development

Something has gone wrong, but honestly, this is a pretty normal part of the development process. There are lots of things that could cause our application to crash, so we need to figure out what the problem is.

Warnings can help find problems first

In general, if your application doesn't build, Xcode won't launch it—but that's not true for warnings. Xcode will happily compile and run an application with warnings and your only indication will be a little yellow yield signs in the gutter of the Xcode editor. Two minutes spent investigating a warning can save hours of debugging time later.

They'll also show up in the corner of the editor window.

Here's what you'll see for a warning and an error.

They will appear in the gutter next to the offending code.

Geek Bits

Some common warning culprits:

- Now that iOS 4.3 is out, code that uses deprecated 2.0 or 3.0 properties triggers warnings.

- Sending a message to an object that it doesn't claim to understand (from a typo or an autocompletion error) will trigger warnings. Your app will compile, but will likely end up in a runtime exception when that code is executed.

That's not our problem, though: at this point our code is (at least it should be) warning and compile-error-free. The good news is that when an app crashes in the Simulator, it doesn't go away completely (like it would on a real device). Xcode stops the app right before the OS would normally shut it down. Let's use that to see what's going on.

Time for some debugging...

First stop on your debugging adventure: the console

We need to figure out why our app crashed, and thankfully, Xcode has a lot of strong debugging capabilities. For now we're just going to look at the information it gave us about the crash, but later in the book, we'll talk about some of the more advanced debugging features.

Since you ran the program in the simulator, Xcode is going to bring up the debugging pane at the bottom of the editor. You'll probably want to resize it to make the log easier to review.

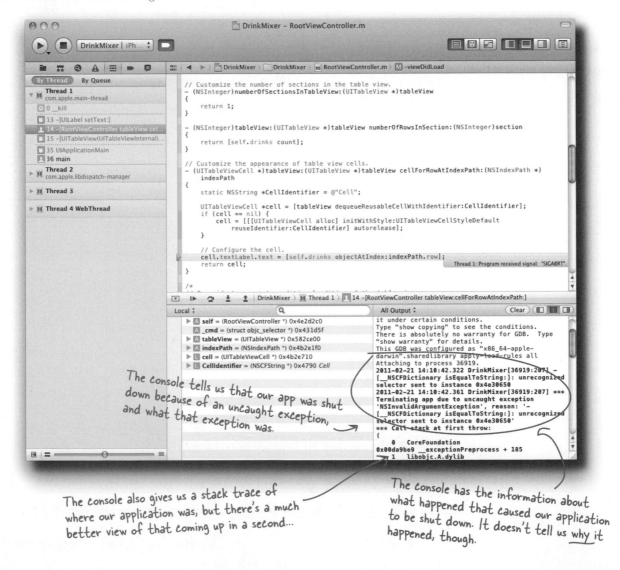

The console tells us that our app was shut down because of an uncaught exception, and what that exception was.

The console also gives us a stack trace of where our application was, but there's a much better view of that coming up in a second...

The console has the information about what happened that caused our application to be shut down. It doesn't tell us <u>why it</u> happened, though.

Interact with your application while it's running

Xcode 4 is a very powerful debugging tool. Some of the best debugging techniques involve well-placed logging messages using NSLog(...). This information is printed into the console and can help you diagnose problems quickly. The console isn't just read-only, though; it is your window into your running application. We'll see log messages displayed in the console, and when your application hits a breakpoint, you'll be placed at the console prompt. From there you can use debugging commands like **print**, **continue**, **where**, **up**, and **down** to inspect the state of your application.

The console debugger is actually the gdb (GNU debugger) prompt, so nearly all gdb commands work here.

And when it's about to stop running

In this case, we're dealing with a nearly dead application, but the idea is the same. Since DrinkMixer has crashed, Xcode provides you with the basic information of what went wrong. In our case, an "unrecognized selector" was sent to an object. Remember that a selector is basically a method call—it means that some code is trying to invoke methods on an object and *those methods don't exist.*

To see this output, you'll need to select "Debugger Output" from this drop-down box.

The console prompt lets you interact with your application at the command line.

But Xcode doesn't stop at the command line. It has a full GUI debugger built right in. Let's take a look...

Xcode supports you after your app breaks, too

So far we've used Xcode to write code and compile and launch our applications. Its usefulness doesn't stop once we hit the "Build and Debug" button. First, we can set breakpoints in our code to let us keep an eye on what's going on. Simply click in the gutter next to the line where you want to set a breakpoint. Xcode will put a small blue arrow next to the line and when your application gets to that line of code, it will stop and let you poke around using the console.

This switch indicates whether the breakpoints are on or not.

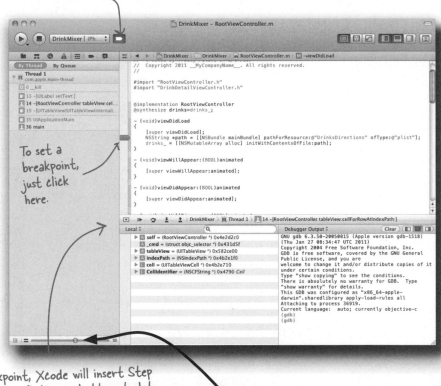

To set a breakpoint, just click here.

Once your app hits a breakpoint, Xcode will insert Step Into, Step Over, Continue, and Debugger buttons to let you walk through your code.

Slide the scrubber all the way to the right to see the full stack from the app...

The Xcode debugger shows you the state of your application

The debugger shows your code and also adds a stack view and a window to inspect variables and memory. When you click on a stack frame, Xcode will show you the line of code associated with that frame and set up the corresponding local variables. There isn't anything in the debugger window you couldn't do with the console, but this provides a nice GUI on top of it.

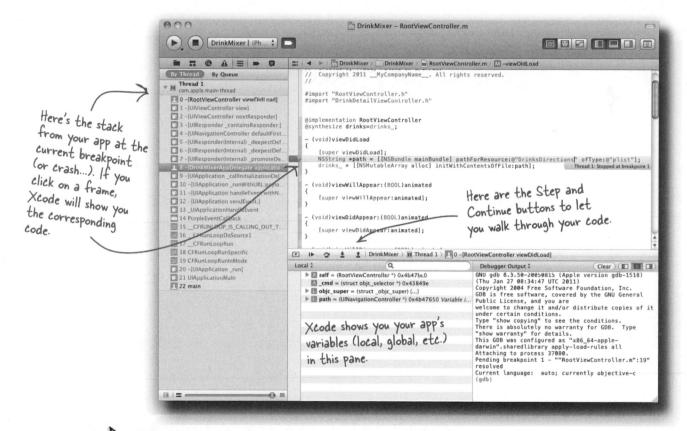

Here's the stack from your app at the current breakpoint (or crash...). If you click on a frame, Xcode will show you the corresponding code.

Here are the Step and Continue buttons to let you walk through your code.

Xcode shows you your app's variables (local, global, etc.) in this pane.

Test Drive

Since we know that we're having a problem near the array, try setting a breakpoint on the line that creates the array. Then build and run the app again and see what happens.

TEST DRIVE

When you step over the breakpoint at the point where you load the array, everything is OK:

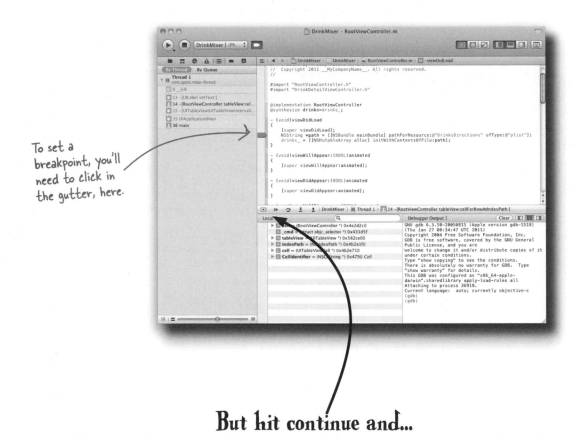

To set a breakpoint, you'll need to click in the gutter, here.

But hit continue and...

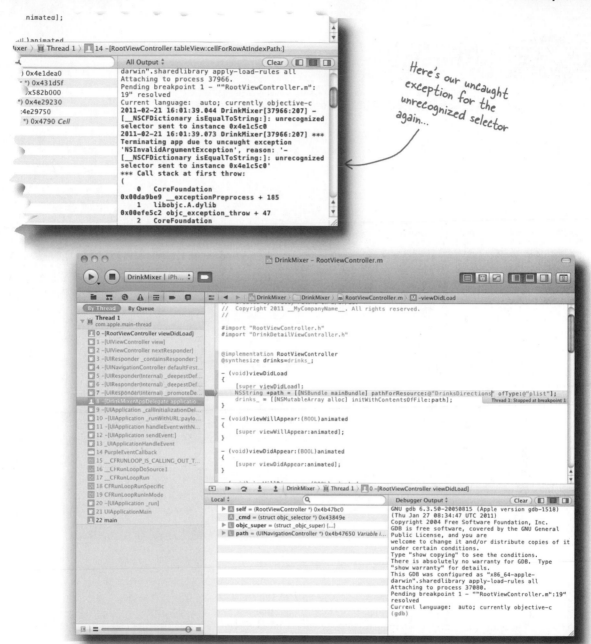

Here's our uncaught exception for the unrecognized selector again...

What the heck is going on?

Our application is crashing, and it's not at the array loading code, so get back into Xcode. It will show you the line that's causing the problem, can you see what's wrong?

To be continued...

MultipleViews cross

Take what you've learned about the Navigation
Controller and multiple views to fill in the blanks.

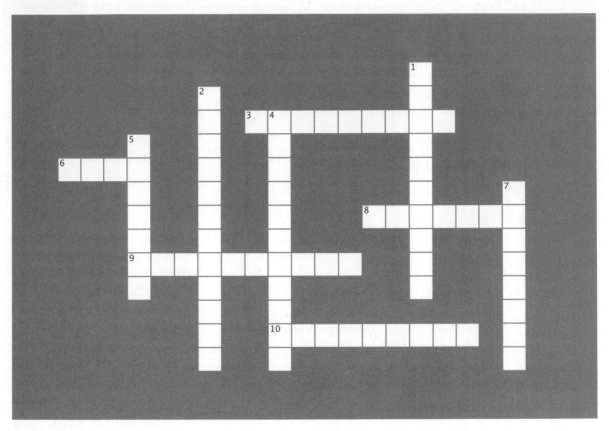

Across

3. The set of views that the nav controller deals with.
6. Dictionaries use _____ to organize data.
8. The screen that gives you output from the app.
9. A template that combines a table view and nav controls.
10. Has cells that need to be customized to work.

Down

1. A more versatile way to manage data beyond an array.
2. DrinkMixer is this type of app.
4. To use a new class you need to _____ it.
5. The @ symbol is shorthand for creating one of these.
7. A tool in Xcode to help fix broken code.

Your iOS Toolbox

You've got Chapter 4 under your belt and now you've added multiple views and the Navigation Controller to your toolbox.

Navigation Template:

Comes with a table view and navigation control built in.

Is great for a productivity app.

Is designed to manage hierarchical data and multiple views.

Has cool animations built in to move between views.

Tables:

Are a collection of cells.

Come with support for editing contents, scrolling, and moving rows.

Can be customized so your cells look like more than one column.

UITableView:

Controls memory by only creating the cells requested in the view. Any other cells are destroyed if iOS needs the memory for something else.

Navigation Controller:

Maintains a view stack for moving between view controllers.

Has a navigation bar for buttons and a title.

Can support custom toolbars at the bottom of the view as needed.

Plists:

Files that can be created and edited in Xcode.

Support Arrays and Dictionaries out of the box.

Are good for handling data, but have some limitations—we'll cover another option, Core Data, in a couple chapters coming up.

Xcode:

Has a built-in console with debugging and logging information.

Gives you errors and warnings as you compile to identify problems.

Has a built-in debugger that allows you to set breakpoints and step through the code to find the bug.

MultipleViews cross Solution

Take what you've learned about the navigation controller and multiple views to fill in the blanks.

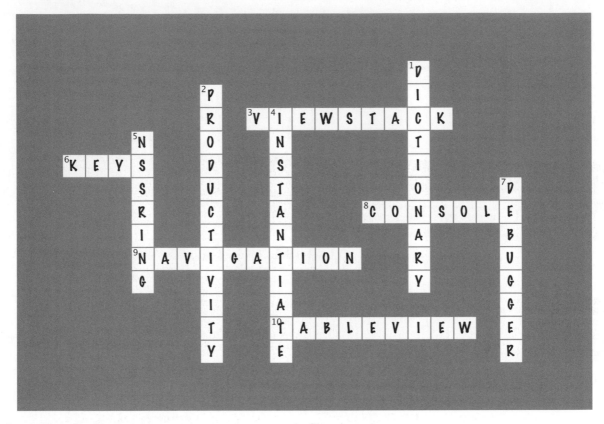

Across

3. The set of views that the nav controller deals with. [VIEWSTACK]
6. Dictionaries use _____ to organize data. [KEYS]
8. The screen that gives you output from the app. [CONSOLE]
9. A template that combines a table view and nav controls. [NAVIGATION]
10. Has cells that need to be customized to work. [TABLEVIEW]

Down

1. A more versatile way to manage data beyond an array. [DICTIONARY]
2. DrinkMixer is this type of app. [PRODUCTIVITY]
4. To use a new class you need to _____ it. [INSTANTIATE]
5. The @ symbol is shorthand for creating one of these. [NSSRING]
7. A tool in Xcode to help fix broken code. [DEBUGGER]

5 plists and modal views

Refining your app

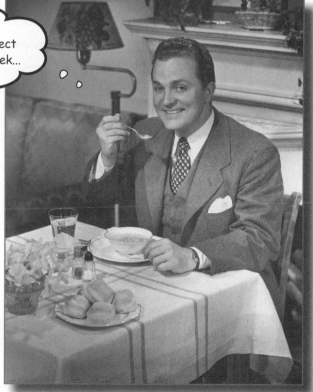

This soup would be even better with the perfect cocktail, maybe a Neon Geek...

So you have this almost-working app...

That's the story of every app! You get some functionality working, decide to add something else, need to do some refactoring, and respond to some feedback from the App Store. Developing an app isn't ~~always~~ ever a linear process, but there's a lot to be learned along the way.

It all started with Sam...

Sam wanted an app to make his bartending work
easier. You got one up and rolling pretty quick,
but hit a snag filling in the details for each drink
because of a plist of dictionaries.

I need to know a ton of drink recipes every night. Is there an app for that?

DrinkMixer has two views: a table view of the drinks and a detail view about each individual drink.

When we last left DrinkMixer, you were in the middle of debugging it...

Anatomy of a Crash

DrinkMixer started and ran happily until it hit our breakpoint at line 19. The debugger stopped our application and displayed the debugging console. By setting a breakpoint in our code, what we discovered at the end of Chapter 4 is that before your app imported the file, there was no crash; so far so good.

Let's walk through loading our plist and make sure that works by typing **next** twice. The first "next" sets up the path to the plist, the second one actually loads the data.

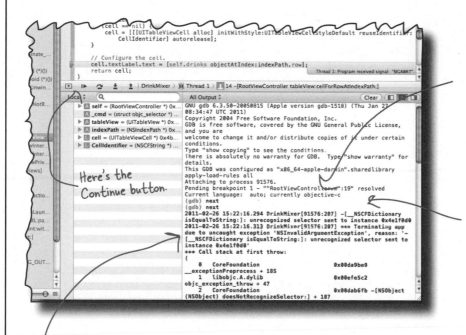

Here's where it stopped at the breakpoint. We told the debugger to let DrinkMixer execute the next two lines.

Here's the Continue button.

It made it past loading the plist, so let's let it continue running...

This exception tells you that an unknown selector (message) is being sent to an NSCFDictionary—specifically, isEqualToString...so where is it coming from?

Loading the plist worked fine; no problems there. The error must be coming after that. Let's have the application continue running and see where it fails. Hit the Continue button (or type **continue** in the console)...and there's our exception again. Where is this actually failing?

Use the debugger to investigate the crash

We can reliably get DrinkMixer to crash, and it doesn't seem to be our plist loading code. Xcode has suspended our application right before iOS shuts it down, so we can use the debugger to see exactly what it was trying to do before it crashed.

Switch back to the debugger and take a look at the stack on the left. This is the call stack that led to the crash.

The stop button will terminate your application.

Here's the stack at the time of the crash. The top 13 frames are framework code, but frame 6 is code we wrote...

Trying to continue now will just keep failing—DrinkMixer has been stopped by iOS.

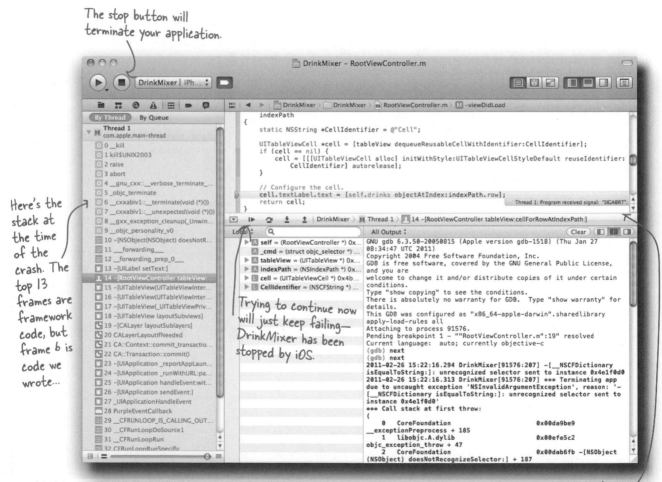

And here's the line that caused the problem. See what's going on yet?

So the exception talks about NSCF Dictionary...maybe it has something to do with the new drinks directions we uploaded for the detail view?

You're on to something there.

Let's take a closer look.

Sharpen your pencil

Using what you've learned so far, figure out what's going on!

The exception talks about NSCF Dictionary. What dictionary is it talking about? Where is it coming from?

....

....

Who's sending messages to the dictionary? Why did we get an unrecognized selector?

....

....

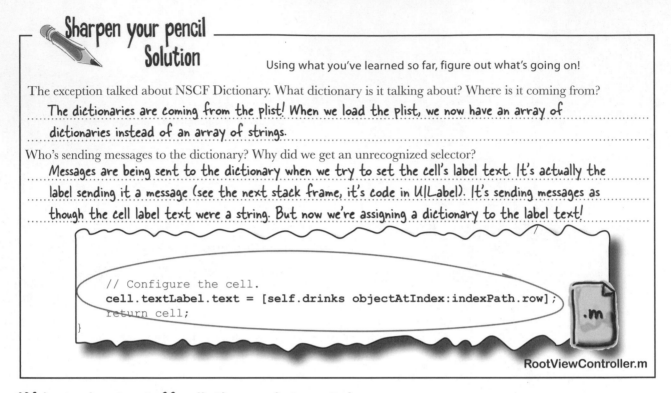

Sharpen your pencil Solution

Using what you've learned so far, figure out what's going on!

The exception talked about NSCF Dictionary. What dictionary is it talking about? Where is it coming from?

The dictionaries are coming from the plist! When we load the plist, we now have an array of
dictionaries instead of an array of strings.

Who's sending messages to the dictionary? Why did we get an unrecognized selector?

Messages are being sent to the dictionary when we try to set the cell's label text. It's actually the
label sending it a message (see the next stack frame, it's code in UILabel). It's sending messages as
though the cell label text were a string. But now we're assigning a dictionary to the label text!

```
// Configure the cell.
cell.textLabel.text = [self.drinks objectAtIndex:indexPath.row];
return cell;
}
```

RootViewController.m

We're trying to stuff a dictionary into a string

Putting a dictionary into the text field of the label, which wants a string, isn't going to work. Our previous array was an array of strings, so that code worked fine. Now that we have an array of dictionaries, we need to figure out how to get the drink name value (a string) out of the dictionary, and then assign that to the text label. If you take another look at the DrinksDirections.plist, you'll see that we have an array of dictionaries— one for each drink. As we saw earlier, dictionaries store their values using keys; they're just a collection of key-value pairs. To get a value out, you simply send the dictionary the objectForKey:@"key" message.

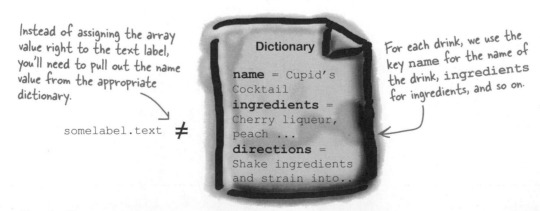

Instead of assigning the array value right to the text label, you'll need to pull out the name value from the appropriate dictionary.

somelabel.text ≠

Dictionary

name = Cupid's Cocktail
ingredients = Cherry liqueur, peach ...
directions = Shake ingredients and strain into...

For each drink, we use the key name for the name of the drink, ingredients for ingredients, and so on.

Update your code to handle a plist of dictionaries

Armed with the knowledge of how the dictionaries are put together, we can use this information to populate the detail view, too. If you give the detail view controller the dictionary of the selected drink, it can populate the view's fields before the view is shown to the user.

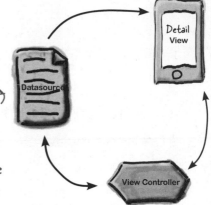

Each dictionary has everything we need for a drink. We need to get that dictionary to the datasource for the detail view.

Sharpen your pencil

Go ahead and make the changes below to your app. After this, it should know that you're using an array of dictionaries, not strings—and the detail view should have a reference to the drink it should display.

① Change the way a table cell is configured.
In RootViewController.m, fix the cell's textLabel.text property to use the name value from the appropriate dictionary.

Don't forget about the NSDictionary documentation if you want to know more about dictionaries.

② Add a reference to a drink dictionary in the detail view.
In DrinkDetailViewController.h, add an NSDictionary* instance variable named drink_ and the corresponding property declaration.

③ Add drink to the DrinkDetailViewController.m file.
Synthesize and dealloc the new dictionary reference.

We'll update the detail view controller to use the values in the new dictionary in a minute...

Sharpen your pencil
Solution

Go through the code and make sure
that you've got everything right...

```
// Configure the cell.
       cell.textLabel.text = [[self.drinks objectAtIndex:indexPath.row]
objectForKey:@"name"];
    return cell;
```

Use objectForKey to get the
name from the dictionary.

RootViewController.m

```
@private
    UITextField *nameTextField_;
    UITextView *ingredientsTextView_;
    UITextView *directionsTextView_;
    NSDictionary *drink_;
}
@property (nonatomic, retain) IBOutlet UITextField *nameTextField;
@property (nonatomic, retain) IBOutlet UITextView *ingredientsTextView;
@property (nonatomic, retain) IBOutlet UITextView *directionsTextView;
@property (nonatomic, retain) NSDictionary *drink;
```

Declare the NSDictionary*
instance variable and a property
with the usual nonatomic, retain
attributes.

This shouldn't be an outlet since we won't be
setting it through Interface Builder.

DrinkDetailViewController.h

Add drink to the synthesize line.

```
@synthesize drink=drink_, nameTextField=nameTextField_, ingredientsText
View=ingredientsTextView_, directionsTextView=directionsTextView_;
```

```
  - (void)dealloc {
      [nameTextField_ release];
      [ingredientsTextView_ release];
      [directionsTextView_ release];
      [drink_ release];
      [super dealloc];
  }
  @end
```

Release our dictionary
reference here.

DrinkDetailViewController.m

TEST DRIVE

Now that we've told DrinkMixer how to deal with dictionaries, go ahead and build and run. Make sure that the breakpoints are off!

It's working again! Now that it's not crashing, it's time to fill in the details.

The Detail View needs data

Now that you've figured out how to deal with dictionaries, it's time to fill in the drink details. But getting the details out of the array of dictionaries to give to the datasource requires another step.

This is the information in DrinksDirections.plist.

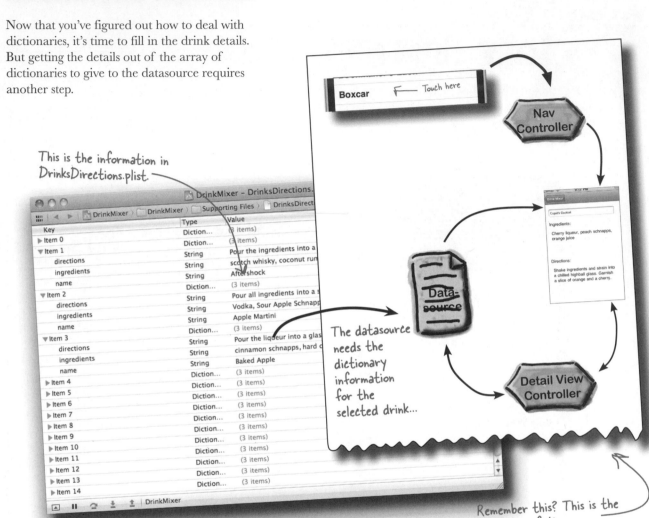

The datasource needs the dictionary information for the selected drink...

Remember this? This is the structure of the app.

BRAIN POWER

How are we going to get the information from DrinksDirections.plist into the Detail View?

The other keys are key

Right now we're just pulling the name of each drink into the app using the **name** key. In order to populate the ingredients and directions, we need to use the other keys. You could just type those right into our code, but you're a better developer than that, so let's pull them up into **constants**. The only thing left is getting the proper dictionary to the detail view controller so it can pull the information it needs. Go ahead and start setting everything up!

Exercise

The View Controller needs direct access to the datasource, and the easiest way to get to that data is going to mean some quick code refactoring.

① **Organize your dictionary constants to avoid bugs.**
Since we're going to need the **name**, **ingredients**, and **directions** keys in the View Controller, we should clean up the code to start using real constants.

Create a new file called **DrinkConstants.h** (right-click on the **DrinkMixer** folder, then choose **New File**, and then choose **Other** and an empty file). Add constants (#define's) for NAME_KEY, INGREDIENTS_KEY and DIRECTIONS_KEY. Import DrinkConstants.h into DrinkDetailViewController.m and RootViewController.m. Finally, update where we use the @"name" key to the new constant, NAME_KEY.

② **Set the detail View Controller's drink property.**
In the root View Controller, after you instantiate the detail View Controller when a cell is tapped, you need to set the drink property on the new controller to the selected drink.

③ **Add code to the detail View Controller to populate values on the UI controls.**
Before the Detail View appears, the View Controller should use the drink dictionary to set the contents of the name, ingredients, and directions components. Don't forget to use the constants you just set up!

Exercise Solution

Here's all the added code to make the Detail View work.

1 Create DrinkConstants.h.

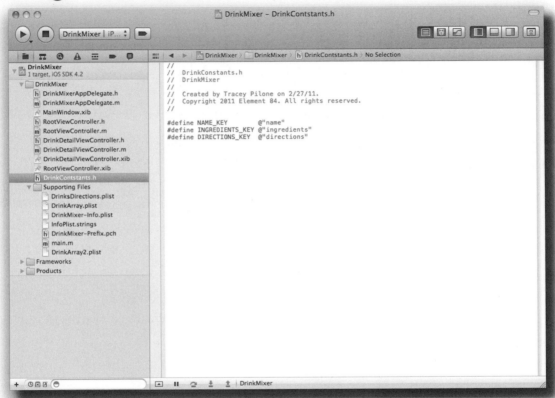

```
//
//  DrinkConstants.h
//  DrinkMixer
//
//  Created by Tracey Pilone on 2/27/11.
//  Copyright 2011 Element 84. All rights reserved.
//

#define NAME_KEY         @"name"
#define INGREDIENTS_KEY  @"ingredients"
#define DIRECTIONS_KEY   @"directions"
```

DrinkDetailViewController.m and RootViewController.m both need
#import "DrinkConstants.h".

We're changing the dictionary keys to constants here...

Then add the constant to display the name:

```
// Configure the  cell.
    cell.textLabel.text = [[self.drinks objectAtIndex:indexPath.row]
objectForKey:NAME_KEY];

    return cell;
```

Change this value from @"name".

RootViewController.m

2 Set the detail view controller's drink property.

```
#pragma mark -
#pragma mark Table view delegate
- (void)tableView:(UITableView *)tableView didSelectRowAtIndexPath:(NSIndex
Path *)indexPath {
        DrinkDetailViewController *detailViewController =
[[DrinkDetailViewController alloc] initWithNibName:@"DrinkDetailViewContro
ller" bundle:nil];

        detailViewController.drink = [self.drinks objectAtIndex:indexPath.
row];

        [self.navigationController pushViewController:detailViewController
animated:YES];

        [detailViewController release];
        }
```

Add this whole line to grab a dictionary from the array.

RootViewController.m

3 Add a method to the detail View Controller to populate the fields.

This whole method is new.

We need to make sure we delegate this up to the UIViewController superclass before we do anything else.

```
- (void) viewWillAppear:(BOOL)animated {
     [super viewWillAppear:animated];
     // Set up our UI with the provided drink
     self.nameTextField.text = [self.drink objectForKey:NAME_KEY];
     self.ingredientsTextView.text = [self.drink
objectForKey:INGREDIENTS_KEY];
     self.directionsTextView.text = [self.drink
objectForKey:DIRECTIONS_KEY];
  }
```

And here are those constants you just created.

DrinkDetailViewController.m

TEST DRIVE

Compile and build and run again...

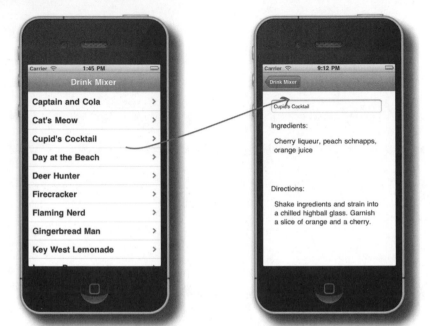

It works!

there are no
Dumb Questions

Q: **We re-create the Detail View every time someone taps on a drink. Couldn't I just reuse that view?**

A: For DrinkMixer, it really won't matter too much; since the view is pretty lightweight, we won't suffer too much overhead re-creating it when a drink is tapped. However, for best performance, you can refactor it to reuse the same detail View Controller and just change the drink it should be showing when a row is tapped.

Q: **Why did we have to pull out the dictionary key names into a separate file?**

A: Having magic string values in your code is generally a bad idea—no matter what programming language or platform you're using. By pulling them up into constants using #define, they are checked by the compiler. So a typo like @"nme" instead of @"name" would end up as a bug at runtime, while mistyping NME_KEY instead of NAME_KEY would prevent things from even compiling.

Q: **I looked at the NSDictionary documentation and there's a valueForKey: and an objectForKey:. What's the difference?**

A: Great question. valueForKey: is used for what's called key value coding, which is a specific pattern typically used in Cocoa Binding. The subtle catch is that NSDictionary usually just turns a call to valueForKey: into a call to objectForKey, and it looks like either one will work. However, valueForKey actually checks the key you pass it and has different behavior depending on your key. That's almost never what you want (unless you're doing Cocoa binding stuff, of course). The correct method to use is objectForKey:.

Overheard at
Head First
Lounge

Is that app up on the App Store? Then I can just download it on my phone and start making even more tips!

Sam, ready for your app to make his (and your) wallet fatter...

Looks like there's a market there!
A quick submission to Apple and...

From: iTunes Store

Subject: DrinkMixer app <u>NOT APPROVED</u>

Your app is NOT APPROVED for distribution on the App Store. It does not conform to iOS's Human Interface Guide in your implementation of the table view. The table views are not using disclosure indicator elements.

Apps that do not conform to the Human Interface Guide may not be distributed. After fixing your implementation, resubmit your app for approval.

Time to investigate the HIG...

Seriously, this can and will happen if you don't follow the HIG. It happened to, um, a friend of the authors...twice.

We'll go through the approval process later.

Later in the book, we'll take you through the process of preparing an app for approval. For now, just worry about how to fix DrinkMixer!

We have a usability problem

We know that the user needs to touch the name of the drink to see the details about each individual drink, but how is the user supposed to know that? The HIG has a number of recommendations for how to deal with drill-down, hierarchical data. We're already on the right track using table views, but the HIG has a number of additional recommendations for helping the user understand how to navigate the app.

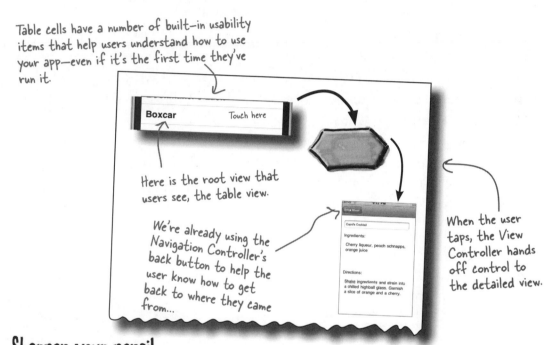

Table cells have a number of built-in usability items that help users understand how to use your app—even if it's the first time they've run it.

Boxcar   Touch here

Here is the root view that users see, the table view.

We're already using the Navigation Controller's back button to help the user know how to get back to where they came from...

When the user taps, the View Controller hands off control to the detailed view.

Sharpen your pencil

It's time to dive into the HIG and figure out what went wrong.

Take a look at disclosure indicator elements—when should we be using these?

....

....

The HIG mentions detail disclosure buttons and disclosure indicators—which should we use? Why?

....

....

Sharpen your pencil
Solution

It's time to dive into the HIG and figure out what went wrong.

Take a look at disclosure indicator elements—when should we be using these?

In the HIG, the "Table View" section, you can pretty quickly find out why you're in violation over those disclosure indicators:

> **"The disclosure indicator element...is necessary if you're using the table to present hierarchical information."**

The HIG mentions detail disclosure buttons and disclosure indicators—which should we use? Why?

The disclosure indicator denotes that there is an additional level of information available about an item when you click it (like drink details); it selects that row and shows the additional data. The button can do something besides select the row—it can kick off an action as well. That's more than we'll need here, so we'll just stick with the disclosure indicator..

Table Cells Up Close

So, what exactly is the detail disclosure button, and where does it go? Let's look a little deeper in the HIG.

The textLabel is the main text area in a cell.

This imageView is used to show images associated with a cell.

Big Font Info
small detailed text

This is the detailTextLabel. Depending on what cell style you use, it can show up in different places, fonts, and colors.

Here's an accessoryType—common ones are disclosure indicator, detail disclosure button, and checkmark.

DrinkMixer uses default cells, but you can easily customize your cells for a different app, besides just adding detail disclosure buttons. There are a few other types of cells in the API: subtitle cell style, a value 1 style (where the first value of the cell is emphasized), or a value 2 cell (where the second value of the style is emphasized). Even though the table only supports one column, you can make it look like more by adding a thumbnail, for example. You can also adjust the font sizes to open up some room for each table cell if you need to.

Most really polished apps use some kind of table cell customizing, so keep that in mind while you're looking through the API. For now, we just need to add the disclosure button to our cells to indicate that there's more information available if a user taps on them.

Use a disclosure button to show that there are more details available

TableViewCells have a lot of built-in functionality—we're just scratching the surface. Adding a detail disclosure indicator is simply a matter of telling the cell what type of accessory icon it should use. Take a look at the UITableViewCell documentation for some of the other options.

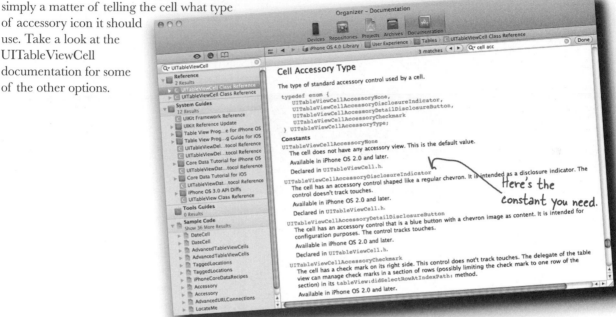

There's just one quick line of code to set the cell's accessory type when we configure the cell:

> Just set the accessory type to the detail disclosure indicator.

```
// Configure the cell.
    cell.textLabel.text = [[self.drinks objectAtIndex:indexPath.row]
valueForKey:NAME_KEY];

    cell.accessoryType = UITableViewCellAccessoryDetailDisclosureIndicator;

    return cell;
    }
```

RootViewController.m

TEST DRIVE

Go ahead and build and run...make sure it's working!

Test Drive

One little line of code fixed all of your App Store approval issues.

There are those disclosure indicators— now the user knows what to do!

After resubmitting to the App Store, DrinkMixer is up on iTunes!

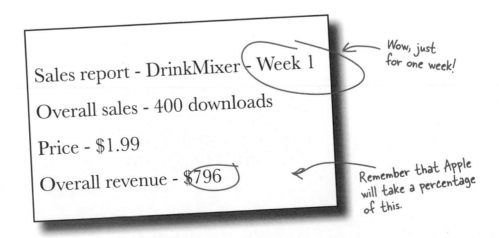

Sales report - DrinkMixer - Week 1

Overall sales - 400 downloads

Price - $1.99

Overall revenue - $796

Wow, just for one week!

Remember that Apple will take a percentage of this.

The reviews are coming in...

Sales were going strong

But then bad reviews started coming in. What's going on?

The reviews are bad...

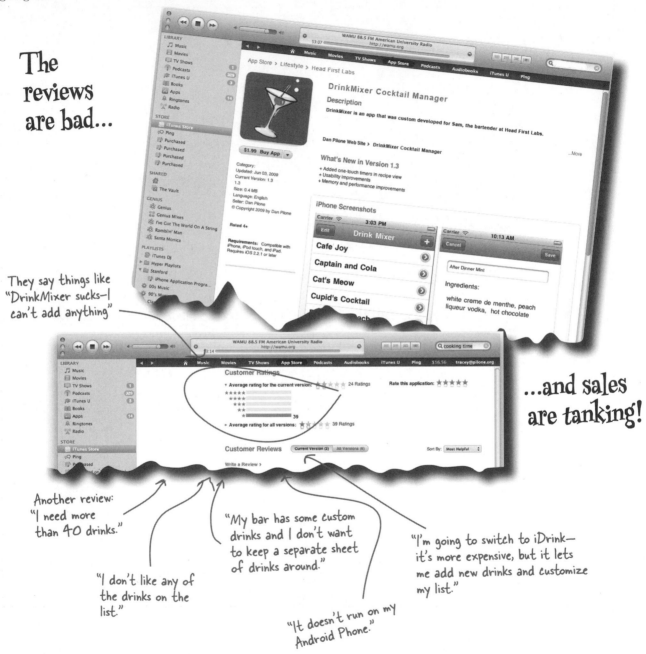

They say things like "DrinkMixer sucks—I can't add anything"

...and sales are tanking!

Another review: "I need more than 40 drinks."

"I don't like any of the drinks on the list."

"My bar has some custom drinks and I don't want to keep a separate sheet of drinks around."

"It doesn't run on my Android Phone."

"I'm going to switch to iDrink—it's more expensive, but it lets me add new drinks and customize my list."

Sharpen your pencil

Think about how you originally designed DrinkMixer, what's not working based on the feedback, and figure out what you'll do next.

1 What would address the users' concerns?

....

....

....

....

2 Given the structure of DrinkMixer, how would you refactor the code to fix the problem?

....

....

....

....

3 Is there an easy way to fix the code? A hard way?

....

....

....

....

Sharpen your pencil
Solution

Think about how you originally designed DrinkMixer, what's not working based on the feedback, and figure out what you'll do next.

1 What would address the users' concerns?

The easiest way to fix the problem is to update the app so users can add more drinks to the list.

2 Given the structure of DrinkMixer, how would you refactor the code to fix the problem?

We could add a new view that lets users enter their drink information. It could look like the detail view, but allow them to type in the information they want. We'll have to save that new information and update the table to show the new drink.

3 Is there an easy way to fix the code? A hard way?

There are lots of hard ways and probably a few good "easy" ways. In general, the easiest way for us to add this functionality is to reuse as much of what we've already done as possible. We can definitely take advantage of our Navigation Controller, and let's see if we can't do something useful with our DetailDrinkView too...

BRAIN POWER

How would you go about implementing a view where users can add drinks to DrinkMixer?

APP LAYOUT CONSTRUCTION

Here is the table view for DrinkMixer with two possible designs. Based on aesthetics, usability, and standard iOS App behavior, which one is better for showing the users where they should add a drink?

Some kind of button in the Navigation Controller to kick off a new view.

Add a new toolbar with some buttons below the Nav Controller.

You'd have room for an add button and others, when you need them.

Option #1   **Option #2**

Which interface is better? ....

Why? (Be specific.) ....

....

Why not the other? ....

APP LAYOUT CONSTRUCTION SOLUTION

Here are two designs. Based on aesthetics, usability, and standard iOS App behavior, which one is better for showing the users where they should add a drink?

The Navigation Controller comes with built-in button support.

This type of interface is good when you have several new views to add, not just one.

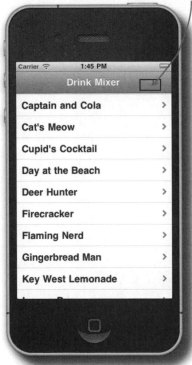

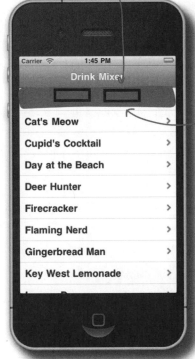

The toolbar will cover up part of the table view, too.

Option #1

Option #2

Which interface is better?   Option #1.

Why? (Be specific.)   Because by putting the icon in the Nav Controller, you don't take space away from the table view. There's also built-in support for that button in the Nav Controller already.

Why not the other?   Option #2 makes the interface a bit more cluttered and requires more code. If there was lots of new functionality coming, it would be worth considering, though.

Use Navigation Controller buttons to add drinks

So far we've used the Navigation Controller to move between views. But if you've spent much time with other iOS apps, you know it's capable of much more. Since a UITableView is almost always embedded in a Navigation Controller, table editing is usually done through buttons on the controller itself. Let's start out by adding a + button to the Navigation Controller that will let the users add a drink when they tap it.

Users will be able to tap the + button to add a drink.

Sharpen your pencil

Using Xcode, add the button to the Nav Controller and the associated IBActions and IBOutlets.

1 **Open RootViewController.xib in the GUI editor.**
Scroll through the library and drag a Bar Button Item to the Main Window (this will add it to the list after the Table View). It won't show up on the Navigation Controller in the editor—we'll need to add code so it shows up at runtime.

It won't show up because the Navigation Controller in Interface Builder is SIMULATED, not real.

2 **Add the instance variable and property declaration for addButton and IBAction for addButtonPressed.**
Just like any other button, we'll have an IBAction for when it gets clicked and a reference to the button itself—all in RootViewController.h.

3 **Add the synthesize, dealloc, and addButtonPressed method for addButton.**
Synthesize the property, release the reference, and implement the addButtonPressed to log a message when the button is clicked—all in RootViewController.m

4 **Finish up in the links.**
Open up RootViewController.xib again and link the new Bar Button Item to the actions and outlets within the Main Window.

Finally, pull up the inspector in the Utilities pane for the Bar Button Item and change the **Identifier** to **Add**.

Sharpen your pencil
Solution

Using Xcode, add the button to the Nav Controller and
the associated IBActions and IBOutlets.

1 **Open RootViewController.xib in the GUI editor.**

Scroll through the library and drag a
Bar Button Item to the Main Window
(it will get added to the list).

2 **Add the instance variable and property declaration for addButton and IBAction for addButtonPressed.**

```
@interface RootViewController : UITableViewController {
    NSMutableArray *drinks_;

    UIBarButtonItem *addButton_;
}
@property (nonatomic, retain) NSMutableArray *drinks;

@property (nonatomic, retain) IBOutlet UIBarButtonItem *addButton;

- (IBAction) addButtonPressed: (id) sender;

@end
```

.h

RootViewController.h

3 **Add the synthesize, dealloc, and addButtonPressed method for addButton.**

```
@synthesize drinks=drinks_, addButton=addButton_;
```

.m

RootViewController.m

```
#pragma mark-
#pragma mark Actions
- (IBAction) addButtonPressed: (id)sender {
    NSLog(@"Add button pressed!");
}
```

*We'll start just by logging the
button press so we can test it
before implementing anything
further...*

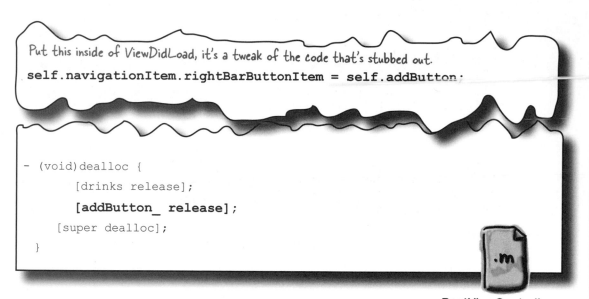

Put this inside of ViewDidLoad, it's a tweak of the code that's stubbed out.

```
self.navigationItem.rightBarButtonItem = self.addButton;
```

```
- (void)dealloc {
    [drinks release];
    [addButton_ release];
    [super dealloc];
}
```

RootViewController.m

④ **Finish up in the view.**

Open up RootViewController.xib again, and link the new Bar Button Item to the actions and outlets within the Main Window, right-clicking and using the menus that pop up.

Finally, pull up the inspector for the Bar Button Item and change the **Identifier** to **Add**.

Test Drive

Go ahead; build and run the app...

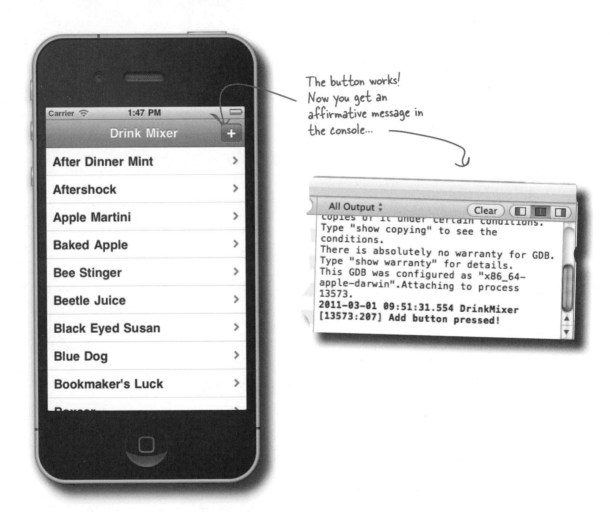

The button works! Now you get an affirmative message in the console...

> All Output ◊   Clear ☐ ▊ ☐
>
> copies of it under certain conditions.
> Type "show copying" to see the
> conditions.
> There is absolutely no warranty for GDB.
> Type "show warranty" for details.
> This GDB was configured as "x86_64-
> apple-darwin".Attaching to process
> 13573.
> 2011-03-01 09:51:31.554 DrinkMixer
> [13573:207] Add button pressed!

Carrier 🛜   1:47 PM

Drink Mixer   ＋

After Dinner Mint	>
Aftershock	>
Apple Martini	>
Baked Apple	>
Bee Stinger	>
Beetle Juice	>
Black Eyed Susan	>
Blue Dog	>
Bookmaker's Luck	>

The button shows up in the view, but now what?

The button should create a new view

Our new button works: the action gets called, but really doesn't do anything useful yet. We need to give our user a place to enter the new drink information, and we can do that with a new view. Just like with the detailed view, we can let the Navigation Controller handle the transition.

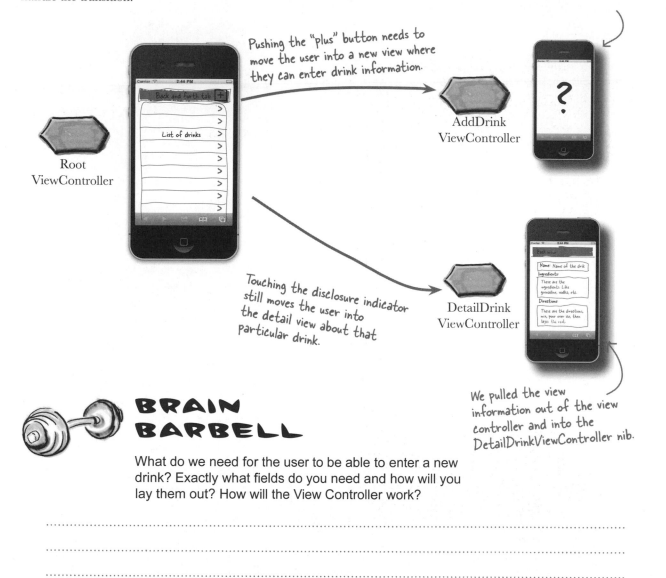

What do we need for the AddViewController's UI? Where does it go?

Pushing the "plus" button needs to move the user into a new view where they can enter drink information.

Root
ViewController

AddDrink
ViewController

Touching the disclosure indicator still moves the user into the detail view about that particular drink.

DetailDrink
ViewController

We pulled the view information out of the view controller and into the DetailDrinkViewController nib.

BRAIN BARBELL

What do we need for the user to be able to enter a new drink? Exactly what fields do you need and how will you lay them out? How will the View Controller work?

....
....
....
....

We need a view...but not necessarily a <u>new</u> view

Our "new" drink view is really just an editable version of our detailed view. So instead of creating a whole new nib, let's take advantage of the fact that the UI (the nib) is separate from our behavior (the UIView subclass in the .m file) and reuse the detail view.

Up until now, we've had a one-to-one pairing between our nibs and our View Controllers. That's definitely the norm, but our View Controllers are really just normal Objective-C classes. That means we can use object-oriented extension mechanisms like **inheritance** to add the behavior we want.

The add drink view needs to contain exactly the same fields as the detail view—it just needs to be editable.

We need to support different behavior than the detail View Controller, though. We'll need a new view controller.

AddDrink
ViewController

When you click on these text fields, the keyboard will pop up and let you enter new information.

`DrinkDetailViewController.xib`

Really, a new view controller but not a new nib? I thought they always go together.

Not necessarily.

Remember that a xib is just the XML representation of a view. Using nibs is a lot easier than trying to lay out your view using code. And since the nib is just graphical information, you need to put the actual code somewhere else. That's where the view controller comes in...

The View Controller defines the behavior for the view

From the user's perspective, we'll have three views: the table view, the detailed view, and the new drink view. But, since we're reusing the .xib to create the "new" view, all we need is a new view controller class that supports adding a drink. That means there isn't any Interface Builder work to do at all!

Here's the new view we need to create. It will look the same, so we can reuse the nib.

When we instantiate the DrinkDetailViewController, we tell it to initialize with a specific nib.

We need this now...

DrinkDetailViewController.xib

DrinkDetailViewController.m

AddDrinkViewController.m

The ViewController defines the behavior for the view—in this case, populating the fields with drink information.

The nib defines the GUI and since both views will look the same, we can reuse it.

Separating the UI from behavior helps you reuse your view.

BRAIN POWER

Reusing both the .xib file and the detail view controller is also an option. But where could we run into problems with that approach?

A nib file contains the UI components and connections...

One way we could reuse the nib is to create a new ViewController and pass it the DrinkDetailViewController.xib file when we initialize it. There are a few challenges with that, though. Remember, we don't just use Interface Builder to lay out the interface; we use it to wire up the components to the class that will load the nib.

The View Controller has the fields and methods that get wired up to the components in the nib.

The view layout information and connections are stored in the nib...

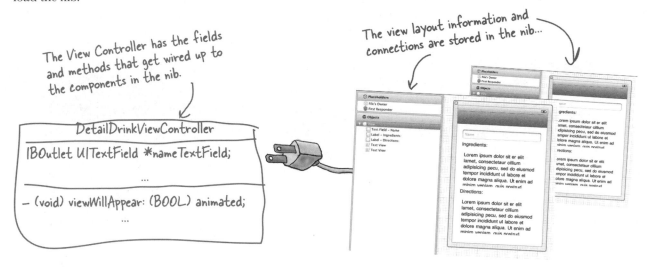

```
DetailDrinkViewController

IBOutlet UITextField *nameTextField;
                ...

– (void) viewWillAppear: (BOOL) animated;
                ...
```

...and information about the nib's File's Owner

The nib doesn't actually contain the ViewController class it's setup to be wired to. Instead, it does this through the nib's File's Owner. When you pass the nib to the view controller, it will deserialize the nib and begin making connections to the outlet names stored in the nib file. This means that if we want to pass that nib into another, new view controller, we need to make sure we have the same outlets with the same names, the same actions, etc.

Watch it!

Reusing our nib gets us what we need for this app, but it's not for every app out there.

Because of the way DrinkMixer is built, we can just subclass our detailed view to get what we need. That works great for this app, but be careful doing this in more complex apps, because your code can get difficult to maintain. Often, it's better to just bite the bullet and build a new view...and sometimes you'll realize they shouldn't even look the same.

You can subclass and extend view controllers like any other class

Instead of reusing just the nib and having to recreate all the outlets and actions, we can just subclass the DetailedViewController and add the behavior we need. Our AddDrinkViewController is the same as a DetailedViewController; it just has the ability to create and save an entirely new drink. Everything else—showing the name, showing the description, etc.—are all exactly the same as the DetailedViewController.

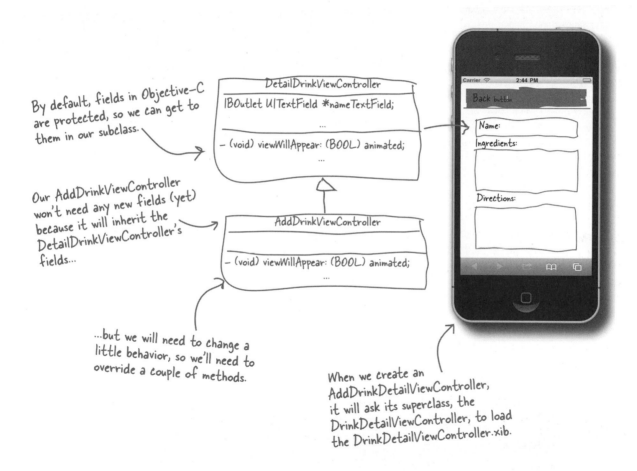

By default, fields in Objective-C are protected, so we can get to them in our subclass.

Our AddDrinkViewController won't need any new fields (yet) because it will inherit the DetailDrinkViewController's fields...

...but we will need to change a little behavior, so we'll need to override a couple of methods.

When we create an AddDrinkDetailViewController, it will ask its superclass, the DrinkDetailViewController, to load the DrinkDetailViewController.xib.

```
DetailDrinkViewController

IBOutlet UITextField *nameTextField;

...

- (void) viewWillAppear: (BOOL) animated;

...
```

```
AddDrinkViewController

- (void) viewWillAppear: (BOOL) animated;

...
```

First, we need to create the new View Controller.

there are no
Dumb Questions

Q: **I still don't get it about the new view controller without a new nib.**

A: There's nothing in that nib that you couldn't create in normal Objective-C by hand. As you've likely discovered with Interface Builder, nibs are generally a lot easier to work with than trying to lay out your view using code, so when you create a new view, you typically create a nib to go with it. But really, you could build an entire application without a single nib.

In our case, we're going to do something somewhere in the middle: we're going to create a new view but reuse the UI information from another view.

Q: **So why the "Watch it" warning about reusing the nib? Is this a good idea or not?**

A: Unfortunately, the answer is: it depends. For DrinkMixer, we can reuse our DetailDrinkView and its nib since we want the layouts to look the same and the DetailDrinkView doesn't really do anything specific. However, in a more complex application, you might run into problems where you're constantly fighting between the two view controllers or you have to expose so much information to the subclass that your code becomes unmaintainable. This isn't a problem unique to iOS development; you always have to be careful when you start subclassing things.

For our app, subclassing works fine, and you'll see it in some of Apple's example applications, too (which is part of the reason we included it here). But it's equally likely that in some other application you'll want views to be similar, but not quite exactly the same. In those cases, create a new view controller and nib.

Q: **Do you usually have all your table cell initialization code in cellForRowAtIndexPath?**

A: It depends on how complex your table view and cells are. If your cell configuration is simple, sure. As you get more complicated table views (in particular, grouped table views with different kinds of cells), it gets unwieldy. Instead, consider creating helper methods that can configure a particular kind of cell.

Another really important thing to keep straight is resetting a cell back to defaults. Your cellForRowAtIndexPath should always reset a cell back to default values before using it—you just don't know where it's been. Obviously, you can factor that code out into a helper method too, but don't forget to do it!

Use Xcode to create a View Controller without a nib

What we'll do is create a new ViewController in Xcode that doesn't have its own nib, and then tweak it to inherit from the DrinkDetailViewController. This new view will get all of the fields, behavior (which we'll change), and the nib we need.

Sharpen your pencil

Get into Xcode and create the AddDrinkViewController files.

☐   Create a new UIViewController subclass named AddDrinkViewController **without** a nib using the **New File** dialog box.

Watch the options in the new file creation...You don't want a xib with the view.

☐   Open up the new AddDrinkViewController.h file and change it to inherit from DrinkDetailViewController instead of the UIViewController. Don't forget to import the DrinkDetailViewController.h file.

We'll add the new behavior we need in a minute...

Sharpen your pencil Solution

Get into Xcode and create the AddDrinkViewController files.

In the **New File** dialog box, you need to create new UIViewController subclass files. Be sure to uncheck the **With XIB for user interface box,** since we don't need that .xib file.

In order to use the DrinkDetailViewController, we need to import the header so the compiler knows what we're talking about.

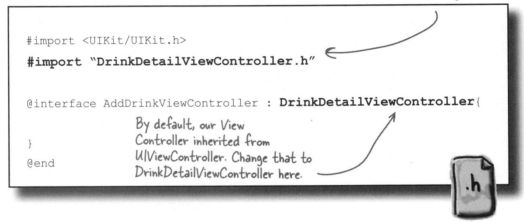

```
#import <UIKit/UIKit.h>
#import "DrinkDetailViewController.h"


@interface AddDrinkViewController : DrinkDetailViewController{



}
@end
```

By default, our View Controller inherited from UIViewController. Change that to DrinkDetailViewController here.

AddDrinkViewController.h

The AddDrinkViewController.m file can stay exactly as it is generated by Xcode.

there are no Dumb Questions

Q: Wait, why aren't we just passing the nib into the AddDrinkViewController? Why all this subclassing stuff?

A: We could do that, but the problem is we're not just dealing with GUI layout. We have text fields and labels in there that need to get populated. Our DetailedDrinkViewController already has outlets for all the fields we need, plus it has the functionality to populate them with a drink before it's shown. We'd have to reimplement that in our new view controller if we didn't subclass.

Q: Is this some kind of contrived Head First example, or should I really be paying attention?

A: You should be paying attention. This pattern shows up pretty often and a lot of Apple's example applications use it. It's very common, particularly in table-driven applications, to have one view that just displays the data and another to edit it when the user puts the table in editing mode (we'll talk about that more later). Sometimes you should use totally different views; sometimes you can reuse one you have.

Q: You mentioned that fields are protected by default. What if I wanted private fields in my class?

A: It's easy—just put @private (or @public for public fields) in your interface definition before you declare the fields. If you don't put an access specifier there, Objective-C defaults to protected for fields.

Jim: Now we have an AddDrinkViewController class, so all we have to do is push it on the stack like we did with the detail view, right?

Joe: That makes sense—we used the Navigation Controller to drill down into the data just by pushing a detailed view on the stack...

Frank: Adding a new drink to our list is a little different, though.

Jim: Why?

Frank: Well, adding a new drink is really a sub-task.

Joe: Huh?

Frank: The users are stepping out of the usual browsing drinks workflow to create a new drink.

Joe: Oh, that's true. Now they're typing, not reading and mixing a drink.

Frank: Right, so for times like this, it's important to communicate to the users that they have to complete the task. Either by finishing the steps or—

Joe: —or by cancelling.

Frank: So, what kind of view is that?

Modal views focus the user on the task at hand...

When users navigate through your app, they are used to seeing views pushed and popped as they move through the data. However, some tasks are different than the normal drill-down navigation and we really need to call the user's attention to what's going on. iOS does this through **modal views**. These are normal views from your (the developer's) perspective, but feel different to the user in a few ways:

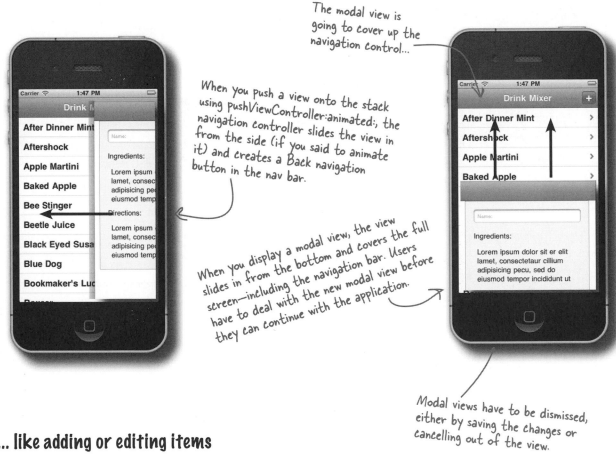

The modal view is going to cover up the navigation control...

When you push a view onto the stack using pushViewController:animated:, the navigation controller slides the view in from the side (if you said to animate it) and creates a Back navigation button in the nav bar.

When you display a modal view, the view slides in from the bottom and covers the full screen—including the navigation bar. Users have to deal with the new modal view before they can continue with the application.

Modal views have to be dismissed, either by saving the changes or cancelling out of the view.

... like adding or editing items

We're going to use a modal view when users want to add a new drink to DrinkMixer. They have to either save the added drink or discard (cancel) it before they can return to the main DrinkMixer app. So we want a view that encourages the user to make that choice.

Any view can present a modal view

Up until now, we've presented new views using our Navigation Controller. Things are a little different for modal views: *any* UIViewController can show a modal view, then dismiss it when necessary. To display a modal view on top of the current view, simply send the current view the presentModalView Controller:animated: message. Since our RootViewController is the View Controller that needs to show the modal view, we can just send this message to ourselves, using self, like this:

```
[self presentModalViewController:addViewController animated:YES];
```

self is the Objective-C keyword for the object that is currently executing the method. It's similar to "this" in Java or C++.

This is the View Controller you want displayed as a modal view, in our case, the new AddDrinkViewController.

If you say NO to animated, then the view just appears. By saying YES, we get the smooth slide in from the bottom.

Sharpen your pencil

Update the RootViewController.m file to display our AddDrinkViewController when the + button is tapped.

☐ Import the AddDrinkViewController.h so the RootViewController knows what class you're talking about.

☐ Change the addButtonPressed:sender: method to create an AddDrinkViewController, and present it as a modal view. Be careful about your memory management—don't leak references to the controllers.

Sharpen your pencil
Solution

Update the RootViewController.m file to display our AddDrinkViewController in a UINavigationController when the + button is tapped.

```
#import "RootViewController.h"
#import "DrinkConstants.h"
#import "DrinkDetailViewController.h"
#import "AddDrinkViewController.h"
```

Not much to say here—just import the file.

RootViewController.m

```
#pragma mark -
#pragma mark Actions
- (IBAction) addButtonPressed: (id) sender {
    NSLog(@"Add button pressed!");

    AddDrinkViewController *addViewController = [[AddDrinkViewController
alloc] initWithNibName:@"DrinkDetailViewController" bundle:nil];
    [self presentModalViewController:addViewController animated:YES];
    [addViewController release];
}
```

Allocate the AddDrinkViewController just like the DetailedDrinkViewController—remember, it's a subclass. It uses the same nib, too.

Now we just need to show the modal view—since RootViewController is a ViewController, we just call presentModalViewController and iOS handles the rest.

The RootViewController will retain a reference to the new View Controller when we present it. Don't forget to release the reference to the View Controller!

RootViewController.m

TEST DRIVE

Now that the add view is fully implemented, build and run the project. Make sure you try out all the functionality: scrolling, drilling down to details, and finally adding a drink. You'll see there's still a little work left to be done...

Try clicking around, between fields.

Touch in the title to bring up the keyboard and make sure it works.

Watch it!

If your keyboard isn't working, your fields might still not be editable.

Back in Chapter 4, we had you make the fields uneditable in the utilities panel. If your keyboard isn't appearing, try going back into Interface Builder and checking that the fields are now editable.

But what about after you finish typing?

That's great, but after I type in the drink, nothing happens! I can't get the view to go away, and I can't add the drink.

That's a problem.

Actually, it's two problems that are related. Earlier, we decided that the add drink detail view needs to go away one of two ways: either the user cancels out or saves the drink. We need to get those buttons in there.

APP LAYOUT CONSTRUCTION

How should we lay out the Save and Cancel buttons? Is there anything unique about this view that we have to deal with?

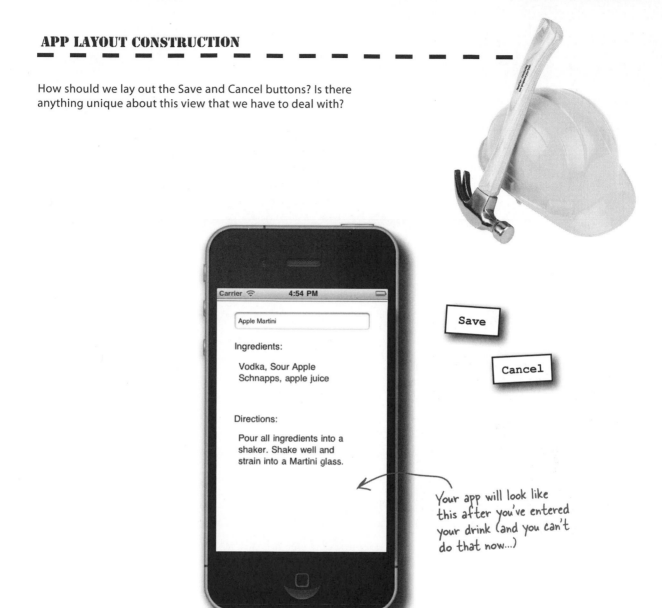

Your app will look like this after you've entered your drink (and you can't do that now...)

Our modal view doesn't have a navigation bar

To be consistent with the rest of DrinkMixer, we really should put the save and cancel buttons at the top of the view in a navigation bar. The problem is, we don't have one in our modal version of the detail view.

A modal view covers the navigation control.

Drink detail view

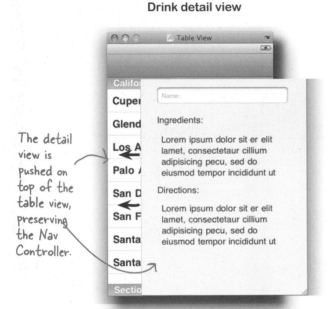

The detail view is pushed on top of the table view, preserving the Nav Controller.

Add drink detail view

We could add one by hand, but remember we're sharing the detail drink view nib, which gets its navigation bar from the navigation controller. Since we're showing the add drink view as a modal view, we cover up the navigation bar.

Instead of trying to solve this from within the detail drink view nib, we can embed our add drink view in a Navigation Controller of its own, like this:

Instead of presenting our addViewController, we can present an addNavController View Controller.

This will add a Nav Controller to wrap the add drink view.

```
UINavigationController *addNavController = [[UINavigationController
alloc] initWithRootViewController:addViewController];
```

Do this!

Allocate the UINavigationController and pass in our addViewController as its root view controller. It will retain the controller, since it needs to display it.

```objc
- (IBAction) addButtonPressed: (id) sender {
    NSLog(@"Add button pressed!");

    AddDrinkViewController *addViewController = [[AddDrinkViewController
alloc] initWithNibName: @"DrinkDetailViewController" bundle:nil];

    UINavigationController *addNavController = [[UINavigationController
alloc] initWithRootViewController:addViewController];

    [self presentModalViewController:addNavController animated:YES];

    [addViewController release];

    [addNavController release];
}
```

Now we just need to show the modal view—since RootViewController is a ViewController, we just call presentModalViewController, and iOS handles the rest.

Don't forget to release references to the AddDrinkViewController and the NavigationController.

RootViewController.m

There's our nav controller.

Now we just need to create those buttons...

Create the Save and Cancel buttons

Since both the Save and Cancel buttons need to dismiss the modal view, let's start by wiring them up to do that. We'll need some actions, and the buttons themselves. We've covered how to do that in Interface Builder—and you can do that now if you want, but this time, let's write them in code so see how that approach works.

```objc
- (IBAction) save: (id) sender;

- (IBAction) cancel: (id) sender;
```

These go just before the @end.

AddDrinkViewController.h

Since we're using the navigation bar, we get built-in support for left and right-hand buttons. We just need to create those buttons and assign them to our leftBarButtonItem and rightBarButtonItem to place them where we want them.

Add a viewDidLoad to the AddDrinkViewController.m file.

Just like when we made an add button, we're going to use the Navigation Controller's left and right buttons for Save and Cancel.

Here are our two buttons in code.

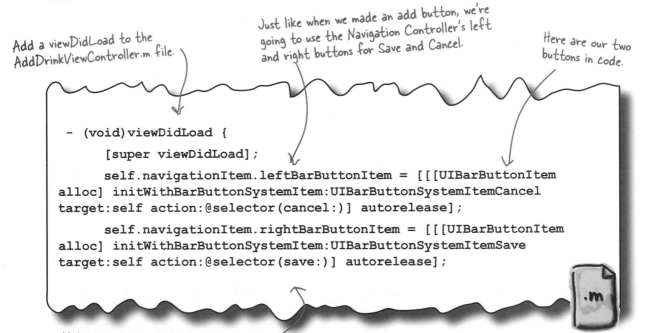

```objc
- (void)viewDidLoad {
    [super viewDidLoad];

    self.navigationItem.leftBarButtonItem = [[[UIBarButtonItem
alloc] initWithBarButtonSystemItem:UIBarButtonSystemItemCancel
target:self action:@selector(cancel:)] autorelease];

    self.navigationItem.rightBarButtonItem = [[[UIBarButtonItem
alloc] initWithBarButtonSystemItem:UIBarButtonSystemItemSave
target:self action:@selector(save:)] autorelease];
```

AddDrinkViewController.m

Notice our "autorelease" here—normally, we alloc a class, assign it to where it needs to go, then release our reference to it. By autoreleasing when we create it, we ask Objective-C to handle releasing it for us later. Not quite as efficient as explicitly handling it ourselves, but a little cleaner looking in the code.

Write the Save and Cancel actions

When the user clicks either Save or Cancel, we need to exit the modal view by asking the View Controller that presented the view to dismiss it. However, to make things easier, we can send the modal view the dismiss message, and it will automatically forward the message to its parent View Controller. Since the AddDrinkViewController is the modal view and gets the button call back, we can just send ourselves the dismiss message and the controller stack will handle it correctly. We need to send ourselves the dismissModalViewControllerAnimated: message, like this:

```
[self dismissModalViewControllerAnimated:YES];
```

Implement the Save and Cancel methods to log which one was called, then clear the modal view. We'll tackle actually saving a new drink once this works.

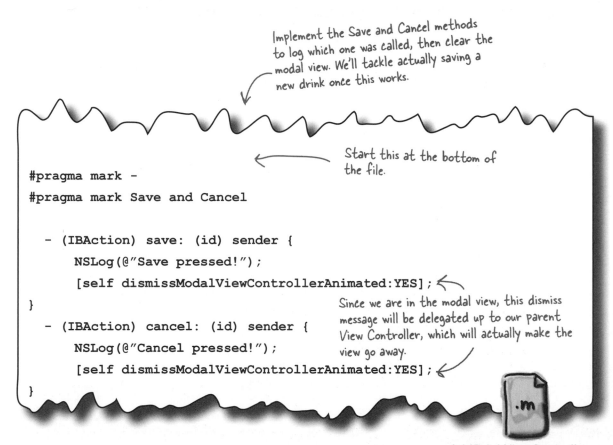

Start this at the bottom of the file.

```
#pragma mark -
#pragma mark Save and Cancel

- (IBAction) save: (id) sender {
    NSLog(@"Save pressed!");
    [self dismissModalViewControllerAnimated:YES];
}
- (IBAction) cancel: (id) sender {
    NSLog(@"Cancel pressed!");
    [self dismissModalViewControllerAnimated:YES];
}
```

Since we are in the modal view, this dismiss message will be delegated up to our parent View Controller, which will actually make the view go away.

AddDrinkViewController.m

Now, to see if those buttons work...

Test Drive

The modal view can be dismissed now, and the keyboard works, too!

Just like that, the buttons are in the detail view.

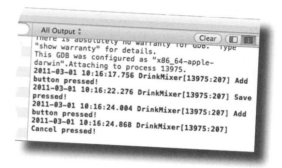

```
                              no warranty for GDB.  Type
"show warranty" for details.
This GDB was configured as "x86_64-apple-
darwin".Attaching to process 13975.
2011-03-01 10:16:17.756 DrinkMixer[13975:207] Add
button pressed!
2011-03-01 10:16:22.276 DrinkMixer[13975:207] Save
pressed!
2011-03-01 10:16:24.004 DrinkMixer[13975:207] Add
button pressed!
2011-03-01 10:16:24.868 DrinkMixer[13975:207]
Cancel pressed!
```

Congratulations, the modal view is working!

You did a lot of view manipulation in this chapter and have a solid foundation of an application to show for it. You can transition to and from detail views and jump into modal views when you need the user to complete a specific task. Next, we just need to tackle saving the new drink.

there are no
Dumb Questions

Q: Why don't we need an outlet for the Save/Cancel button? And what about Interface Builder?

A: We don't need to do anything with the Save and Cancel buttons after we've created them (like disabling one, or swapping one out for something else briefly), so we create them and immediately hand them off to our navigationItem to put in the upper left and upper right. If we needed to do anything with them later, we'd probably want to hang onto a reference, and we could use an instance variable for that.

As for Interface Builder, we created the buttons in code this time. Depending on what you're trying to do with a control, sometimes it's easier to just create them (or set sizes or configure controls, etc.) in code. For many developers, it's just personal preference. In our case, we only needed to create simple buttons, so we did that in code. We didn't need any IBActions because when creating the buttons programmatically, you can pass in a selector (using the @selector(...) syntax) that should be called. That's how we hooked the buttons up to our Save and Cancel methods.

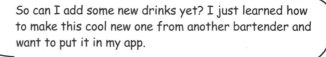

So can I add some new drinks yet? I just learned how to make this cool new one from another bartender and want to put it in my app.

To be continued...

iOSDev cross

Using all the stuff you've learned about how to work with different plists and views, fill in the puzzle.

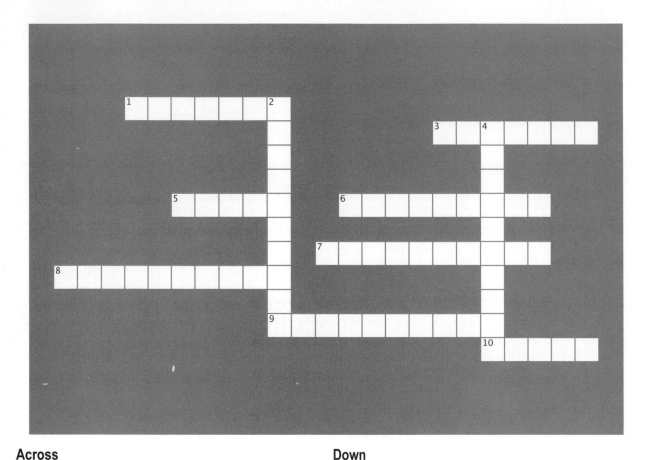

Across

1. User _____ on itunes stick with the app even after a new version is released.
3. The navigation controller has support for _____ buttons to fix stuff.
5. A _____ view has to be dealt with by the user before doing anything else.
6. Use these to organize names of things.
7. You can create _____ bars in IB or in code.
8. A nib file has UI _____.
9. The HIG requires some kind of _____ element in a cell if there is more information availible.

Down

2. Views can be _____ and extended like any other class.
4. An _____ specifies what a button should look like.

Your iOS Toolbox

You've got Chapter 5 under your belt and now you've added plists and modal views to your toolbox. For a complete list of tooltips in the book, go to *http://www .headfirstlabs.com/books/hfiphonedev.*

Debugging

If you know where your problem is likely to be, set the breakpoint there.

You can use the debugger to step through the problem area.

If your application does crash, pay close attention to the call stack. Your code frames are in black; framework code (code without source) is in grey.

AppStore Basics

1. Submitting your app to the store means it HAS TO CONFORM TO THE HIG.

2. Approvals can take time, so try and get it right with the first submission.

3. Once your app is up for sale, the reviews stay with it, even with updates.

Dictionaries

Are useful ways to expand the contents of a plist

Store key-value pairs of data

Typically use NSStrings for keys but don't require it.

Views

Are typically used in a view stack with a Navigation Controller or presented modally.

Can be subclassed and extended like any other class.

Modal views help communicate to a user that they have to complete a distinct task or abandon it entirely.

 # iOSDev cross Solution

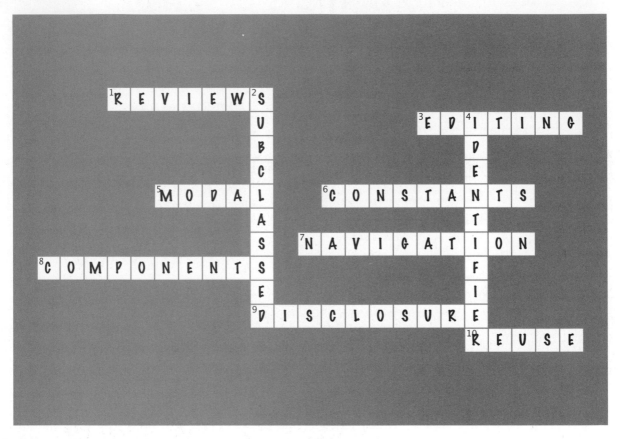

Across

1. User _____ on itunes stick with the app even after a new version is released. [REVIEWS]
3. The navigation controller has support for _____ buttons to fix stuff. [EDITING]
5. A _____ view has to be dealt with by the user before doing anything else. [MODAL]
6. Use these to organize names of things. [CONSTANTS]
7. You can create _____ bars in IB or in code. [NAVIGATION]
8. A nib file has UI _____. [COMPONENTS]

Down

2. Views can be _____ and extended like any other class. [SUBCLASSED]
4. An _____ specifies what a button should look like. [IDENTIFIER]

6 saving, editing, and sorting data

Everyone's an editor...

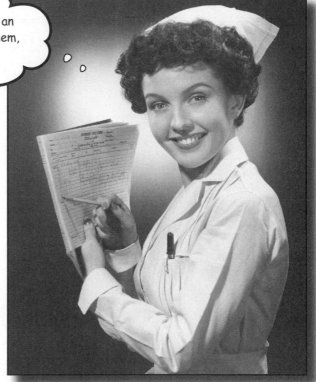

> If these records were on an iPhone and I could edit them, life would be grand!

Displaying data is nice, but adding and editing information is what makes an app really hum.

DrinkMixer is great—it uses some cell customization, and works with plist dictionaries to display data. It's a handy reference application, and you've got a good start on adding new drinks. Now it's time to give the user the ability to modify the data—saving, editing, and sorting—to make it more useful for everyone. In this chapter, we'll take a look at editing patterns in iOS apps and how to guide users with the Nav Controller.

Sam is ready to add a Red-Headed School Girl...

A new drink at the Lounge

Sam went to try DrinkMixer with the new add view and ran into problems right away.

Sam was clicking around, ready to add his new drink.

The directions field is hidden under the keyboard.

You can't see the directions at all, and part of the ingredients information is covered up.

We have a problem with our view, since we can't get to some of the fields.

Sam, the bartender

...but the keyboard is in the way

We're back to the keyboard problem we saw earlier with InstaEmail. When Sam taps on a control, it gets focus (becomes the **first responder**) and asks iOS to show the keyboard. Generally, that's a good thing. However...

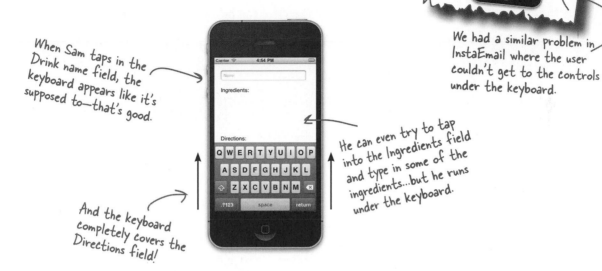

We had a similar problem in InstaEmail where the user couldn't get to the controls under the keyboard.

When Sam taps in the Drink name field, the keyboard appears like it's supposed to—that's good.

He can even try to tap into the Ingredients field and type in some of the ingredients...but he runs under the keyboard.

And the keyboard completely covers the Directions field!

BRAIN BARBELL

How did we deal with the keyboard last time? Will that work this time? What do you want the view to **do** when the keyboard appears?

....

....

....

....

BRAIN BARBELL

How did we deal with the keyboard last time? Will that work this time?
What do you want the view to *do* when the keyboard appears?

Resigning first responder worked last time. In DrinkMixer, it would be fine for the name field, but what about the directions and the ingredients fields? As soon as the keyboard comes up, they're covered. The user has a smaller screen to work with once the keyboard shows up—we need to set up the view to scroll things in when the user needs them. We can do this with a UIScrollView.

UIScrollView Up Close

UIScrollView is just like the basic UIView we've been using except that it can handle having items (like buttons, text fields, etc.) be off the screen and then scrolling them into view. The scroll view draws and manages a scroll bar, panning and zooming, and controlling which part of the content view is displayed. It does all of this by knowing how big the area it needs to show is (called the contentSize) and how much space it has to show it in (the frame). UIScrollView can figure out everything else from there.

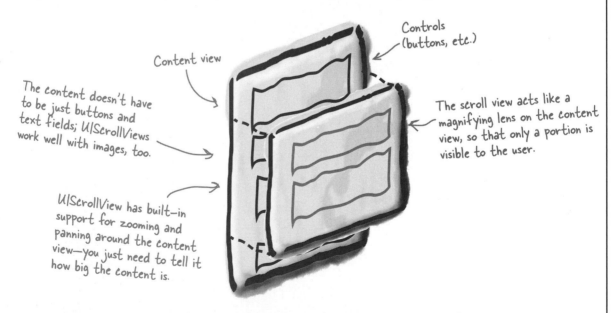

Content view

Controls (buttons, etc.)

The content doesn't have to be just buttons and text fields; UIScrollViews work well with images, too.

The scroll view acts like a magnifying lens on the content view, so that only a portion is visible to the user.

UIScrollView has built-in support for zooming and panning around the content view—you just need to tell it how big the content is.

Remember, in CocoaTouch, components are subclasses of UIView. All a scroll view needs to care about are the subviews it has to manage. It doesn't matter if it's one huge UIImageView that shows a big image you can pan around, or if it's lots of text fields, buttons, and labels.

To get a scrollable view, we need to move our components into a UIScrollView instead of a UIView. Time to get back into Interface Builder...

Wrap your content in a scroll view

We want the user to be able to scroll through our controls when the keyboard covers some of them up. In order to do that, we need to add a UIScrollView to our view and then tell it about the controls (the content view) we want it to handle.

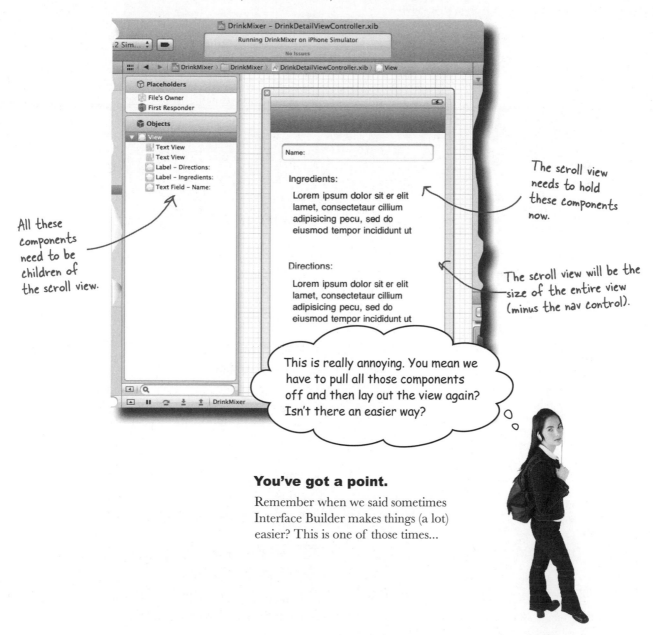

All these components need to be children of the scroll view.

The scroll view needs to hold these components now.

The scroll view will be the size of the entire view (minus the nav control).

This is really annoying. You mean we have to pull all those components off and then lay out the view again? Isn't there an easier way?

You've got a point.

Remember when we said sometimes Interface Builder makes things (a lot) easier? This is one of those times...

EASY GUI RECONSTRUCTION

Apparently we aren't the first people to realize after
we've built a view that it needs to be scrollable.
Interface Builder has built-in support for taking an
existing view and wrapping it in a UIScrollView.

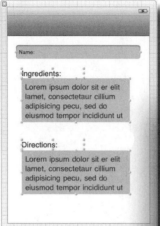

Highlight all the widgets (as shown
here) in the detail view, then go to the
Editor→**Embed**→**Scroll View** menu option.
Interface Builder will automatically create a new
scrolled view and stick all the widgets in the same
location on the scrolled view.

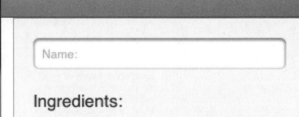

Interface Builder
will create a
UIScrollView just
big enough to hold
all our components.
Since we want
the whole view
to scroll, grab the
corners of the new
UIScrollView and
drag them out to
the corners of the
screen, right up
to the edge of the
navigation bar (we
don't want that to
scroll).

Now you have the
same listing of
widgets as before,
but they are
under a scroll view.

How will this new scroll view know how much
content needs to be scrolled?

The scroll view is the same size as the screen

Interface Builder created the UIScrollView, but there are a few finishing touches necessary to make this work the way we want. You need to tell the UIScrollView how big its content area is so it knows what it will need to scroll—you do that by setting its contentSize property. Then you'll need to add an outlet and property for the UIScrollView, then wire it up in Interface Builder so we can get to it.

So how do we figure out how big the contentSize should be? When the UIScrollView is the same size as our screen, we don't have anything outside of the visible area that it needs to worry about. Since the scroll view is the same size as our UIView that it's sitting in, we can grab the size from there, like this:

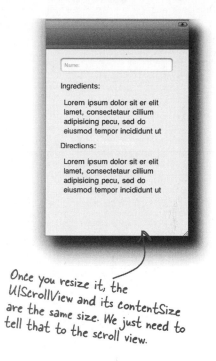

```
scrollView.contentSize = self.view.frame.size;
```

Once you've added that line, you'll have a scroll view that takes up all of the available space, and it thinks its content view is the same size.

Once you resize it, the UIScrollView and its contentSize are the same size. We just need to tell that to the scroll view.

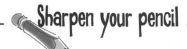

Sharpen your pencil

Update DrinkDetailViewController.h and DrinkDetailViewController.m to handle our new UIScrollView.

1 Add an attribute named scrollView to DrinkDetailViewController to hold a reference to the UIScrollView. You'll need the field declaration and IBOutlet property, then you will synthesize it in the .m and release it in dealloc.

2 Wire up the new property to the UIScrollView in Interface Builder by adding a new Referencing Outlet to the UIScrollView connected to your scrollView property.

3 Set the initial contentSize for the scrollView in viewDidLoad:. Remember, we're telling the scrollView that its content is the same size as the view it's sitting in.

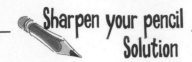

Sharpen your pencil
Solution

Update your DrinkDetailViewController.h and
DrinkDetailViewController.m to handle our new UIScrollView.

1 Add an attribute named scrollView to DrinkDetailViewController to hold a reference
to the UIScrollView. You'll need the field declaration, an IBOutlet property, to
synthesize it in the .m and release it in dealloc.

```
@interface DrinkDetailViewController : UIViewController {
@private
    UITextField *nameTextField_;
    UITextView *ingredientsTextView_;
    UITextView *directionsTextView_;
    NSDictionary *drink_;
    UIScrollView *scrollView_;
}
@property (nonatomic, retain) IBOutlet UIScrollView *scrollView;
```

Add a field and a property for
the new scrollView.

DrinkDetailViewController.h

Synthesize the property,
then set the contentSize
in viewDidLoad.

```
@synthesize scrollView=scrollView_;
```

```
-   (void)viewDidLoad {
    [super viewDidLoad];
    self.scrollView.contentSize = self.
view.frame.size;
}
```

Set the initial
contentSize.

Clean up our
reference in dealloc.

```
- (void)dealloc {
    [scrollView_ release];
    [nameTextField_ release];
    [ingredientsTextView_
 release];
...
```

DrinkDetailViewController.m

2 Wire up the new property to the UIScrollView in Interface Builder.

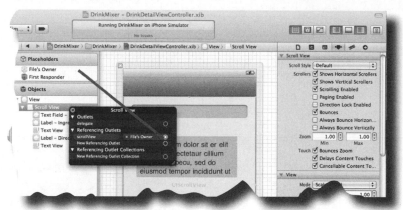

TEST DRIVE

Tap in the text field and the keyboard appears...but nothing's scrolling!

BRAIN POWER

Why isn't it working yet? Think about all the things that you have going into this view—the scroll view, the main view, and the keyboard...

The keyboard changes the visible area

The problem is that the keyboard changes the visible area but the scroll view has no idea that just happened. The scroll view still thinks it has the whole screen to display its content, and from its perspective, that's plenty of room. We need to tell the scroll view that the visible area is smaller now that the keyboard is there.

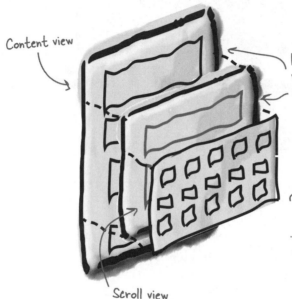

Content view

In DrinkMixer, the content view is the same size as our scroll view's initial size, which is the whole screen...

Scroll view

...but then the keyboard appears over the scroll view and covers up a large part of the visible area. We need to tell the scroll view it has less space to work with.

iOS tells you about the keyboard, but doesn't tinker with your views.

Just because iOS knows that the keyboard is there, it doesn't know how your app wants to handle it. That's up to you!

iOS notifies you about the keyboard

Interacting with the keyboard and the scroll view brings us to a part of the iOS we haven't talked about yet called **Notifications**. Just like component events being passed around our application, there are system-level events, called Notifications, that are being passed by iOS. The secret to knowing what's going on with the keyboard is knowing about these events.

 Sam taps in the Drink name field and the field becomes the first responder. Now the iOS needs to show the keyboard.

 The iOS posts a notification to the default NSNotificationCenter named UIKeyboardDidShowNotification.

Event	Object	Selector
UIKeyboardDidShowNotification	DetailDrinkViewController	keyboardDidShow

NSNotificationCenter

 The NSNotificationCenter invokes the target selector and passes it information about the object that triggered the event, along with event-specific details.

```
[registeredObject
keyboardDidShow:eventInfo];
```

3 NSNotificationCenter looks up the event to see if anyone is registered to be told when that event happens. Objects are registered by providing a selector (method) to call if the event is triggered.

Register with the default notification center for events

iOS supports more than one NSNotificationCenter, but unless you have specific needs for your own, you can just use the default system-level one. You can get a reference to the default one by calling this:

```
[NSNotificationCenter defaultCenter];
```

With the notification center, you can register for events by passing the object you want the notification center to call back to (usually yourself), the method to call, an event you are interested in (or nil for any event), and, optionally, the sender you want to listen to (or nil for all senders).

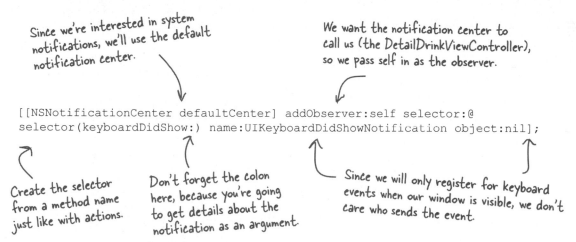

Since we're interested in system notifications, we'll use the default notification center.

We want the notification center to call us (the DetailDrinkViewController), so we pass self in as the observer.

```
[[NSNotificationCenter defaultCenter] addObserver:self selector:@
selector(keyboardDidShow:) name:UIKeyboardDidShowNotification object:nil];
```

Create the selector from a method name just like with actions.

Don't forget the colon here, because you're going to get details about the notification as an argument.

Since we will only register for keyboard events when our window is visible, we don't care who sends the event.

Then unregister when you're done

Just like memory management, we need to clean up our registrations from the notification center when we don't need them any longer. We'll register for events in viewWillAppear: and unregister in viewWillDisappear:. Unregistering for an event is easy—just ask the notification center to removeObserver for the object you registered.

```
[[NSNotificationCenter defaultCenter] removeObserver:self];
```

Make sure you unregister from the same notification center you registered with.

We simply ask the notification center to remove us from everything we've registered for. If you only want to stop receiving certain notifications, you can specify the notification as well.

The notification center exposed

**This week's interview:
Why do you talk so much?**

Head First: Um, this is embarrassing, but I'm not entirely sure I have the right Notification Center here...

Notification Center: Well, unless you need something weird, it's probably me. I'm the guy everybody goes to by default. Heads up! An app's shuttin' down. Be with you in a second.

Head First: Wow—so you know about every app that starts and stops?

Notification Center: Yup. I'm the default center; all the system events go through me. Now, not everybody is interested in what's going on, but if they want to know, I'm the guy to see.

Head First: So when someone wants to know what's going on, they tell you what they're interested in, right?

Notification Center: Exactly. If somebody wants to know about somethin' in the system, they register with me. They tell me the notification they want me to watch for, who I should tell when it happens, and, if they're really picky, who should have sent it.

Head First: So then you tell them when that notification happens?

Notification Center: Right—they tell me what message to send them when I see the notification they were interested in. I package up the notification information into a nice object for them and then call their method. Doesn't take me long at all; the sender almost always waits for me to finish telling everyone what happened before it does anything else.

Interviewer: Almost always?

Notification Center: Well, the sender could use a notification queue to have me send out the notifications later, when the sender isn't busy, but that's not typically how it's done.

Head First: Hmm, this sounds a lot like message passing. The sender wants to tell somebody that something happened, you call a method on that somebody...what's different?

Notification Center: It's similar to message passing, but there are some differences. First, the senders don't need to know who to tell. They just tell me that something happened and I'll figure out if anyone cares. Second, there might be lots of people interested in what's going on. In normal message passing, the senders would have to tell each one individually. With notifications, they just tell me once and I'll make sure everyone knows. Third, unlike the delegate pattern—where the message gets sent to only one object—I can send messages to any number of objects. Finally, the receiver of the notification doesn't need to care who's sending the message. If some object wants to know that the application is shutting down, it doesn't care who's responsible for saying the app's quitting, the object just trusts me to make sure they'll know when it happens.

Head First: So can anyone send notifications?

Notification Center: Sure. Anybody can ask me to post a notification and if anyone's registered to get it, I'll let them know.

Head First: How do they know which notifications to send?

Notification Center: Ah, well that's up to the sender. Different frameworks have their own messages they pass around; you'll have to check with the framework to see what they'll send out. If you're going to be posting your own notifications, you almost certainly don't want to go blasting out someone else's notifications; you should come up with your own. They're just strings—and a dictionary if you want to include some extra info—nothing fancy.

Head First: I see. Well, this has been great, Notification Center. Thanks for stopping by!

So registering for the keyboard event sounds pretty easy, but there's more to do after that, right?

Exactly.

We need to tell the scroll view what to do once the keyboard does pop up (and when it goes away).

Sharpen your pencil

Fill in the blanks and get a plan for the next step!

We need to .... for the ....

and .... events in ....

We'll add two .... that will be called by the ....

when the notifications are posted.

We'll adjust the size of the .... when the keyboard appears and disappears.

We need to .... for events in ....

Bonus Question: What file will you put all these changes in?

Sharpen your pencil
Solution

Now you have a plan for what to do next.

We need to ....**register**.......... for the ...**UIKeyboardDidShowNotification**...

and ...**UIKeyboardDidHideNotification**... events in ....**viewWillAppear**.........:

We'll add two ...**methods**... that will be called by the ...**notification center**...

when the notifications are posted.

We'll adjust the size of the .....**scroll view**..... when the keyboard appears and disappears.

We need to ....**unregister**......... for events in ....**viewWillDisappear**........:

This code needs to go into AddDrinkViewController, since that's the only view where we're going to be using the keyboard.

there are no
Dumb Questions

Q: **I can't find the list of notifications that are sent by the iOS. Where are they listed?**

A: There isn't a central list of all the notifications that could be sent. Different classes and frameworks have different notifications they use. For example, the UIDevice class offers a set of notifications to tell you about when the battery is being charged or what's happening with the proximity sensor. Apple's documentation is usually pretty clear about what notifications are available and what they mean. The keyboard notifications are described in the UIWindow class documentation.

Q: **Why would I want to create my own notifications?**

A: It depends on your application. Remember, notifications let you decouple the sender from the receiver. You could use this in your application to let multiple distinct views know that something happened in your application.

For example, let's say you had a view that let you add or remove items from your application and your app has several different ways to view those things. Notifications could give you a nice way to announce to all the other views that something has changed without your add/remove view needing to have a reference to each of them.

Exercise

Go ahead and make the changes to your code to register for the keyboard events. We'll implement the code to handle the scroll view shortly.

1 **Add keyboardDidShow and keyboardDidHide methods to the AddDrinkViewController.**
For now, just have them print out an NSLog when they are called. We'll add the meat in a second. Both methods should take an NSNotification*, as they'll be called by the notification center and will be given notification information.

2 **Register for the UIKeyboardDidShowNotification and UIKeyboardDidHideNotification in viewWillAppear(...).**
You should use the default NSNotificationCenter and register to receive both events regardless of who sends them out.

3 **Unregister for all events in viewWillDisappear(...).**
Create this method and use it to add the code to unregister for events.

4 **Add a BOOL to AddDrinkViewController that keeps track of whether the keyboard is visible or not.**
We'll talk more about this in a minute, but you're going to need a flag to keep track of whether the keyboard is already visible. Set it to NO in your viewWillAppear(...) for now.

Exercise
Solution

Go ahead and make the changes to your code to register
for the keyboard events. We'll implement the code to handle
the scroll view shortly.

These are both new methods for the
keyboard notifications in the implementation
file. We'll get to those in a minute.

```objc
- (void)viewWillAppear: (BOOL)animated {
    [super viewWillAppear:animated];

    NSLog(@"Registering for keyboard events");
    [[NSNotificationCenter defaultCenter] addObserver:self selector:@
selector(keyboardDidShow:)
        name:UIKeyboardDidShowNotification object:nil];
    [[NSNotificationCenter defaultCenter] addObserver:self selector:@
selector(keyboardDidHide:)
        name:UIKeyboardDidHideNotification object:nil];
    // Initially the keyboard is hidden, so reset our variable
    keyboardVisible_ = NO;
}
```

We need to keep track of whether the keyboard is
showing or not. More on this in a minute.

If you don't give it a notification to
unregister from, it will remove you
from anything you've registered for.

```objc
- (void)viewWillDisappear:(BOOL)animated {
    NSLog(@"Unregistering for keyboard events");
    [[NSNotificationCenter defaultCenter] removeObserver:self];
}
#pragma mark -
#pragma mark Keyboard handlers

- (void)keyboardDidShow:(NSNotification *)notif {
    NSLog(@"Received UIKeyboardDidShowNotification.");
}

- (void)keyboardDidHide:(NSNotification *)notif {
    NSLog(@"Received UIKeyboardDidHideNotification.");
}
```

.m

AddDrinkViewController.m

```objc
@interface AddDrinkViewController : DrinkDetailViewController {
    BOOL keyboardVisible_;
}
- (void)keyboardDidShow: (NSNotification *) notif;
- (void)keyboardDidHide: (NSNotification *) notif;
```

.h

AddDrinkViewController.h

Keyboard events tell you the keyboard state and size

The whole point of knowing when the keyboard appears or disappears is to tell the scroll view that the visible area has changed size. But, how do we know the new size? Thankfully, the keyboard notification events (UIKeyboardDidShowNotification and UIKeyboardDidHideNotification) include all the information we need.

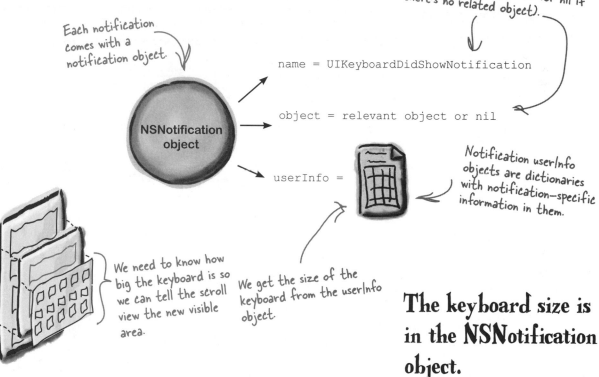

Each notification comes with a notification object.

The notification object contains the name of the notification and the object it pertains to (or nil if there's no related object).

NSNotification object

name = UIKeyboardDidShowNotification

object = relevant object or nil

userInfo =

Notification userInfo objects are dictionaries with notification-specific information in them.

We need to know how big the keyboard is so we can tell the scroll view the new visible area.

We get the size of the keyboard from the userInfo object.

The keyboard size is in the NSNotification object.

Watch it!

Getting the notification is easy, but we get told every time the keyboard is shown, even if it's already there.

That's why we need the BOOL to keep track of whether or not the keyboard is currently displayed. If the keyboard isn't visible when we get the notification, then we need to tell our scroll view its visible size is smaller. If the keyboard is hidden, we set the scroll view back to full size.

Keyboard Code Magnets Part I

Below are the code magnets you'll need to implement the
keyboardDidShow method. Use the comments in the code
on the right to help you figure out what goes where.

```objc
NSDictionary *info = [notif userInfo];
```

```objc
CGRect viewFrame = self.view.bounds;
viewFrame.size.height = keyboardTop - self.view.bounds.origin.y;
```

```objc
NSValue *aValue = [info objectForKey:UIKeyboardFrameEndUserInfoKey];
```

```objc
self.scrollView.frame = viewFrame;

keyboardVisible_ = YES;
```

```objc
if (keyboardVisible_) {
  NSLog(@"%@",@"Keyboard is already visible.  Ignoring
notification.");
  return;
}
```

```objc
CGRect keyboardRect = [aValue CGRectValue];
keyboardRect = [self.view convertRect:keyboardRect fromView:nil];
CGFloat keyboardTop = keyboardRect.origin.y;
```

```objc
NSLog(@"Resizing smaller for keyboard");
```

```
-  (void)keyboardDidShow:(NSNotification *)notif {



        // The keyboard wasn't visible before


        // Get the origin of the keyboard when it finishes animating.




        // Get the top of the keyboard in view's coordinate system.
        // We need to set the bottom of the scroll view to line up with it




        //Resize the scroll view to make room for the keyboard




}
```

AddDrinkViewController.m

Keyboard Code Magnets Part II

Below are the code magnets you'll need to implement the keyboardDidHide method. Use the comments in the code on the right to help you figure out what goes where.

```
self.scrollView.frame = self.view.bounds;
        keyboardVisible_ = NO;
```

```
if (!keyboardVisible_) {
        NSLog(@"%@",@"Keyboard already hidden.   Ignoring
notification.");

return;

}
```

```
NSLog(@"%@",@"Resizing bigger with no keyboard");
```

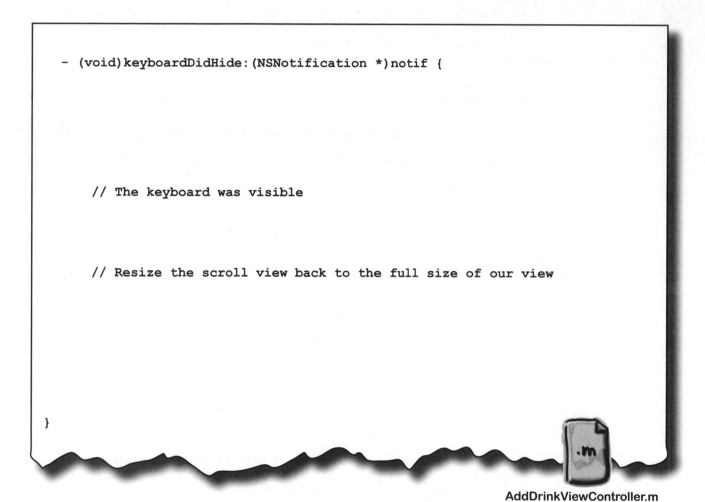

```objc
- (void)keyboardDidHide:(NSNotification *)notif {



    // The keyboard was visible



    // Resize the scroll view back to the full size of our view



}
```

AddDrinkViewController.m

Keyboard Code Magnets Part I Solution

Below are the code magnets to SHOW the keyboard.

```objc
- (void)keyboardDidShow:(NSNotification *)notif {

    if (keyboardVisible_) {
        NSLog(@"%@",@"Keyboard is already visible.  Ignoring
    notification.");
        return;
    }
```
We will get this notification whenever the user switches text fields, even if the keyboard is already showing. So we keep track of it and bail if it's a repeat.

```objc
    // The keyboard wasn't visible before

    NSLog(@"Resizing smaller for keyboard");

    // Get the origin of the keyboard when it finishes animating.
    NSDictionary *info = [notif userInfo];
```
NSNotification contains a dictionary with the event details; we pull that out here.

We get the keyboard size from the dictionary...

```objc
    NSValue *aValue = [info objectForKey:UIKeyboardFrameEndUserInfoKey];

    // Get the top of the keyboard in view's coordinate system.
    // We need to set the bottom of the scroll view to line up with it

    CGRect keyboardRect = [aValue CGRectValue];
    keyboardRect = [self.view convertRect:keyboardRect fromView:nil];
    CGFloat keyboardTop = keyboardRect.origin.y;

    //Resize the scroll view to make room for the keyboard

    CGRect viewFrame = self.view.bounds;
    viewFrame.size.height = keyboardTop - self.view.bounds.origin.y;
```
...then figure out how big the scroll view really is now (basically how big our view is, minus the size of the keyboard).

```objc
    self.scrollView.frame = viewFrame;

    keyboardVisible_ = YES;
```
Finally, update the scroll view with the new size and mark that the keyboard is visible.

```objc
}
```

AddDrinkViewController.m

Keyboard Code Magnets Part II Solution

Below are the code magnets to HIDE the keyboard. Handling the UIKeyboardDidHideNotification works almost exactly the same way, except this time the scroll view needs to be expanded by the size of the (now missing) keyboard.

```objc
- (void)keyboardDidHide:(NSNotification *)notif {

    if (!keyboardVisible_) {
        NSLog(@"%@",@"Keyboard already hidden.  Ignoring
notification.");
    return;

    }

// The keyboard was visible

    NSLog(@"%@",@"Resizing bigger with no keyboard");


// Resize the scroll view back to the full size of our view


    self.scrollView.frame = self.view.bounds;
        keyboardVisible_ = NO;

}
```

Ignore this notification if we know the keyboard isn't visible.

Then resize the scroll view to the new visible area.

AddDrinkViewController.m

Test Drive

Go ahead and build and run. Once you get into the detail view, you should be able to scroll the view to all the fields, and the messages in the console help you keep track of what's going on.

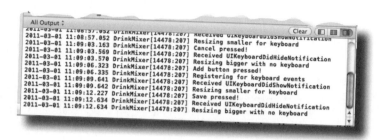

there are no
Dumb Questions

Q: Manipulating that scroll view size is kind of tricky—how would I have figured that out without magnets?

A: A great reference for the code samples and information for programming apps in general is the *Text, Web and Editing Programming Guide for iOS* that is available on the Apple developer website. That has sample code for common problems like managing the keyboard and text views.

Q: Tell me again why we need to keep track of whether the keyboard is already visible? Isn't iOS doing that?

A: The iOS knows the state of the keyboard, but it sends keyboard events out when different controls get focus. So, when the user taps in the first field, you'll get a UIKeyboardWillShowNotification followed

by a UIKeyboardDidShowNotification. When the user taps into another field, you'll get another UIKeyboardDidShowNotification so you know the keyboard focus has changed, but you won't get the keyboard hide event, since it never actually went away. You need to keep track of whether you already knew it was visible so you don't resize the scroll view to the wrong size.

Q: The scroll view works, but depending on what the users pick, they still have to scroll to the widget?

A: Yes—and that's not ideal. You can ask the scroll view to scroll to a particular spot on the content view if you keep track of which control has the focus. The *Text, Web and Editing Programming Guide for iOS* has good sample code for that.

Q: Don't we know the dimensions of the keyboard that pops up? Why do we

have to figure out the boundaries with all that code? Isn't it always the same?

A: It's not always the same! If your application is landscape, your keyboard is wider than it is tall. If your app is portrait, then it's taller than it is wide. And the iPad is a completely different size. Apple also makes it clear that they may change the size of the keyboard if necessary and you should never assume you know how big it is. Always get size information directly from the keyboard notifications.

Q: What are the animation and curve properties in the notification about?

A: The Keyboard notification includes information on how quickly the keyboard is animating in. You can use this information to animate the size change of your content so the keyboard comes in as your content view shrinks.

Everything scrolls OK, and I can put a drink in, but as soon as I get back to the list, the drink I added isn't there!

Sam's drink is missing.

As soon as he leaves the drink detail view, the new drink no longer shows up in the main list. We need to figure out how to keep it around longer...

Sharpen your pencil

Work through the following questions to think about what this means for our app.

What happens to new drinks when the user hits Save? ....
....

Where do we need to add code? ....
....

How are we going to save the new drink? ....
....

Sharpen your pencil
Solution

Work through the following questions to think about what this means for our app.

What happens to new drinks when the user hits save? We dismiss the view and the drink information is lost.

Where do we need to add code? We need to add some code that actually stores the values that the user entered.

How are we going to save the new drink? Since we already store our drinks in dictionaries, we can create a new dictionary with the information and add it to the drink array.

We can create a new dictionary by allocing it, but we're going to need to get a reference to the array from somewhere. Could the RootViewController help with that?

That's not a bad idea.

Creating a new NSMutableDictionary is easy enough, we can do that by allocing and initializing it. We can set the drink interaction on the dictionary using setObjectForKey:. What's going to take a little more work is adding it to the drink array. We need to give the AddDrinkViewController a reference to the whole drink array. Let's start by having the RootViewController pass the new drink in after we've created it.

Exercise

Go back and update the RootViewController and AddDrinkViewController to support saving new drinks.

① **Give the AddDrinkController a reference to the master drink array.**
You're going to need to add a drinkArray field to the class, a corresponding property, and then synthesize it and release the reference in dealloc. Finally, you need to make sure that the RootViewController passes on a reference to the drink array when it's setting up the AddDrinkController.

② **Create and add a new dictionary to the array.**
You need to update the save: method to get the drink details from the controls and store them in a new dictionary. After that, add the dictionary to the master drink array using addObject:.

Exercise Solution

Go back and update the RootViewController and AddDrinkViewController to support saving new drinks.

1 **Give the AddDrinkController a reference to the master drink array.**

```
@                                          interface
AddDrinkViewController : DrinkDetailViewController{
     BOOL keyboardVisible_;
     NSMutableArray *drinkArray_;
}
@property (nonatomic, retain) NSMutableArray *drinkArray;
```

We need a reference to the array so we can add a new drink later.

AddDrinkViewController.h

```
- (IBAction) addButtonPressed: (id) sender {
     NSLog(@"%@", @"Add button pressed.");

     AddDrinkViewController *addViewController = [[AddDrinkViewController alloc] ini
tWithNibName:@"DrinkDetailViewController" bundle:nil];
     addViewController.drinkArray = self.drinks;
```

Give our newly created AddDrinkViewController a reference to the master drink array for when the user adds a new drink.

RootViewController.m

```
#import "DrinkConstants.h"

@implementation AddDrinkViewController

@synthesize drinkArray=drinkArray_;
```

We need the constant key names so we can populate the new dictionary.

We need to synthesize the new property.

AddDrinkViewController.m

2 Create and add a new dictionary to the array.

```
- (IBAction) save: (id) sender {
        NSLog(@"%@", @"Save pressed!");
```

Since we want to add keys and objects, we need to create a mutable dictionary. What problems could you run into later if you created an immutable version?

```
// Create a new drink dictionary for the new values
      NSMutableDictionary *newDrink = [[NSMutableDictionary alloc] init];
      [newDrink setValue:self.nameTextField.text forKey:NAME_KEY];
      [newDrink setValue:self.ingredientsTextView.text forKey:INGREDIENTS_
KEY];
      [newDrink setValue:self.directionsTextView.text forKey:DIRECTIONS_KEY];

// Add it to the master drink array and release our reference
      [drinkArray_ addObject:newDrink];
      [newDrink release];

// Pop the modal view and go back to the list
      [self dismissModalViewControllerAnimated:YES];
}
```

Since we alloc'ed it, we need to release our reference.

Use the key constants to add the drink information, then append it to the drink array.

```
- (void)dealloc {
      [drinkArray_ release];
      [super dealloc];
}
```

And release our reference to the drinkArray when we clean up.

AddDrinkViewController.m

Nicole, ready to pamper her VIP guests.

Five-Minute Mystery

The Case of the Missing Reservations

Nicole has been a maitre d' at Chez Platypus since it opened nearly 10 years ago. This upscale restaurant has a number of distinguished customers who like their dining experience to be just perfect. The VIP guest list hasn't changed in years and Nicole knows everyone's face. She takes them right to their favorite table when they show up and makes sure everything is just right. She's extremely efficient and the restaurant couldn't do without her... that is, until her recent, tragic, mistake.

Earlier this month, Chez Platypus got a new investor. A prominent, if eccentric, Nobel Prize-winning scientist who is known for his particular tastes. Restaurant management dug up the dusty VIP list and added the scientist's name at the bottom, along with all the detailed instructions for making sure everything was "just so" when he arrived. They trusted that Nicole would take good care of him and didn't give it another thought.

Last night, their new investor arrived a few minutes before some of the other VIP guests. Nicole didn't even notice him. She continued to move the regular VIPs to their seats and, for all she knew, their new investor did not even exist.

Why would Nicole ignore such an important new guest?

to be continued...

Test Drive

That was a lot of code! Run the app and make sure everything is working. Here's a drink to add to the list (it's the new house drink in the Head First Lounge).

Add this to your app.

Red-Headed School Girl

Canadian whiskey

Cream soda

Add the whiskey, then the cream soda to a shot glass and drink.

Test Drive

To properly test the app now, click the Add button and enter the data for the new drink in the detail view. When you're finished, click Save.

Now, what happens back in the list view?

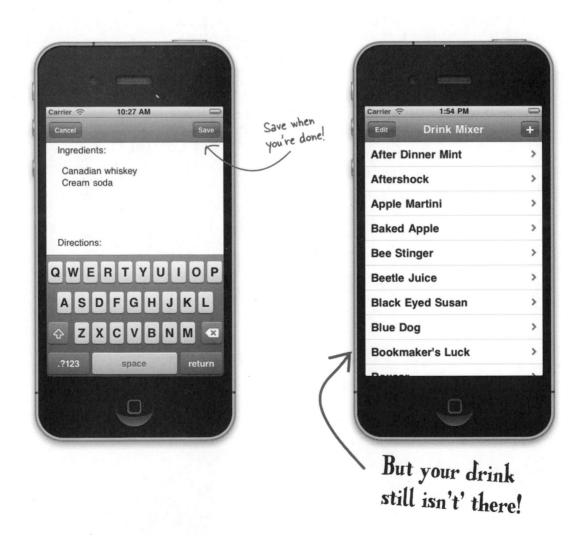

Save when you're done!

But your drink still isn't' there!

Debugging Exercise

Something's wrong. We implemented the Save method, created a new drink, added it to the array...and we're pretty sure all that code works. Before we move on, let's use the debugger and do a quick sanity check. Uncomment the viewWillAppear in RootViewController.m and set a breakpoint. If the breakpoints are on, it will launch the debugger when you run.

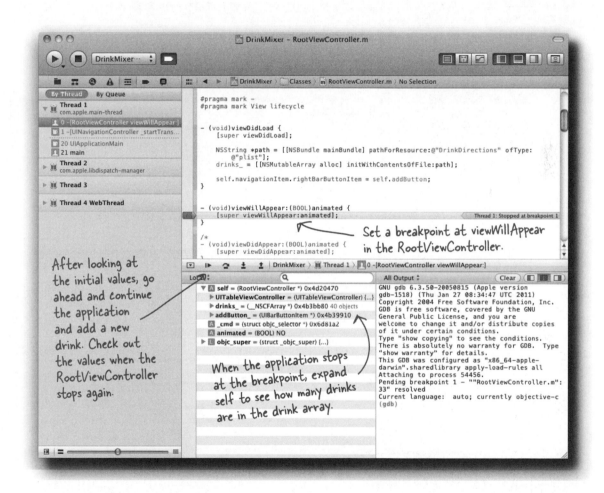

Set a breakpoint at viewWillAppear in the RootViewController.

After looking at the initial values, go ahead and continue the application and add a new drink. Check out the values when the RootViewController stops again.

When the application stops at the breakpoint, expand self to see how many drinks are in the drink array.

What did you find? ....

....

What's going on? ....

....

Debugging

Exercise Solution

Now we're going to use the debugger to help us figure out what's going on.

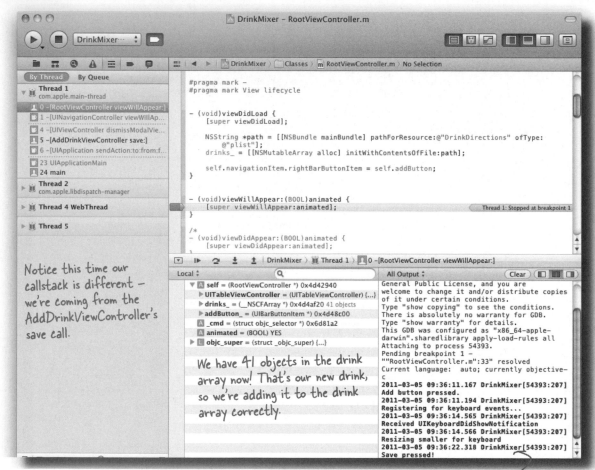

Notice this time our callstack is different — we're coming from the AddDrinkViewController's save call.

We have 41 objects in the drink array now! That's our new drink, so we're adding it to the drink array correctly.

*If you want to see the name in each dictionary, you can use this command in the console:
`p (char*)[[[self.drinks objectAtIndex:0] objectForKey:@"name"] UTF8String]`

What did you find?   The array initially has 40 dictionaries in it; after adding our new drink, it
has one more. If we use that console command, we can step through them and see that it's right.

What's going on?   The tableview isn't picking up the new drink. We've added it to the drink array,
but it's not getting added to the actual view. It's like the table view doesn't know it's there...

The Case of the Missing Reservations Solved

Why would Nicole ignore such an important new guest?

Nicole hasn't needed to look at the VIP list in years. She was so concerned that their important customers feel welcome that she didn't want to have to do something as crass as go back and read a list every time someone arrived. She made a point of memorizing that list so when they came to the restaurant she could recognize and seat them immediately. As far as Nicole knew, there were 10 VIPs on that list and she knew them all.

The problem was that the list was changed and no one told her. All it would have taken was a simple "heads up" to Nicole that there was a change to the list and the restaurant's newest investor wouldn't have disappeared...along with his money.

Five-Minute
Mystery
Solved

The table view doesn't know its data has changed

The table view does a number of things to improve performance as much as possible. As a result, if you just change values in the datasource without telling it, it won't know that something has changed. In our case, we added a new value to the array used by our datasource but didn't let the table view know about it.

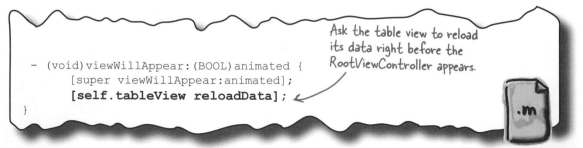

The Save button controller modified the drink array used by the datasource...

...but nothing ever told the table view it happened.

Datasource

View Controller

You need to ask the table view to reload its data

Since we're modifying the underlying data used by the datasource, the easiest way to refresh the table is to ask it to reload its data. You do this by sending it the reloadData message. This tells the tableview to reconstruct everything—how many sections it thinks it has, the headers and footers of those sections, its data rows, etc.

Ask the table view to reload its data right before the RootViewController appears.

```
- (void)viewWillAppear:(BOOL)animated {
    [super viewWillAppear:animated];
    [self.tableView reloadData];
}
```

RootViewController.m

TEST DRIVE

Update your RootViewController.m to tell the table view to refresh its data before the tableview is shown, and let's try adding a new drink again.

Add this to
your app.

Red-Headed School Girl

Canadian whiskey

Cream soda

Add the whiskey, then the cream soda to a
shot glass and drink.

TEST DRIVE

To properly test the app now, click the Add button and enter the data for the new drink in the detail view. When you're finished, click Save.

Now, what happens back in the list view?

Save when you're done!

There it is...

there are no Dumb Questions

Q: Telling the table to reload all its data seems pretty drastic. Is that really how I should do it?

A: It's the simplest way to refresh the table data, but not necessarily the most efficient. It depends on what you're doing to the table. If you're modifying the table while it's visible, you can call beginUpdates and endUpdates to tell it you're about to make a number of changes and it will animate those changes for you and let you avoid a reloadData call. There are also versions that only reload the specified rows or for a given section. Which you use depends on your application, how much you know about what changed in your data, and how big your dataset is.

Q: We didn't add any code to the cancel button. Don't we have to do something there?

A: Nope—the cancel button is coded to just dismiss the AddDrinkViewController. This will clean up any memory associated with the controller and throw away any data the user entered in the fields. As long as we don't manipulate the drink array, we've properly canceled any action the user started.

Q: Why can't I see the drink information in the debugger when I expand the drinks array and dictionaries?

A: This is one of the disadvantages of using a generic class like NSMutable Dictionary for storing our drinks. The debugger knows the class is a dictionary, but that's about all it can tell us, since all the keys and values are dynamic. You can get to them through the debugging console, but that's not as convenient as seeing real attributes on classes when you debug something.

Q: Did we really need to use the debugger back there? Couldn't I have just printed out how many items were in the array using NSLog?

A: Sure, but then you wouldn't have been able to practice debugging again... :-)

Q: Why can't we use the po command for the GDB debugger to see the names in the dictionary?

A: You can use po [[self.drinks objectAt Index:0] objectForKey:@"name"] and simplify the command we used earlier. The catch is that sometimes Xcode has trouble figuring out which object you want, so use the command from earlier if that happens.

Uhh—that drink is at the end of the list, not in with the Rs.

⚛ BRAIN POWER

Look back at your debugging work. Why is the drink showing up at the bottom of the table? What do we need to do?

The array is out of order, too

Our table view gets its information directly from our drink array.
In fact, we just map the row number into an index in our array
in cellForRowAtIndexPath:.

We map the row number right into an index value for the array. So, row 41 is going to be whatever we have in the 41st spot in the array—namely, our new drink.

```
// Configure the cell.
cell.textLabel.text = [[self.drinks objectAtIndex:indexPath.row]
objectForKey:NAME_KEY];
```

RootViewController.m

Sort your array using NSSortDescriptor

In order to get the table view properly sorted, we need to sort our data
array. NSSortDescriptors can do exactly that. You tell descriptors **what**
to compare by specifying a property, **how** to compare them with an
optional selector, and then **which order** to display the information in.
In our case, we're looking for alphabetical sorting by the name of the
drink.

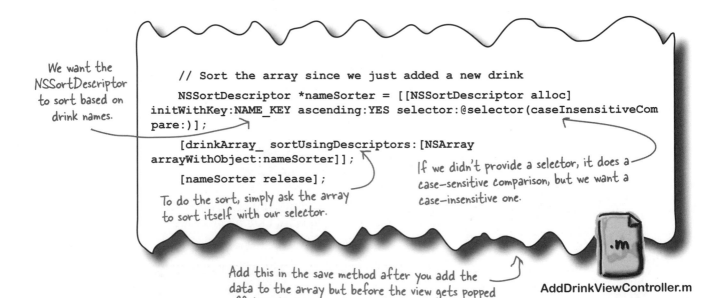

We want the NSSortDescriptor to sort based on drink names.

```
// Sort the array since we just added a new drink
NSSortDescriptor *nameSorter = [[NSSortDescriptor alloc]
initWithKey:NAME_KEY ascending:YES selector:@selector(caseInsensitiveCom
pare:)];

    [drinkArray_ sortUsingDescriptors:[NSArray
arrayWithObject:nameSorter]];

    [nameSorter release];
```

If we didn't provide a selector, it does a case-sensitive comparison, but we want a case-insensitive one.

To do the sort, simply ask the array to sort itself with our selector.

Add this in the save method after you add the data to the array but before the view gets popped off the stack.

AddDrinkViewController.m

Test Drive

Add the sorting code to AddDrinkViewController, then run the app. Let's add another drink; this one should end up in the right place.

Guesswork Cocktail

Peach schnapps, gin, dry sherry, passion fruit juice, pineapple juice and lime juice

Shake together, strain into a cocktail glass and serve.

> Great, that new drink is there, but what about the Red-Headed School Girl from before? Don't we need to deal with saving more permanently?

All our data is lost when we quit...

We're positive we're updating the array with our new drink, but obviously that new array doesn't survive quitting and restarting our app.

What do we need to do? When should it happen?

Frank

Joe

Jim

Jim: OK, so we should save the array after each new drink is added, right? That will make sure we always have the right data.

Frank: Not so fast. Keep in mind the whole speed/memory management thing.

Joe: What's the problem? It's just a little array.

Frank: But that means you could be saving every time you add a drink.

Jim: Oh, I see, that means we'll have to go through reading in the array and saving it back out multiple times. That does seem like a waste.

Joe: Well then, when are we supposed to do it?

Frank: When we background the app! With multitasking, apps don't really close anymore, but when it goes to background, we can save it.

Jim: How do we do that? How can we tell when the user backgrounds the app?

Frank: Hmm...what about that applicationDidEnterBackground method on our app delegate?

Joe: But the app delegate doesn't know anything about our drink list or where to save it...

Frank: Good point. The UIApplicationDelegate says there's a notification that goes out, too. I bet we could use that...

there are no
Dumb Questions

Q: What notification tells us the application is going into the background?

A: The iOS will send out an UIApplicationDidEnterBackground when your app is put in the background. Since iOS 4, iPhone supports multitasking, so they can do limited tasks in the background, but in general, they suspend shortly after entering the background state.

Q: Do I need to register to receive it?

A: Yup—just like any other notification.

Q: What if the user hits the home button or the phone rings or...?

A: In general, if the user answers the phone, views a text message, or does something else to trigger the iPhone or iPad to switch applications, you'll get the applicationDidEnterBackgournd. There's really only one case where you won't...

Q: What happens if my app crashes?

A: Then you're not going to get the notification. The data would be lost in this case. You need to balance how critical it is to make sure no data is lost with the performance impact of saving more frequently. In our case, we're just going to save on background. In general, Apple advises you to save as close to the user interaction as possible—we'll build an app that behaves that way later in the book.

Sharpen your pencil

Use Jim, Frank, and Joe's discussion and your skills at working with the API to figure out what to implement to save the array. Update RootViewController.m and RootViewController.h to handle saving.

① **Add the code to save out the new plist of dictionaries.**

Implement the method that will be called when the UIApplicationDidEnterBackground Notification is sent to save the plist. We're going to give you a little code snippet to use. **This code will only work on the simulator**, but we'll revisit this issue in a later chapter.

```
NSString *path = [[NSBundle mainBundle]
    pathForResource:@"DrinksDirections" ofType:@"plist"];

[self.drinks writeToFile:path atomically:YES];
```

② **Register for the UIApplicationDidEnterBackgroundNotification.**

We know that the applicationDidEnterBackground: method will be called on the AppDelegate when the application is sent to the background, but our RootViewController really owns all of the data. Have the RootViewController register for the UIApplication DidEnterBackgroundNotifcation just like the AddDrinkViewController did, except add the registration and unregistration code to viewDidLoad and viewDidUnload, respectively.

This code will only work in the simulator!

The code used to save the plist will work fine on the simulator, but fail miserably on a real device. The problem is with file permissions and where apps are allowed to store data. We'll talk a lot more about this in Chapter 8, but for now, go ahead with this version. This is a perfect example of things working on the simulator but behaving differently on a real device.

Sharpen your pencil
Solution

Use Jim, Frank, and Joe's discussion and your skills at working with the API to figure out what to implement to save the array. Update RootViewController.m and RootViewController.h to handle saving.

Add this to viewDidLoad.

RootViewController.m

```
// Register for application backgrounding so we can save data
[[NSNotificationCenter defaultCenter] addObserver:self
      selector:@selector(applicationDidEnterBackground:)
      name:UIApplicationDidEnterBackgroundNotification object:nil];
```

Implement this in RootViewController.m.

```
- (void)applicationDidEnterBackground:(NSNotification *)notification
{
    NSString *path = [[NSBundle mainBundle]
          pathForResource:@"DrinksDirections" ofType:@"plist"];
    [self.drinks writeToFile:path atomically:YES];
}
```

This is the code that's going to give us problems on a real device. We'll run into this again (and fix it) in the next chapter—bear with us for now....

Add this to viewDidUnload.

```
// Unregister for notifications
[[NSNotificationCenter defaultCenter] removeObserver:self];
```

Test Drive

Here it is!

Purple Crayon

Raspberry liqueur, vodka, and pineapple juice

Pour the liqueur and vodka over ice and then fill with pineapple juice and garnish with a grape.

Make sure when you run DrinkMixer the second time you tap on the icon in the simulator; don't hit Build and Debug again!

Author's note: we thought about showing the same screenshot twice, but figured that still wouldn't prove that it saves after hitting the home key and coming back in.

Watch it!

Stopping and hitting "Build and Debug" in Xcode is NOT the same as pushing the Home key and relaunching the app in the simulator!

When you stop the app using Xcode's Stop button, you are killing the app right then and there. No termination notifications are sent, no saving is done—it's just stopped. Likewise, when you click Build and Debug, Xcode will reinstall the application on your device before launching it. To test our load and save code, make sure you restart the app by tapping the icon in the simulator.

there are no
Dumb Questions

Q: So arrays know how to save themselves...Can I just put any object in there and have it save to a plist?

A: No—not just any old object. Arrays load and save using a Cocoa technique called NSCoding. Any objects you want to load and save must conform to the NSCoding protocol, which includes initWithCoder and encodeWithCoder method—basically, load and save. You'd need to conform to the NSCoding protocol and provide those methods to so that objects can be archived and distributed. However, NSDictionaries do conform to NSCoding (as do the strings inside of them), and that's why we can load and save so easily.

Q: What is the deal with giving us code that won't work on the device? What happens?

A: Well, to find out what happens, we encourage you to run it on a real device. Then think about why it isn't working the way you'd expect. We'll talk a lot more about this in the next app. To give you a hint, it has to with where we're trying to save the data. This is also a real-world example of something working just fine in the simulator only to behave differently on a real device. You always need to test on both.

Q: Instead of registering for that backgrounding notification, couldn't

we have just updated the AppDelegate to get the drink array from the RootViewController and save it in the delegate?

A: Yes, you could. It's more of a style and design question than anything else. Right now, the AppDelegate doesn't know anything about our plist, our drink array, or even the RootViewController, for that matter (other than making it visible). You could argue we'd be breaking encapsulation if we exposed what needs to be loaded and saved for each view up to the AppDelegate. Since we only need to save a single array, it's not a big deal either way, but if you have a number of views that need to save information or complex persistence code, it's often cleaner to leave it with the class that needs to know about it rather than lumping it all into the AppDelegate. Technically speaking, though, either one would work.

Q: Why did we register and unregister in the viewDidLoad and viewDidUnload methods instead of the *Appear methods?

A: The problem is when and how often those methods are called. viewWillAppear is called whenever the view is about to be shown. That starts out OK—we'll get that call before the table view shows up and we can register. However, the viewWillDisappear will be called right before we show the detail or add drink view controllers (since our RootViewController is about to be hidden).

If we unregister there, we won't get the backgrounding notification if the user decides to quit while looking at the details for a drink.

For example, say the user adds a new drink, goes back to the RootViewController, then taps on his drink to make sure he entered it correctly. We show the detailed view, he's happy, then he quits the app. Our RootViewController has unregistered for the backgrounding notification and the drink is lost. Instead, we use the load and unload methods, which are called when the view is loaded from the nib or unloaded. Since that view is in use throughout the application, those won't be called except at startup and shutdown.

Q: What's the deal with hitting "Build and Run" versus tapping on the icon to start DrinkMixer the second time?

A: It's because of how we're saving the data. We'll talk more about it in the next chapter, but the problem is when you hit "Build and Debug," Xcode compiles and installs the application onto the simulator. This means it's replacing the modified drink plist with the one that we ship with the application and you lose your drink. Which, everyone can agree, is very, very sad.

That's great! Now I can add the extra drinks I need. But there are a couple of other things that I need to really make this app work for me. Think you can help?

DrinkMixer ideas:

Delete drinks that I don't use to keep the list smaller.

Edit the ingredients for drinks that are in the list. I like to experiment and change things up!

BRAIN POWER

How can we implement these things? Where in the app do we need to handle this stuff?

Table views have built-in support for editing and deleting

Good news! The table view comes complete with almost everything we need for deleting data. This is behavior that acts a bit like implementing a Save or Cancel button, and a lot of it comes preloaded.

Editing mode adds an Edit button to the Navigation Control in the main view, and when it's pressed, indicators appear to the left of the table cell that can be selected and deleted like this:

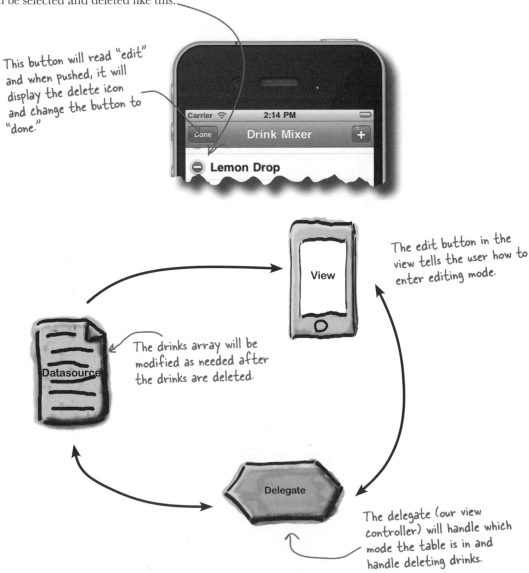

This button will read "edit" and when pushed, it will display the delete icon and change the button to "done."

The edit button in the view tells the user how to enter editing mode.

The drinks array will be modified as needed after the drinks are deleted.

The delegate (our view controller) will handle which mode the table is in and handle deleting drinks.

saving, editing, and sorting data

EDITING VIEW CONSTRUCTION

Using the view below, write what each part of the editing view does.

EDITING VIEW CONSTRUCTION SOLUTION

Using the view below, write what each part of the editing view does.

The Done button turns
off editing mode and
puts the table back to
normal.

The + button is
unchanged: it lets us add
a new drink.

The delete icons let the
user delete a row from
the table.

When tapping on a row
in edit mode, we should
be able to edit a drink
instead of just displaying
it.

LONG EXERCISE

The Xcode template we chose for this app comes with a good bit of the code we'll need, and at this point, you're pretty familiar with the RootViewController and the table view. We'll give you some hints on what to implement next, but let you take it from here.

① Add the Edit button to the root view.
We need an Edit button in the upper left of the navigation bar. The templated code for the UITableViewController comes with everything we need built-in; it's just a matter of uncommenting the line in viewDidLoad.

② Implement tableView:commitEditingStyle:forRowAtIndexPath.
Once the table view is in editing mode, we'll get a call when the user tries to delete a row either by swiping across the row or tapping the delete indicator. Most of this method is stubbed out for us too, but you'll need to add code to update the datasource with the change. Remember, we've been mapping rows to indexes in our array. Finally, you don't need to call reloadData after this change because we ask the tableView to explicitly remove the row.

③ Update the didSelectRowAtIndexPath to add a drink.
Our AddDrinkViewController has nearly everything we need to be able to edit an existing drink. Update didSelectRowAtIndexPath to invoke the AddDrinkViewController instead of the DrinkDetailViewController if we're in editing mode.

You'll need to create a Navigation Controller for this display of AddDrinkViewController, since it's being presented modally.

④ Make sure Interface Builder knows it's editable.
Verify that "Allow Selection While Editing" is checked for the Drinks table view.

⑤ Add the ability to edit a drink in our AddDrinkViewController.
You'll need to tell the app that it must edit a drink instead of creating a new one, then have it populate the controls with the existing information, and finally update the drink on save.

LONG EXERCISE
SOLUTION

The Xcode template comes with a good bit of the code we'll need, and at this point you're pretty familiar with the RootViewController and the table view. We'll give you some hints on what to implement next, but let you take it from here.

① Add the Edit button to the root view.
We need an Edit button in the upper left of the navigation bar. The templated code for the UITableViewController comes with everything we need built-in; it's just a matter of uncommenting the line in viewDidLoad.

In viewDidLoad

```
self.navigationItem.leftBarButtonItem = self.editButtonItem;
```
The UITableViewController comes with built-in support for an edit button. All we need to do is add it to the nav bar.

RootViewController.m

② Implement the tableView:commitEditingStyle:forRowAtIndexPath.
Once the table view is in editing mode, we'll get a call when the user tries to delete a row either by swiping across the row or tapping the delete indicator. Most of this method is stubbed out for us too, but you'll need to add code to update the datasource with the change. Remember, we've been mapping rows to indexes in our array. Finally, you don't need to call reloadData after this change because we ask the tableView to explicitly remove the row.

```
// Override to support editing the table view.
- (void)tableView:(UITableView *)tableView commitEditingStyle:(UITableViewCellEdi
tingStyle)editingStyle forRowAtIndexPath:(NSIndexPath *)indexPath {
   if (editingStyle == UITableViewCellEditingStyleDelete) {          Use removeObjectAtIndex to
      // Delete the row from the data source.                        clean up our datasource.
      [self.drinks removeObjectAtIndex:indexPath.row];
      [tableView deleteRowsAtIndexPaths:[NSArray arrayWithObject:indexPath]
         withRowAnimation:UITableViewRowAnimationFade];
   }
   else if (editingStyle == UITableViewCellEditingStyleInsert) {
   }
}
```

RootViewController.m

③ **Update the `didSelectRowAtIndexPath` to add a drink.**

Our AddDrinkViewController has nearly everything we need to be able to edit an existing drink. Update didSelectRowAtIndexPath to invoke the AddDrinkViewController instead of the DrinkDetailViewController if we're in editing mode.

```objc
// Override  to  support  row  selection   in  the
table view.
- (void)tableView:(UITableView *)tableView didSelectRowAtIndexPath:(NSIndexPath *)
indexPath {
  if (!self.editing) {
    DrinkDetailViewController *drinkDetailViewController =
[[DrinkDetailViewController alloc] initWithNibName:@"DrinkDetailViewController"
bundle:nil];
    drinkDetailViewController.drink = [self.drinks objectAtIndex:indexPath.row];
    [self.navigationController pushViewController:drinkDetailViewController
animated:YES];
    [drinkDetailViewController release];
  }
  else {
    AddDrinkViewController *editingDrinkVC = [[AddDrinkViewController
alloc] initWithNibName:@"DrinkDetailViewController" bundle:nil];

    editingDrinkVC.drink = [self.drinks objectAtIndex:indexPath.row];
    editingDrinkVC.drinkArray = self.drinks;


    UINavigationController *editingNavCon = [[UINavigationController
alloc] initWithRootViewController:editingDrinkVC];


    [self.navigationController presentModalViewController:editingNavCon
animated:YES];
    [editingDrinkVC release];
    [editingNavCon release];
  }
}
```

↖ First, we need to check to see if we're in editing mode. If not, just display the normal detail view.

↖ If we are in editing mode, create an AddDrinkViewController and set the drink to edit in addition to our drink array. We'll fix up the AddDrinkViewController in a minute...

RootViewController.m

Just the AddDrink ViewController left...

LonG ExErcise
SoLutioN

The Xcode template comes with a good bit of the code we'll need, and at this point you're pretty familiar with the RootViewController and the table view. We'll give you some hints on what to implement next, but let you take it from here.

4 **Make sure Interface Builder knows it's editable.**
Verify that "Allow Selection While Editing" is checked for the Drinks table view.

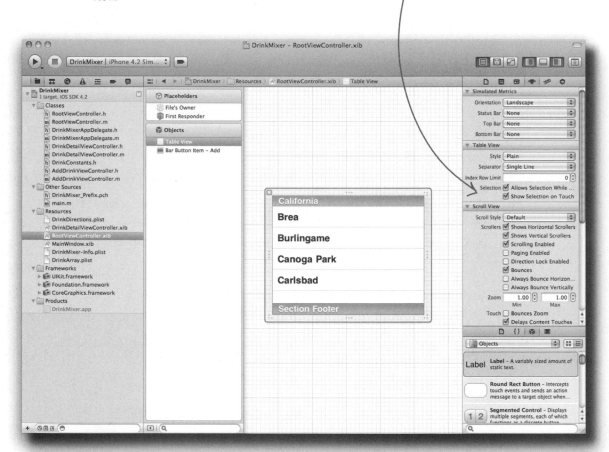

⑤ **Add the ability to edit a drink in our AddDrinkViewController.**

You'll need to tell it that it must edit a drink instead of creating a new one, then have it populate the controls with the existing information, and finally update the drink on save.

```
- (IBAction) save: (id) sender {
      NSLog(@"Save pressed!");


      if (self.drink != nil) {
            // We're working with an existing drink, so let's remove
            // it from the array to get ready for a new one
            [drinkArray_ removeObject:self.drink];
            self.drink = nil; // This will release our reference too
      }


      // Now create a new drink dictionary for the new values
      NSMutableDictionary* newDrink = [[NSMutableDictionary alloc] init];
```

If there's a drink set, then we need to update it. We can either update the existing object or replace it. Since we need to re-sort the whole array anyway (in case the drink name changed), we just remove the old one and re-add it.

AddDrinkViewController.m

TEST DRIVE

Try removing or editing drinks now. You should be able to remove drinks and fine-tune them all you want. Remember to restart your app by tapping on the icon, though; otherwise, you'll lose your changes.

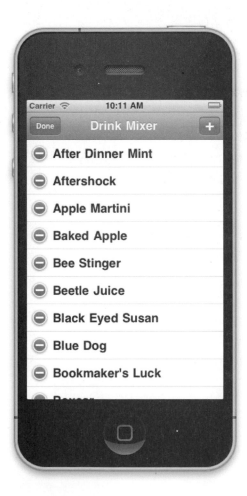

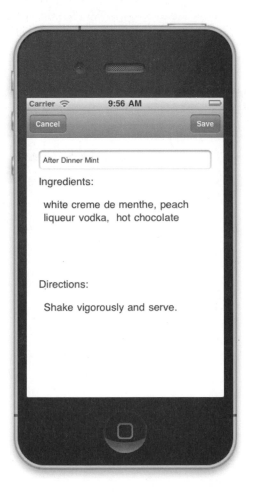

Resubmit your app to the store and...

Here's DrinkMixer at #1!
Congratulations!

NavigationController cross

Let's check your scroll view, nav control, and table view buzz words!

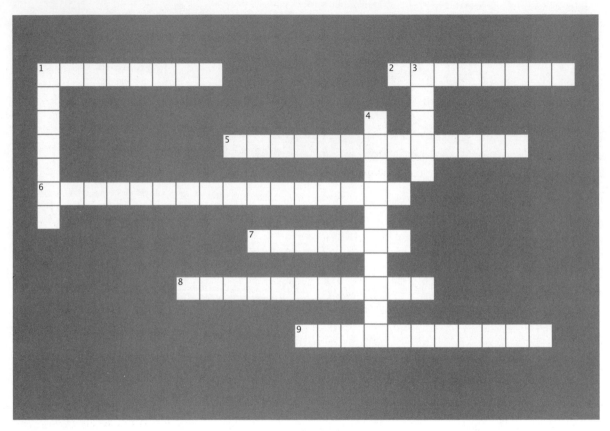

Across

1. A field that the user can change is _____.
2. Arrays load and save using _____.
5. System-level events that can be passed are called _____.
6. Sort data using the _____.
7. All the sytem events go through the _____ center.
8. The scroll view won't work without setting the _____.
9. viewWillAppear and _____ are called at different times.

Down

1. Table views have built-in support for _____.
3. Keyboard events tell you about the _____ and size of the keyboard.
4. The _____ handles the scroll bar, panning, zooming, and what content is displayed in the view.

there are no
Dumb Questions

Q: **I like the automatic editing support in the table view, but how do I do those cool "Add New Address" rows that the iPhone has when you edit a contact?**

A: It's a lot easier than you think. Basically, when you're in editing mode, you tell the table view you have one more row than you actually have in your data. Then, in cellForRowAtIndexPath, check to see if the row the table view is asking for is one past the end. If it is, return a cell that says "Add New Address" or whatever. Finally, in your didSelectRowAtIndexPath, check to see if the selected row is one past your data, and if so, you know it was the selected row.

Q: **We haven't talked about moving rows around, but I've seen tables do that. Is it hard?**

A: No, the table view part is really easy; it's the datasource part that can be tricky. If you support moving rows around, simply implement the method tableView:move RowAtIndexPath:toIndexPath: (the tableview checks to see if you provide this method before allowing the user to rearrange cells). The users will see a row handle on the side of the cells when they're in editing mode. When they move a row, you'll get a call to your new method that provides the IndexPath the row started at and the IndexPath for the new position. It's your job to update your datasource to make sure they stay that way. You can also implement tableview:canMoveRowAtIndexPath to only allow the users to move certain rows. There are even finer-grained controls in

the delegate if you're interested, such as preventing the users from moving a cell to a certain section.

Q: **What if I don't want the users to be able to delete a row? Can I still support editing for some of the rows?**

A: Absolutely. Just implement tableview: canEditRowAtIndexPath: and return NO for the rows you don't want to be editable.

Q: **When we edit a drink, we replace the object in the array. What if we had some other view that had a reference to the original?**

A: Great question. The short answer is you're going to have a problem, no matter how you handle it. If some other view has a reference to the object we removed, that's not tragic since the retain count should still be at least 1; the object won't get deallocated when we remove it. However, the other views obviously won't see any of the changes the user made since we're putting them in a new dictionary. Even if they had the old dictionary, they wouldn't have any way of knowing the values changed. There are a few ways you could handle this. One option is you could change our code to leave the original object in the array and modify it in place, then make sure that any other view you have refreshes itself on viewWillAppear or something along those lines. Another option is you could send out a custom notification that the drink array changed or that a particular drink was modified. Interested views can register to receive that notification.

Q: **Aren't we supposed to be concerned about efficiency? Isn't removing the drink and reading it inefficient?**

A: It's not the most efficient way since it requires finding the object in the array and removing it before reinserting it, but for the sake of code clarity, we decided it was simpler to show. We'd have to re-sort the array regardless of which approach we took, however, since the name of the drink (and its place alphabetically) could change with the edit.

Q: **We added the edit button on the left-hand side of the detail view, but what about a back button? Isn't that where they usually go?**

A: That's true. When you get into having an add button, an edit button, and a back button, you run into a real estate problem. The way we solved it was fine, but you'll need to make sure that your app flows the way you need it to when your Navigation Controller starts to get crowded.

Q: **We still have some oddities like the drink being editable in the detail view. Should we worry about that?**

A: Yes. So much of what has made iOS and the app store successful is the polish that Apple and iOS developers have put on their applications. It's the difference between a pretty good app and a chart-topping, wow-inducing success purchased by hundreds of thousands of users.

 NavigationController cross Solution

Let's check your scroll view, nav control, and table view buzz words!

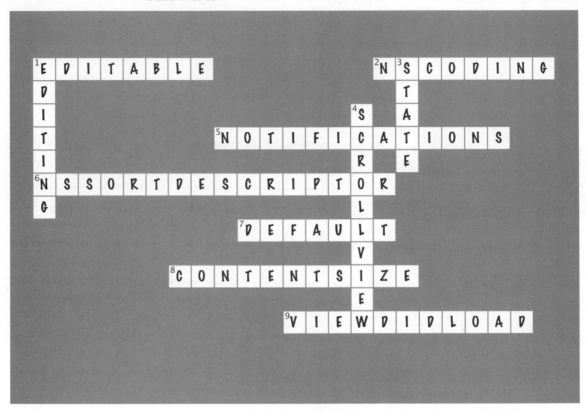

Across

1. A field that the user can change is _____. [EDITABLE]
2. Arrays load and save using _____. [NSCODING]
5. System-level events that can be passed are called _____. [NOTIFICATIONS]
6. Sort data using the _____. [NSSORTDESCRIPTOR]
7. All the sytem events go through the _____ center. [DEFAULT]
8. The scroll view won't work without setting the _____. [CONTENTSIZE]
9. viewWillAppear and _____ are called at different times. [VIEWDIDLOAD]

Down

1. Table views have built-in support for _____. [EDITING]
3. Keyboard events tell you about the _____ and size of the keyboard. [STATE]
4. The _____ handles the scroll bar, panning, zooming, and what content is displayed in the view. [SCROLLVIEW]

Your iOS Development Toolbox

You've got Chapter 6 under your belt and now you've added saving, editing, and sorting data to your toolbox.

Scroll View

Acts like a lens to show only the part of the view you need and scrolls the rest off the screen.

Needs to be given a contentSize to work properly.

Can be easily constructed in Interface Builder

Sorting

Arrays can be sorted using NSSortDescriptors.

Table View Editing

There's built-in support for editing a table view.

The edit button comes with lots of functionality, including methods to delete rows from the table view.

Notifications

Are system-level events that you can monitor and use in your app.

The default notification center handles most notifications.

Different frameworks use different notifications, or you can create your own.

Sam has another project in mind...

Congrats on the app. So, we all just got iPads as a bonus. I bet DrinkMixer would look awesome on mine!

7 migrating to iPad

We need more room

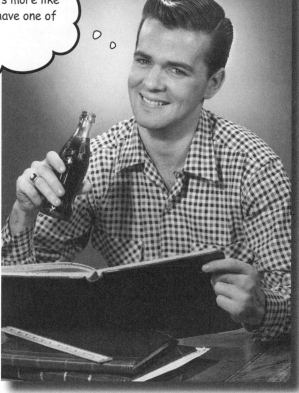

I need a device that's more like a book. Does Apple have one of those?

iPhones are great, but a bigger screen can be better.

When the iPad first launched, some panned it by saying that it was "just a big iPhone" (but uh, without the phone). In many ways it is, but that screen opens up many opportunities for better user interaction. More screen real estate means that reading is comfortable, web pages are easily viewed, and the device can act more like a book. Or a calendar. Or many other things that you already know how to use, like a menu...

DrinkMixer on the iPad

It happens all the time: a new device comes out and now your clients want to use it. iPad and iPhone apps have lots of overlap. iOS runs both devices, which are touch screen–based, and only one app is allowed to be visible at a time to users.

The big difference? The screen size!

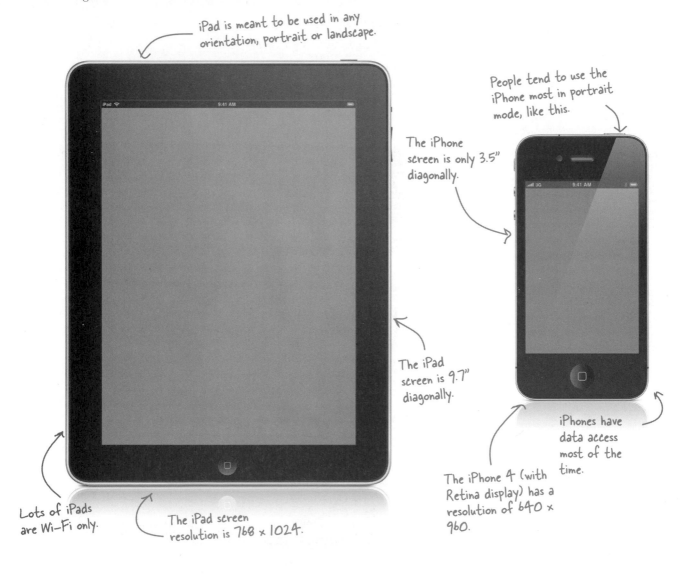

iPad is meant to be used in any orientation, portrait or landscape.

People tend to use the iPhone most in portrait mode, like this.

The iPhone screen is only 3.5" diagonally.

The iPad screen is 9.7" diagonally.

iPhones have data access most of the time.

The iPhone 4 (with Retina display) has a resolution of 640 × 960.

Lots of iPads are Wi-Fi only.

The iPad screen resolution is 768 × 1024.

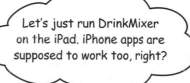

Let's just run DrinkMixer on the iPad. iPhone apps are supposed to work too, right?

Yes, they do.

Every iPhone app on the App Store will run on iPads right out of the box, but there's a catch.

Do this! Open up DrinkMixer in Xcode and run it in the iPad simulator. Then you can see what we're dealing with.

Click here and select iPad Simulator.

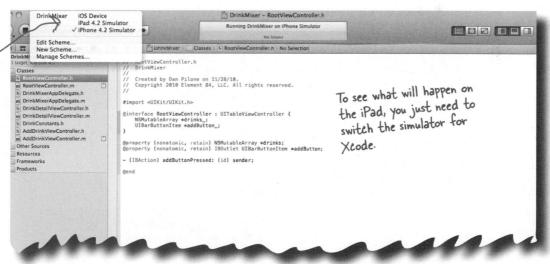

To see what will happen on the iPad, you just need to switch the simulator for Xcode.

Build and run...

The iPad simulator

The simulator will launch the iPad with the DrinkMixer iPhone app, as is. You didn't have to change a line of code, and it does work. Of course, the simulator is enough to show you that just running the iPhone app on the iPad isn't ideal.

First off, it's the size of an iPhone app, but on an iPad. Ugh. You can change the size of the view to fill the entire screen by "doubling" the pixels, but that doesn't change the *resolution* of the view, so the graphics don't look as good. Play with it in the simulator, too, and we'll bet it doesn't really feel right, either...

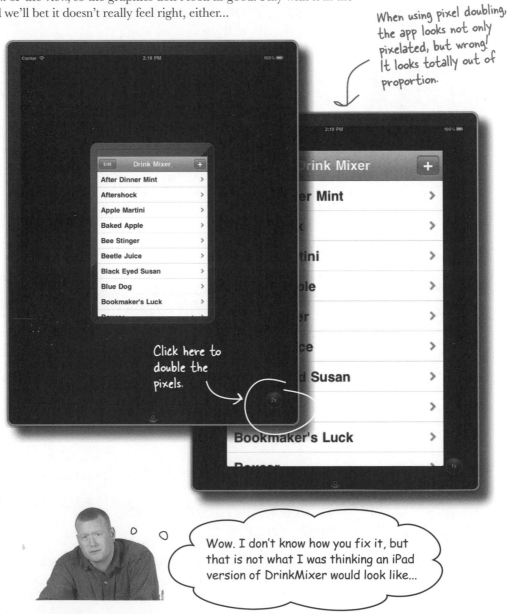

When using pixel doubling, the app looks not only pixelated, but wrong! It looks totally out of proportion.

Click here to double the pixels.

Wow. I don't know how you fix it, but that is not what I was thinking an iPad version of DrinkMixer would look like...

The HIG covers iPads, too

Since the device has changed, let's go back to the HIG. If you work your way through the iOS Human Interface Guidelines, you'll find a section called "For iPad: Restrain Your Information Hierarchy." For DrinkMixer, that means we need to use the extra real estate that comes from the big screen to **reduce the number of screen transitions**. For example, you can easily display a detail view next to a list view using a **Split View Controller**.

The view shows two levels of data, called a Split View Controller.

Organizer – Documentation

Devices Repositories Projects Archives Documentation

iOS 4.2 Library › User Experience › iOS Human Interface Guidelines › User Experience Guidelines

For iPad: Restrain Your Information Hierarchy

Use the large iPad screen and iPad-specific UI elements to give people access to more information in one place. Although you don't want to pack too much information into one screen, you also want to prevent people from feeling that they must visit many different screens to find what they want.

In general, focus the main screen on the primary content and provide additional information or tools in an auxiliary view, such as a popover. This gives people easy access to the functionality they need, without requiring them to leave the context of the main task.

With the large iPad screen, and UI elements such as split view and popover, you have alternatives to the one-level-per-screen structure of many iPhone applications. (For specific guidelines on how to use these elements, see "Split View (iPad Only)" and "Popover (iPad Only).") For example, you can:

Use a navigation bar in the right pane of a split view to allow people to drill down into a top-level category that is persistently displayed in the left pane. This flattens your information hierarchy by at least one level, because two levels are always onscreen at the same time. For example, Settings displays device and application settings using a navigation bar in the right pane of a split view.

This is a pop-over. It's used in portrait mode.

This is the segmented control. It's another way to consolidate information into a single view rather than introduce a hierarchy.

BRAIN BARBELL

What are some apps that you've used for both iPad and iPhone? Are there any elements that are iPad-specific?

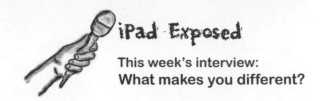

iPad Exposed

This week's interview:
What makes you different?

Head First: Hi, iPad! It really exciting to be interviewing a famous device like you.

iPad: Thank you! I'm happy to be here. There are lots of other tablets out there, but once you know me, you know the best.

Head First: That's a great lead-in for me. How do you answer the critics that say you're just a big iPhone?

iPad: Would that really be such a bad thing? People who say that just don't understand us. We do have some things in common, like the touch screen, iOS, accelerometers, and awesome apps, but the apps are usually different.

Head First: Well, your apps are bigger, right?

iPad: Yes, but you're missing the point. My screen is bigger, but because of that, you interact with me very differently.

Head First: How so? People still use the same gestures?

iPad: When you pick me up, I'm more like a book than iPhone. iPhone is more about getting things done quickly and moving on. Me, you want to sit down and spend some time with. I might even write my own book: *iPhones Are From Mars, iPads Are From Venus*. Don't you agree?

Head First: Ummm, that's probably true. I've noticed that you move around more, too.

iPad: My Apps need to support all four orientations, so no matter how you pick me up, it just works. And there should be less bouncing around.

Head First: What?

iPad: When you're using iPhone, the screen is really small (but pretty, I wish I had that awesome display). Anyway, because the screen is small, you're going between screens a lot on iPhone. With me, designers usually put a lot on one screen. They call that "restraining the hierarchy."

Head First: Interesting. Do you have any special views?

iPad: I do. To reduce the number of views, there is a Split View Controller just for my apps. In landscape, it shows a table view on the left side of the screen and the detail view on the other side. So as soon as you pick something, you can see the details without hiding the list.

Head First: Is that what you use for mail?

iPad: Yup, it's perfect for that. And if you shift that Split View Controller to portrait, it just shows the detail view, until you click on a navigation button and see the popover.

Head First: The what?

iPad: The popover. It's another one of my own special controls. It's like a dialog box that appears on the screen without covering the whole thing up.

Head First: Like a speech bubble?

iPad: Exactly. Great for little bits of information, color settings, stuff like that.

Head First: What don't you have?

iPad: I'm like an iPod Touch. Limited GPS, sometimes no camera. Those are the biggies.

Head First: Anything you'd like to add?

iPad: Well, people should really take advantage of my size. Use visual clues from the real world to help people use your app. You have lots of space to work with and room for lots of fingers touching things. Think about how real books, calendars, switches, dials, and real physical controls look and feel. Take advantage of that.

Head First: Thanks, iPad. Can't wait to get started!

Sketch up the UI for the new DrinkMixer iPad app. You've got more room, so be sure to use it well! Consult the HIG and make sure you know what information is going in which element of the view.

Remember, we want to convert this whole app into an iPad app, with the right iPad controls.

Exercise
Solution

Now we have an idea of the UI for the new iPad app. Having this all put together first is going to help keep everything going in the right place as you code.

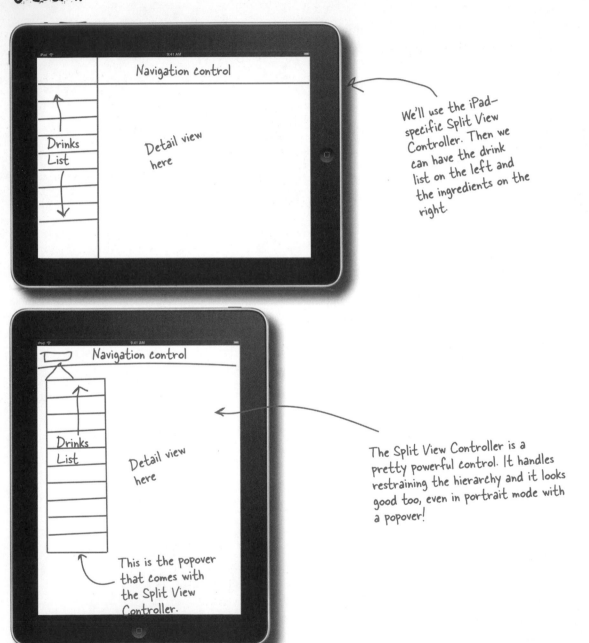

We'll use the iPad–specific Split View Controller. Then we can have the drink list on the left and the ingredients on the right.

The Split View Controller is a pretty powerful control. It handles restraining the hierarchy and it looks good too, even in portrait mode with a popover!

This is the popover that comes with the Split View Controller.

there are no Dumb Questions

Q: Is building an app for iPad really that different than building for iPhone?

A: From a coding and development perspective, no, they're nearly identical. But from a design and UI perspective, yes, they're very different. It's important to spend time with an iPad to make sure you "get it." When designing iPad apps, there will be a point where an app will just start to feel like an iPad app. It's lots of little design elements like the use of space, textures on controls and UI components, interaction patterns, etc. iPhone apps are much more about ease of use with your thumb, quick access to data, etc. iPad apps are "bigger" than that. People sit on couches and really soak in iPad apps. Give them that kind of depth.

Q: Does "restraining the hierarchy" just mean using a split-view control?

A: No. That's one way to help get there, but it's definitely not the only way. We'll

use a split view control for DrinkMixer, but there are lots of other things to consider. For example, let's say you have summary information about chapters in a book. In an iPhone app, you might have a table view listing the chapters, and tapping on a chapter will show that summary information. In an iPad app, you might want to have a fancy table of contents only showing three or four summaries at a time but indicate to the user that they can turn the page to see the next set. Hook that up with a swipe gesture and a nice page curl animation and you have a much more natural way of flipping through the same material without needing to slide views in and out as the user moves through data.

Q: Are we going to have the same hardware issues with iPad as we did with iPhone? Specifically different capabilities and features?

A: Absolutely. You already had that to some extent with just the first iPad—there are 3G iPads with a GPS while the

Wi-Fi–only ones obviously don't have 3G connectivity or a true GPS. The iPad 2 has two cameras while the original iPad doesn't have any. iPad 2's graphics and processing capabilities are substantially better, too. The good news is that you should handle it just like iPhone and iPod Touch differences— simply check for device capabilities and code around not having them.

Q: Does the iPad run a different version of iOS or anything?

A: No; well, no more so than iPod Touch vs. iPhone. There are some controls that are only available on the iPad (and you need to check for them if you build a universal app— more on that later), but the basic OS is the same and you can have a single build that runs on all iOS devices. Speaking of running on lots of devices...

Building a project for iPhone + iPad = Universal App

Behind the Scenes — Creating an App for iPhone and iPad

Now that you're ready to build this thing, what exactly is it called? When Apple designed the iPad and iPhone to share one OS, Apple introduced the concept of a **Universal app,** an app that is built for both devices. That still means different views for iPhone and iPad, but only one code base that gets submitted to the App Store. Users get both a native iPhone app and native iPad app when they buy your application instead of needing to purchase two separate apps.

It's a big factor in distribution, actually...

Fireside Chats

Tonight's talk: **Universal App Distribution or not?**

Universal:

Ha! Two apps. That's really inefficient. It really just makes more sense to support iPhones and iPads everywhere, like I do.

True, but if I'm written right, most of my code is shared between the devices. It's really not that hard to just use the right view controllers on the right device and everything else goes from there.

I'd be happy to trade worrying about a couple more devices for better sales and reviews.

The reviews I see have a lot of people complaining about needing to purchase the same app again just to use it on another device. I'm usually a little more expensive, but users love getting more value for their money.

Two Apps:

You do support everyone, that's true, but that makes you kinda hefty, right? You have to check for like, everything!

See, my apps don't have that much to worry about. If it's iPhone, that's it. Well, except for touches...but I don't need to deal with everything in one..

Wait a sec. I'm really the moneymaker. If you build two apps, then you can sell twice per user. Every person out there with an iPhone and an iPad has to pay twice to get all of me.

Hmm. I don't buy it. I cost less but only work on a specific kind of device.

Universal:

Let's talk maintenance. I think we both agree that you don't want two completely separate code bases, right?

Two Apps:

Oh, absolutely. Even if you are going to make two different apps, you should be sharing a code base. You definitely don't want to be in a situation where you're fixing the same bug in multiple projects or trying to keep them in sync.

Totally agree. So I guess really we're arguing about a packaging issue. Do the users want to pay a little more and get iPhone and iPad support, or do they want to pay a little less when they only want support for one device, but end up paying more if they want both?

You know, I bet there isn't a simple answer to that. There are lots of users who have lots of different opinions. It probably depends on the app and how the developer wants to interact with the users. I guess there's room for both of us...

BRAIN POWER

Sam doesn't want to deal with multiple applications. He wants the iPad version of DrinkMixer to be tied in with the original iPhone app. What kind of app distribution are we going to have to use?

Use Xcode to build your Universal app

Since we're looking to support Sam and keep things easier, it makes more sense to build a universal app that creates one software bundle. This isn't too hard to implement, because when the code is cleanly separated in the MVC pattern, we just need to talk to another view.

Do this!

Upgrade your app

Highlight the project in the Navigator window and you'll see the basic project settings. Make sure that **Targets** is highlighted.

Under devices, the drop-down box will let you select iPhone, iPad, or **Universal.** Select **Universal**.

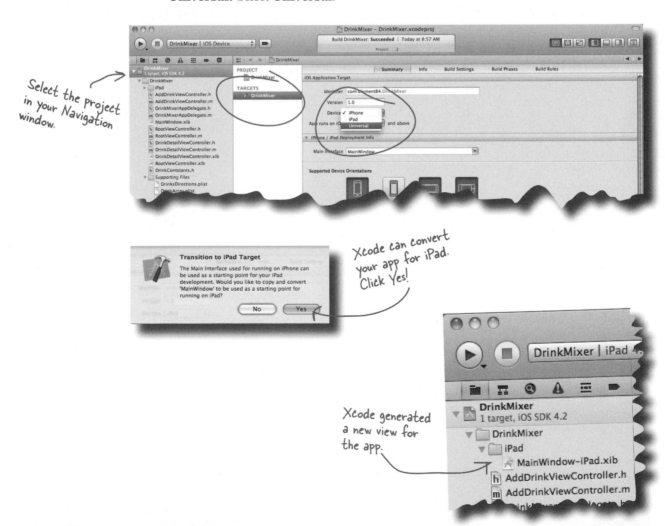

Select the project in your Navigation window.

Xcode can convert your app for iPad. Click Yes!

Transition to iPad Target

The Main Interface used for running on iPhone can be used as a starting point for your iPad development. Would you like to copy and convert 'MainWindow' to be used as a starting point for running on iPad?

No   Yes

Xcode generated a new view for the app.

DrinkMixer | iPad 4.

DrinkMixer
1 target, iOS SDK 4.2
DrinkMixer
iPad
MainWindow-iPad.xib
AddDrinkViewController.h
AddDrinkViewController.m

Wait—what's a target? What does it have to do with iPads?

Targets are used in the build process.

Xcode completes the build process based on the *targets* that you identify. A target keeps track of which files and the instructions of what to do with them for a build. We upgraded our target to be a universal build, so now it has everything it needs to build an app that runs on iPhones, iPod Touches, and iPads.

As part of the upgrade process, Xcode introduced the new .xib for us and added it to the target.

Geek Bits

Since Xcode is used for Mac development too, there are lots of reasons to create several targets, such as frameworks or libraries. Targets are frequently used to build unit tests or application tests as well. The test code is only included in the test targets and won't be in the release builds. Xcode only builds the **active target**, so you can build just one piece at a time. We only have one target for DrinkMixer, so it's always active.

TEST DRIVE

Make sure that the iPad simulator is still selected for the build and build and run the app. It should look much more iPad-specific now...

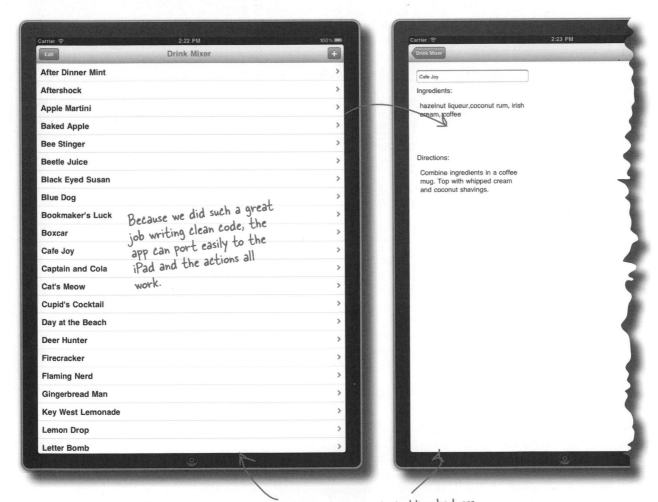

Because we did such a great job writing clean code, the app can port easily to the iPad and the actions all work.

We got rid of the pixel-doubling badness, but it still feels like an overgrown iPhone app...

The detail view looks really bad, and it's just a regular table view—we never told it to use the Split View Controller.

You're right.

Since we're working with iPhone and a new view, Xcode just ported what we had over to the iPad—in this case, a table view. To put the new Split View Controller into play, we need to fix that.

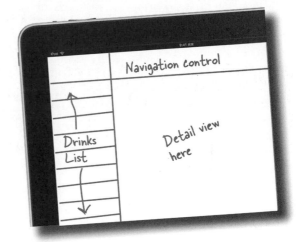

Navigation control

Drinks List

Detail view here

Split-view Magnets

We'll walk you through the coding, you just get them in order!

Adding the split view isn't really that hard if you think about it a bit. Use these magnets to order the steps we need to work through.

> Declare and add the UISplitViewController instance variable and its IBOutlet to the DrinkMixerAppDelegate files

> Delete the Navigation Controller

> Add in the DrinkMixer Detail View

> Change the Table View to the Root View

> Wire up the Split View Controller reference

> Add a Split View Controller from the library

> Add a Navigation Controller to the Detail View

> Open up MainWindow-iPad.xib in Xcode

Split-view Magnets Solution

Adding the split view isn't really that hard if you think about it a bit.
Use these magnets to order the steps we need to work through.

Open up MainWindow-iPad.xib in Xcode

This is the initial
file listing that was
created by Xcode
when the new
target was created.

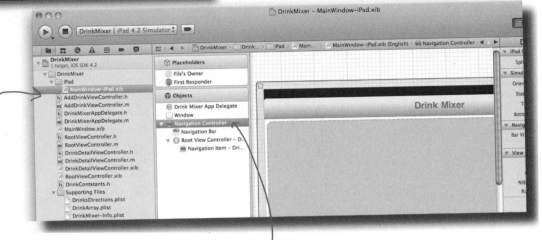

Delete the Navigation Controller

This Navigation Controller is going
to be replaced with a Split View
Controller. So, delete this now.

Add a Split View Controller from the library

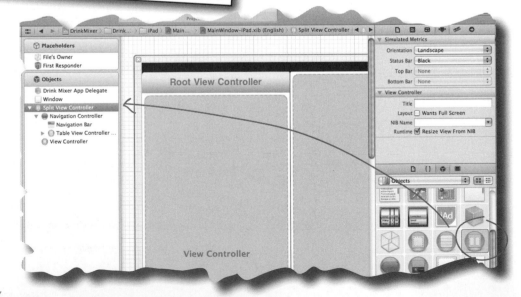

Add a Navigation Controller to the Detail View

For the Split View Controller to work, you need to have two **children**. By default, they are a Navigation Controller with an embedded Table View and a standard view controller. We want a Navigation Control on top of the View Controller for the right-hand pane. Using a real navigation controller for the detail view gets us access to a navigation bar and the usual edit buttons, like we had for the iPhone version of the app.

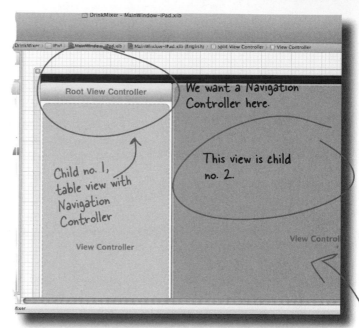

We want a Navigation Controller here.

This view is child no. 2.

Child no. 1, table view with Navigation Controller

The easiest way to swap out the right view controller is to drag and drop a Navigation Controller into the right pane. Interface Builder will update the right view controller to be a Navigation Controller for us and drop the navigation bar right where we want it.

Drop a Navigation Controller right into the right View Controller. It should change to look like this...

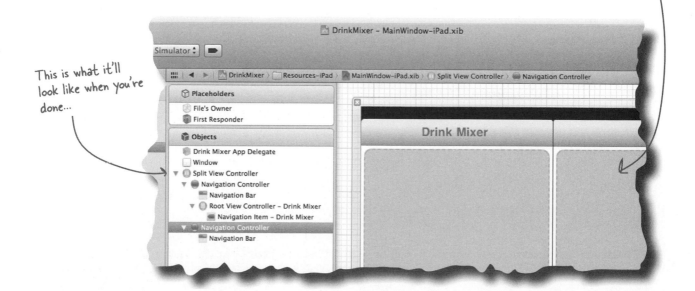

This is what it'll look like when you're done...

Split-view Magnets Solution (cont.)

Add in the DrinkMixer Detail View

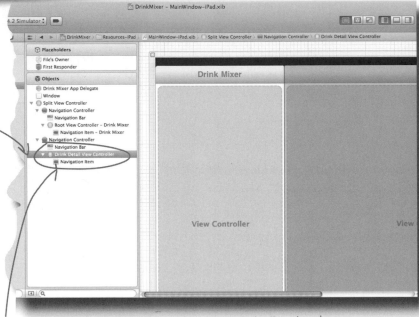

This view controller is the detail view on the landscape view of the Split View Controller. It needs to be our detail view.

To change this, highlight the View Controller, and change the view controller class to "DrinkDetailViewController" from the drop-down list in the inspector.

Declare and add the UISplitViewController instance variable and its IBOutlet to the DrinkMixerAppDelegate files

```objc
@interface DrinkMixerAppDelegate : NSObject <UIApplicationDelegate> {

    UIWindow *window;
    UINavigationController *navigationController;
    UISplitViewController *splitViewController_;
}

@property (nonatomic, retain) IBOutlet UISplitViewController
*splitViewController;
```

DrinkMixerAppDelegate.h

```
@synthesize splitViewController=splitViewController_;
```

```
- (void)dealloc {
        [splitViewController_ release];
        [navigationController release];
        [window release];
        [super dealloc];
}
@end
```

DrinkMixerAppDelegate.m

Wire up the Split View controller reference

Right-click on the App Delegate and connect the splitViewController outlet
to the Split View Controller.

Change the table view to the root view

Just like we did with the detail view, change the class type for the table view controller
to "Root View Controller."

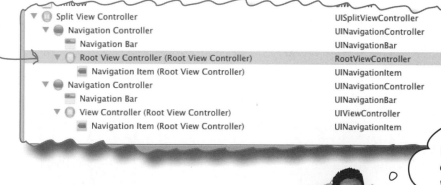

▼ 🔘 Split View Controller	UISplitViewController
▼ 🔵 Navigation Controller	UINavigationController
🖼 Navigation Bar	UINavigationBar
▼ 🔘 Root View Controller (Root View Controller)	RootViewController
🖼 Navigation Item (Root View Controller)	UINavigationItem
▼ 🔵 Navigation Controller	UINavigationController
🖼 Navigation Bar	UINavigationBar
▼ 🔘 View Controller (Root View Controller)	UIViewController
🖼 Navigation Item (Root View Controller)	UINavigationItem

But the App
Delegate is for the iPhone
and the iPad, right? Don't
we need to tell it which
view to use?

Check your devices

This is where the code paths for the iPhone and the iPad are going to intersect—in the App Delegate. Because we're migrating an existing iPhone application, we already have an AppDelegate and it's set up to add our RootViewController to the window when the application launches.

Now that we've added iPad-specific views, we need to update our AppDelegate to add the correct one to the window depending on the device. iOS makes it easy to determine which device you're on through a macro named UI_USER_INTERFACE_IDIOM(). This returns a constant that tells you the type of device your application is running on; we can use this to figure out which view controller to show in the window.

> Here we check the UI_USER_INTERFACE_IDIOM() and if it's an iPad, we add the splitViewController's view to the window. Otherwise, we add the navigationController's view.

```objc
- (BOOL)application:(UIApplication *)application didFinishLaunchingWithOptions
:(NSDictionary *)launchOptions {

    // Override point for customization after application launch.

    // Add the navigation controller's view to the window and display.
    if (UI_USER_INTERFACE_IDIOM() == UIUserInterfaceIdiomPad) {
        [self.window addSubview:self.splitViewController.view];
    }
    else {
        [self.window addSubview:navigationController.view];
    }
    [self.window makeKeyAndVisible];
    return YES;
}
```

DrinkMixerAppDelegate.m

Now it's ready to run...

TEST DRIVE

Save everything and then build and run. You may need to switch Xcode back to the iPad setting for the Simulator...

This is the view that we should see in portrait. Just the detail view.

We don't have the popovers working yet, so there's no way to show the full drink list.

To see the split view, go up to the Hardware→Rotate Right menu option.

TEST DRIVE

Rotating DrinkMixer should expose the Split View Controller that we've been working on. But there's a problem...

That isn't
working!

Rotation is key with iPad

An important part of coding for the iPad is that is has to support all orientations, since Apple is big on there being no wrong way to use an iPad. Users will expect to be able to pick up their iPad any way and have it work. To start supporting *all* orientations, we need each of our controllers to know that we want to do that.

This method is in all your view implementation files, just commented out.

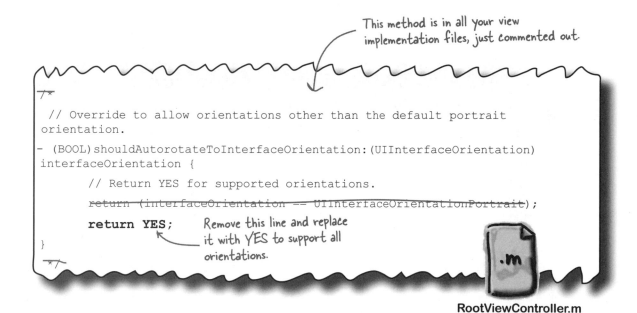

```
/*

  // Override to allow orientations other than the default portrait
  orientation.
- (BOOL)shouldAutorotateToInterfaceOrientation:(UIInterfaceOrientation)
interfaceOrientation {

      // Return YES for supported orientations.

      return (interfaceOrientation == UIInterfaceOrientationPortrait);

      return YES;

}

*/
```

Remove this line and replace it with YES to support all orientations.

RootViewController.m
DrinkDetailViewController.m

Test Drive

Now you're supporting all the orientations, everything is linked, and devices are checked. The split view should be working now...

Now, push the home key and launch it again.

> Wait. The app looked OK once it got started, but something weird happened at startup.

We're not fully supporting rotations yet.

The code is all set up to handle a rotation *when you're in the app*.

At startup, iPad apps should show a launch image first, while they're loading, like a splash screen. Apple's HIG recommends that the image should be your actual initial user interface (minus specific data). Depending on the application, though, some people use actual splash screens.

Once the images are set up, iOS will pick the image that goes with the current orientation and avoid that awkward rotation of the interface that you saw without appropriate launch images.

Sharpen your pencil

We have two images you can use for launch images, you just need to download them and drop them in your project.

☐ Go to *http://www.headfirstlabs.com/books/hfiphonedev* and download the launch images for this chapter.

☐ Select the project in Xcode and scroll down to iPad Deployment Info. Enable all four support device orientations.

☐ Drop the portrait launch image into the Portrait Launch image box and the landscape image into the Landscape Launch Image box. Let Xcode copy both into your project.

Sharpen your pencil
Solution

We're just about ready to fully support the launch in any orientation. Here's what your final resources directory should look like.

In the iPad Deployment Info, you should have all launch orientations selected and the images dropped into Launch Images.

Xcode will have added the images to your project, but notice that it changed the names to Default-<orientation>~ipad.png. This ~ipad notation is standard in iOS and can be used to provide device specific resources.

Test Drive

Now we're supporting all the different orientations, right from the beginning. Try stopping it and relaunching in the simulator from landscape. Everything works!

Test Drive — Continued...

What if you tap on one of those rows in the horizontal split-view orientation?

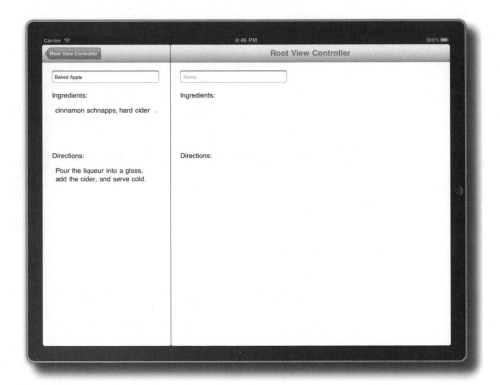

That's not right!

BE the Detail View Controller
Your job is to play Detail View Controller and figure out why you're not displaying the right thing. Look at the code below and see if you can figure out what's going wrong...

When does this code actually get called?

_____

_____

_____

```objc
- (void)viewWillAppear:(BOOL)animated {
    [super viewWillAppear:animated];

    // Setup our UI with the provided drink
    self.nameTextField.text = [self.drink objectForKey:NAME_KEY];
    self.ingredientsTextView.text = [self.drink
objectForKey:INGREDIENTS_KEY];
    self.directionsTextView.text = [self.drink objectForKey:DIRECTIONS_
KEY];
}
```

DrinkDetailViewController.m

When <u>should</u> it get called?

_____

_____

_____

What classes are you going to need to update?

_____

_____

_____

What's the difference here between the iPad and the iPhone?

_____

_____

_____

BE the Detail View Controller
Your job is to play Detail View Controller and figure out why you're not displaying the right thing. Look at the code below and see if you can figure out what's going wrong...

When does this actually get called?

viewWillAppear gets called only when the view gets presented to the user. Not as the user interacts with the view.

DrinkDetailViewController.m

```
- (void)viewWillAppear:(BOOL)animated {
    [super viewWillAppear:animated];

    // Setup our UI with the provided drink
    self.nameTextField.text = [self.drink objectForKey:NAME_KEY];
    self.ingredientsTextView.text = [self.drink
objectForKey:INGREDIENTS_KEY];
    self.directionsTextView.text = [self.drink objectForKey:DIRECTIONS_
KEY];
}
```

When **should** it get called?

The detail view needs to be updated each time the user selects a row.

What classes are you going to need to update?

DrinkDetailViewController,
RootViewController

What's the difference here between the iPad and the iPhone?

That restrained hierarchy thing. The iPhone has to show two different views for the detail view and the root view. Since the views are together for the Split View Controller on the iPad, the view isn't being presented, but it still has to change.

A persistent view problem

We built things for the iPhone to populate the detail view when it's *about* to be displayed. The problem is that with the iPad version, it's *always* displayed. What worked well on the iPhone (repopulating the data as the view was presented) doesn't work well on the iPad, since it will only get one viewWillAppear message—right after the app launches. So what should we do?

The wrong solution would be to duplicate our viewWillAppear code. We're better developers than that, so we're going to refactor the code into a new method in the DrinkDetailViewController called refreshView that will repopulate the view when the drink changes (via a drinkChanged method).

Yeah, we said it. Duplicating that code would be bad. Not "maybe not a good idea" or "for now we can...blah blah". It would be BAD. Your code needs its dignity, too.

✷ Add this! ✷

.m
DrinkDetailViewController.m

```
-      (void)viewWillAppear:(BOOL)
animated {
       [super viewWillAppear:animated];
       [self refreshView];
}

- (void)refreshView {
      // Setup our UI with the provided drink
      self.nameTextField.text =         [self.drink objectForKey:NAME_KEY];
      self.ingredientsTextView.text = [self.drink objectForKey:INGREDIENTS_KEY];
      self.directionsTextView.text =    [self.drink objectForKey:DIRECTIONS_KEY];
}

- (void)drinkChanged:(NSDictionary *)newDrink {
      self.drink = newDrink;
      [self refreshView];
   }
```

Make sure you add a call to our new refreshView method in viewWillAppear.

This is code that has been pulled from viewWillAppear

Here's our new drinkChanged method, which updates the drink we're showing, then delegates to our new method to update the view.

.h
DrinkDetailViewController.h

```
-(void) refreshView;
-(void) drinkChanged:(NSDictionary *)newDrink;

@end
```

Don't forget the tableview

Instead of swapping out the table view when a row is selected, the detail view needs to change and the table view should stay the same—but only for the iPad, not the iPhone.

To fix that problem, we need to split the code, just like we did in our AppDelegate.

> What's the difference here between the iPad and the iPhone?
>
> That restrained hierarchy thing. The iPhone has to show two different views for the detail view and the root view. Since the views are together for the split view controller on the iPad, the view isn't being presented, but it still has to change.

 Add this!

```objc
@class DrinkDetailViewController;
@interface RootViewController : UITableViewController {
    NSMutableArray *drinks_;
    UIBarButtonItem *addButton_;
    DrinkDetailViewController *splitViewDetailView_;
}


@property (nonatomic, retain) IBOutlet DrinkDetailViewController
*splitViewDetailView;
```

RootViewController.h

```objc
@synthesize drinks=drinks_, addButton=addButton_, splitViewDetailView=spli
tViewDetailView_;
```

RootViewController.h

```objc
-    (void)dealloc             {
    [splitViewDetailView_ release];
    [drinks_ release];
    [addButton_ release];
    [super dealloc];
}
```

We need to check to see if we're on an iPad, and if so, use the new
drinkChanged method on our detailViewController. If we're not on an
iPad, just create and push a new detail view controller like before.

```objc
- (void)tableView:(UITableView *)tableView didSelectRowAtIndexPath:(NSIndexPath *)indexPath {

    if (!self.editing) {

        if (UI_USER_INTERFACE_IDIOM() == UIUserInterfaceIdiomPad) {

            [self.splitViewDetailView drinkChanged:[self.drinks objectAtIndex:indexPath.row]];

        }
        else {

            DrinkDetailViewController *detailViewController = [[DrinkDetailViewController alloc] initWithNibName:@"DrinkDetailViewController" bundle:nil];
            detailViewController.drink = [self.drinks objectAtIndex:indexPath.row];
            [self.navigationController pushViewController:detailViewController animated:YES];
            [detailViewController release];

        }
    }
    else {

        AddDrinkViewController *editingDrinkVC = [[AddDrinkViewController
```

RootViewController.h

Test Drive

Before you build and run, go into Interface Builder and link up the detail view in the split
pane to our new split ViewDetailView property on the RootViewController. Now you're
pushing the detail view onto the right-hand side of the pane, while the left-hand side is
still showing the table view.

Test Drive

Build and run the application. Now you're pushing the detail view onto the right-hand side of the pane, while the left-hand side is still showing the table view.

Everything's working!
In landscape at least...

But if you rotate the thing, it still doesn't look right.

Right.

To fully implement the Split View Controller, we need to have the **popover** working in the portrait view. If it doesn't, the user will be stuck in the detail view unless they rotate back to landscape.

WHO DOES WHAT?

Match each control in the landscape view (table, detail view, nav control) to its equivalent in the portrait view. Then you'll have an idea of what needs to go where!

Landscape

Portrait

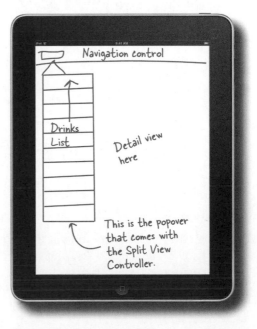

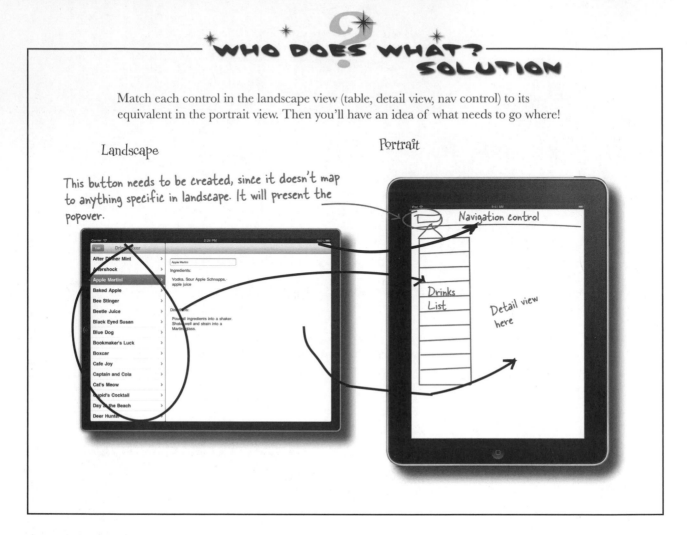

Present the popover!

The UISplitViewController, while awesome, doesn't do anything except manage the two views inside it. When the iPad is rotated to portrait, the views that we're working with are the same, just like you saw in the exercise. While DrinkMixer supports the detail view in portrait, we need to enable the other hidden view, the table view. We'll do this with the **popover**.

The **popover** is an iPad exclusive control that is used to present a table view temporarily, just to allow the user to select another detail view and keep working with the data. To manage moving the views around, we need to conform to the UISplitViewController delegate protocol and present the popover. We also need to set up a button to allow the user to access the popover view in the navigation control of the detail view in portrait.

Long Exercise

Go dive into the documentation and find out about the UISplitViewController delegate protocol. Use that to figure out how to implement the items below.

1   **Add the UIPopoverController to DrinkDetailViewController.h.**
Create an instance variable named popOver_ and a corresponding property that's an IBOutlet.

2   **Synthesize and dealloc popOver_ in DrinkDetailViewController.m.**

3   **Implement UISplitViewDelegate methods in DrinkDetailView Controller.m.**
Get started based on what you can find in the documentation. We're going to implement the button in code. If you get stuck, it's on the next page.

4   **Use Xcode to edit the view so that the SplitViewController delegate outlet is connected to our DrinkDetailViewController.**
You'll have to open up the iPad main window and expand the Split View Controller to make the connection.

Note that it's the DrinkDetailViewController acting as the Split View Controller's delegate. That's the view that's visible when we go to portrait, so that's the view that has to handle the popover.

Once you're finished implementing the Split View Controller delegate, it can handle all the information properly in landscape and portrait.

1 **Add the UIPopoverController to DrinkDetailViewController.h.**
Create an instance variable named popOver_ and a corresponding property that's an IBOutlet.

```
@interface DrinkDetailViewController : UIViewController
<UISplitViewControllerDelegate> {
@private
     UITextField *nameTextField_;
     UITextView *ingredientsTextView_;
     UITextView *directionsTextView_;
     UIScrollView *scrollView_;
     NSDictionary *drink_;
   UIPopoverController *popOver_;
}


@property (nonatomic, retain) UIPopoverController *popOver;
```

DrinkDetailViewController.h

2 **Synthesize and dealloc popOver_ in DrinkDetailViewController.m.**

```
@synthesize drink=drink_,
nameTextField=nameTextField_, ing
redientsTextView=ingredientsTextVi
ew_, directionsTextView=directions
TextView_, scrollView=scrollView_,
popOver=popOver_;
```

DrinkDetailViewController.m

```
- (void)dealloc {
     [nameTextField_ release];
     [ingredientsTextView_ release];
     [directionsTextView_ release];
     [scrollView_ release];
     [drink_ release];
     [popOver_ release];
     [super dealloc];
}
```

③ **Implement UISplitViewDelegate methods in DrinkDetailViewController.m.**
Get started based on what you can find in the documentation. We're going to implement the button in code. If you get stuck, it's on the next page.

```objc
#pragma mark - UISplitViewDelegate methods


- (void)splitViewController:(UISplitViewController *)svc willHideViewContr
oller:(UIViewController *)aViewController withBarButtonItem:(UIBarButtonIt
em *)barButtonItem forPopoverController:(UIPopoverController *)pc {

    barButtonItem.title = @"Drinks";


    [self.navigationItem setLeftBarButtonItem:barButtonItem animated:YES];
    self.popOver = pc;

}

- (void) splitViewController:(UISplitViewController *)svc willShowViewContr
oller:(UIViewController *)aViewController invalidatingBarButtonItem:(UIBarB
uttonItem *)barButtonItem {


    [self.navigationItem setLeftBarButtonItem:nil animated:YES];
    self.popOver = nil;

}
```

This method will be called by the splitViewController when it has to hide the left-hand view controller. This method gives us a popover controller and button that we can use to show that hidden view when necessary.

This method gets called when the splitViewController can put the left-hand view controller back. We just ditch the button.

DrinkDetailViewController.m

LONG EXERCISE SOLUTION

④ **Use Xcode to edit the view so that the SplitViewController delegate outlet is talking to the DrinkDetailViewController.**

You'll have to open up the iPad main window and expand the Split View Controller to make the connection.

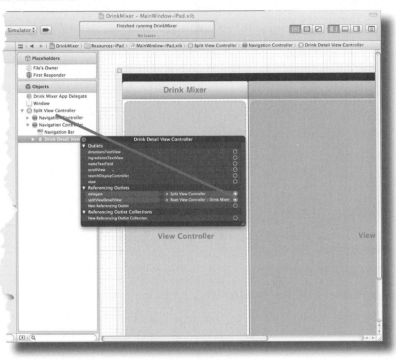

Do this! ✱

One last thing—the drinkChanged method needs a quick update.

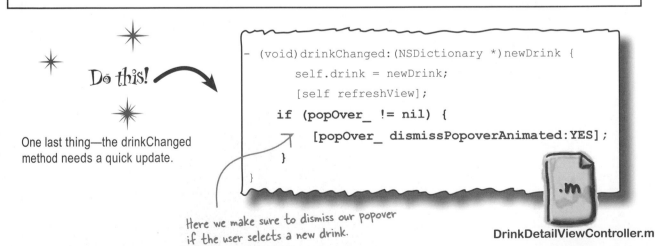

```
- (void)drinkChanged:(NSDictionary *)newDrink {
        self.drink = newDrink;
        [self refreshView];
    if (popOver_ != nil) {
        [popOver_ dismissPopoverAnimated:YES];
    }
}
```

Here we make sure to dismiss our popover if the user selects a new drink.

DrinkDetailViewController.m

TEST DRIVE

Everything should be working now! Try using the button and rotating the simulator.

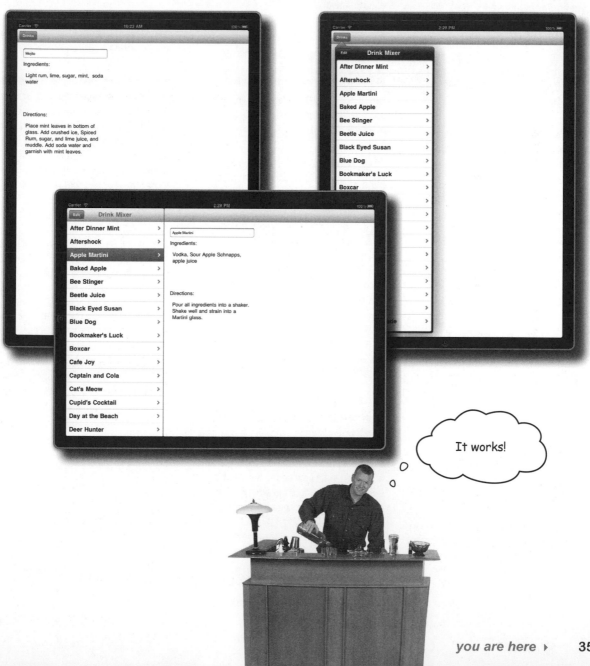

It works!

there are no
Dumb Questions

Q: **The detail view still doesn't look all that great. Shouldn't we fix that?**

A: If we were going up on the App Store, yes. In our next iPad app, later in the book, we're going to focus a lot more on look and feel. For now, we wanted you to get the controls figured out.

Q: **When we enabled various launch orientations in Xcode, what did that actually do?**

A: If you take a look at your Info.plist in your project, you'll see that Xcode quietly added an array of enumerations that list the launch orientations you support. The GUI option we used is just a convenience (and new in Xcode 4) for setting those values. iOS looks at your app's Info.plist to figure out what launch orientations it can use.

Q: **You mentioned the ~ipad thing was standard. Standard for what?**

A: Before the iPad, launch screens were simply named Default.png, then Default-Portrait.png and Default-Landscape.png. Once the iPad entered the scene, Apple added the concept of ~<device> to filenames. iOS will pick the most appropriate file based on device type. It does something similar with the @2x notation for high-resolution (iPhone 4 Retina display).

Q: **Are popovers only used with Split View Controllers?**

A: Most definitely not! Popovers are used pretty often in iPad applications. They're very straightforward to use—they simply wrap a view and you can tell them which control they should appear next to. See the documentation for UIPopoverController for more information.

Q: **We really didn't do much to support the various screen orientations. Is that normal?**

A: It really depends on your application. When you edit the size information of a control in Xcode, you can set its Autoresizing properties. With those properties, you can anchor a control to the top, bottom, or sides and control whether it stretches when the view changes size (which is typically due to a rotation). If you're using roughly the same layout for both landscape and portrait (which we are, minus the table view), you can use Autosizing to get you what you want.

For more complicated views, you might hide or show entire controls or resize and re-layout controls depending on the orientation. There are a number of view controller callbacks that will get called while the view is rotating to its new orientation, and in there you can update the size, position, and visibility of your controls if necessary.

Typically, you'll use view animations here to make sure things transition smoothly.

Q: **What happens if I try to use a popover on the iPhone?**

A: Very, very bad things. There are controls and features that only exist on a particular device (and within a particular iOS version). When the iPad first came out, you couldn't even rely on there being a class name UIPopoverController on the iPhone. Now that's gotten a little simpler, but you must always check that you're on a particular device or that the device has the feature you are about to use before trying to do it.

Depending on what versions of iOS you support, you will also need to check to make sure certain classes exist before doing anything with them. For example, older code will often have the popover reference we added in the detail view controller declared as type "id" since you couldn't assume the UIPopoverController was a valid type on iPhones. If you support old versions of iOS, you'll need to do the same. Apple has excellent documentation on writing backward compatible code that you should look into if you're going to support older versions of iOS.

iPad Cross

Let's get the right brain working. Here are some vocab words from your first iPad chapter.

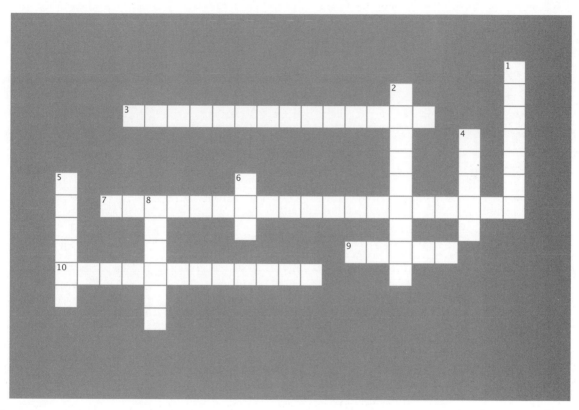

Across

3. _____ is what you're doing when you implement code that differs by device
7. This control is iPad specific and controls other views.
9. These are not just big iphones
10. iPads need to support all _____.

Down

1. This control is used only on iPad
2. Apps compiled for both iPhone and iPad are
4. The Split View Controller keeps track of _____ views
5. To implement the popover, you need to add a _____ to the portrait view.
6. This covers UI for iPhone and iPad
8. The images display when the app is starting up

iPad Cross Solution

Let's get the right brain working. Here are some vocab words from your first iPad chapter.

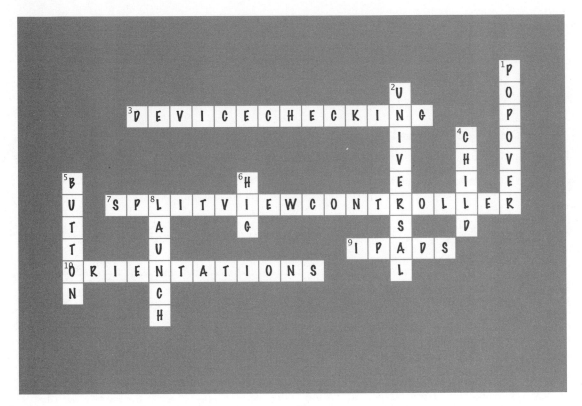

Across

3. _____ is what you're doing when you implement code that differs by device [DEVICECHECKING]
7. This control is iPad specific and controls other views. [SPLITVIEWCONTROLLER]
9. These are not just big iphones [IPADS]
10. iPads need to support all _____. [ORIENTATIONS]

Down

1. This control is used only on iPad [POPOVER]
2. Apps compiled for both iPhone and iPad are [UNIVERSAL]
4. The Split View Controller keeps track of _____ views [CHILD]
5. To implement the popover, you need to add a _____ to the portrait view. [BUTTON]
6. This covers UI for iPhone and iPad [HIG]
8. The images display when the app is starting up [LAUNCH]

Your iOS Development Toolbox

You've got Chapter 7 under your belt and now you've added a bunch of iPad controls to your toolbox.

iPad HIG

There are iPad-specific controls, and some rules differ between iPhone and iPad.

The Split View Controller and popovers are iPad-specific controls.

Universal Apps

Depending on how you want to distribute your app, you can build two apps or a Universal app. Universal apps are only sold once, but they contain code for both the iPhone and iPad, which makes maintenance easier and the customers happy!

Device Checking

Once you build a Universal app, you'll need to check for different devices so your app can behave differently as needed.

Split View Controller

This controller's job is to keep track of two child views that are displayed differently in portrait and landscape. Once you set it up properly, you can have a small number of views that display lots of different ways.

8 tab bars and Core Data

Enterprise
~~Bounty hunter apps~~

Here's what I 've found: we just can't be competitive anymore without an iPhone app!

Enterprise apps mean managing more data in different ways.

Companies large and small are a significant market for iPhone and iPad apps. A small handheld device with a custom app can be huge for companies that have staff on the go. Most of these apps are going to manage lots of data, and since iOS 3.0, there has been built-in Core Data support. Working with that and another new controller—the tab bar controller—we're going to build an app for justice!

HF bounty hunting

> With my business, I'm out of the office a lot. The courts will let me submit evidence from my iPhone now, so I need an app for that to get paid. I picked up an iPad while I was at it, since I figured it would help me do more detailed research during boring stakeouts. Can you help me with some apps for both?

Bob the bounty hunter

Bob needs some help.

Bounty hunting is *not* a desk job; Bob needs lots of information to pick up fugitives on the go. His iPhone is ideal to take along while he's chasing bad guys, while his iPad will great for more detailed background work. Here's what Bob needs in his apps:

iPhone App

1. Bob needs a list of fugitives. He has to keep track of everyone he's looking for, along with people he's captured.

2. He wants to be able to quickly display a list of just the captured fugitives.

3. He also needs a display of the detailed information about each fugitive, like what they're wanted for, where they were last seen, and how much their bounty is.

iPad App

1. Details on past whereabouts. They'll have a location and details about what the fugitive was doing there.

2. For research, Bob needs the full dossier on each fugitive. Picture and details should all be in the same view.

3. All the information he uses in the iPhone app, too.

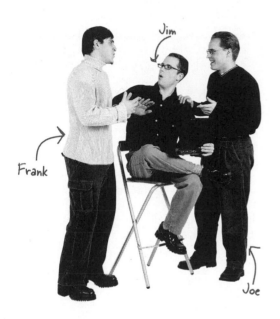

Jim: OK, so he wants the entire package, iPhone and iPad. Where do we start?

Frank: Well, we're going to want to create another universal app.

Joe: Right, then we can keep the logic and everything together, just like we did last time, but with different views.

Jim: OK, so what do we do first?

Joe: What if we start with the iPad, write that, and then do the iPhone, since it's smaller?

Frank: Two things. First, we need to design everything.

Jim: Why?

Frank: Because we want to figure out what the two views will have in common and make sure it's set up right.

Jim: Oh.

Frank: Second, since the customer gets paid based on using the iPhone app, pretty sure he's going to want that first.

Joe: But it's smaller! I think we should do the hardest one first.

Frank: Listen, we work for Bob and this is what he wants.

Joe: OK, so the plan is...

Jim: We'll start with designing both views, then code up the iPhone and the backend together.

Frank: Right, then we can lay the iPad view on top.

Jim: OK, let's get started.

Make it Stick

Universal Apps

If you're planning on supporting both devices from the beginning, it's best to start with an app set up to do just that. Remember, a universal app comes with all this stuff built right in:

● **One binary file to maintain.**
The files will compile together and support both devices. That means that changes only need to be tracked once.

● **UIs will be separate.**
Universal apps have two separate view controllers and Interface Builder files, one each for the iPhone view and the iPad view.

● **Shared code needs device checking.**
Since all of the logic code will be shared (if we do our job right), there's going to need to be more device checking than before. Instead of just 4 generations of iPhones and iPod Touches, you'll also need to watch out for iPad-specific stuff.

● **Universal apps are sold once, used twice.**
The way the App Store is set up, universal apps are sold as an app that will run on both devices. Users buy the app, put it in their iTunes libraries, and then those who have iPhones and iPads can install it on both as a native app. It may look and act differently, like iBountyHunter will, but you only get paid once.

It's something to consider. The iPad app store is full of XD and XL versions of apps that you can charge for again.

Now for some UI work...

 Sharpen your pencil

Now, what is this iPad app going to look like? Since iPad apps MUST support both landscape and portrait, you need to think about both.

<u>Portrait Orientation</u>

Remember—the HIG wants you to have different-looking views for the different orientations...

<u>Landscape Orientation</u>

Sharpen your pencil
Solution

Here's what we came up with for this iPad app—don't worry if yours is a bit different! Since iPad apps are expected to support both orientations differently, we're using the Split View Controller that we used for DrinkMixer.

To show the list of fugitives, we'll have a popover that can appear in this corner with this full list.

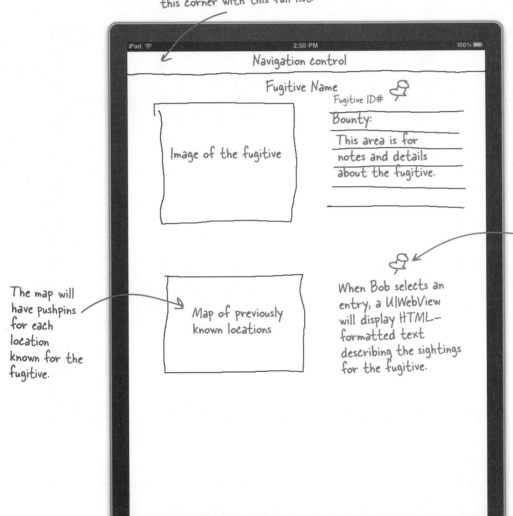

We'll add some fun UI touches, too, like a pushpin holding the description.

The map will have pushpins for each location known for the fugitive.

When Bob selects an entry, a UIWebView will display HTML-formatted text describing the sightings for the fugitive.

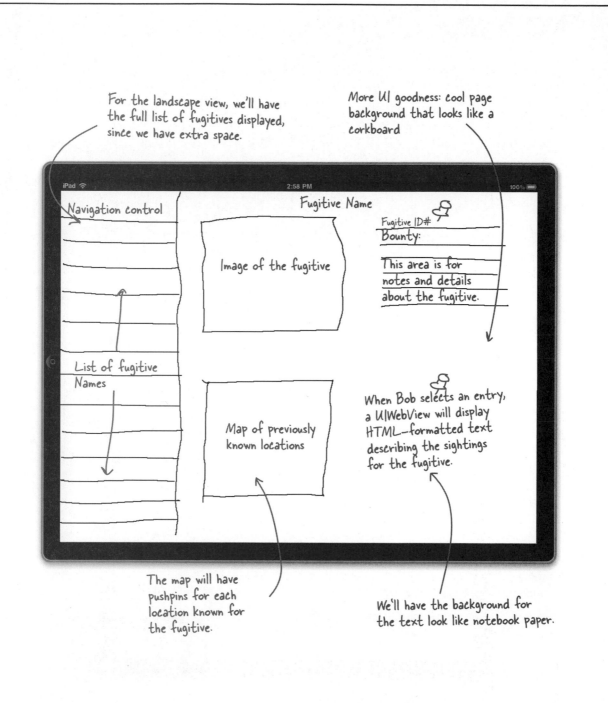

For the landscape view, we'll have the full list of fugitives displayed, since we have extra space.

More UI goodness: cool page background that looks like a corkboard

Navigation control

Fugitive Name

Fugitive ID#
Bounty:

Image of the fugitive

This area is for notes and details about the fugitive.

List of fugitive Names

When Bob selects an entry, a UIWebView will display HTML—formatted text describing the sightings for the fugitive.

Map of previously known locations

The map will have pushpins for each location known for the fugitive.

We'll have the background for the text look like notebook paper.

A new iPhone control

Now that we've designed the larger interface, we need to get into the iPhone views. In some ways, designing an iPhone view after an iPad is more difficult. Smaller screen size and shorter interaction times are the key things to consider in creating this view, especially when there's plenty of data to display.

To leverage the smaller screen, we're going to use a new controller: the **tab bar**.

iPhone App

① Bob needs a list of fugitives. He has to keep track of everyone he's looking for, along with people he's captured.

② He wants to be able to quickly display a list of just the captured fugitives.

③ He also needs a display of the detailed information about each fugitive, like what they're wanted for, where they were last seen, and how much their bounty is.

Tab Bar Up Close

The Tab Bar Controller is another common iPhone interface. Unlike the Navigation Controller, there isn't really a stack. All the views are created up front and easily accessed by clicking the tab, with each tab being tied to a specific view.

Tab bars are better suited to tasks or data that are related, but not necessarily hierarchical. The UITabBarController keeps track of all of the views and swaps between them based on user input.

Standard iPhone apps that have tab bar controllers include the phone app and the iPod.

The tab bar can contain any view you need.

The tabs themselves can contain text and/or an image.

Sharpen your pencil

Take a second to go back to Bob's requirements and your iPad UI—think about how many views you'll need for the iPhone version and then sketch up what you think you'll need to build.

Sharpen your pencil
Solution

For the iPhone app, we're going to need three views.
Using Bob's parameters, here's what we came up with.

1 Bob needs a list of fugitives. He keeps track of everyone he's looking for or has captured.

2 Bob wants to be able to quickly display a list of just the captured fugitives.

We'll keep track of the fugitive data sorted by name.

The quickest way to switch between different lists is with a tab bar controller.

For each list, we'll use a table view, like we did with DrinkMixer.

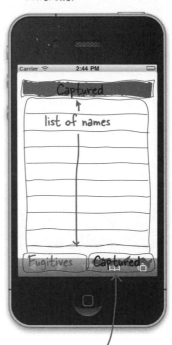

With the tab bar controller, the user can click on the tab at the bottom of the screen to jump between views.

Sharpen your pencil
Solution

3 Bob wants a separate display with the detailed information about each fugitive.

For managing these data, we're going to use a technology introduced with the 3.0 iOS SDK, Core Data. It can manage a lot of different data types for your app.

The detail view for each fugitive will be available by clicking on any name.

This area is for notes and details about the fugitive.

The tab bar controller will still be visible.

Fugitive Name
Fugitive ID#

Bounty:

Fugitives   Captured

---

there are no
Dumb Questions

Q: Why are there so many UI touches in the iPad version?

A: The iPad is all about eye candy, so we're going to show you how to add some! To get an idea of the importance of realistic UI to Apple, go check out the iPad HIG.

Another good way to get an idea of what they're focused on is to go play with the Mail app on an iPad. There are a lot of little touches aimed at realism.

Q: How do I keep track of integrating the iPad and the iPhone UIs together?

A: Good question. Now that we have the UI worked out for the iPad, it's a good idea to sit down and make up a list of the fields that we've included. Since the iPhone app is smaller, we should take the iPad list of fields and pick and choose the ones we need.

Q: Can I embed a Navigation Control inside of a tab bar controller?

A: Yes, you can, but NOT the other way around. If you have too much information to fit within one tab, but the contents are related, this may be the way to go.

Choose a template to start iBountyHunter

This time around, we have a lot going on in our app. A universal app with a Navigation Controller, a tab bar, and Core Data, too. As we saw earlier, the only template that supports universal apps right now is the window-based app; so we'll start there and add the tab bar and the Navigation Controller with Interface Builder and a little bit of code.

After you pick the window-based application, you get this dialog box.

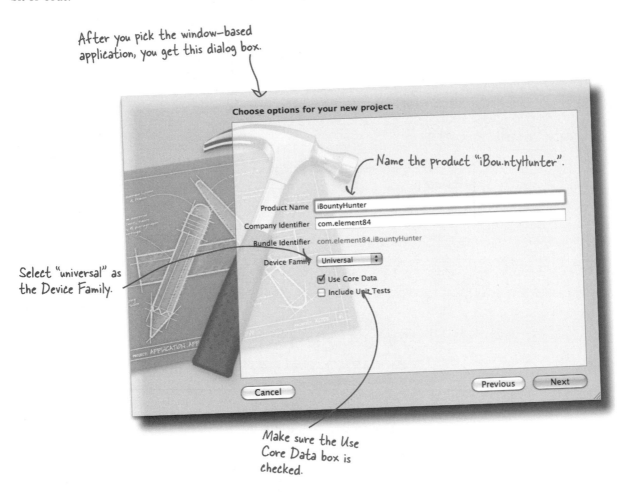

Name the product "iBou.ntyHunter".

Select "universal" as the Device Family.

Make sure the Use Core Data box is checked.

I just checked out the new file folders. They're completely different than what we had earlier when we upgraded our target to be a universal app for DrinkMixer.

Yes!

This app is being designed with two front ends in mind from the start. That means that we need to be smart about how we split up the functionality, with some of the logic shared for both UIs and some for each device.

Let's take a closer look...

There's a different structure for universal apps

Since we're starting out building an app that will build for both devices, there's a different structure from the beginning. Some logic will be shared between the two devices, like data management, while the UI logic will be separated for each device.

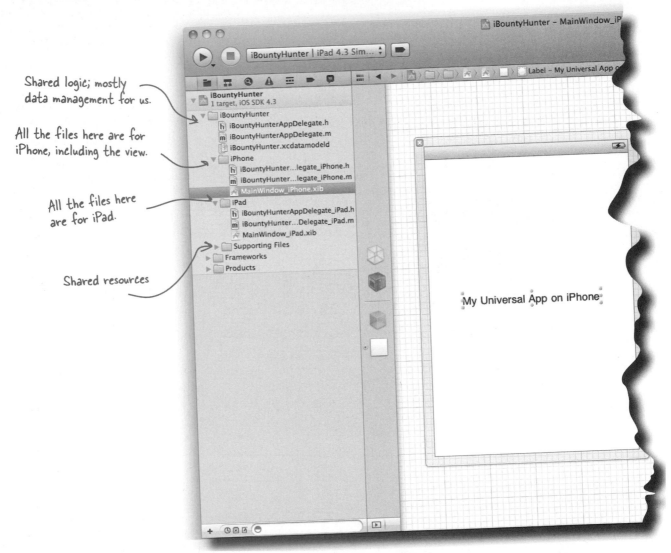

Shared logic; mostly data management for us.

All the files here are for iPhone, including the view.

All the files here are for iPad.

Shared resources

Now that we have the files in place, let's focus on the iPhone stuff first...

Jim: OK, what do we do now? All we have is an empty view.

Joe: Well, we need to add two table views, the tab bar navigation controller to switch between those views, and the detail view.

Frank: So do we need a bunch of new nib files to handle all these views and controls?

Jim: Ugh. This basic template gave us nothing!

Joe: It's not so bad. I like to think of it as a blank slate. Let's see, we can start with the tab bar and tab bar controller...

Frank: Right, that will switch between the two table views for Fugitive and Captured. Those views will each need nav controllers as well, to get in and out of the detailed view.

Joe: So do we need separate nibs for the tab bar and those two views? It seems like maybe we could have all those controls in just one nib, for the tab bar and the two views, since they're basically the same.

Jim: Yeah, but we'd still need view controllers, headers, and .m files for each of those views.

Joe: Yup, they're the views that need the tables in them. We'd also need a detail view with it's own nib and view controller, with the .h and .m files, right?

Frank: That sounds about right. We can use Interface Builder to create the tab bar and navigation controllers.

Joe: What do we do about the rest of the stuff? Add new files in Xcode?

Frank: That'll work—like before, we just need to specify that the nib files are created at the same time, and we should be good to go.

Jim: I think that all makes sense—it's a lot to keep track of.

Joe: Well, we're combining like three different things now, so it's definitely going to get more complicated! Maybe it would help to diagram how this will all fit together?

Drawing how iBountyHunter iPhone works...

The main tab controller is going to be responsible for presenting a few different views to the user, and our data will be stored in a SQLite database. Putting all this info together is definitely easier if you can see how it all works.

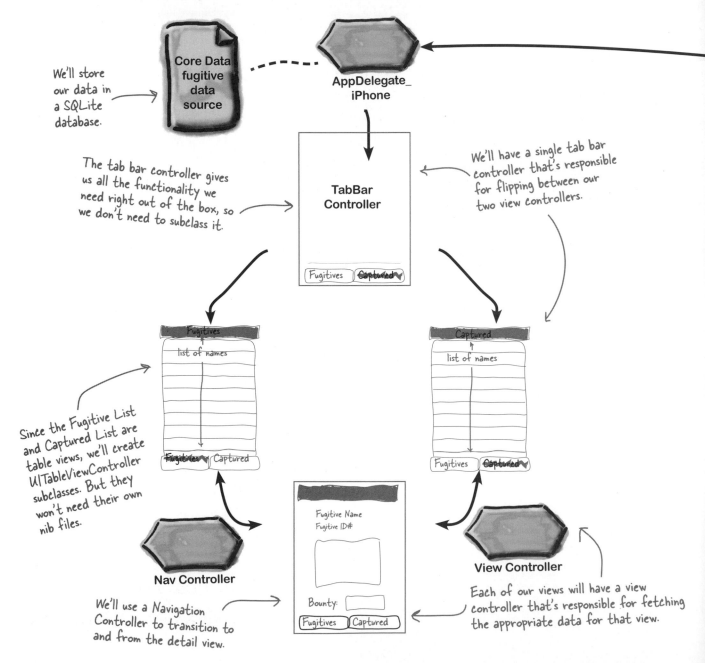

We'll store our data in a SQLite database.

The tab bar controller gives us all the functionality we need right out of the box, so we don't need to subclass it.

We'll have a single tab bar controller that's responsible for flipping between our two view controllers.

Since the Fugitive List and Captured List are table views, we'll create UITableViewController subclasses. But they won't need their own nib files.

We'll use a Navigation Controller to transition to and from the detail view.

Each of our views will have a view controller that's responsible for fetching the appropriate data for that view.

...and how it fits with the universal app

The AppDelegate_Shared class works for controlling views and data within the entire app structure. Once you get into either the iPhone or the iPad app, each one has its own AppDelegate to control the views and data within each individual app.

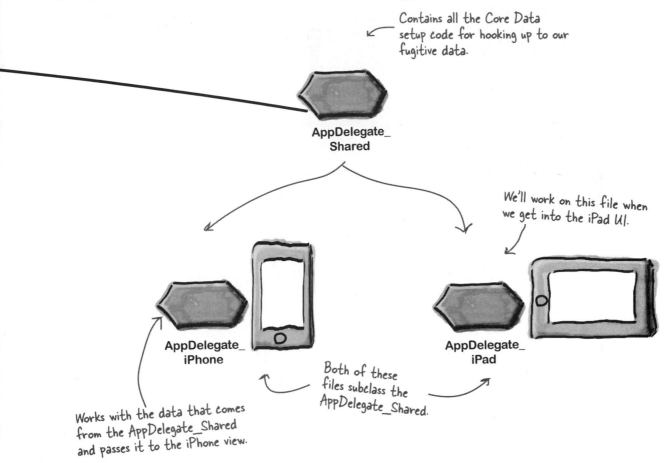

Contains all the Core Data setup code for hooking up to our fugitive data.

AppDelegate_Shared

We'll work on this file when we get into the iPad UI.

AppDelegate_iPhone

AppDelegate_iPad

Both of these files subclass the AppDelegate_Shared.

Works with the data that comes from the AppDelegate_Shared and passes it to the iPhone view.

Now that you know how the views all fit together...

Jim

Joe

Frank

Joe: That helps a lot. So we only need two nibs: one to handle the controls for the tab bar switching between Fugitive and Captured views and another to handle the detail view.

Frank: I get it. We need to put the table view components somewhere, and we can either create new nibs for each view and have the tab controller load them...

Jim: ...or we can just include it all in one nib. Easy!

Frank: Exactly. Since we don't plan to reuse those table views anywhere else and they're not too complicated, we can keep everything a bit simpler with just one nib.

Jim: And we need view controllers for the two table views, along with the detail view. They'll handle getting the right data, depending on which view the user is in.

Frank: Plus a Navigation Controller for the table views to transition to and from the detail view.

Joe: I think we're ready to start building!

Jim: Call me picky, but I'd still like to list it all out...

iBountyHunter To Do List

1. Create view controllers (both .h and .m files) for the Fugitive and Captured views.
2. Create the tab bar view and add the tab bar controller to it, along with a reference from the app delegate.
3. Add the Nav Controllers for the Fugitive and Captured views.
4. Build the table views for the Fugitive and Captured views.
5. Create a detail view with a nib and a view controller with .h and .m files.

there are no
Dumb Questions

Q: Why are we using a tab bar controller *and* a table view?

A: Our Fugitive data is hierarchical and lends itself well to a table view. The problem is, we have two table views: the Fugitive list and the Captured list. To support two top-level lists, we chose a tab bar.

Q: Couldn't you have done something similar with a toggle switch, like a UISegmentControl?

A: Yes, we could have. It's really a UI design choice. The two lists are really different lists, not just different ways of sorting or organizing the same data. It's subjective, though.

Q: OK, I'm still a bit confused about the business with using just one nib for the tab controller and the two table views.

A: Well, there is a lot going on in this app, and we could have done this a different way. We could create two more nibs, each with a Nav Controller and a table view in it. Then we'd tell the Tab Bar Controller to load the first one as the Fugitive List and the second one as the Captured List. Rather than do that, since the views look the same, we just put all those controls for the list in the same nib as the tab bar. Remember, the nib is just the UI controls, not the behavior.

Q: Can you use a tab bar controller for the iPad, too?

A: Yup, but you might not need them. With the Split View Controller (which we'll be using), you can display both a list and some details on the same screen, so you may be able to handle your data filtering with other elements.

Exercise

Create a new class for the Fugitive view controller in Xcode, and then add your tab bar controller in Interface Builder.

① **Create one new class with .m and .h. files.**
These will be the view controllers for the Fugitive List and the Captured List. We'll start with FugitiveListViewController.h and .m for now, which needs to be a subclass of UITableViewController, so select "UITableViewController subclass" from the drop-down in the Utilities pane.

② **Add the tab bar controller.**
In Interface Builder, open the MainWindow_iPhone.xib to get started, and drop the tab bar controller in the view.

We'll help you take it from there!

Create a new class for the Fugitive view controller in Xcode, and then add your tab bar controller in Interface Builder.

Exercise Solution

① **Create one new class with .m and .h files.**

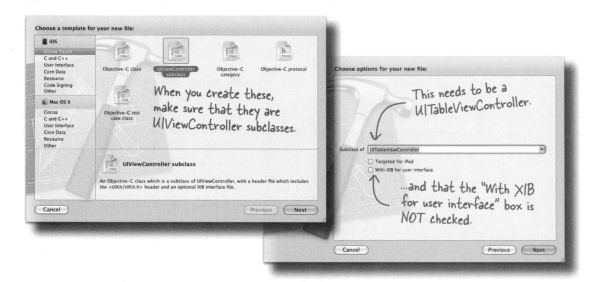

When you create these, make sure that they are UIViewController subclasses.

This needs to be a UITableViewController.

...and that the "With XIB for user interface" box is NOT checked.

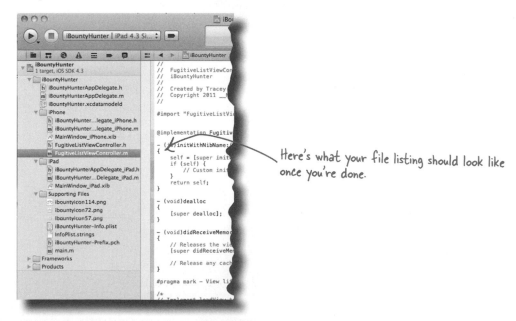

Here's what your file listing should look like once you're done.

2 **Add the tab bar controller.**

The window template doesn't give us a whole lot out of the box. We're going to use Xcode to assemble our views and view controllers the way we want them.

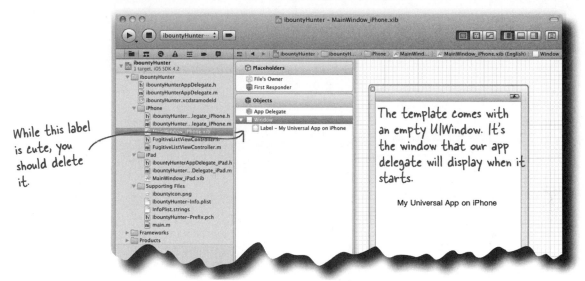

While this label is cute, you should delete it.

The template comes with an empty UIWindow. It's the window that our app delegate will display when it starts.

Drag the tab bar controller from the Library into your main window listing. This will create your TabController view.

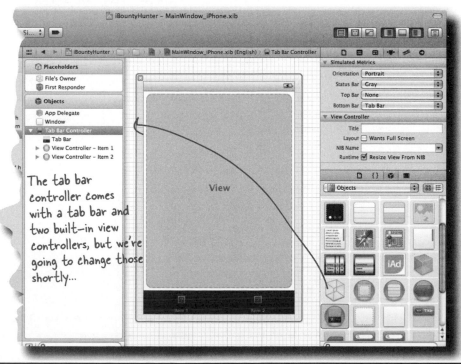

The tab bar controller comes with a tab bar and two built-in view controllers, but we're going to change those shortly...

Build the fugitive list view

We're going to focus on the Fugitive List first, but the same steps will apply to the Captured List when we get to it.

1 **Delete those two view controllers and replace them with Navigation Controllers.**
Since we want all the functionality that comes with a Nav Controller, delete those View Controllers and drag two new Nav Controllers in their place from the Library. Make sure they're listed underneath the tab bar controller.

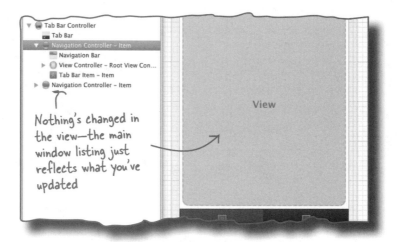

Nothing's changed in the view—the main window listing just reflects what you've updated

2 **Change the view controller to the FugitiveListView controller.**
Highlight the view controller under the first Navigation Controller and use the inspector in the utility panel to change the **Class** to FugitiveListViewController.

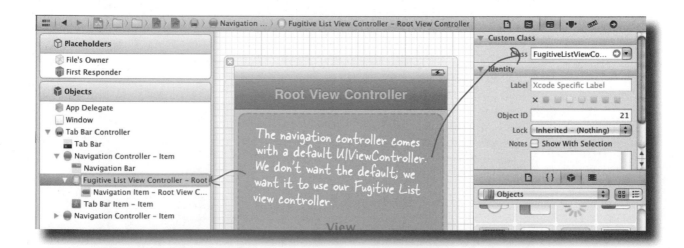

The navigation controller comes with a default UIViewController. We don't want the default; we want it to use our Fugitive List view controller.

❸ **Set the names in the tabbar and navbar.**

To change the title for the Fugitive List view controller, double-click on the title in the nav bar and type "Fugitives". For the tab, in the Utilities pane, change the **Bar Item Title** to "Fugitives".

Updated Nav Controller title is changed with the badge item.

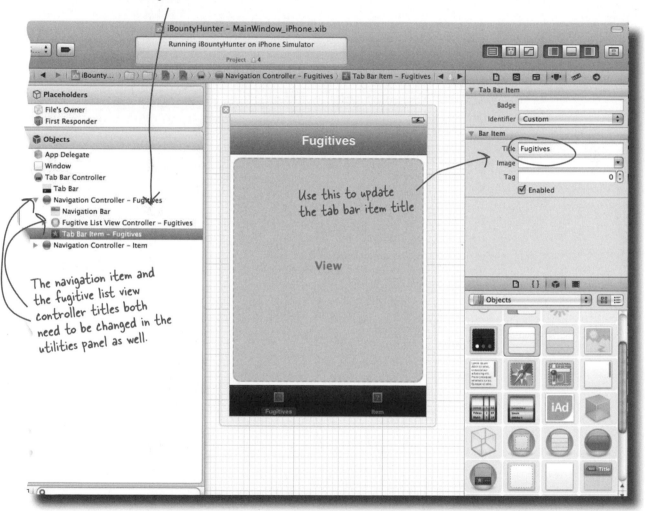

Use this to update the tab bar item title

The navigation item and the fugitive list view controller titles both need to be changed in the utilities panel as well.

We see the warnings.

Yes, there are a couple in there. Don't worry, we're going to fix them soon. If you want to figure out what they are, it wouldn't hurt!

Next up: the Captured view

You've just gone through and created the classes for your two table views and
dropped in a tab controller to switch between the two. You've already checked
quite a few things off your list!

Remember this from the
conversation earlier?

iBountyHunter To Do List

1. ~~Create view controllers (both .h and .m
files) for the Fugitive and Captured views.~~
2. ~~Create the tab bar view and add the
tab bar controller to it,~~ along with a
reference from the app delegate.
3. ~~Add the nav controllers for the Fugitive
and Captured views.~~
4. ~~Build the table views for the Fugitive
and Captured views.~~
5. Create a detail view with a nib and a
view controller with .h and .m files.

We haven't done this
yet. That's going to
mean some code and IB
work; we'll come back to
it in a minute.

Just do the same
thing we did earlier
with the Fugitives
view for these two
items.

BE the Developer

Your job is to be the developer and finish up the work in Xcode and Interface Builder to get the Fugitive and Captured views working with the tab bar controller. Use the To Do list from Jim, Frank, and Joe to figure out what's left.

It's up to you to create the captured view and then connect the views up with the tab bar controller...

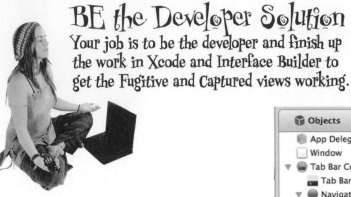

BE the Developer Solution
Your job is to be the developer and finish up the work in Xcode and Interface Builder to get the Fugitive and Captured views working.

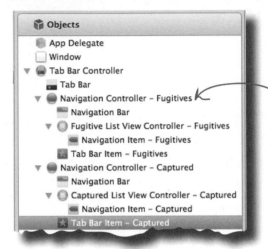

You should end up with a list that looks like this.

Create your Captured view.
Follow the same steps from earlier for creating the Fugitive view.

Then wire up the tab bar controller.
To do this, we need to go back to IBountyHunterAppDelegate_iPhone.h. Right now, there isn't an outlet to connect the tab bar controller to anything, so it won't work. You should be pretty familiar with how to do this by now. Here's the outlet you need for a tab controller:

Since the tab bar doesn't apply to the iPad

iBountyHunterAppDelegate_iPhone.h

```
#import <UIKit/UIKit.h>
#import "iBountyHunterAppDelegate.h"


@interface iBountyHunterAppDelegate_iPhone : iBountyHunterAppDelegate {
    UITabBarController *tabBarController_;
    }


@property (nonatomic, retain) IBOutlet UITabBarController *tabBarController;
@end
```

Almost there...

Here, we'll need to wire up the App Delegate to the Tab Bar Controller.

```
@implementation iBountyHunterAppDelegate_iPhone
@synthesize tabController=tabBarController_;
```

```
- (void) dealloc {
      [tabBarController_release];
      [super dealloc];
  }
```

iBountyHunterAppDelegate_iPhone.m

Clear up the warnings.

The UITableViewController in XCode 4 comes with the numberOfSectionsInTableView: and numberOfRowsInSection: methods declared with #warnings so you don't forget to set them up.

Make sure that you delete the #warning lines.

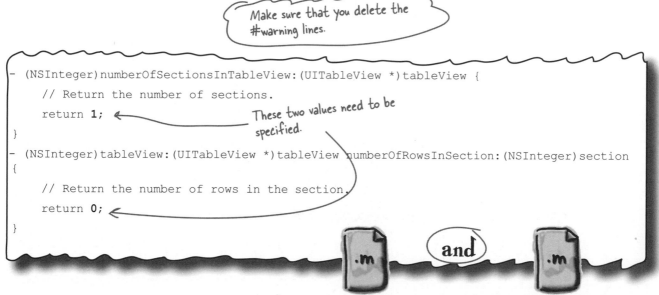

```
- (NSInteger)numberOfSectionsInTableView:(UITableView *)tableView {
    // Return the number of sections.
    return 1;
}
- (NSInteger)tableView:(UITableView *)tableView numberOfRowsInSection:(NSInteger)section
{
    // Return the number of rows in the section.
    return 0;
}
```

These two values need to be specified.

FugitiveListViewController.m and **CapturedListViewController.m**

TEST DRIVE

You've just done a lot of work on your app—new view controllers, new Nav Controllers, table views—all from scratch. Build and run to make sure that everything's working.

Check and make sure that you have the iPhone Simulator scheme selected in Xcode, so the iPad doesn't launch instead.

Ugh! Nothing! Why isn't the tab bar controller (or anything else) being displayed?

Sharpen your pencil

Figure out why all you see is an empty view. Look at what we did earlier in Interface Builder (shown below) and see if you can figure out what's missing. Write what you think on the lines below.

The window template doesn't give us a whole lot out of the box. We're going to use Xcode to assemble our views and view controllers the way we want them.

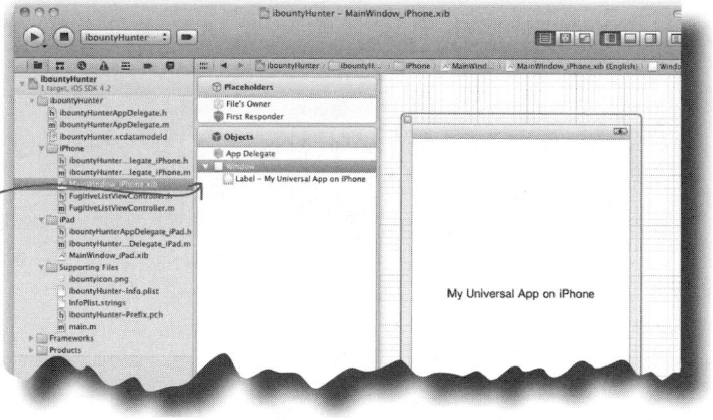

While this label is cute, you should delete it.

My Universal App on iPhone

Drag the tab bar controller from the Library into your main window listing. This will create your TabController view:

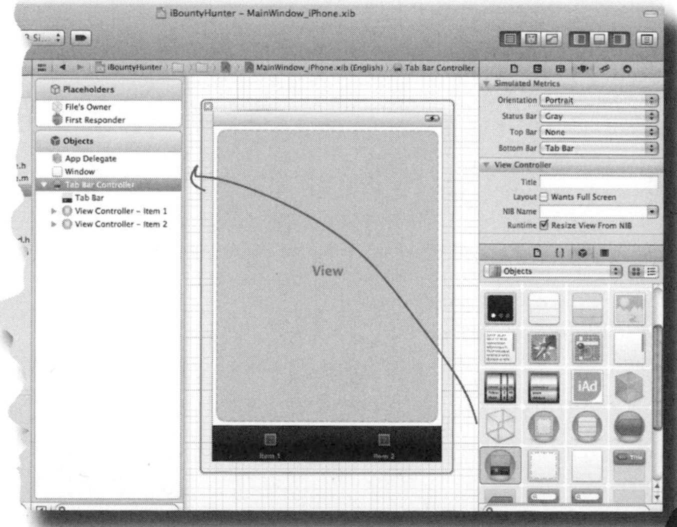

....

....

....

....

....

....

....

....

there are no
Dumb Questions

Q: **We have a lot jammed in our main window nib. It still seems kinda strange to me.**

A: The nib for iBountyHunter contains five controllers (the tab bar, two Nav Controllers, and our FugitiveListViewController and CapturedListViewController) and their associated components. If you're still having trouble with the idea, it might help to open the MainWindow.xib file in Interface Builder and view it in tree mode. Expanding the hierarchy shows the structure of our app. We have a single nib with a tab bar controller, which internally has two Nav Controllers nested underneath it that are instances of FugitiveListViewController and CapturedListViewController, respectively.

Q: **Can I add icons to the tab bar tabs?**

A: Absolutely. The easiest way is to pick a standard icon using Interface Builder. To do that, click on the question mark icon on the tab you want to change, then change the Identifier in the Inspector. If you want to use a custom image, set the Identifier to custom, then select your image in the Image field (you'll need to add it to your project, just like we did with the application icon earlier). There are a couple of peculiarities with Tab Bar icons, though: they should be 30x30, and the alpha values in the icon are used to actually create the image. You can't specify colors or anything like that.

Q: **How many views can I have in a tabbar?**

A: As many as you want. If you add more views than can fit across the tab bar at the bottom, the UITabBarController will automatically add a "More" item and show the rest in a table view. By default, the UITabBarController also includes an Edit button that lets the user edit which tabs are on the bottom bar.

Q: **Is there any way of knowing when a user switches tabs?**

A: Yes, there's a UITabBarDelegate protocol you can conform to and set as the tab bar delegate. You'll be notified when the users are customizing the bottom bar and when they change tabs.

Q: **Why did we add a reference to the tab bar controller in the App Delegate?**

A: We've added the tab bar controller to the nib, but there's a little more tweaking we're going to have to do to get everything displaying properly. Go ahead and give it a Test Drive to see what's going on...

BULLET POINTS

- As apps get more complex, building the UI becomes more difficult.

- The hierarchy view for the xib files helps visualize how the components go together.

- Separating the iPhone and iPad UIs is important, but the logic needs to remain consistent.

Sharpen your pencil Solution

Figure out why all you see is an empty view. Look at what we did earlier in Interface Builder (shown below) and see if you can figure out what's missing. Write what you think on the lines below.

The window template doesn't give us a whole lot out of the box. We're going to use Xcode to assemble our views and view controllers the way we want them.

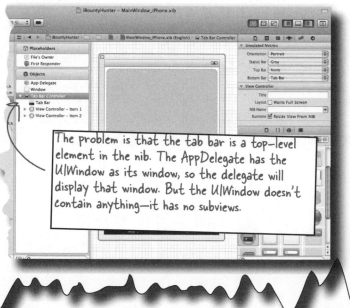

While this label is cute, you should delete it.

We need to embed the tab bar controller into the UIWindow, then it will have the subviews that it needs and will display them correctly.

Drag the tab bar controller from the Library into your main window listing. This will create your TabController view.

The problem is that the tab bar is a top-level element in the nib. The AppDelegate has the UIWindow as its window, so the delegate will display that window. But the UIWindow doesn't contain anything—it has no subviews.

A view's contents are actually subviews

All the UI components we've used are *subclasses* of UIView. By dropping them into a view, we've made them subviews of some bigger container view. We need to do the same thing with our tab bar. We just need to go back into the GUI and add one more link between the main view and the Tab Bar Controller.

Test Drive

Link up the rootViewController outlet to the Tab Bar Controller. Then everything should be working! Interface Builder knows how to work with tableviews and Nav Controllers, so the datasource and delegate will be automatically handled.

Test Drive

It's time to see everything working. Build and run and you can see both tab views working with tables.

Looks good! So now we need to get some data in those tables, right?

After a quick meeting with Bob...

Here's my list of fugitives to track. While the court is in the process of going digital, I still only have this on paper.

Managing Bob's data is the next step.

Now that the iPhone app is up and running, you need to fill in the blanks. The list is pretty simple right now, so we can make the data into any form we want and then import it.

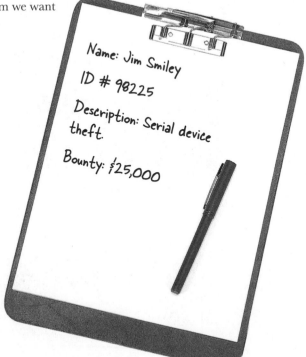

Name: Jim Smiley

ID # 98225

Description: Serial device theft.

Bounty: $25,000

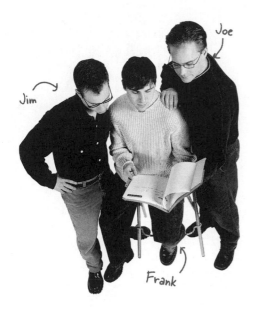

Frank: I was thinking—I'm not sure a plist is such a good idea this time.

Jim: Why not? We used it for DrinkMixer, and it worked fine.

Frank: Well, this list could get pretty big—remember, the list of fugitives is going to be ongoing: the ones that Bob is trying to catch and those that he already has.

Joe: So?

Frank: So...a big list means lots of memory.

Joe: Oh, that's right—and the plist loaded everything *every* time.

Frank: Exactly.

Jim: What about that Core Data thing, that's supposed to handle large amounts of data, right?

Frank: That was a new data framework introduced in iOS 3.0. That would probably work.

Jim: Why use that and not just a database? Doesn't iPhone have SQLite support?

Frank: It does, but I'm not a SQL expert, and Core Data can support all kinds of data, including SQL, but you don't have to talk SQL directly.

Joe: I thought you said we weren't using SQLite?

Frank: We are, but we'll use Core Data to access it.

Joe: How does that work?

Frank: Core Data handles all the dirty work for us—we just need to tell it what data we want to load and save...

What are some other limitations with how we stored data in plists and dictionaries with DrinkMixer?

Core Data lets you focus on your app

Loading and saving data, particularly lots of data, is a major part (often a painful one) of most applications. We've already spent a lot of time working with plists and moving objects in and out of arrays. But what if you wanted to sort that data in a bunch of different ways, or only see fugitives worth more than $1,000,000, or handle 100,000 fugitives? Writing code to handle that kind of persistence gets really old, really quickly. Enter **Core Data**...

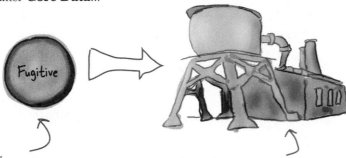

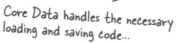

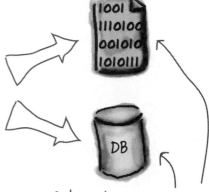

Core Data works with objects. You define what your classes (called Entities) look like.

Core Data handles the necessary loading and saving code...

...and can store data in a number of different formats, like in a database or simple binary file.

But wait, there's more!

Core Data makes loading and saving your data a snap, but it doesn't stop there. It's a mature framework that Apple brought over from Mac OS X to iOS in version 3.0 and gives you:

- **The ability to load and save your objects**
  Core Data automatically loads and saves your objects based on Entity descriptions. It can even handle relationships between objects, migrating between versions of your data, required and optional fields, and field validation.

- **Different ways to store your data**
  Core Data hides how your data is actually stored from your application. You could read and write to a SQLite database or a custom binary file by simply telling Core Data how you want it to save your stuff.

- **Memory management with undo and redo**
  Core Data can be extremely efficient about managing objects in memory and tracking changes to objects. You can use it for undo and redo, paging through huge databases of information, and more.

But before we do any of that, we need to tell Core Data about our objects...

Core Data needs to know what to load

We need Core Data to load and save the fugitive information that we need to populate our detailed view. If you think back to DrinkMixer, we used dictionaries to hold our drink information and accessed them with keys, like this:

```
nameTextField.text = [drink objectForKey:NAME_KEY];
ingredientsTextView.text = [drink objectForKey:INGREDIENTS_KEY];
directionsTextView.text = [drink objectForKey:DIRECTIONS_KEY];
```

The problem with dictionaries and plists was that we had to store all our data by using basic types and get to this data with dictionary keys. We could have easily had a bug if we put the wrong type in the Dictionary or used the wrong key, causing lots of problems down the road. What we really want is to use normal Objective-C classes and objects where we can declare properties for the fields, use real data types, etc. You know, stuff you're already really good at. That's exactly what Core Data lets us do.

DrinkMixer used dictionaries to store drink information. It worked, but was pretty primitive.

We can use Core Data to populate this.

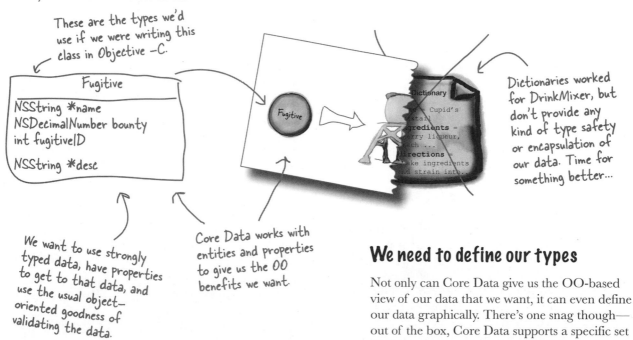

These are the types we'd use if we were writing this class in Objective-C.

Fugitive

NSString *name
NSDecimalNumber bounty
int fugitiveID

NSString *desc

Dictionaries worked for DrinkMixer, but don't provide any kind of type safety or encapsulation of our data. Time for something better...

We want to use strongly typed data, have properties to get to that data, and use the usual object-oriented goodness of validating the data.

Core Data works with entities and properties to give us the OO benefits we want.

We need to define our types

Not only can Core Data give us the OO-based view of our data that we want, it can even define our data graphically. There's one snag though— out of the box, Core Data supports a specific set of data types, so we need to define our entity using the types it offers...

Core Data describes entities with a Managed Object Model

Entities controlled by Core Data are called **Managed Objects**. The way you deal with your *entity* descriptions (properties, relationships, type information, etc.) for Core Data is through a Managed Object Model. Core Data looks at that Managed Object Model at runtime to figure out how to load and save data from its persistent store (e.g., a database). The Xcode template we used comes with an empty Managed Object Model to get us started. Let's take a closer look.

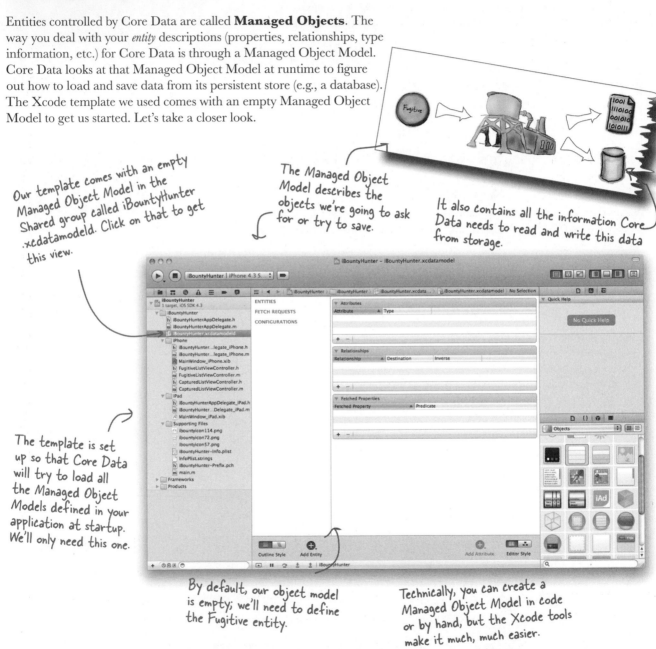

Our template comes with an empty Managed Object Model in the Shared group called iBountyHunter .xcdatamodeld. Click on that to get this view.

The Managed Object Model describes the objects we're going to ask for or try to save.

It also contains all the information Core Data needs to read and write this data from storage.

The template is set up so that Core Data will try to load all the Managed Object Models defined in your application at startup. We'll only need this one.

By default, our object model is empty; we'll need to define the Fugitive entity.

Technically, you can create a Managed Object Model in code or by hand, but the Xcode tools make it much, much easier.

Let's go ahead and create our Fugitive entity...

Build your Fugitive entity

We need to create a Fugitive entity in our Managed Object Model. Since our Fugitive doesn't have any relationships to other classes, we just need to add properties. Open up iBountyHunter.xcdatamodeld to create the Fugitive data type.

① To add the Fugitive entity, click the "plus" button all the way down here at the bottom of the window and change the **name** to "Fugitive".

② Once the entity exists, you can add attributes to the data model, using this plus button here.

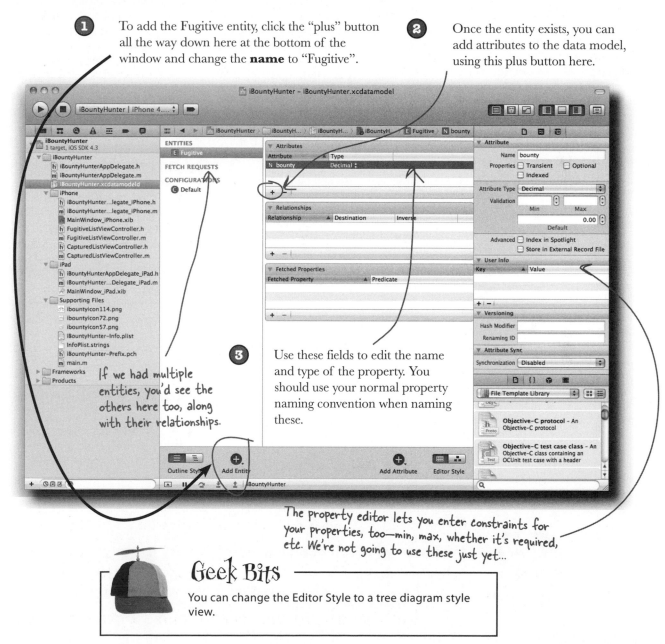

If we had multiple entities, you'd see the others here too, along with their relationships.

③ Use these fields to edit the name and type of the property. You should use your normal property naming convention when naming these.

The property editor lets you enter constraints for your properties, too—min, max, whether it's required, etc. We're not going to use these just yet...

Geek Bits

You can change the Editor Style to a tree diagram style view.

there are no
Dumb Questions

Q: Why did you use an NSDecimalNumber for the bounty? Why not a float or a double?

A: We're going to store a currency value in the bounty field, so we want precision with the decimal part of the figure. Floats and Doubles are approximations, so you tend to get things like $9.999999998 instead of $10.00 when using them for currency calculations. Our choice of NSDecimalNumber for the bounty has nothing to do with Core Data and everything to do with what we're trying to store.

Q: What are the Transient and Indexed checkboxes for in Xcode when you create properties?

A: The Transient checkbox indicates that Core Data doesn't need to load or save that property. Transient properties are typically used to hold values that you only want to calculate once for performance or convenience reasons, but can be calculated based on the other data you save in the Entity. If you use transient properties, you typically implement a method named awakeFromFetch: that is called right after Core Data loads your Entity. In that method, you can calculate the values of your transient properties and set them.

The Indexed checkbox tells Core Data it should try to create an index on that property. Core Data can use indexes to speed up searching for items, so if you have a property that you use to look up your entities (customer IDs, account numbers, etc.), you can ask Core Data to index them for faster searching. Indexes take up space and can slow down inserting new data into the store, so only use them when they can actually improve search performance.

Q: I've seen constants declared with a "k" in front of them. Are they different somehow?

A: Nope. It's just a naming convention. C and C++ programmers tend to use all caps, while Apple tends to use the lowercase "k" instead.

Q: What if I need to use a type that Core Data doesn't support?

A: The easiest way is obviously to try to make your data work with one of the built-in types. If that doesn't work, you create custom types and implement methods to help Core Data load and save those values. Finally, you could stick your data into a binary type (binary data or BLOB) and write some code to encode and decode it at runtime.

Q: What other types of persistence does Core Data support?

A: Core Data supports three types of persistence stores on the iPhone: Binary files, SQLite DBs, and in-memory. The SQLite store is the most useful and what we're using for iBountyHunter. It's also the default. Binary files are nice because they're atomic, meaning that either everything is successfully stored at once, or nothing is. The problem with them is that in order to be atomic, the iPhone has to read and write the whole file whenever something changes. They're not used too often on the iPhone. The in-memory persistence store is a type of store that isn't actually ever saved on disk, but lets you use all the searching, sorting, and undo-redo capabilities that Core Data offers with data you keep in-memory.

Q: What SQL datatypes/table structures does Core Data use when it writes to a SQLite database?

A: The short answer is you don't need to know. Even though it's writing to a SQLite database, the format, types, and structures are not part of the public API and could potentially be changed by Apple. You're supposed to treat the SQLite database as a blackbox and only access it through Core Data.

Q: So this is a nice GUI and all, but I still don't see what this gets us over dictionaries. It seems like a lot of work.

A: We had to tell Core Data what kind of information we're working with. Now that we've done that, we can start putting it to work.

Watch it!

Make sure your object model matches ours exactly!

When you're writing your own apps, there are lots of ways to set up your data model, but since we're going to give you a database for iBountyHunter, your model must match ours exactly!

MANAGED OBJECT MODEL CONSTRUCTION

Finish building the Fugitive entity in the Managed Object Model based on the Fugitive information we want to store. Remember, Core Data Types won't match our Objective-C types exactly. Make sure you name your properties the same as we have in the Fugitive diagram shown below.

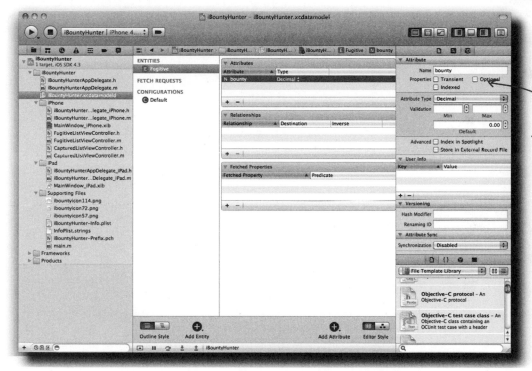

You should uncheck "Optional" for each of the properties you add—we want them all to be required.

Fugitive

NSString *name
NSDecimalNumber bounty
int fugitiveID

NSString *desc

Make sure you use the same property names as we did.

These are the Objective-C types we want to use; you'll need to pick the right Core Data types when you build the entity.

MANAGED OBJECT MODEL CONSTRUCTION SOLUTION

Finish building the Fugitive entity in the Managed Object Model based on the Fugitive information we want to store. Remember, Core Data Types won't match our Objective-C types exactly. Make sure you name your properties the same as we used in the Fugitive diagram.

Make sure that the "optional" box is unchecked for all the properties.

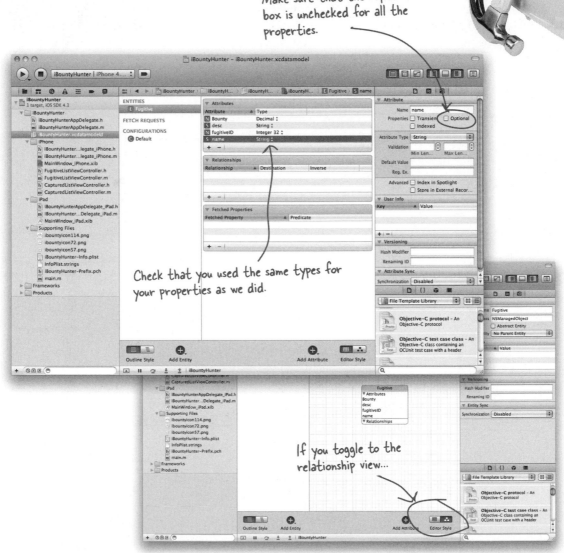

Check that you used the same types for your properties as we did.

If you toggle to the relationship view...

...your Fugitive entity should have four properties and no relationships.

 Core Data Up Close

Core Data is about managing objects

So far we've talked about how to describe our objects to Core Data, but not how we're actually going to *do* anything with them. In order to do that, we need to take a quick look inside Core Data.

Inside Core Data is a stack of three critical pieces: the Managed Object Context, the Persistent Store Coordinator, and the Persistent Object Store.

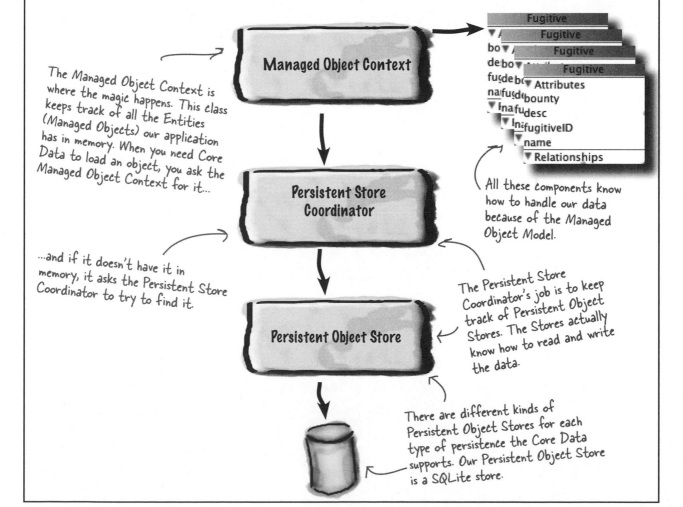

The Managed Object Context is where the magic happens. This class keeps track of all the Entities (Managed Objects) our application has in memory. When you need Core Data to load an object, you ask the Managed Object Context for it...

Managed Object Context

All these components know how to handle our data because of the Managed Object Model.

...and if it doesn't have it in memory, it asks the Persistent Store Coordinator to try to find it.

Persistent Store Coordinator

The Persistent Store Coordinator's job is to keep track of Persistent Object Stores. The Stores actually know how to read and write the data.

Persistent Object Store

There are different kinds of Persistent Object Stores for each type of persistence the Core Data supports. Our Persistent Object Store is a SQLite store.

So, if we want to load or save anything using Core Data, we need to talk to the Managed Object Context, right?

Exactly!

But, the next question is how do we get data in and out of it?

The Xcode template we used set up the Core Data stack for us, but we still need to figure out how to talk to the Managed Object Context. Given what you know about Core Data so far, how would you go about asking the framework to load and save data for you?

☐ Use SQLite commands. ⟵ We're using a SQLite store, but Core Data supports other kinds of stores. Everything about how it uses SQLite is hidden from you. Trying to access it with straight SQL would be dangerous.

☐ Write custom save and load code to update the data. ⟵ This has two problems: first, you still don't know how the data is actually stored (or even the type of store being used), and second, one of the big reasons we're using Core Data is to avoid writing this kind of code.

☑ Use Core Data to generate classes to do the work for you.

This is what we're after! Because of our Managed Object Model, Core Data knows everything it needs to know to create classes for us and do all the loading and saving—we just need to ask it.

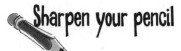

Sharpen your pencil

Xcode can create a Fugitive class from our Managed Object Model that we can use like any other class. Follow the steps below to create the Fugitive class you need.

1 **Select the iBountyHunter.xcdatamodel and click on the Fugitive Entity.**
You need to have a Core Data entity selected before you ask Xcode to generate a class for you.

2 **Create a new Managed Object Class.**
Select **File→New→New File.** There will be a new type of file that you can add, the **NSManaged Object Class.** Select this file and click **Next**.

After confirming the save location for the new file (iBountyHunter should be the **Group**)...

3 **Generate the .h and .m files.**
Click Create and you should have a Fugitive.h and a Fugitive.m added to your project. Go ahead and drag these up to the **/Supporting Files** group.

Sharpen your pencil Solution

Xcode can create a Fugitive class from our Managed Object Model that we can use like any other class.

1 **Select the iBountyHunter .xcdatamodel and click on the Fugitive Entity.**
You need to have a Core Data entity selected before you ask Xcode to generate a class for you.

2 **Create a new Managed Object Class...**
Select **File→New→New File.** There will be a new type of file that you can add, the **NSManaged Object Class.** Select this file and click **Next.**

After confirming the save location for the new file (iBountyHunter should be the **Group**)...

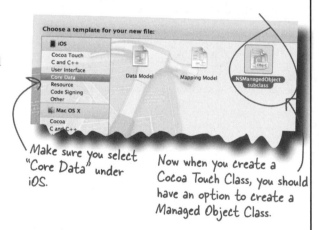

Make sure you select "Core Data" under iOS.

Now when you create a Cocoa Touch Class, you should have an option to create a Managed Object Class.

3 **Generate the .h and .m files.**
Click Create and you should have Fugitive.h and a Fugitive.m added to your project. Go ahead and drag these up to the **/Supporting Files** group.

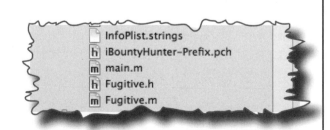

InfoPlist.strings
iBountyHunter-Prefix.pch
main.m
Fugitive.h
Fugitive.m

Your generated Fugitive class matches the Managed Object Model

Xcode created two new files from our Fugitive entity: a Fugitive.h header file and a Fugitive.m implementation file. Open up both files and let's take a look at what was created.

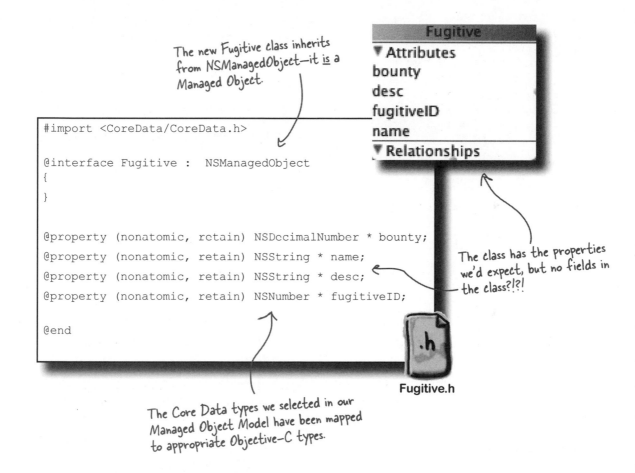

The new Fugitive class inherits from NSManagedObject—it is a Managed Object.

```
#import <CoreData/CoreData.h>

@interface Fugitive :  NSManagedObject
{
}


@property (nonatomic, retain) NSDecimalNumber * bounty;

@property (nonatomic, retain) NSString * name;

@property (nonatomic, retain) NSString * desc;

@property (nonatomic, retain) NSNumber * fugitiveID;

@end
```

Fugitive

▼ Attributes
bounty
desc
fugitiveID
name
▼ Relationships

The class has the properties we'd expect, but no fields in the class?!?!

Fugitive.h

The Core Data types we selected in our Managed Object Model have been mapped to appropriate Objective-C types.

NSManagedObject handles storage and memory for generated properties

The generated Fugitive class has properties for name, description, etc., but no fields in the class. The Core Data framework (and NSManagedObject in particular) are responsible for handling the memory associated with those properties. You can override this if you want, but in most cases, this does exactly what you need.

Things get even more interesting in Fugitive.m...

There's no code in there either... but I'm guessing that I'm not going to need to worry about that?

Right! The Core Data framework takes care of it.

The Fugitive.m class is nearly empty, and instead of synthesizing the properties, they're declared with a new directive, @dynamic.

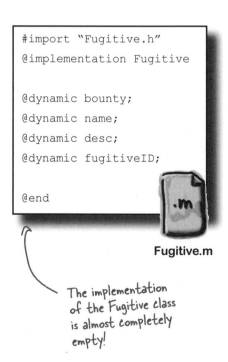

```objc
#import "Fugitive.h"
@implementation Fugitive

@dynamic bounty;
@dynamic name;
@dynamic desc;
@dynamic fugitiveID;

@end
```

Fugitive.m

The implementation of the Fugitive class is almost completely empty!

NSManagedObject also implements the properties

The new @dynamic directive tells the compiler not to worry about the getter and setter methods necessary for the properties. They need to come from somewhere, though, or else code is going to crash at runtime when something tries to access those properties. This is where NSManagedObject steps in again. Because NSManagedObject handles the memory for the fields backing the properties, it also provides runtime implementations for the getter and setter methods. By having NSManagedObject implement those methods, you get a number of other neat benefits:

- The NSManagedObject knows when properties are changed, can validate new data, and can notify other classes when changes happen.

- NSManagedObject can be lazy about fetching property information until someone asks for it. For example, it does this with relationships to other objects.

- NSManagedObject can keep track of changes to properties and provide undo-redo support.

You get all of this without writing a line of code!

BRAIN POWER

How do you think you'll get Core Data to load a Fugitive from the persistent store?

Use an NSFetchRequest to describe your search

In order to tell the Managed Object Context what we're looking for, we need to create an NSFetchRequest. The NSFetchRequest describes what kind of objects we want to fetch, any conditions we want when it fetches them (like bounty > $1,000), and how Core Data should sort the results when it gives them back. Yeah, it does all that for us.

Entity Info

You tell the request what type of data to look for by picking an entity from your managed object model.

NSFetchRequest

An NSFetchRequest describes the search we want Core Data to execute for us.

Predicate

You can provide a predicate that describes conditions the entities must meet, like if you wanted only entities beginning with the letter B. We want them all, so no predicate for us.

Sort Descriptor

The sort descriptor tells Core Data how you want the data sorted before it sends it back. These are just like the sort descriptors we used in DrinkMixer.

Ask the Managed Object Context to fetch data using your NSFetchRequest

All that's left is to ask the Managed Object Context to actually execute your NSFetchRequest. That means we'll need a reference to a Managed Object Context. Fortunately, the template set one up for us in the App Delegate. We can get to it like this:

```
iBountyHunterAppDelegate *appDelegate =
    (iBountyHunterAppDelegate*)[[UIApplication sharedApplication] delegate];
NSManagedObjectContext *managedObjectContext =
    appDelegate.managedObjectContext;
```

```
    NSFetchRequest *request = [[NSFetchRequest alloc] init];
    NSEntityDescription *entity = [NSEntityDescription
entityForName:@"Fugitive" inManagedObjectContext:managedObjectContext];
    [request setEntity:entity];
```

We specify the entity by name, a Fugitive.

```
    NSSortDescriptor *sortDescriptor = [[NSSortDescriptor alloc]
initWithKey:@"name" ascending:YES];
```

We want the Fugitives sorted alphabetically by name.

```
    NSArray *sortDescriptors = [[NSArray alloc]
initWithObjects:sortDescriptor, nil];

    [request setSortDescriptors:sortDescriptors];

    [sortDescriptors release];

    [sortDescriptor release];


    NSError *error;

    NSMutableArray *mutableFetchResults = [[managedObjectContext
executeFetchRequest:request error:&error] mutableCopy];

    if (mutableFetchResults == nil) {

        // Might want to do something more serious...

        NSLog(@"Can't load the Fugitive data!");

    }


    self.items = mutableFetchResults;

    [mutableFetchResults release];

    [request release];
```

All that's left is to ask our Managed Object Context to go ahead and execute our fetch request. We'll ask it to give us back the results in an array and clean up our references.

BRAIN BARBELL

Where do we put all this code? And where are we going to store the results? What about actually displaying the fetched data?

BRAIN
BARBELL SOLUTION

Where do we put all this code? And where
are we going to store the results? What about
actually displaying the fetched data?

Since Bob is going to want to see his list as soon as his view shows up, the fetching
code needs to go into viewWillAppear in FugitiveListViewController.m.

As for storing the results, we'll get back an array, but we release it right away. We
need to keep a reference to that array in our view controller.

In order to actually show this data, we're going to need to implement the
cellForRowAtIndexPath to pull the data from the array.

The next two exercises together will get you all the
code you need to view the fetched data properly...

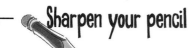

Sharpen your pencil

Let's get all of these pieces into the app.

1 **Create the mutable array to hold the fetched items.**
Create an array in the FugitiveListViewController called items to hold the
results of the fetch. Don't forget to synthesize the property and clean up memory.

2 **Import the appropriate headers into FugitiveListViewController.m.**
Make sure that you #import headers for the App Delegate and the Fugitive
classes into FugitiveListViewController.m.

3 **Implement the fetch code inside viewWillAppear.**
Take what we learned on the previous couple of pages and get the fetch working.
You'll need to get the Managed Object Context from the delegate, create the fetch,
and then execute it. Remember to update the code to actually hang onto the results
by assigning them to the array we just created.

Table Cell Magnets

Use the code snippets below to customize the table cells for the fugitive list.

```objc
- (NSInteger)numberOfSectionInTableView:(UITableView *)tableView {
        return 1;
}


// Customize the number of rows in the table view.
  - (NSInteger)tableView:(UITableView *)tableView numberOfRowsInSection:
(NSInteger)section {

        _____

}


// Customize the appearance of table view cells.
  - (UITableViewCell *)tableView:(UITableView *)tableView cellForRowAtIndexPath:
(NSIndexPath *)indexPath {
        static NSString *CellIdentifier = @"Cell";

        UITableViewCell *cell = [tableView dequeueReusableCellWithIdentifier:
CellIdentifier];
        if (cell == nil) {
                cell = [[[UITableViewCell alloc] initWithStyle:
                        UITableViewCellStyleDefault reuseIdentifier:CellIdentifier
autorelease];
        }
        // Configure the cell...
        _____
        _____
        _____
        return cell;
```

```objc
cell.accessoryType
```

```objc
= fugitive.name;
```

```objc
Fugitive *fugitive
```

```objc
cell.textLabel.text
```

```objc
= UITableViewCellAccessoryDisclosureIndicator;
```

```objc
#pragma mark Table view data source
```

```objc
- (NSInteger) numberOfSectionsInTableView:
```

```objc
return [items count];
```

```objc
= [items objectAtIndex:indexPath.row];
```

Sharpen your pencil
Solution

It's a lot of code to implement, but when you're done, Core Data
will be fetching the data you need for the fugitive list.

① **Create the mutable array to hold the fetched items.**

```
#import <UIKit/UIKit.h>
@interface FugitiveListViewController : UITableViewController {
        NSMutableArray *items_;
}
@property(nonatomic, retain) NSMutableArray *items;
@end
```

.h

FugitiveListViewController.h

② **Import the appropriate headers into
FugitiveListViewController.m.**

```
#import "FugitiveListViewController.h"
#import "iBountyHunterAppDelegate.h"
#import "Fugitive.h"
@implementation FugitiveListViewController
@synthesize items=items_;
```

.m

FugitiveListViewController.m

```
- (void)dealloc {
    [items_ release];
    [super dealloc];
}
```

③ Implement the fetch code inside viewWillAppear.

```objc
- (void) viewWillAppear:(BOOL)animated {
    [super viewWillAppear:animated];
 iBountyHunterAppDelegate *appDelegate = (iBountyHunterAppDelegate*)
[[UIApplication sharedApplication] delegate];
    NSManagedObjectContext *managedObjectContext = appDelegate.
managedObjectContext;
    NSFetchRequest *request = [[NSFetchRequest alloc] init];
    NSEntityDescription *entity = [NSEntityDescription
entityForName:@"Fugitive"  inManagedObjectContext:managedObjectContext];
    [request setEntity:entity];

    NSSortDescriptor *sortDescriptor = [NSSortDescriptor
sortDescriptorWithKey:@"name" ascending:YES];
    [request setSortDescriptors:[NSArray arrayWithObject:sortDescriptor]];

    NSError *error;
    NSMutableArray *mutableFetchResults = [[managedObjectContext
executeFetchRequest:request error:&error] mutableCopy];
    if (mutableFetchResults == nil) {
        // Handle the error;
    }

    self.items = mutableFetchResults;
    [mutableFetchResults release];
    [request release];
}
```

FugitiveListViewController.m

Table Cell Magnets Solution

Use the code snippets below to customize the table cells for the fugitive list.

```
#pragma mark Table view data source
```

```objc
- (NSInteger)numberOfSectionsInTableView:(UITableView *)tableView {
    return 1;
}


// Customize the number of rows in the table view.
- (NSInteger)tableView:(UITableView *)tableView numberOfRowsInSection:
(NSInteger)section {
        return [items_ count];
}


// Customize the appearance of table view cells.
- (UITableViewCell *)tableView:(UITableView *)tableView cellForRowAtIndexPath:
(NSIndexPath *)indexPath {
    static NSString *CellIdentifier = @"Cell";

    UITableViewCell *cell = [tableView dequeueReusableCellWithIdentifier:
CellIdentifier];
    if (cell == nil) {
        cell = [[[UITableViewCell alloc] initWithStyle:
UITableViewCellStyleDefault reuseIdentifier:CellIdentifier] autorelease];
    }
```

Here's Core Data at work. The data is stored in normal Objective-C Fugitive objects. No more magic dictionary keys here...

```objc
    // Configure the cell...
    Fugitive *fugitive = [items_ objectAtIndex:indexPath.row];
    cell.textLabel.text = fugitive.name;
    cell.accessoryType = UITableViewCellAccessoryDisclosureIndicator;

    return cell;}
```

 Do this! → To completely wire up your table view, in Interface Builder make sure that the table view in the Fugitive List has its datasource as the FugitiveListViewController.

Wow, the court got its digital program together fast! Here's a URL for the data I'm getting.

Very cool. Let's grab the data.

Browse over to *http://www.headfirstlabs .com/books/iphonedev* and download iBountyHunter.sqlite. In XCode, right-click on your iBountyHunter project and select "**Add Files to iBountyHunter**" and make sure it is copied into the project's **/Supporting Files** directory.

As you do that, think about what this means for your app. Will adding in a new database mean a bunch of refactoring, or can Core Data help out here, too?

Bob's database is a resource

We have all this code already in place to load data—it came with the Core Data template. But how do we get from there to actually loading the database?

We've handled the object model, the Managed Object Context, and the Fugitive Class.

Now we need to look at the other end. We need to connect Core Data to our Fugitive Database.

Back to the Core Data stack

Remember the Core Data stack we talked about earlier? We've gotten everything in place with the Managed Object Context, and now we're interested in where the data is actually coming from. Just like with the Managed Object Context, the template set up the rest of the stack for us.

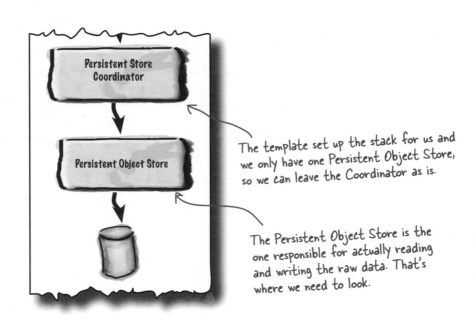

The template set up the stack for us and we only have one Persistent Object Store, so we can leave the Coordinator as is.

The Persistent Object Store is the one responsible for actually reading and writing the raw data. That's where we need to look.

Let's take a look at what the template set up for us in the App Delegate...

The template sets things up for a SQLite DB

The Core Data template set up the Persistent Store Coordinator to use a SQLite database named after our project. As long as the database is named iBountyHunter.sqlite, then Core Data should be ready to go.

```
- (NSPersistentStoreCoordinator *)persistentStoreCoordinator
{
    if (__persistentStoreCoordinator != nil)
    {
        return __persistentStoreCoordinator;
    }


    NSURL *storeURL = [[self applicationDocumentsDirectory] URLByAppending
PathComponent:@"iBountyHunter.sqlite"];
    NSError *error = nil;
    __persistentStoreCoordinator = [[NSPersistentStoreCoordinator alloc]
initWithManagedObjectModel:[self managedObjectModel]];
    if (![__persistentStoreCoordinator addPersistentStoreWithType:NSSQLite
StoreType configuration:nil URL:storeURL options:nil error:&error])
    {

  NSLog(@"Unresolved error %@, %@", error, [error userInfo]);
  abort();
    }
  return persistentStoreCoordinator;
}
```

The template sets things up to use a DB named the same as your project.

The template code adds a Persistent Object Store to the coordinator configured with the NSSQLiteStoreType.

iBountyHunterAppDelegate.m

TEST DRIVE

Now that the database is in place and the Persistent Object Store can be used as-is, go ahead and run the app.

TEST DRIVE

Where is the data?

We added the database to the project. The code looks right. This all worked with DrinkMixer. What's the deal??

Core Data is looking somewhere else.

Our problem is with how Core Data looks for the database. Well, it's actually a little more complicated than that.

iOS Apps are read-only

Back in DrinkMixer, we loaded our application data from a plist by using the application bundle. This worked great and our data loaded without a problem. But remember how we talked about how this would only work in the simulator? It's time to sort that out. As part of iOS security, applications are installed on the device as read-only. You can access any resources bundled with your application, but you can't *modify* them. The Core Data template assumes you're going to want to read and write to your database, so it doesn't even bother checking the application bundle. It checks the application documents directory instead.

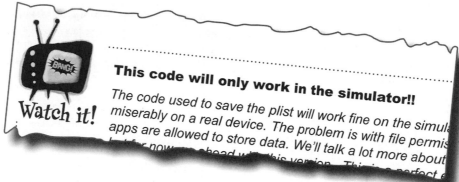

Watch it!

This code will only work in the simulator!!

The code used to save the plist will work fine on the simul~~ator~~
miserably on a real device. The problem is with file permis~~sion~~
apps are allowed to store data. We'll talk a lot more about ~~this~~
~~but for now~~ ~~ahead with this version. This is a perfect~~

The Core Data template looks in the application documents directory for the database, not the application bundle.

```
NSURL *storeUrl = [NSURL fileURLWithPath: [[self
applicationDocumentsDirectory] URLByAppendingPathComponent:
@"iBountyHunter.sqlite"]];
```

iBountyHunterAppDelegate.m

**Let's take a closer look at how
those directories are set up...**

The iPhone's application structure defines where you can read and write

For security and stability reasons, iOS locks down the filesystem pretty tight. When an application is installed, the iOS creates a directory under /User/Applications on the device using a unique identifier. The application is installed into that directory, and a standard directory structure is created for the app.

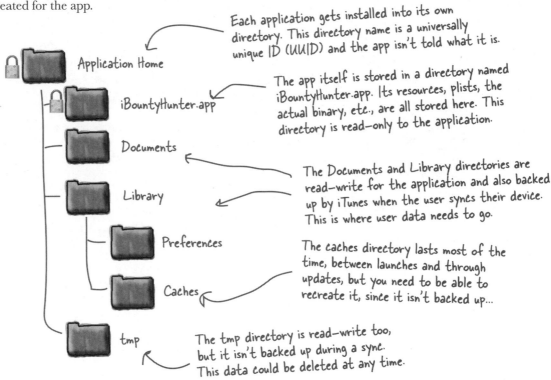

Application Home

Each application gets installed into its own directory. This directory name is a universally unique ID (UUID) and the app isn't told what it is.

iBountyHunter.app

The app itself is stored in a directory named iBountyHunter.app. Its resources, plists, the actual binary, etc., are all stored here. This directory is read-only to the application.

Documents

Library

The Documents and Library directories are read-write for the application and also backed up by iTunes when the user syncs their device. This is where user data needs to go.

Preferences

Caches

The caches directory lasts most of the time, between launches and through updates, but you need to be able to recreate it, since it isn't backed up...

tmp

The tmp directory is read-write too, but it isn't backed up during a sync. This data could be deleted at any time.

Use the Documents directory to store user data

Since most Core Data applications want to read and write data, the template sets up our Core Data stack to read and write from the Documents directory. An application can figure out where its local directories are by using the NSSearchPathForDirectoriesInDomains, just like the template does in the App Delegate:

```
- (NSURL *)applicationDocumentsDirectory
{
    return [[[NSFileManager defaultManager] URLsForDirectory:NSDocumentDirectory
                                        inDomains:NSUserDomainMask] lastObject];
}
```

Copy the database to the Documents directory

When the application first starts, we need to check to see if there's a copy of the database in our Documents directory. If there is, we don't want to mess with it. If not, we need to copy one there.

Add this!

You'll need to declare this method in AppDelegate_Shared.h.

```objc
- (void) createEditableCopyOfDatabaseIfNeeded {
    // First, test for existence - we don't want to wipe out a user's DB
    NSFileManager *fileManager = [NSFileManager defaultManager];
    NSURL *documentsDir = [self applicationDocumentsDirectory];
    NSURL *writableDBPath = [documentsDir URLByAppendingPathComponent:@"iBoun
tyHunter.sqlite"];

    BOOL dbexists = [fileManager fileExistsAtPath:writableDBPath];
    if (!dbexists) {
    // The writable database does not exist, so copy the default to the
    appropriate location.
    NSURL *defaultDBPath = [[[NSBundle mainBundle]
URLForResource:@"iBountyHunter" withExtension:@"sqlite"];

    NSError *error;
    BOOL success = [fileManager copyItemAtURL:defaultDBPath
toURL:writableDBPath error:&error];
    if (!success) {
    NSAssert1(0, @"Failed to create writable database file with message
'%@'.", [error localizedDescription]);
        }
    }
}
```

Here, we grab the master DB from our application bundle; this is the read-only copy.

Copy it from the read-only to the writable directory.

```objc
- (BOOL)application:(UIApplication *)application didFinishLaunchi
  ngWithOptions:(NSDictionary *)launchOptions
{
    // Override point for customization after application launch.
    [self createEditableCopyOfDatabaseIfNeeded];
    [self.window makeKeyAndVisible];
    return YES;
}
```

iBountyHunterAppDelegate.m

You need to uninstall the old version of your app from the simulator.

This deletes the empty database that Core Data created earlier. When you build and run again, your new code will copy the correct DB into place.

Now that the app knows where to find the database, it should load.

All the data is in there!

there are no
Dumb Questions

Q: Why didn't we have to do all of this directory stuff with the plist in DrinkMixer?

A: We only ran DrinkMixer in the simulator, and the simulator doesn't enforce the directory permissions like the real device does. We'd basically have the same problem with DrinkMixer on a device. The reason this was so obvious with iBountyHunter is that Core Data is configured to look in the correct place for a writable database, namely the application's Documents directory.

Q: How do I get paths to the other application directories?

A: Just use NSSearchPathForDirectories InDomains but with different NSSearch PathDirectory constants. Most of them you won't ever need; NSDocumentsDirectory is the most common. You should never assume you know what the directory structure is or how to navigate it—always look up the specific directory you want.

Q: So what happens to the data when someone uninstalls my application?

A: When an application is removed from a device, the entire application directory is removed, so data, caches, preferences, etc., are all deleted.

Q: The whole Predicate thing with NSFetchRequest seems pretty important. Are we going to talk about that any more?

A: Yes! We'll come back to that in Chapter 9.

Q: So is there always just one Managed Object Context in an application?

A: No, there can be multiple if you want them. For most apps, one is sufficient, but if you want to separate a set of edits or migrate data from one data source to another, you can create and configure as many Managed Object Contexts as you need.

Q: I don't really see the benefit of the Persistent Store Coordinator. What does it do?

A: Our application only uses one Persistent Object Store, but Core Data supports multiple stores. For example, you could have a customer's information coming from one database but product information coming from another. You can configure two separate persistent object stores and let the persistent store coordinator sort out which one is used based on the database attached.

Q: How about object models? Can we have more than one of those?

A: Yup—in fact, we're going to take a look at that in Chapter 9, too.

Q: Do I always have to get my NSManagedObjects from the Managed Object Context? What if I want to create a new one?

A: No, new ones have to be added to the context—however, you can't just alloc and init them. You need to create them from their entity description, like this: [NSEntityDescription insertNewObjectFor EntityForName:@"Fugitive" inManaged ObjectContext:managedObjectContext].

That will return a new Fugitive instance and after that you can use it like normal.

Now we need to build the detail view, right?

Exactly.

We have the database loading with detailed information, but the user can't see it yet. Now, we just need to build out the detail view to display that information as well.

iBountyHunter To Do List

You're almost done with your list!

~~1. Create view controllers (both .h and .m files) for the Fugitive and Captured views.~~

~~2. Create the tab bar view, and add the tab bar controller to it along with a reference from the app delegate.~~

~~3. Add the nav controllers for the Fugitive and Captured views.~~

~~4. Build the table views for the Fugitive and Captured views.~~

5. Create a detail view with a nib, and a view controller with .h and .m files.

And you definitely know how to do this...

LONG EXERCISE

Building the detail view isn't anything new for you—so get to it! Here is what you're working with from our earlier sketch for the detail view.

☐ Create a new view controller and nib called the FugitiveDetailViewController.

☐ Lay out the nib using Interface Builder to have the fields we need.

☐ Then update the new view controller to have outlets for the fields we'll need to set and a reference to the Fugitive it's displaying.

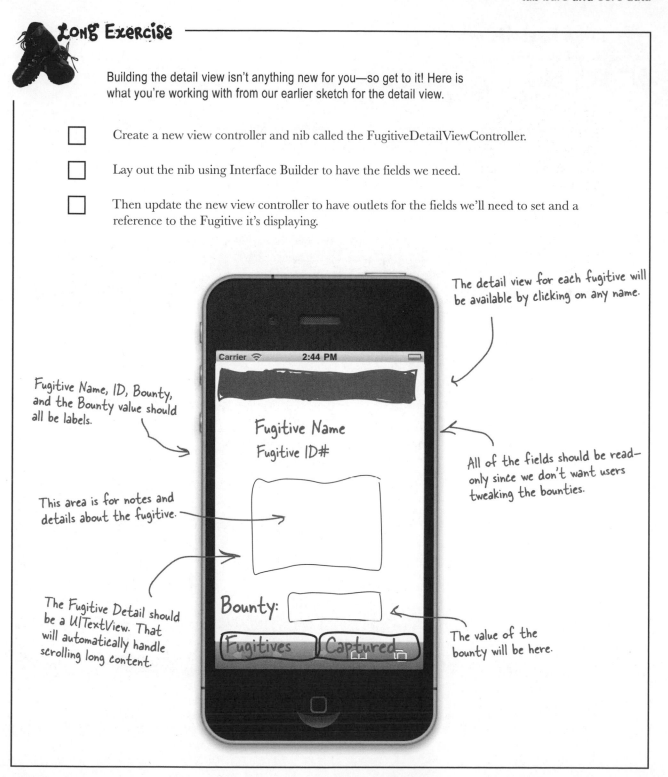

The detail view for each fugitive will be available by clicking on any name.

Fugitive Name, ID, Bounty, and the Bounty value should all be labels.

All of the fields should be read-only since we don't want users tweaking the bounties.

This area is for notes and details about the fugitive.

The Fugitive Detail should be a UITextView. That will automatically handle scrolling long content.

The value of the bounty will be here.

Long Exercise Solution

Go through and check the code, outlets, declarations, and dealloc.

The files that you need for the new view are: FugitiveDetailViewController.h, FugitiveDetailViewController.m, and FugitiveDetailViewController.xib.

To create them, just select **File→New File** and create a UIViewController file and check the box that says "With XIB for User Interface." After that, you'll need to move the .xib file into **/iPhone** directory within Xcode.

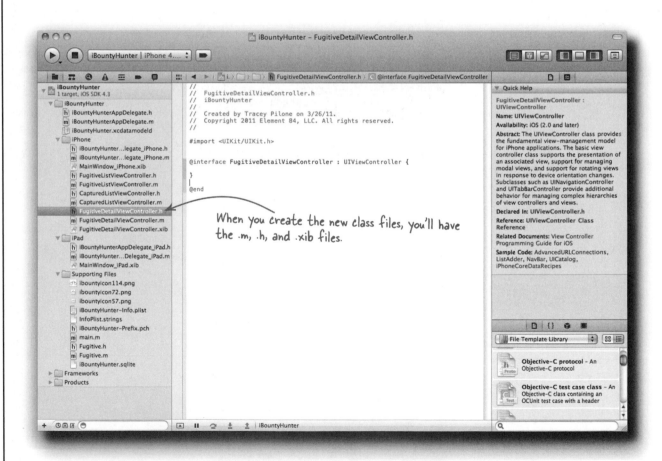

When you create the new class files, you'll have the .m, .h, and .xib files.

```
@interface FugitiveDetailViewController : UIViewController {
@private
    Fugitive *fugitive_;
    UILabel *nameLabel_;
    UILabel *idLabel_;
    UITextView *descriptionTextView_;
    UILabel *bountyLabel_;
}


@property (nonatomic, retain) Fugitive *fugitive;
@property (nonatomic, retain) IBOutlet UILabel *nameLabel;
@property (nonatomic, retain) IBOutlet UILabel *idLabel;
@property (nonatomic, retain) IBOutlet UITextView *descriptionTextView;
@property (nonatomic, retain) IBOutlet UILabel *bountyLabel;
@end
```

FugitiveDetailViewController.h

```
@implementation FugitiveDetailViewController

@synthesize fugitive=fugitive_;
@synthesize nameLabel=nameLabel_;
@synthesize idLabel=idLabel_;
@synthesize descriptionTextView=descriptionTextView_;
@synthesize bountyLabel=bountyLabel_;
```

FugitiveDetailViewController.m

```
- (void)dealloc
{
    [fugitive_ release];
    [nameLabel_ release];
    [idLabel_ release];
    [descriptionTextView_ release];
    [bountyLabel_ release];
    [super dealloc];
}
```

Long Exercise Solution

Now build the view in Interface Builder.

Start out by getting all the elements in the right spots, and then go back and customize them.

To get the simulated navigation bar, in the Utilities Panel, set the Top Bar to "Navigation Bar".

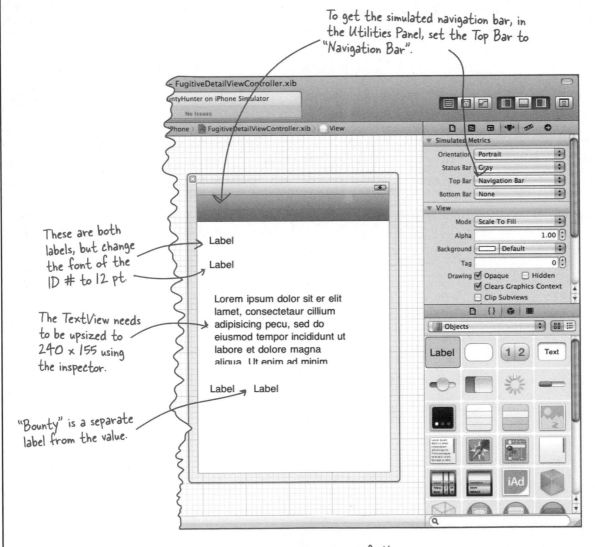

These are both labels, but change the font of the ID # to 12 pt.

The TextView needs to be upsized to 240 x 155 using the inspector.

"Bounty" is a separate label from the value.

Use the inspector to change the default values of each of these elements to "Fugitive Name", "Fugitive ID", etc.

Here's the final listing of the components of the detail view.

Make sure that all the added elements are children of the main view.

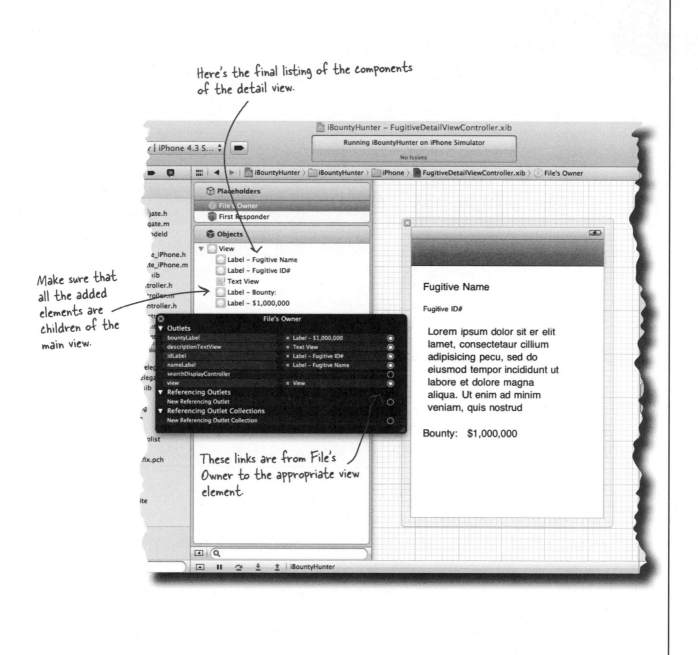

These links are from File's Owner to the appropriate view element.

UI Geek Bits

We're going to add some spit and polish to this view. It's fine the way it is, but here's some iPhone coolness to add.

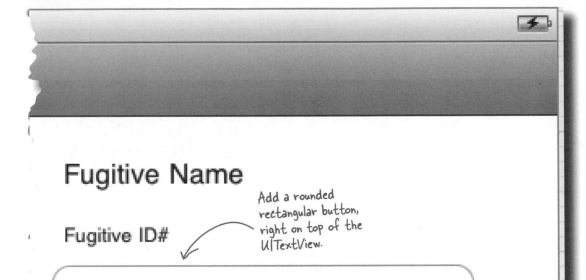

Add a rounded rectangular button, right on top of the UITextView.

We'll make this button function as a border. To do that, you need to do two things:

1 In the element listing for the view, move the button above the Text View. This will move the button behind the text.

2 With the button still selected, use the Utilities pane to uncheck the **enabled** box (under the Attributes panel).

Exercise

Now, populate the detail view from the Fugitive List.
You know how to do this from what we did earlier with
DrinkMixer.

① **The other files need to know that the detail view exists.**
In some implementation file, you'll need to #import FugitiveDetailViewController.h.

You should be able to figure out which one.

② **The detail view needs to be displayed.**
In that same implementation file, the table view needs some selection
code. It'll be similar to the code that we used in DrinkMixer.

③ **The fields need to be populated with the data.**
The detail view code needs to populate the existing fields with the data
from the fields that were set up with the Fugitive.h and Fugitive.m
classes and the Core Data code. In viewWillAppear:

These are just a couple of examples but should give you all the hints you'll need.

```
fugitiveNameLabel.text = fugitive.name;
fugitiveIdLabel.text = [fugitive.fugitiveID stringValue];
```

Exercise Solution

Now, populate the detail view. You know enough from before to do this.

1 **The other files need to know that the detail view exists.**
In some implementation file, you'll need to
#import FugitiveDetailViewController.h

Just add this to the top of the FugitiveListViewController.m file.

2 **The detail view needs to be displayed.**
In that same implementation file, the table view needs some selection code. It'll be similar to the code that we used in DrinkMixer.

```
#pragma mark - Table view delegate

- (void)tableView:(UITableView *)tableView didSelectRowAtIndexPath:(NSIndexPath
*)indexPath
{

    FugitiveDetailViewController *detailViewController =
[[FugitiveDetailViewController alloc] initWithNibName:@"FugitiveDetailV
iewController" bundle:nil];

        detailViewController.fugitive = [items_ objectAtIndex:indexPath.
row];

    [self.navigationController pushViewController:detailViewController
animated:YES];

    [detailViewController release];

}
```

Here, we tell the detail View Controller which fugitive it should display.

FugitiveListViewController.m

③ **The fields need to be populated with the data.**

```objc
#import "FugitiveDetailViewController.h"

@implementation FugitiveDetailViewController
@synthesize fugitive, fugitiveNameLabel, fugitiveIdLabel,
fugitiveDescriptionView, fugitiveBountyLabel;

- (void) viewWillAppear:(BOOL)animated {
    [super viewWillAppear:animated];

    self.nameLabel.text = fugitive_.name;
    self.idLabel.text = [fugitive_.fugitiveID stringValue];
    self.descriptionTextView.text = fugitive_.desc;
    self.bountyLabel.text = [fugitive_.bounty stringValue];
}
```

Adding the stringValue on the end of these two declarations handles the fact that they were not strings, but NSNumber and NSDecimalNumbers.

FugitiveDetailViewController.m

Test Drive

After populating the detail view, you can see
the information about each fugitive.

The back button is working thanks to
the nav control.

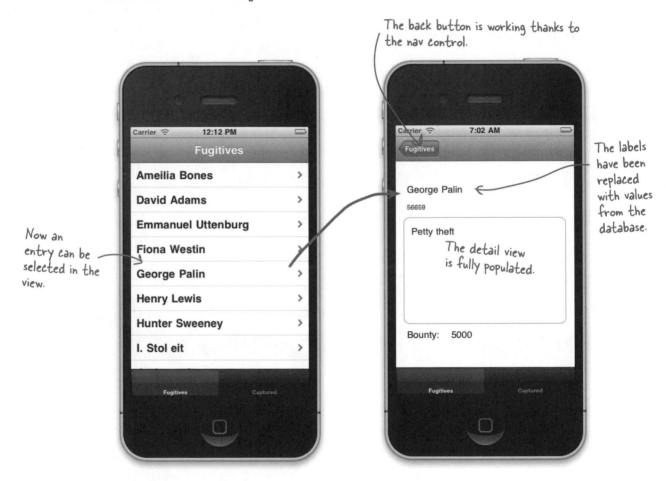

Now an
entry can be
selected in the
view.

The labels
have been
replaced
with values
from the
database.

The detail view
is fully populated.

It all works!

It works great! Having all that information with me makes it much easier to catch outlaws. I should be able to almost double my business with this app!

Great!

After a couple of weeks, Bob is back with a new request...

That really worked! I've caught a ton of people already! How can I keep track of who I've caught? And when do I get the iPad app?

To be continued...

CoreData cross

There's a lot of terminology with Core Data; let's make sure you remember it!

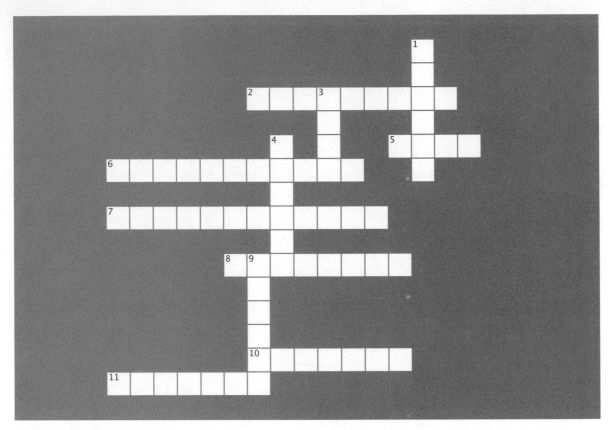

Across

2. Each app has a _____ directory.
5. NS_____Descriptor captures how data should be sorted.
6. In the middle of the Core Data stack is the Persistent Store _____.
7. The _____ template is pretty basic.
8. _____ can manage different types of data.
10. The managed object _____ is the top of the Core Data stack.
11. NSFetch_____ describes a search.

Down

1. The Persistent Object Store is at the _____ of the Core Data stack.
3. Core Data has _____ and redo.
4. The _____ controller is good for switching views.
9. The managed _____ model describes entities.

Match each field we need to implement for the data view to its Core Data type.

Field for the Detail View   **Core Data Type**

Name

Bounty

Fugitive ID#

Description

Int32   A 32 bit integer

String   Equivalent to an NSString attribute

Boolean   A BOOL value (YES or NO)

Decimal   A fixed-point decimal number

Date

A bunch of Core Data code in full costume are playing a party game, "Who am I?" They'll give you a clue—you try to guess who they are based on what they say. Assume they always tell the truth about themselves. Fill in the blanks to the right to identify the attendees.

Tonight's attendees: Managed Object Model, NSManagedObject, Managed Object Context, NSFetchRequest, and NSSortDescriptor.

Any of the charming items you've seen so far just might show up!

Who am I?

Name

Describes the search you want to execute on your data. Includes type of information you want back, any conditions the data must meet, and how the results should be sorted.

_____

Responsible for keeping track of managed objects active in the application. All your fetch and save requests go through this.

_____

Captures how data should be sorted in a generic way. You specify the field the data should be sorted by and how it should be sorted.

_____

Describes entities in your application, including type information, data constraints, and relationships between the entities.

_____

A Objective-C version of a Core Data entity. Subclasses of this represent data you want to load and save through Core Data. Provides the support for monitoring changes, lazy loading, and data validation.

_____

CoreData cross Solution

So, did you remember all those words?

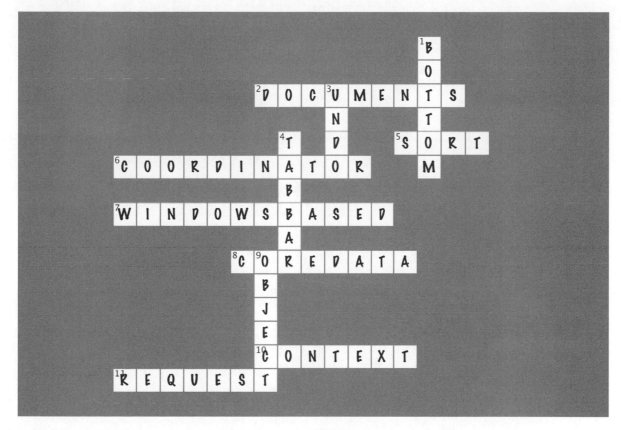

Across

2. Each app has a _____ directory. [DOCUMENTS]
5. NS_____Descriptor captures how data should be sorted. [SORT]
6. In the middle of the Core Data stack is the Persistent Store _____. [COORDINATOR]
7. The _____ template is pretty basic. [WINDOWSBASED]
8. _____ can manage different types of data. [COREDATA]
10. The managed object _____ is the top of the Core Data stack. [CONTEXT]
11. NSFetch_____ describes a search. [REQUEST]

Down

1. The Persistent Object Store is at the _____ of the Core Data stack. [BOTTOM]
3. Core Data has _____ and redo. [UNDO]
4. The _____ controller is good for switching views. [TABBAR]
9. The managed _____ model describes entities. [OBJECT]

Match each field we need to implement for the data view to its Core
Data type.

Field for the Detail View   **Core Data Type**

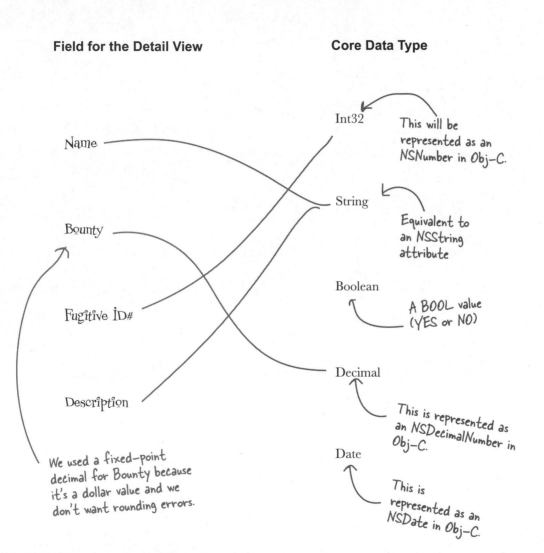

Name

Bounty

Fugitive ID#

Description

We used a fixed-point
decimal for Bounty because
it's a dollar value and we
don't want rounding errors.

Int32

This will be
represented as an
NSNumber in Obj-C.

String

Equivalent to
an NSString
attribute

Boolean

A BOOL value
(YES or NO)

Decimal

This is represented as
an NSDecimalNumber in
Obj-C.

Date

This is
represented as an
NSDate in Obj-C.

Who am I?

SOLUTION

A bunch of Core Data code in full costume are playing a party game, "Who am I?" They'll give you a clue—you try to guess who they are based on what they say. Assume they always tell the truth about themselves. Fill in the blanks to the right to identify the attendees.

Tonight's attendees: Managed Object Model, NSManagedObject, Managed Object Context, NSFetchRequest, and NSSortDescriptor.

Any of the charming items you've seen so far just might show up!

Name

Describes the search you want to execute on your data. Includes type of information you want back, any conditions the data must meet, and how the results should be sorted.

NSFetchRequest

Responsible for keeping track of managed objects active in the application. All your fetch and save requests go through this.

Managed Object Context

Captures how data should be sorted in a generic way. You specify the field the data should be sorted by and how it should be sorted.

NSSortDescriptor

Describes entities in your application, including type information, data constraints, and relationships between the entities.

Managed Object Model

A Objective-C version of a Core Data entity. Subclasses of this represent data you want to load and save through Core Data. Provides the support for monitoring changes, lazy loading, and data validation.

NSManagedObject

Your Core Data Toolbox

You've got Chapter 8 under your belt and now you've added Core Data to your toolbox.

The Data Model

Works with entities that have properties called attributes.

Can be edited directly in Xcode.

Has several different data types.

Tab Bars

Each tab means a separate view.

Tabs work well with tasks that are not hierarchical.

Core Data

Provides a stack that manages the data so you don't have to.

Can manage different types of data.

Great for memory management and tracking changes.

BULLET POINTS

- Core Data is a **persistence framework** that offers loading, saving, versioning and undo-redo.

- **Core Data** can be built on top of SQLite databases, binary files, or temporary memory.

- The **Managed Object Model** defines the **Entities** we're going to ask Core Data to work with.

- The **Managed Object Context** is our entry point to our data. It keeps track of active **Managed Objects**.

- The Managed Object Context is part of the Core Data stack that handles reading and writing our data.

9 migrating and optimizing with Core Data

Things are changing

How about this one? I just can't seem to decide which outfit to wear...

We have a great app in the works.

iBountyHunter successfully loads the data Bob needs and lets him view the fugitives easily. But what about when the data has to change? Bob wants some new functionality, and what does that do to the data model? In this chapter, you'll learn how to handle changes to your data model and how to take advantage of more Core Data features.

Bob needs documentation

To get paid, I need to be able to show who was captured when...

Bob needs to record more information.

Bob has to keep track of his work so he can be paid. That means we need somewhere to store the day and time of a capture and then use that to build the Captured view...

Remember that Captured view we built in the last chapter?

How are we going to update iBountyHunter to handle the new information?

Sharpen your pencil

We need to figure out how to update iBountyHunter
to handle this new data. Look at each piece of our
application and write what, if anything, needs to change.

**iPhone
Views**

....

....

....

....

....

**SQLite
Database**

....

....

....

....

....

View Controllers

....

....

....

....

**Managed
Object
Model**

....

....

....

....

....

Where do we start? ....

Sharpen your pencil
Solution

We need to figure out how to update iBountyHunter
to handle this new data. Look at each piece of our
application and write what, if anything, needs to change.

iPhone Views

– A spot to mark
fugitives as caught.

– Show the date and
time of capture.

– Populate the
Captured list.

SQLite Database

– Add a captured flag
to fugitives.

– Add the captured
time for the fugitive.

– Add the captured
date for the fugitive.

– Fill in the date and
time of capture data.

– Display only the
captured fugitives in
the Captured view.

View Controllers

Managed Object Model

– Add information
about the changes to
the data for display in
the app.

Where do we start?   Since nearly everything depends on the new data
we need to add, let's get that in our object model
first; then we can update the rest.

Everything stems from our object model

So now you've figured out that the Fugitive entity needs a few more fields: the date and time, and something to indicate whether the fugitive has been captured. The database is built from the data model, so we can just update the data model to add the information we need. The Core Data date type includes both a date and time, so we only need two more properties on our Fugitive entity:

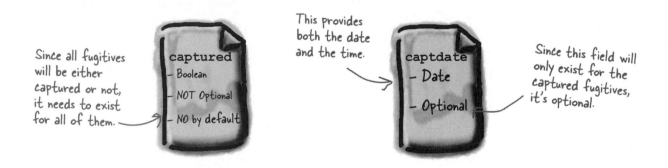

Since all fugitives will be either captured or not, it needs to exist for all of them.

captured
- Boolean
- NOT Optional
- NO by default

This provides both the date and the time.

captdate
- Date
- Optional

Since this field will only exist for the captured fugitives, it's optional.

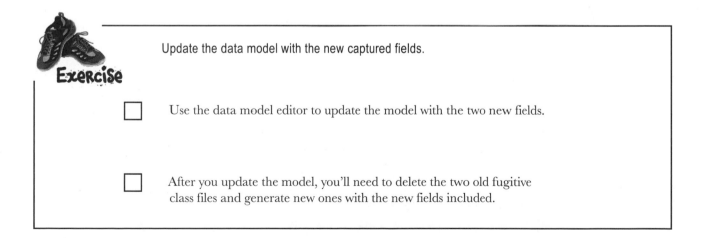

Exercise

Update the data model with the new captured fields.

☐ Use the data model editor to update the model with the two new fields.

☐ After you update the model, you'll need to delete the two old fugitive class files and generate new ones with the new fields included.

EXERCISE SOLUTION

Use the tools that Xcode comes with to quickly make those changes.

☑ Use the Data Model Editor to update the model with the two new fields.

Here's the updated entity

captured
- Boolean
- NOT Optional
- NO by default

Make sure that your attributes match ours.

captdate
- Date
- Optional

☑ After you update the model, you'll need to delete the two old fugitive class files and generate new ones with the new fields included.

```objc
@interface Fugitive : NSManagedObject {
@private
}
@property (nonatomic, retain) NSDecimalNumber *
bounty;
@property (nonatomic, retain) NSString * name;
@property (nonatomic, retain) NSNumber * fugitiveID;
@property (nonatomic, retain) NSString * desc;
@property (nonatomic, retain) NSNumber * captured;
@property (nonatomic, retain) NSDate * captdate;


@end
```

These two fields are the new generated classes.

Fugitive.h

```
#import "Fugitive.h"


@implementation Fugitive
@dynamic bounty;
@dynamic name;
@dynamic fugitiveID;
@dynamic desc;
@dynamic captured;
@dynamic captdate;


@end
```

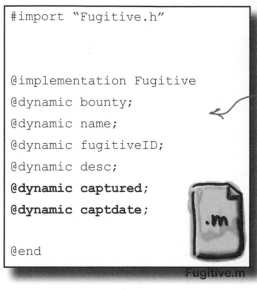

The new fields have been added as dynamic properties, just like the earlier ones.

Fugitive.m

TEST DRIVE

Once you've made the changes, go ahead and run iBountyHunter.

```
All Output ‡                                                                    Clear
   7 : <CFString 0xe268b0 [0x100a400]>{contents = "NSStoreUUID"} = <CFString 0x5a16300 [0x100a400
]>{contents = "E711F65F-3C5A-4889-872B-6541E4B2863A"}
   8 : <CFString 0xe26720 [0x100a400]>{contents = "NSStoreType"} = <CFString 0xe268f0 [0x100a400]
>{contents = "SQLite"}
   9 : <CFString 0x5a164f0 [0x100a400]>{contents = "NSStoreModelVersionHashesVersion"} = <CFNumbe
r 0x590b4a0 [0x100a400]>{value = +3, type = kCFNumberSInt32Type}
   10 : <CFString 0x5a165b0 [0x100a400]>{contents = "_NSAutoVacuumLevel"} = <CFString 0x5a166b0 [
0x100a400]>{contents = "2"}
}
, reason=The model used to open the store is incompatible with the one used to create the store},
{
    metadata =     {
        NSPersistenceFrameworkVersion = 248;
        NSStoreModelVersionHashes =         {
            Fugitive = <e33370b6 e7ca3101 f91d2595 1e8bfe01 3e7fb4de 6ef2a31d 9e50237b b313d390>;
        };
        NSStoreModelVersionHashesVersion = 3;
        NSStoreModelVersionIdentifiers =         (
        );
        NSStoreType = SQLite;
        NSStoreUUID = "E711F65F-3C5A-4889-872B-6541E4B2863A";
        "_NSAutoVacuumLevel" = 2;
    };
    reason = "The model used to open the store is incompatible with the one used to create the sto
re";
}
sharedlibrary apply-load-rules all
Current language:  auto; currently objective-c
(gdb)
```

It crashed! What did we miss?

The data hasn't been updated

If you take a close look at the console report of the crash,
you can figure out what's wrong...

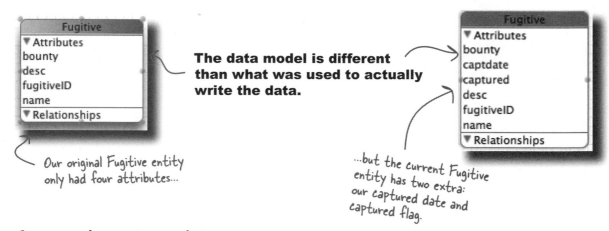

This error seems to be
coming from Core Data.

It's complaining that our
data model isn't compatible
with the one that created
the database.

**The data model is different
than what was used to actually
write the data.**

Our original Fugitive entity
only had four attributes...

...but the current Fugitive
entity has two extra:
our captured date and
captured flag.

Core Data caught a mismatch between our DB and our model

We created this problem when we added new fields to the
Fugitive entity. Our initial fugitive database was created
with the old model, and Core Data has no idea where to
get those new fields from. Rather than risk data corruption,
it aborted our application with an error. That's good, but
we still need to figure out how to fix it.

Data migration is a common problem

Realizing you need to add new data or changing the way you store old data is a pretty common problem in application development. But just because it's common doesn't mean it's easy. Core Data works hard to make sure it doesn't corrupt or lose any data, so we're going to have to tell it what to do with our new Fugitive entity.

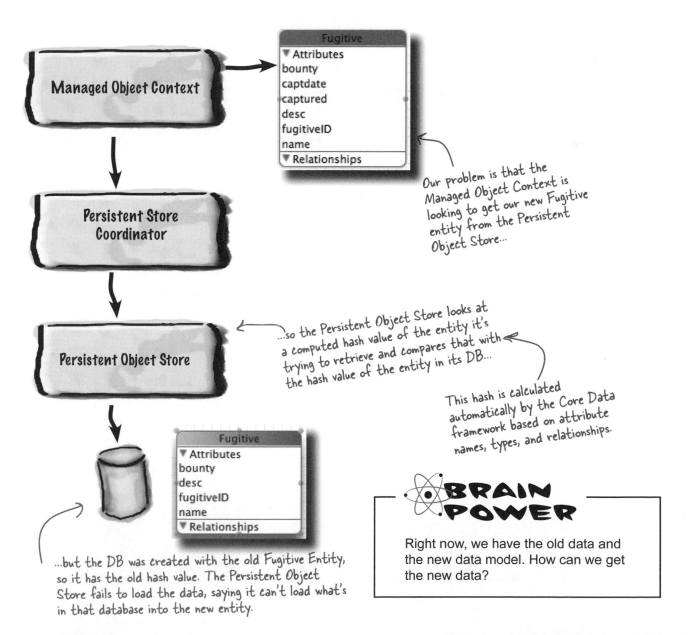

Our problem is that the Managed Object Context is looking to get our new Fugitive entity from the Persistent Object Store...

...so the Persistent Object Store looks at a computed hash value of the entity it's trying to retrieve and compares that with the hash value of the entity in its DB...

This hash is calculated automatically by the Core Data framework based on attribute names, types, and relationships.

...but the DB was created with the old Fugitive Entity, so it has the old hash value. The Persistent Object Store fails to load the data, saying it can't load what's in that database into the new entity.

BRAIN POWER

Right now, we have the old data and the new data model. How can we get the new data?

Migrate the old data into the new model

We made the changes to the data model, but we need everything up and down the Core Data stack to be able to deal with those changes. In order to do that, we need to **migrate the data**.

To migrate anything, you need to go *from* somewhere *to* somewhere. Core Data needs to have both of these data models to make data migration work for the entire stack. We need a new approach to changing the data model, besides just changing the old one. Let's undo what we did earlier so we can load the data from the database again.

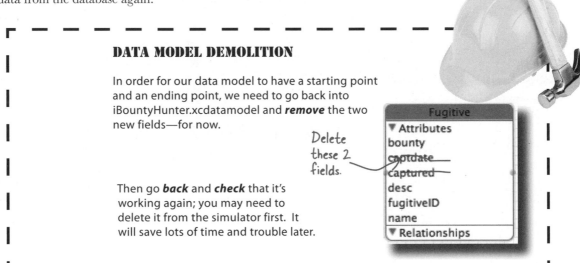

DATA MODEL DEMOLITION

In order for our data model to have a starting point and an ending point, we need to go back into iBountyHunter.xcdatamodel and *remove* the two new fields—for now.

Delete these 2 fields.

Then go *back* and *check* that it's working again; you may need to delete it from the simulator first. It will save lots of time and trouble later.

Fugitive
▼ Attributes
bounty
captdate
captured
desc
fugitiveID
name
▼ Relationships

Our two models need different versions

It's easy enough to change the data model by hand, but Core Data needs to be able to work with both the old and new data. We need to give Core Data access to both, but tell them they're different versions of the same model. Even more importantly, we need to tell Core Data which one we consider our current version.

The Persistent Object Store needs to know that this is what we consider our current version.

This is what we started with, and the Persistent Object Store is expecting this data model.

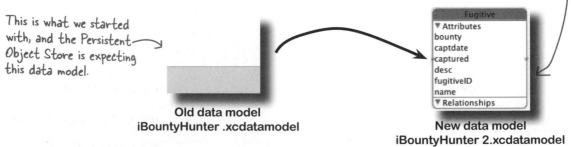

Old data model
iBountyHunter .xcdatamodel

Fugitive
▼ Attributes
bounty
captdate
captured
desc
fugitiveID
name
▼ Relationships

New data model
iBountyHunter 2.xcdatamodel

Xcode makes it easy to version your data model

Fortunately, it's pretty easy to create a new version of your data model using Xcode:

1 **Highlight iBountyHunter.xcdatamodeld.**
Then go to the **Editor**→**Add Model Version** menu option. That will generate a new file under the iBountyHunter.xcdatamodeld directory called iBountyHunter 2.xcdatamodel.

2 **Set the current version.**
Highlight the iBountyHunter.xcmodeld directory, then select the File Inspector on the Utilities Pane. Then in the Versioned Data Model section, select "iBountyHunter 2" as the **Current** version.

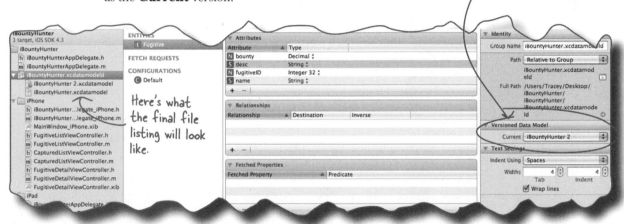

Here's what the final file listing will look like.

3 **Update the new data model.**
Select iBountyHunter 2.xcdatamodel and re-edit the data model to add the captdate and captured fields back in as we did before. Now the old version is preserved and the changes are where they belong.

Geek Bits

Normally, you'd also need to delete and regenerate the Fugitive class, but since we made the same changes to the new file, the generated class would be the same.

How does the app map between the two versions?

Jim: Ugh. I guess we need to write a bunch of migration code or something.

Joe: Why?

Jim: I assume we're going to have to tell Core Data how to get from the old version of the data to the new one, right?

Frank: Well, actually, I think we can do it automatically.

Jim: What?

Frank: Core Data has a feature that allows you to tell the app about both models and it can migrate the data for you.

Jim: Nice! When does the data actually get migrated?

Frank: Runtime, when the Persistent Object Store sees that the data is in the old format. That means that we'll just need some code to tell iBountyHunter to actually do the migration.

Joe: OK, so it looks like some of that code is auto-generated, and some of it needs to be added.

Jim: This is great; so we can just change whatever we want?

Frank: There are certain data changes that Core Data can handle automatically, like adding new attributes. More complex changes to the data need to be handled manually.

Joe: Yeah, it says here that we can do automatic migration if we're adding attributes, or changing the optional status of an attribute.

Jim: What about renaming?

Frank: Renaming gets tricky—sometimes you can and sometimes you can't.

Joe: So, how can we migrate the data we have?

Core Data can "lightly" migrate data

Lightweight data migration is a powerful Core Data tool that allows you to cleanly update your underlying data to match a new data model without needing a mapping model. It only works with basic data changes: adding new attributes, changing a required attribute to an optional one, or making an optional attribute required with a default value. It can also handle limited renaming of attributes, but that gets trickier.

Automatic data migration happens at runtime, which means that your app needs to know that it's going to happen so that the data can be migrated. You'll do that in the AppDelegate:

iBountyHunterAppDelegate.m

```
- (NSPersistentStoreCoordinator *)persistentStoreCoordinator
{
    if (__persistentStoreCoordinator != nil)
    {
        return __persistentStoreCoordinator;
    }
    NSURL *storeURL = [[self applicationDocumentsDirectory] URLByAppendingPathComponent
:@"iBountyHunter.sqlite"];
    NSError *error = nil;
    NSDictionary *options = [NSDictionary dictionaryWithObjectsAndKeys:[NSNumb
er numberWithBool:YES], NSMigratePersistentStoresAutomaticallyOption, [NSNumber
numberWithBool:YES], NSInferMappingModelAutomaticallyOption, nil];

    __persistentStoreCoordinator = [[NSPersistentStoreCoordinator alloc] initWithManaged
ObjectModel:[self managedObjectModel]];
    if (![__persistentStoreCoordinator addPersistentStoreWithType:NSSQLiteStoreType
configuration:nil URL:storeURL options:options error:&error])
    {
        NSLog(@"Unresolved error %@, %@", error, [error userInfo]);
                        abort();
```

Remember, by default, Core Data will load all the object models in your app bundle. That means it will see both the old version and the current version of our model.

All we need to do to enable lightweight migration is turn it on.

We changed this from nil: options to pass the options to the persistentStoreCoordiator.

TEST DRIVE

After adding the code to the app delegate, build and debug...

If you run into issues here, try Build→ Clean first, then Build and Debug. Strangely, Xcode doesn't always properly recompile the first time you version your model, but cleaning should fix it.

Test Drive

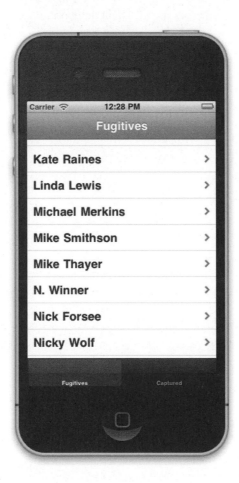

Awesome! It's working with a whole new data model.

The Persistent Object Store Exposed

**This week's interview:
Do you really have any
staying power?**

Head First: Hi, Persistent Object Store, mind if I call you POS for short?

Persistent Object Store: I'd rather you didn't. Just "Store" is fine.

Head First: OK, Store, so I understand you're part of the Core Data stack?

Store: Yep—one of the most important parts, actually. It's my job to read and write your actual data.

Head First: Right, you're the guy who translates into a bunch of different formats.

Store: Exactly. When you use Core Data, you don't really need to know if your data is going into a simple file or a sophisticated database. You just ask me to read and write a bunch of data and I handle it.

Head First: That's convenient. I understand you can be pretty particular, though. I hear you don't take well to change.

Store: I don't think you're getting the whole picture. See, it's my job to make sure your data is loaded and saved exactly right.

Head First: I get that, but still, small changes are OK, right?

Store: Sure—I just need to make sure you really want me to do them. You need to tell me what data I'm looking at and then tell me how you want me to return it to you. Tell me it's OK to infer the differences and do the mapping and I'll take care of the rest.

Head First: So do you actually migrate the data or just translate it when you load it?

Store: Oh, I actually migrate the data. Now, here's where things get cool. Simple stores like the binary file ones just create a new file with the migrated data. But if I'm using a SQLite DB, I can usually do the migration right in place. Don't need to load the data and the whole migration is nearly instant.

Head First: Nice! I thought lightweight migration was kind of a noob's migration.

Store: Oh no, if you can let me do the migration through lightweight migration, that's definitely the way to go. Now if you need to do something more complicated, like split an old attribute into two new ones or change the type of something, you'll need to help me out.

Head First: And people do that through code?

Store: Sort of. Basically, you need to give me one more model, a mapping model. That tells me how to move your data from the old format to the new format.

Head First: Hmm, OK, makes sense. I guess this applies to renaming variables too?

Store: Actually, most of the time I can handle that too, as long as you tell me what the old name was. If you look at the details of an attribute in your object model, you can give me the old name of an attribute. If it's there, and I have to do a migration, I can handle renaming, too.

Head First: Wow, you're not nearly as boring as I thought...

Store: Thanks, I guess.

there are no
Dumb Questions

Q: How many versions of a data model can I have?

A: As many as you need. Once you start adding versions, you'll need to keep track of your current version so that Managed Object Model knows what you want when you ask for an entity. By keeping all the old versions around, Core Data can migrate from any prior version to the current one.

Q: When is renaming something OK for a lightweight migration? When isn't it?

A: You can rename variables as long as you don't change the type. If you rename them, click on the little wrench on the attribute properties in Xcode and specify the renaming identifier to be the old attribute. Core Data will handle the migration automatically from there.

Q: Can I use migration to get data I have in some other format into Core Data?

A: No. Migration (lightweight or otherwise) only works with existing Core

Data. If you have legacy data you want moved into Core Data, you'll need to do that yourself. Typically, you just read the legacy data with your own code, create a new NSManagedObject to hold it, populate the new object, and save it using Core Data. It's not pretty, but it works. There are a couple other approaches you can look at if you have large amounts of data to migrate or streaming data (for example, from a network feed). Take a look at the Apple Documentation on Efficiently Importing Data with Core Data for more details.

Q: Does it make a difference if I use lightweight migration or migrate data myself?

A: Use lightweight migration if you can. It won't work for all cases, but, if it can be done, Core Data can optimize the migration if you're using a SQLite store. Migration time can be really, really small when done through lightweight migration.

Q: What do I do if I can't use lightweight migration?

A: You'll need to create a mapping model. You can do that in Xcode by selecting

Design→Mapping Model, then picking the two models you want to map between. You'll need to select your source entities and attributes, then select the destination entities and attributes. You can enter custom expressions to do data conversions if you need to. To find out more information on mapping models, check out the Apple Documentation on Core Data Migration.

Q: Xcode lets me enter a hash modifier in the Versioning Settings for an attribute. What are those for?

A: Core Data computes a hash for entities using attribute information so it can determine if the model has changed since the data store was created. However, it's possible that you need to change the way your data is stored without actually changing the data model. For example, let's say you always stored your time values in seconds, but then decided you needed to store milliseconds instead. You can continue to store the value as an integer but use the version hash modifier to let Core Data know that you want two models to be considered different versions and apply your migration code at runtime.

BULLET POINTS

- Lightweight automatic migration needs **both versions** of the data model before it will work.

- Automatic migration can change a SQLite database **without** loading the data.

- Migration of data happens **at runtime**.

- You can use lightweight migration to **add variables**, make a required variable **optional**, make an optional one **required** with default, and to do some **renaming**.

Here's what you've done so far...

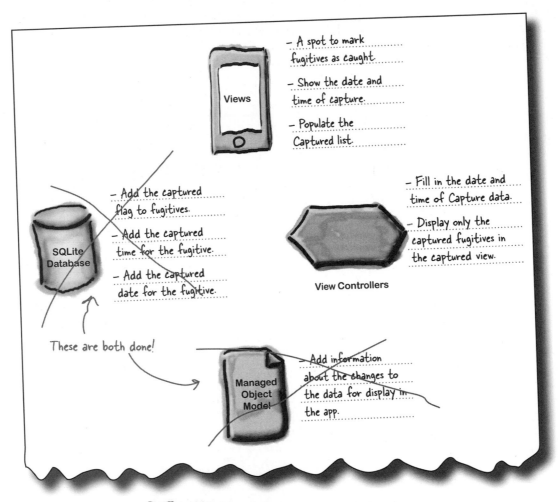

Views
- A spot to mark fugitives as caught.
- Show the date and time of capture.
- Populate the Captured list.

SQLite Database
- ~~Add the captured flag to fugitives.~~
- ~~Add the captured time for the fugitive.~~
- ~~Add the captured date for the fugitive.~~

These are both done!

View Controllers
- Fill in the date and time of Capture data.
- Display only the captured fugitives in the captured view.

Managed Object Model
- ~~Add information about the changes to the data for display in the app.~~

BRAIN POWER

What kind of changes do we need to make to the UI to add the captured information?

Bob has some design input

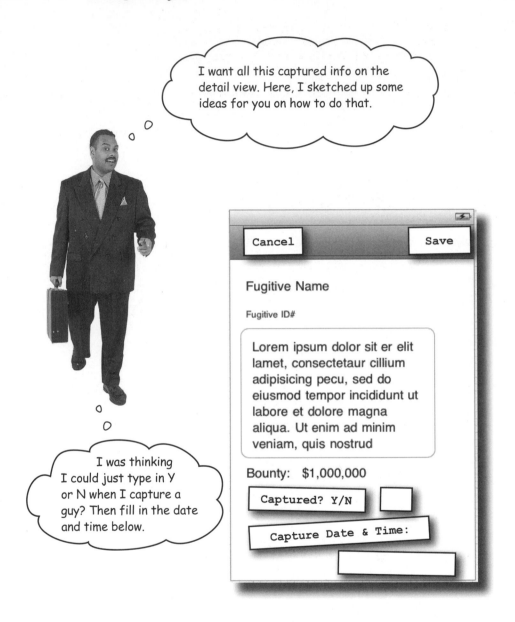

I want all this captured info on the detail view. Here, I sketched up some ideas for you on how to do that.

I was thinking I could just type in Y or N when I capture a guy? Then fill in the date and time below.

Cancel   **Save**

Fugitive Name

Fugitive ID#

Lorem ipsum dolor sit er elit lamet, consectetaur cillium adipisicing pecu, sed do eiusmod tempor incididunt ut labore et dolore magna aliqua. Ut enim ad minim veniam, quis nostrud

Bounty: $1,000,000

Captured? Y/N

Capture Date & Time:

But Bob's sketch has some problems...

Sharpen your pencil

Bob's view needs some improving. As an experienced iOS developer, you can probably come up with some better UI designs. Time for you to help him out.

1 Can Bob's view actually work with the app as it's currently written? (Circle one)   **Yes   No**

2 If not, why not? ....

....

....

3 To properly implement this view, you need to know what data is editable. What data can the user edit and what is the best way to handle that input? ....

....

....

4 Sketch up *your* plan for the final detail view:

Fugitive Name

Fugitive ID#

Lorem ipsum dolor sit er elit lamet, consectetaur cillium adipisicing pecu, sed do eiusmod tempor incididunt ut labore et dolore magna aliqua. Ut enim ad minim veniam, quis nostrud

Bounty: $1,000,000

Don't forget about the Tab Bar Controller down here.

Sharpen your pencil
Solution

Now that you've thought through the design implications, what should the detail view look like?

1 Can Bob's view actually work as is with the app as written? (Circle one)   **Yes**   **No**

2 If not, why not?   We already have a Back button where Bob wants to put a Cancel button. Asking the user to input the "Y" or "N" and type the date and time is not a great UI.

3 To properly implement this view, you need to know what data is editable. What data can the user edit and what is the best way to handle input?   The only data that will need to change is the Captured field and the Captured date and time. Since Captured is a boolean, a switch or some kind of control will work better than typing. Since Bob will hit the control when he captures the bad guy, we can just get the current date and time from iOS and save even more typing.

4 Sketch up *your* plan for the final detail view:

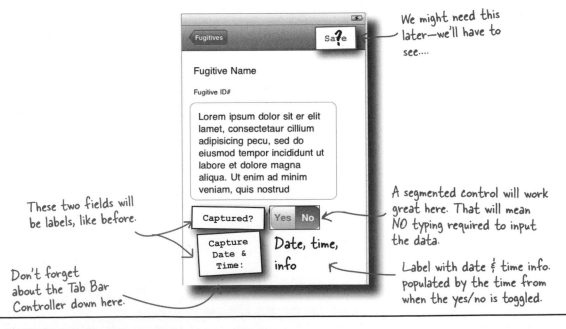

We might need this later—we'll have to see....

Sa**?**e

Fugitives

Fugitive Name

Fugitive ID#

Lorem ipsum dolor sit er elit lamet, consectetaur cillium adipisicing pecu, sed do eiusmod tempor incididunt ut labore et dolore magna aliqua. Ut enim ad minim veniam, quis nostrud

These two fields will be labels, like before.

Captured?   Yes   No

Capture Date & Time: Date, time, info

A segmented control will work great here. That will mean NO typing required to input the data.

Label with date & time info. populated by the time from when the yes/no is toggled.

Don't forget about the Tab Bar Controller down here.

Exercise

Make the additions you need to the detail view
to include the additional fields.

1 **Open up FugitiveDetailViewController.xib in Interface
Builder.**
Go ahead and add the visual elements you need: the three labels and the
segmented control. You'll need to add a simulated tab bar to make sure
everything will fit. Don't worry about the Save button for now.

2 **In FugitiveDetailViewController.m (and .h), add properties
and initialization code.**
Now that all those interface elements exist, give them the back end in
Xcode, but don't worry about linking them just yet...

Exercise Solution

Here are the additions to the view and
the code to support them.

1 Open up FugitiveDetailViewController.xib in Interface Builder.

The segmented control
needs to be configured
(it says first/second
by default).

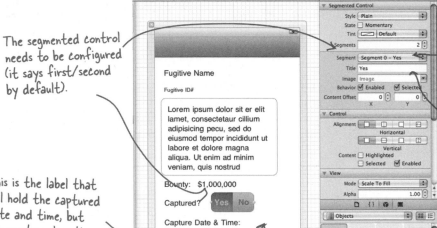

Toggle this selection
to get to the other
half of the control.

This is the label that
will hold the captured
date and time, but
it's empty unless the
switch is toggled to
Yes.

Make sure "Segment 0 –
Yes" is selected and both
segments are enabled. We'll
need this in a minute.

2 In FugitiveDetailViewController.m (and .h), add properties
and initialization code.

```
UISegmentedControl *capturedToggle_;
UILabel *capturedDateLabel_;
```
Add this inside
the @interface.

Add this with
the other @
properties.

```
@property (nonatomic, retain) IBOutlet UISegmentedControl
*capturedToggle;

@property (nonatomic, retain) IBOutlet UILabel
*capturedDateLabel;
```

FugitiveDetailViewController. h

```
@synthesize bountyLabel=bountyLabel_;
@synthesize capturedToggle=capturedToggle_;
@synthesize capturedDateLabel=c apturedDateLabel_;
```

FugitiveDetailViewController.m

```
- (void) viewWillAppear:(BOOL)animated {
    [super viewWillAppear:animated];

    self.nameLabel.text = fugitive_.name;
    self.idLabel.text = [fugitive_.fugitiveID stringValue];
    self.descriptionTextView.text = fugitive_.desc;
    self.bountyLabel.text = [fugitive_.bounty stringValue];
    self.capturedDateLabel.text = [fugitive_.captdate description];
    self.capturedToggle.selectedSegmentIndex = [fugitive_.captured
boolValue] ? 0 : 1;
}
```

Convert the date to a label for the description.

Set the selectedSegmentIndex based on whether they are captured: 0 = YES, 1 = NO.

```
- (void)dealloc
{
    [fugitive_ release];
    [nameLabel_ release];
    [idLabel_ release];
    [descriptionTextView_ release];
    [bountyLabel_ release];
    [capturedToggle_ release];
    [capturedDateLabel_ release];
    [super dealloc];
}
```

FugitiveDetailViewController.m

Do this!

Finally, link the capturedToggle outlet for the segmented control to File's Owner in Interface Builder.

Test Drive

All the view
elements look good!
Now we just need
to implement their
behaviors...

there are no Dumb Questions

Q: Why didn't we use the switch instead of the segmented control?

A: Because there's no Apple-sanctioned way to change the text of the switch. By default, the options are On and Off, which won't work for us.

Q: Why didn't we use a checkbox for the captured field?

A: It turns out that the checkbox isn't a standard control. It's certainly surprising, since you see them so often in iOS apps.

They can be done, however, by creating a custom button with three images (an empty box, a selected box, and a checked box), and switching between them.

Toggle Code Magnets

Now that we have the controls laid out the way we want them, we need to actually give them some behavior. Use the magnets below to implement the method that will handle the segmented control switching. Then everything will be ready for linking to the segmented control in Interface Builder.

```objc
- (IBAction) capturedToggleChanged: (id) sender {

    if (_____    _____) {
        _____ = [NSDate _____
        self.capturedDateLabel.text = [fugitive_captdate
description];
        _____ = [NSNumber numberWithBool:YES];
    }
    else {
        _____ = nil;
        fugitive_.captured = [NSNumber numberWithBool:NO];
    }

    self.capturedDateLabel.text = [_____];
}
```

`x == 1`	`@""`
`fugitive_.captured`	`date];`
`self.capturedToggle.selectedSegmentIndex`	`== 0`

`fugitive_.captdate`

`fugitive_.captdate`

`NSDate`

`text`

Toggle Code Magnets Solution

Now that we have the controls laid out the way we want them, we need to actually give them some behavior. Use the magnets below to implement the method that will handle the segmented control switching. Then everything will be ready for linking to the segmented control in Interface Builder.

This will only be called if the value actually changed, so if the selected index is now 0, the fugitive wasn't captured prior to this call.

```
- (IBAction) capturedToggleChanged: (id) sender {

    if ( self.capturedToggle.selectedSegmentIndex == 0) ) {

        fugitive_.captdate = [NSDate date];
        self.capturedDateLabel.text = [fugitive_captdate
    description];

        fugitive_.captured = [NSNumber numberWithBool:YES];

    }
    else {

        fugitive_.captdate = nil;
        fugitive_.captured = [NSNumber numberWithBool:NO];

    }

    self.capturedDateLabel.text = @""  ;

}
```

Remember, segment 0 is YES on our control.

This will return an NSDate set to the current date and time.

Core Data stores booleans as NSNumbers, so we need to convert our boolean YES/NO values to NSNumbers to update the fugitive.

If the fugitive isn't captured, clear the old capture date if there was one.

This will return a text representation of an NSDate.

`date];`

`text`

`NSDate`

`x == 1`

These were extras...

Test Drive

Add the code above to FugtiveDetailViewController.m and don't forget the corresponding declaration in the .h file:

```
- (IBAction) capturedToggleChanged:
(id) sender;
```

→ Link the Value Changed event from the segmented control to the capturedToggleChanged and the captureDateLabel action to the empty Date & Time label in the Files's Owner in Interface Builder.

Test Drive

Now that all that work is done, you should have a functioning detail view. Give it a try...

The view looks great and the segmented control is set to No, just like it should be.

If you toggle the segmented control, the date and time are filled in.

OK, but if I come in and out of the app, it's not restarting. What's the deal with that? I thought that only one app was running at a time...

That was true before iOS 4.

Now developers can access **multitasking** behavior on iPhone. That means that apps don't terminate when you leave them, or the phone rings, or you flip over to your iPod to change your music. So what does that mean for iBountyHunter?

Your app has a lifecycle all its own...

The Core Data template we used tries to save our data when our application quits (look in applicationWillTerminate). The problem is, as of iOS 4, most iOS devices support multitasking and the application lifecycle has changed.

Because of the constraints of mobile hardware, the applications aren't running in a full multitasking model like you'd see on a desktop. Instead, applications have a very specific lifecycle they go through as iOS starts and stops them.

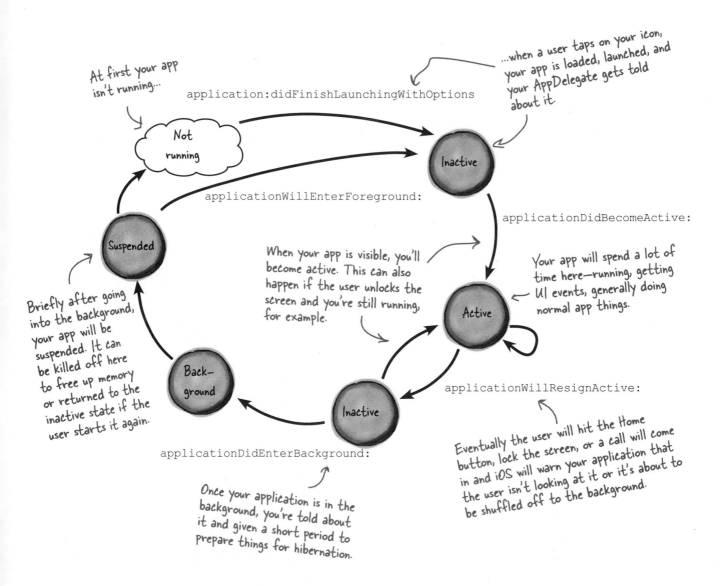

At first your app isn't running...

...when a user taps on your icon, your app is loaded, launched, and your AppDelegate gets told about it.

application:didFinishLaunchingWithOptions

applicationWillEnterForeground:

applicationDidBecomeActive:

When your app is visible, you'll become active. This can also happen if the user unlocks the screen and you're still running, for example.

Your app will spend a lot of time here—running, getting UI events, generally doing normal app things.

Briefly after going into the background, your app will be suspended. It can be killed off here to free up memory or returned to the inactive state if the user starts it again.

applicationWillResignActive:

Eventually the user will hit the Home button, lock the screen, or a call will come in and iOS will warn your application that the user isn't looking at it or it's about to be shuffled off to the background.

applicationDidEnterBackground:

Once your application is in the background, you're told about it and given a short period to prepare things for hibernation.

Multitasking rules of engagement

Apple provides excellent documentation in the iOS Application Programming guide detailing each state transition and the corresponding method calls and notifications you'll receive. A couple points are critical, however:

● You have a limited time to handle moving to the background.
You have approximately 5 seconds to return from applicationDidEnterBackground before iOS takes action and suspends or kills you. At a minimum, **you should save any modified user data** when moving into the background. You should also save application state information you might want to restore the application to where the user left it. They shouldn't know that your application was terminated between when they left it and when it restarted.

● You can request more background time if you need it.
There are limited things you can do in the background state, but if you need more time or want to maintain some network connectivity, for example, you can request it in your applicationDidEnterBackground: method.

● Once you enter the background state, you won't be told if you're killed.
Once you enter the background state, iOS will try to keep you in memory in the suspended state. However, applications are terminated based on resource availability, so if you can reduce memory usage, your app may run longer. Your app will not receive any further notifications before it's killed off, which is why it's so important to persist everything you need to start up again later as soon as you get backgrounded.

● If the device doesn't support multitasking, your app will be terminated.
If the device your app is running on doesn't support multitasking (iPhone 3G, for example) or you have opted out of multitasking support, your application is simply terminated when the user leaves it. This is similar to the pre-iOS 4 behavior and you will receive an applicationWillTerminate: call before you're shut down.

Sharpen your pencil

Add the save code to the right place to handle multitasking.

☐ Copy [self saveContext] from applicationWillTerminate in iBountyHunterAppDelegate.m.

The application isn't going to terminate anymore, it's going to go into the background, thanks to multitasking support.

☐ Paste [self saveContext] in applicationDidEnterBackground in iBountyHunterAppDelegate.m.

Sharpen your pencil
Solution

Relocate the save code to the right place to handle multitasking.

```
- (void)applicationDidEnterBackground:(UIApplication *)application
{

    [self saveContext];

}
```

There are some notes that came with the template that you can delete in here...

```
- (void)applicationWillTerminate:(UIApplication *)application
{

    // Saves changes in the application's managed object context before the
application terminates.
    [self saveContext];

}
```

iBountyHunterAppDelegate.m

The Managed Object Context saves new or changed items

We've used the managed object context to load our Fugitives, but it is also responsible for coordinating saving your data. Remember how NSManagedObject can keep track of changes to entities? The Managed Object Context can take advantage of this information to tell if you if there are any changes in the objects it's managing. Similarly, if you create a new instance of an NSManagedObject, you need to tell it which Managed Object Context it belongs to and that Managed Object Context knows it has new entities to keep track of. The Core Data template takes advantage of this during application exit to see if the Managed Object Context has any new or changed data. If it does, the application simply asks the context to save them.

This template code from iBountyHunterAppDelegate.m is checking for changes as you exit the app.

```
- (void)saveContext
{

    NSError *error = nil;

    NSManagedObjectContext *managedObjectContext = self.
managedObjectContext;

    if (managedObjectContext != nil)

    {

        if ([managedObjectContext hasChanges] &&
                    ![managedObjectContext save:&error])...
```

there are no
Dumb Questions

Q: You said if I create new instances of NSManagedObjects, I need to tell them which Managed Object Context they belong to. How do I do that?

A: It's part of the EntityDescription we mentioned earlier. If you want to create a new instance of an NSManagedObject, you just do this: [NSEntityDescription insertNewObjectForEntityForName:@"Fugitive" inManagedObjectContext:managedObjectContext];. The Managed Object Context is provided right from the start.

Q: What's the "&error" that's being passed to the save call?

A: Most Core Data load/save operations point to an NSError in case something goes wrong. The "&" in Objective-C behaves just like it does in C or C++ and returns the "address of" the item. We declare a pointer to an NSError, then pass the address of that pointer into the save method in case something happens. If the save call fails, Core Data will populate that error argument with more detailed information. Keep in mind that just checking for an NSError does not work for determining if a method succeeded. For that, you should check the BOOL return value, since the error is only tracking if success was NO.

Q: Speaking of errors, what should I do if this comes back with an error?

A: That's really application-specific. Depending on when you detect the problem, you can warn the user and try to recover; other times, there's not too much you can do. For example, if the error happens during the applicationWillTerminate method, there's not much you can do other than tell the user the save failed and possibly stash the data somewhere else.

Q: Should I only ever call save in applicationWillTerminate?

A: No, not at all. The Core Data template set it up this way for convenience, but you should save whenever it's appropriate in your application. In fact, if you're using a SQLite database backend for your data, saves are significantly faster than when we were working with plists in DrinkMixer. You should consider saving additions or changes to the data as soon as possible after they are made to try to avoid any kind of data loss.

Q: You said Core Data could do data validation; where does that fit into all of this?

A: At a minimum, Core Data will validate objects before they're stored in the Persistent Store. So, it's possible that you could get a validation error when you try to save your changes if you have invalid data in one of your managed objects. To avoid such late notice, you should validate your NSManagedObjects as close to the time of change as possible. You can explicitly validate a new NSManagedObject like this: [fugitive validateForInsert:&error]. Similarly, there are methods for validating updates and deletes. You can call these methods at any time to verify that the NSManagedObject is valid against constraints you put in the data model. If it's not, you can notify the user and ask them to correct the problem.

Q: What if I don't want to save the changes in the Managed Object Context? Can I reset it?

A: It's easier than that—just send it the rollback: message. When a Managed Object Context is told to roll back, it will discard any newly inserted objects, deletions, and unsaved changes to existing objects. You can think of the Managed Object Context as managing transactions—changes to entities, including insertion and deletions, are either committed with a save: message or abandoned with a rollback: message.

A quick demo with Bob

After seeing the detailed view and all the captured stuff,
Bob's thrilled, but has one quick comment:

This is definitely way easier
than what I came up with.
But, um, where is that list of
captured people?

**After all that, we
forgot to populate the
Captured list!**

OK, I know how to populate the table cells and stuff—but how can I only pick captured guys?

We can use Core Data to filter our results.

We already have capture information in our Fugitive data; we just need to use it to get the Captured list. We need a way to tell Core Data we only want Fugitives where the captured flag is true.

BRAIN POWER

Where is a natural place to put this kind of filtering?

Use predicates for filtering data

In database languages all over the world, **predicates** are used to scope (or limit) a search to only find data that match certain criteria. Remember the NSFetchRequest we talked about in Chapter 8? For that we used the Entity Information and Sort Descriptor, but we haven't needed the predicate support...until now.

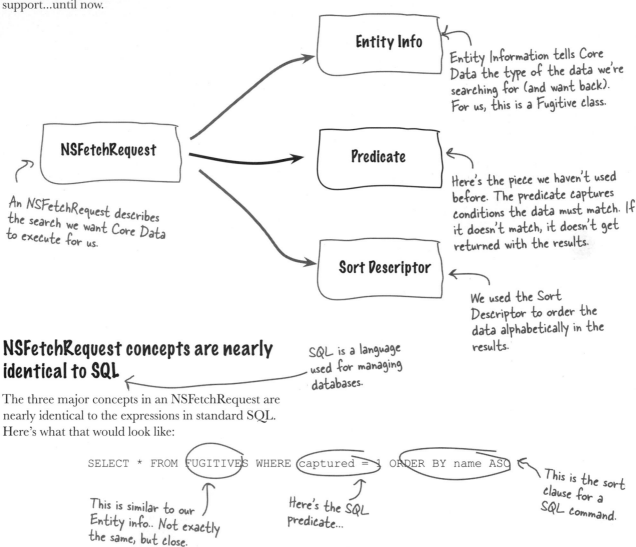

Entity Info

Entity Information tells Core Data the type of the data we're searching for (and want back). For us, this is a Fugitive class.

NSFetchRequest

An NSFetchRequest describes the search we want Core Data to execute for us.

Predicate

Here's the piece we haven't used before. The predicate captures conditions the data must match. If it doesn't match, it doesn't get returned with the results.

Sort Descriptor

We used the Sort Descriptor to order the data alphabetically in the results.

NSFetchRequest concepts are nearly identical to SQL

SQL is a language used for managing databases.

The three major concepts in an NSFetchRequest are nearly identical to the expressions in standard SQL. Here's what that would look like:

```
SELECT * FROM FUGITIVES WHERE captured = 1 ORDER BY name ASC
```

This is similar to our Entity info.. Not exactly the same, but close.

Here's the SQL predicate...

This is the sort clause for a SQL command.

All we need to do is provide the predicate information to our NSFetchRequest and Core Data handles the rest. We can use an NSPredicate for that...

We need to set a predicate on our NSFetchRequest

NSPredicate is a deceptively simple class that lets us express logical constraints on our NSFetchRequest. You use entity and attribute names along with comparison operators to express your constraint information. You can create a basic NSPredicate with a string format syntax similar to NSString, like this:

```
NSPredicate *predicate = [NSPredicate
predicateWithFormat:@"captured == YES"];
[request setPredicate:predicate];
```

But NSPredicates don't stop with simple attribute comparisons. Apple provides several subclasses like NSComparisonPredicate, NSCompoundPredicate, and NSExpression, as well as a complex grammar for wildcard matching, object graph traversal, and more. You can even build complex fetch requests graphically in Xcode. For iBountyHunter, a simple attribute condition is all we need to get Bob's view working, so we'll create the predicate programmatically.

Exercise

Time to populate the Captured view! There's some work to get the Captured view updated to where the fugitive view is, and then a tweak to display what we need.

1 **Set some captured fugitives.**
Build and run the old version of the app and toggle a handful of the fugitives to "captured" before making any changes. You'll need that for testing.

2 **Update the Captured view to match the Fugitive view.**
When we left off in Chapter 8, we hadn't yet done the work to populate the Captured list. Since we're just going to be filtering the data that's in the Fugitive list, the easiest way is to start with the entire list and then add the filtering code. Don't forget the tableview datasource and delegate methods.

3 **Add the predicate code.**
Update your NSFetchRequest to use an NSPredicate so it only finds captured fugitives. This needs to go into the viewWillAppear method in the CapturedViewController.m.

Exercise
Solution

You should recognize the code from Chapter 8 to get the captured
view working, and then add the predicate code to get the filtered data.

① Set some captured fugitives. ⬅ Just do this through the
app—any 5 that you want!

② Update the Captured view to match the Fugitive view.

```
@interface CapturedListViewController : UITableViewController {
@private
        NSMutableArray *items_;                    Create the array to store the
}                                                  captured fugitives.

@property (nonatomic, retain) NSMutablearray *items;

@end
```

CapturedListViewController.h

```
#import "CapturedListViewController.h"         Make sure the Captured
#import "Fugitive.h"                            view is importing all the
#import "iBountyHunterAppDelegate.h"            delegates and data that
#import "FugitiveDetailViewController.h"        we need.
@synthesize items=items_;
```

CapturedListViewController.m

Authors' note: Step 2 code continues on pages 482–483.

```
- (void)viewWillAppear:(BOOL)animated
{
    [super viewWillAppear:animated];
```

> This code is exactly the same code that we used for the FugitiveListViewController.

```
    iBountyHunterAppDelegate *appDelegate = (iBountyHunterAppDelegate*)
[[UIApplication sharedApplication] delegate];
    NSManagedObjectContext *managedObjectContext = appDelegate.
managedObjectContext;
    NSFetchRequest *request = [[NSFetchRequest alloc] init];
    NSEntityDescription *entity = [NSEntityDescription
entityForName:@"Fugitive"  inManagedObjectContext:managedObjectContext];
    [request setEntity:entity];

    NSSortDescriptor *sortDescriptor = [NSSortDescriptor
sortDescriptorWithKey:@"name" ascending:YES];
    [request setSortDescriptors:[NSArray arrayWithObject:sortDescriptor]];

    NSPredicate *predicate = [NSPredicate predicateWithFormat:@"captured
== YES"];
    [request setPredicate:predicate];
```

3 Add the predicate code.

```
    NSError *error;
    NSMutableArray *mutableFetchResults = [[managedObjectContext
executeFetchRequest:request error:&error] mutableCopy];
    if (mutableFetchResults == nil) {
        // Handle the error;
    }

    self.items = mutableFetchResults;
    [mutableFetchResults release];
    [request release];

    // Since the user could have changed how many fugitives are captured,
we need to reload our table view
    [self.tableView reloadData];
}
```

CapturedListViewController.m

You should recognize the code from Chapter 8 to get the captured
view working, and then the predicate code to get the filtered data.

 Get the Captured view to match the Fugitive view (continued).

```objc
#pragma mark Table data source
- (NSInteger)numberOfSectionsInTableView:(UITableView *)tableView
{
    // Return the number of sections.
    return 1;
}
- (NSInteger)tableView:(UITableView *)tableView numberOfRowsInSection:(NSInteger)section
{
    // Return the number of rows in the section.
    return [items_ count];
}


- (UITableViewCell *)tableView:(UITableView *)tableView cellForRowAtIndexPath:(NSIndexPath *)indexPath
{
    static NSString *CellIdentifier = @"Cell";
    UITableViewCell *cell = [tableView dequeueReusableCellWithIdentifier:CellIdentifier];
    if (cell == nil) {
        cell = [[[UITableViewCell alloc] initWithStyle:UITableViewCellStyleDefault reuseIdentifier:CellIdentifier] autorelease];
    }

    // Configure the cell...
    Fugitive *fugitive = [items_ objectAtIndex:indexPath.row];
    cell.textLabel.text = fugitive.name;
    cell.accessoryType = UITableViewCellAccessoryDisclosureIndicator;
    return cell;
}
```

CapturedListViewController.m

```
#pragma mark - Table view delegate
- (void)tableView:(UITableView*)tableView didSelectRowAtIndexPath:(NSIndexPa
th *)indexPath {

        FugitiveDetailViewController *detailViewController =
[[FugitiveDetailViewController alloc] initWithNibName:@"FugitiveDetail
ViewController" bundle:nil];

        detailViewController.fugitive = [self.resultsController
objectAtIndexPath:indexPath];

        [self.navigationController pushViewController:fugitiveDetailVie
wController animated:YES];

        [detailViewController release];
}


- (void)dealloc {
        [items_ release];
        [super dealloc];
}
```

CapturedListViewController.m

Test Drive

Go ahead and fire it up—the captured
view should be ready to go!

TEST DRIVE

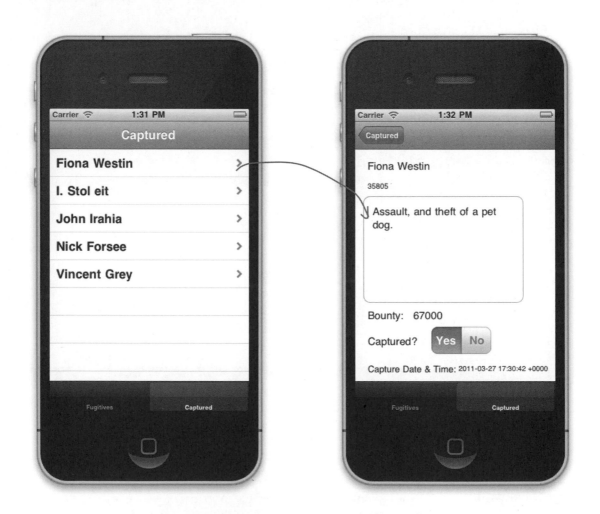

It works! These are the five
fugitives we marked as captured.

> Hang on—you said we should be careful with memory and performance and blah blah...Now we have two arrays of fugitives and we reload them every time the view appears. It seems pretty dumb. What if we moved this code to viewDidLoad so it's only done once per view?

True, we can make this a lot more efficient.

But not by moving it to viewDidLoad. If we move the code there, we're going to end up with two new problems. We need another solution...

BRAIN BARBELL

What problems would we introduce if we moved the fetching code to viewDidLoad? What else could we do to improve performance?

Core Data controller classes provide efficient results handling

The code for both the FugitiveListViewController and the CapturedListViewController is in viewWillAppear. The problem is that viewWillAppear gets called every time the view is shown, which means we're reloading all the fugitives and all the captured fugitives every time, regardless of whether anything's changed.

We could move the code to viewDidLoad, but that only gets called when the views are loaded from their nibs. That causes two problems. First, if we mark a fugitive as captured, the Captured List won't reflect that since it only loads its data once. The second problem is that viewDidLoad gets called *before* our applicationDidFinishLaunching, which means the views will try to get their data before the app delegate gets a chance to copy the master database in place. What we need is a better way to manage our fetched data.

Table views and NSFetchedResultsControllers are made for each other

Since UITableViews are such a common component and frequently deal with large amounts of data, there's a special Core Data class designed to support them. The NSFetchedResultsController works together with the Managed Object Context and your NSFetchRequest to give you some pretty impressive abilities:

Very efficient memory usage
The NSFetchedResultsController works with the NSFetchRequest and the ManagedObjectModel to minimize how much data is actually in memory. For example, even if we have 10,000 fugitives to deal with, the NSFetchedResultsController will try to keep only the ones the UITableView needs to display in memory, probably closer to 10 or 15.

High performance UITableView support
UITableView needs to know how many sections there are, how many rows there are in each section, etc. NSFetchedResultsController has built-in support for figuring that information out quickly, without needing to load all the data.

Built-in monitoring for data changes
We've already talked about how the Managed Object Context knows when data is modified. NSFetchedResultsController can take advantage of that to let you (well, its delegate) know when data that matches your fetch results is modified.

Time for some high-efficiency streamlining

We need to do a little refactoring to get NSFetchedResultsController in there, but when it's done, Bob could give us a database of 100,000 fugitives and iBountyHunter wouldn't blink. We're going to do this for the CapturedListViewController, but the same refactoring can be applied to the FugitiveListViewController, too.

First, we need to replace our items array with an instance of an NSFetchedResultsController, like this:

We want the controller to tell us when data changes—we need to conform to its delegate protocol.

```objc
@interface CapturedListViewController : UITableViewController
<NSFetchedResultsControllerDelegate> {

@private

        NSFetchedResultsController *resultsController_;

}


@property (nonatomic, readonly) NSFetchedResultsController
*resultsController;

@end
```

We're creating a read-only property since we don't want anyone setting it.

CapturedListViewController.h

```objc
@implementation CapturedListViewController

@synthesize items=items_;
```

Remove the items array and its property. We won't need those any longer.

```objc
- (void)dealloc {
    [resultsController_ release];
    [super dealloc];
}
@end
```

Delete the reference to the items array here and release the new controller.

CapturedListViewController.m

Next we need to change the search to use the controller...

Create the new FetchedResultsController getter method

```
- (NSFetchedResultsController *)resultsController {
// If we've already initialized our results controller, just return it
    if (resultsController_ != nil) {
        return resultsController_;
    }
```

Since the NSFetchedResultsController can tell us when data changes, we only need to actually fetch once. If we've already done this (the view is being shown again), we can just bail.

```
// This must be the request for our results controller.  We don't have one
// yet so we need to build it up.
iBountyHunterAppDelegate *appDelegate = (iBountyHunterAppDelegate*)[[UIApplication
sharedApplication] delegate];
    NSManagedObjectContext *managedObjectContext = appDelegate.
managedObjectContext;
    NSFetchRequest *request = [[NSFetchRequest alloc] init];
    NSEntityDescription *entity = [NSEntityDescription entityForName:@"Fugitive"
inManagedObjectContext:managedObjectContext];
    [request setEntity:entity];

    NSSortDescriptor *sortDescriptor = [NSSortDescriptor
sortDescriptorWithKey:@"name" ascending:YES];
    [request setSortDescriptors:[NSArray arrayWithObject:sortDescriptor]];

    NSPredicate *predicate = [NSPredicate predicateWithFormat:@"captured == YES"];
    [request setPredicate:predicate];
```

Create and initialize the NSFetchedResultsController with our fetch request and the Managed Object Context.

```
    resultsController_ = [[NSFetchedResultsController alloc]
        initWithFetchRequest:request
            managedObjectContext:managedObjectContext
            sectionNameKeyPath:nil cacheName:@"captured_list.cache"];
    resultsController_.delegate = self;

    NSError *error;
    BOOL success = [resultsController_ performFetch:&error];
    if (!success) {
        // Handle the error;
    }
    [request release];
    return resultsController_;
}
```

Now instead of asking the Managed Object Model to perform the fetch, we ask the controller.

CapturedListViewController.m

Hmm, so if we get rid of the array of Fugitives, then we're going to have to re-implement the datasource and delegate methods too, right? My guess is we're going to use the NSFetchedResultsController there as well?

Yes.

The NSFetchedResultsController gives us everything we need to access the fetched data. In fact, it can do it a lot more efficiently.

Sharpen your pencil

We've given you the code to set up the NSFetchedResultsController. Now you need to update the tableview delegate and datasource methods to use the controller instead of the view.

1 **Refactor numberOfSectionsInTableView and numberOfRowsInSection to use the controller.**
NSFetchedResultsController has a sections property that is an array of NSFetchedResultsSectionInfo objects. Use those to figure out how many sections there are and how many rows in each section.

2 **Refactor cellForRowAtIndexPath and didSelectRowAtIndexPath to use the controller.**
NSFetchedResultsController makes it easy to implement these methods using its objectAtIndexPath method.

Sharpen your pencil
Solution

Here is the final code for CapturedListViewController.m table methods.

```objc
#pragma mark Table data source


- (NSInteger)numberOfSectionsInTableView:(UITableView *)tableView {
       return [[self.resultsController sections] count];
}
// Customize the number of rows in the table view.
- (NSInteger)tableView:(UITableView *)tableView numberOfRowsInSection:(NSInteger)
section {
       return [[[self.resultsController sections] objectAtIndex:section]
numberOfObjects];

}
// Customize the appearance of table view cells.
- (UITableViewCell *)tableView:(UITableView *)tableView cellForRowAtIndexPath:(NS
IndexPath *)indexPath {
       static NSString *CellIdentifier = @"Cell";
       UITableViewCell *cell = [tableView dequeueReusableCellWithIdentifier:CellI
dentifier];
       if (cell == nil) {
       cell = [[[UITableViewCell alloc] initWithStyle:UITableViewCellStyleDefault
reuseIdentifier:CellIdentifier] autorelease];
       }
       // Set up the cell...
       Fugitive *fugitive = [self.resultsController
objectAtIndexPath:indexPath];
       cell.textLabel.text = fugitive.name;
       cell.accessoryType = UITableViewCellAccessoryDisclosureIndicator;
       return cell;

}
```

For the number of sections, we can just return the count of the sections in the controller.

Nothing fancy here—just get the Fugitive at the given indexPath.

.m

CapturedListViewController.m

```
#pragma mark - Table view delegate
- (void)tableView:(UITableView*)tableView didSelectRowAtIndexPath:(NSIndexPa
th *)indexPath {

        FugitiveDetailViewController *detailViewController =
[[FugitiveDetailViewController alloc] initWithNibName:@"FugitiveDetail
ViewController" bundle:nil];

        detailViewController.fugitive = [self.resultsController
objectAtIndexPath:indexPath];

        [self.navigationController pushViewController:fugitiveDetailVie
wController animated:YES];

        [detailViewController release];

}


- (void)dealloc {

        [resultsController_ release];

        [super dealloc];

}
```

One more lookup for the indexPath to get the Fugitive, and we're all set.

CapturedListViewController.m

Test Drive

Go ahead and run iBountyHunter to make sure the changes didn't break anything. The views should be loading just like they were...sort of. Do some quick testing—if you mark a fugitive as captured, does he switch lists? What if you exit and come back into the app using the Home key?

TEST DRIVE

Now that you're using the controller instead of just a predicate, the behavior of the app should be the same. But people are showing up in the Captured list even when they're not marked as captured!

BRAIN POWER

Why aren't fugitives properly changing lists when you change their captured status? Hint: think back to the "Five-Minute Mystery" from Chapter 6...

We need to refresh the data

The fugitives aren't properly changing lists when you change their status because we're not refreshing the data every time the Captured list view is displayed. We need to set up the NSFetchedResultsController to let us know when things have changed so we can update the table.

Do this!

```
- (void)controllerDidChangeContent:(NSFetchedResultsController *)controller
{
        [self.tableView reloadData];
}
```

You can add this anywhere in the CapturedListViewController.m file.

We ask the whole tableview to reload its data when we detect a change. There are more efficient means of just reloading modified rows when you have larger tableviews.

NSFetchedResultsController can check for changes

Now that we've set up the app to work with the NSFetchedResultsController instead of just an array, we can leverage the methods embedded with the controller to help us. The view controller has built-in support for monitoring the data for changes through a delegate. We had set ourselves up as that delegate but never implemented the code to handle data changing.

Having the view completely reload when it detects a change can become cumbersome if you are dealing with a large amount of data; however, the FetchedResultsController delegate also has support built-in for notifying you of the specific cell that is changed, and you can modify just that. Check Apple's documentation for more details.

TEST DRIVE

Implement the controllerDidChangeContent method from above, and make sure everything's working.

CapturedListViewController.m

Test Drive

Do the same thing you did last time, build and run, and then change the status of one of the fugitives to pull him dynamically out of the captured list.

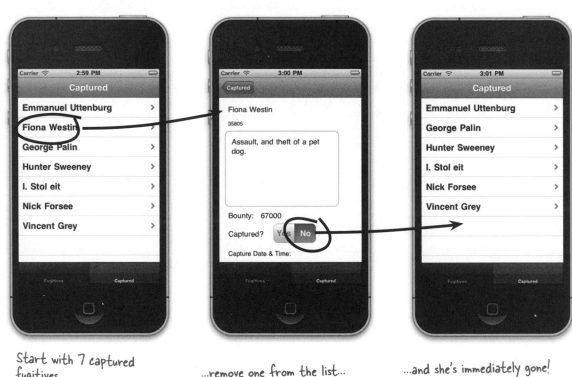

Start with 7 captured fugitives...

...remove one from the list...

...and she's immediately gone!

It works!

This is awesome! The advantage I'm going to have over the competition is great, and having all that information with me means that I'll be making way fewer trips back to the police station. Thanks!

There's nothing like a satisfied customer!

there are no
Dumb Questions

Q: **Where can I find the full syntax for NSPredicate?**

A: NSPredicate has a pretty complex syntax available for expressing constraints on your data. There's a simple summary available in the NSPredicate class documentation, but Apple has an entire document available to help you write advanced predicates.

Q: **It seems like it would be pretty easy to make a mistake typing predicate syntax into code like that. Isn't that sort of like embedding SQL?**

A: Yes, and Xcode can offer a lot of help here. Instead of embedding your predicates in code, you can build them graphically using Xcode's data modeler, just like we did with the Managed Object Model. To build a predicate graphically, select an entity in Xcode, then click on the plus as though you were adding an attribute. Select "Add Fetch Request" to create a new fetch request and click Edit Predicate to bring up the graphical editor. You can name your fetch requests whatever you like. You'll need to retrieve them in code like this:

```
NSFetchRequest *fetchRequest
= [managedObjectModel
fetchRequestFromTemplateWithName:
@"capturedFugitives" substitutionVariables:[
NSDictionary dictionaryWithObject:capturedF
lag forKey:@"captured"]];
```

Then just use that fetch request instead of one created in code. You can also use Xcode's builder to assemble a predicate, then just cut and paste that into your code if you'd prefer to keep them there.

Q: **Reloading the whole table when data changes seems pretty inefficient. Aren't we trying to optimize things?**

A: Yes it is, and yes, we are. There are a number of delegate methods you can implement to get finer-grained information about what's happening with the Managed Object Context. With that information, you can find out if you just need to update a specific table view cell, insert a cell, or remove a cell. We took the easier route and just asked the table view to reload completely.

Q: **What's with that cache value we gave to the results controller?**

A: The results controller will use that file name to cache information like the number of items, number of sections, etc. It will keep an eye on the data store and regenerate the cache if something changes. You can also forcibly ask it to remove a cache, but in general, you shouldn't need to.

Q: **Our results controller only has one section. How do I get it to split things into multiple sections?**

A: Just provide an attribute name for the sectionNameKeyPath. The NSFetchedResultsController will group your results using that attribute and return each grouping as a section. You can get really sophisticated and create a transient property if you want to group them by something you're not actually storing in the database and calculate the value using a custom getter added to your object model.

BULLET POINTS

- NSFetchRequest can take an NSPredicate to **filter data** based on logical conditions.

- You can express NSPredicate **conditions** in code or using Xcode's predicate builder.

- NSFetchedResultsController provides highly efficient memory management and **change monitoring** for UITableViews

- Be careful about what you put in viewWillAppear, as it will be called **every time** your view is shown.

DataMigration cross

We have some new data lingo to try out, so flex those verbal skills...

Across

2. viewDidLoad and view_____ both load views, but with different frequency.
5. The _____ is responsible for reading and writing data.
7. Automatic migration is called _____ data migration.
8. To update the data, we need to _____ it.
9. The FetchedResultsController is good at _____ management.
10. NSFetchResultsController can _____ for changes.

Down

1. _____ concepts are similar to NSFetchResults concepts.
3. _____ are used for filtering data.
4. The new model is the current _____.
6. The Managed Object Context saves new or _____ items.

DataMigration cross Solution

We have some new data lingo to try out, so flex those verbal skills...

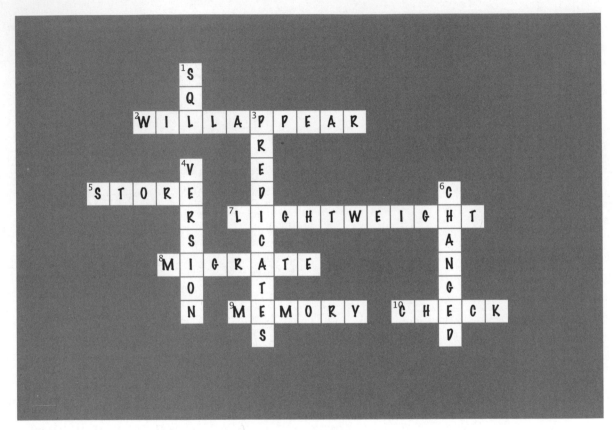

Across

2. viewDidLoad and view_____ both load views, but with different frequency. [WILLAPPEAR]
5. The _____ is responsible for reading and writing data. [STORE]
7. Automatic migration is called _____ data migration. [LIGHTWEIGHT]
8. To update the data, we need to _____ it. [MIGRATE]
9. The FetchedResultsController is good at _____ management. [MEMORY]
10. NSFetchResultsController can _____ for changes. [CHECK]

Down

1. _____ concepts are similar to NSFetchResults concepts. [SQL]
3. _____ are used for filtering data. [PREDICATES]
4. The new model is the current _____. [VERSION]
6. The Managed Object Context saves new or _____ items. [CHANGED]

Your Data Toolbox

You've got Chapter 9 under your belt and now you've added migrating and optimizing data to your toolbox.

Data Migration

Core Data can use lightweight migration to automatically make database changes.

Versioning is used to keep track of the data migrations.

Lightweight migration can be used to add attributes or changing optional status.

Persistent Obj Store

Actually reads and writes the data.

Does data migration, sometimes without actually needing to load the data.

Uses mapping models if the changes are too much for lightweight migration.

Saving

The Managed Object Context handles saving new or changed items.

NSFetchResultsControllers

Maximizes memory efficiency.

Has high-performance UITableView support.

Built-in support for monitoring data changes.

Filtering Data

Predicates are used for filtering results data.

The predicate needs to be set on the NSFetchRequest.

It's a good thing the iPhone comes with a camera...

10 camera, map kit, and core location

Proof in the real world

I can take a perfectly fine picture with this. I don't need a fancy iPhone...

iOS devices know where they are and what they see.

As any iPhone, iPod Touch, or iPad user knows, these devices go way beyond just managing data: they can also take pictures, figure out your location, and put that information together for use in your app. The beauty of incorporating these features is that just by tapping into the tools that iOS gives you, suddenly you can import pictures, locations, and maps without much coding at all.

For Bob, payment requires proof

Bob is working hard on getting as many fugitives off the street as he can, but to get paid he has to document his captures.

I need a picture of the arrest when it happens, and since my phone has a camera, I was thinking you might be able to help out. This is more important than the iPad app, that can wait...

That should be easy enough.

Bob wants a picture of his catch and he's going to need it to be pretty big—so let's go ahead and put it on its own view.

Those pictures will be great for advertising too, not to mention that it will speed up payment!

Sharpen your pencil

Here's what the app looks like so far. Where and how should we add photos?

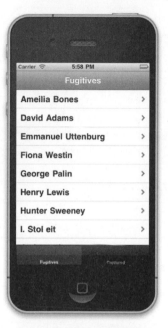

Your ideas go here.

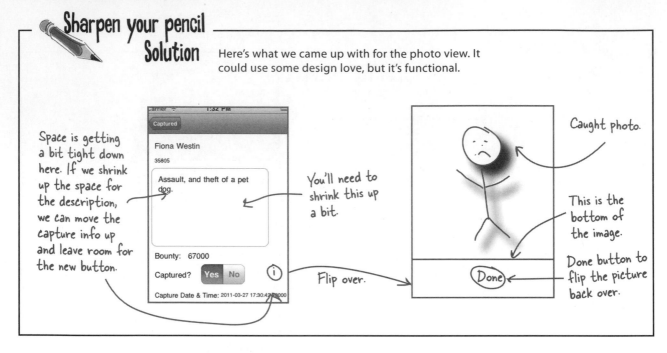

Sharpen your pencil
Solution

Here's what we came up with for the photo view. It could use some design love, but it's functional.

Space is getting a bit tight down here. If we shrink up the space for the description, we can move the capture info up and leave room for the new button.

You'll need to shrink this up a bit.

Flip over.

Caught photo.

This is the bottom of the image.

Done button to flip the picture back over.

Flip over for the detail view

We can use a built-in animation for some nice usability with a little flair here. Since Bob will only want the photo after drilling down through to the detail view (what he'll use to find his fugitive), it makes sense to stick it on the back of the detail view.

This is a really common interface for the utility apps on the iPhone. Typically, there will be two views, one with an info button on it, and another that is revealed by flipping over when the info button is clicked. The flipping is just another transition that comes with UIKit. We can steal the idea to give a nice baseball-card look to our fugitive detail view.

BRAIN POWER

What kind of view will you need to implement for this? Hint: You used it for DrinkMixer...

Long Exercise

Enough planning and hints. Build the view
and get it implemented!

① **Build the new CapturedPhotoViewController.**
That's going to mean a view with a UIImageView and a Done button.
Don't forget the action to tie in with the button and dismiss the view.

*Don't worry about an IBOutlet for the
UIImageView yet; we'll get to that in a second.*

② **Start with the FugitiveDetailViewController updates.**
The detail view needs a new info button, and an action to trigger the
new flip view. The info button is just a regular button with the Info Dark
type.

*Don't forget to connect the button
and the IBAction in Interface Builder!*

③ **Use a custom animation to show the new view when the
info button is pressed.**
You already know how to present a modal view, but this time we
want to do it with a custom animation. The animation you want to
use is the UIModalTransitionStyleFlipHorizontal. Take a look at the
UIViewController documentation if you're stuck on how to use it.

Long Exercise Solution

This one is a whole bunch of functionality that you added without much help! Here's what we came up with:

1 **Build the new CapturedPhotoViewController.**
Start by creating a new UIViewController subclass, with a .xib file to use for our image. Make sure they're under the **/iPhone** folder.

```
@interface CapturedPhotoViewController : UIViewController {

}
- (IBAction) doneButtonPressed;

@end
```

Declare the action for the button.

CapturedPhotoViewController.h

```
- (IBAction) doneButtonPressed {
    [self dismissModalViewControllerAnimated:YES];
}
```

When the done button is pressed, we want the view to go away.

CapturedPhotoViewController.m

2 **Start with the FugitiveDetailViewController updates.**

Add the action to respond to the button press.

```
- (IBAction) showInfoButtonPressed;
```

FugitiveDetailViewController.h

```
#import "CapturedPhotoViewController.h"
```

FugitiveDetailViewController.m

③ Use a custom animation to show the new view
when the info button is pressed.

Instantiate the view controller and
open up the flip view nib.

```objc
- (IBAction) showInfoButtonPressed {
    CapturedPhotoViewController *vc = [[CapturedPhotoViewController
alloc] initWithNibName:@"CapturedPhotoViewController" bundle:nil];
    vc.modalTransitionStyle = UIModalTransitionStyleFlipHorizontal;
    [self presentModalViewController:vc animated:YES];
    [vc release];

}
```

Ah ha! It's a modal view...

Wire this up to File's Owner, at
the top of the dialog box.

FugitiveDetailViewController.m

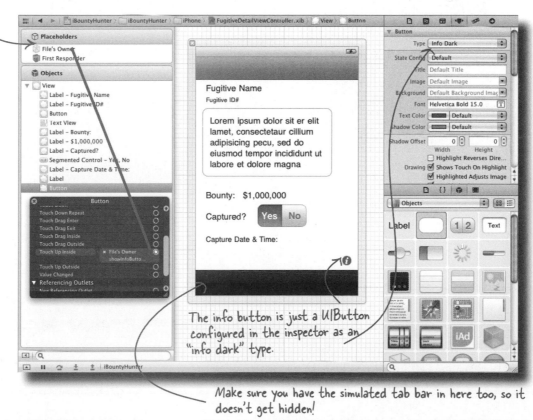

The info button is just a UIButton
configured in the inspector as an
"info dark" type.

Make sure you have the simulated tab bar in here too, so it
doesn't get hidden!

Long Exercise Solution

This one is a whole bunch of functionality that you added
without much help! Here's what we came up with:

1 **Build the new `CapturedPhotoViewController` (continued).**

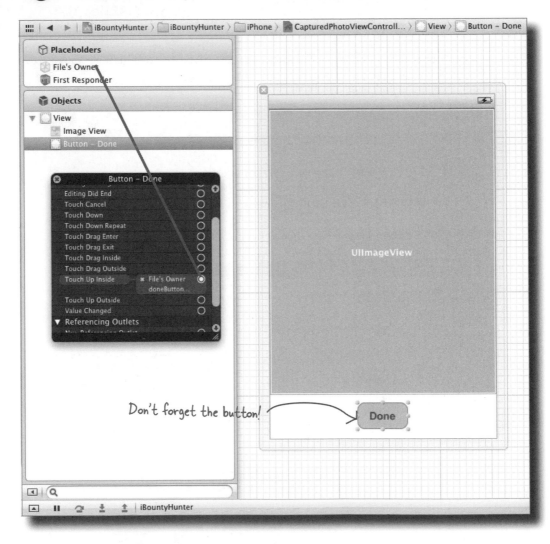

Don't forget the button!

Test Drive

Run the app and see the cool animation working!

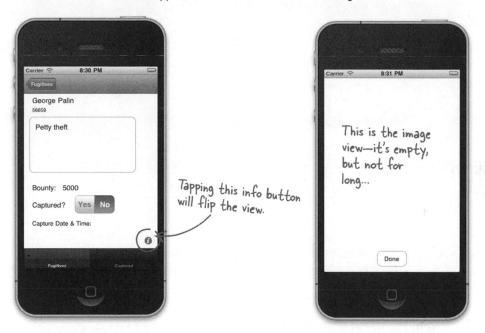

Tapping this info button will flip the view.

This is the image view—it's empty, but not for long...

Sharpen your pencil

Now the views and animations are all working properly, what about the image itself? Think about the data model when you fill in the blanks below.

The UIImage will be stored in the ....

The .... and the .... need to be .... again so this will work.

The .... has to know about the image and where to display it.

The image has to come from the .... or the ....

Sharpen your pencil
Solution

Now the views and animations are all working properly, what about the image itself? Think about the data model when you fill in the blanks below.

The UIImage will be stored in the .... *database* ....

The ..... *database* ..... and the ..... *data model* ..... need to be ..... *migrated* ..... again so this will work.

The ..... *CapturedPhotoViewController* ..... has to know about the image and where to display it.

The image has to come from the ..... *camera* ..... or the ..... *photo library* ..... .

 Do this! You've migrated a database before, and you're going to need to do it again. Just so it's handled and out of the way, get into Xcode and do another database migration.

① **Highlight iBountyHunter 2.xcdatamodel.**
Then go to the **Editor→Add Model Version** menu option. You will have iBountyHunter 3.xcdatamodel in the iBountyHunter .xcdatamodel directory.

② **Set the current version.**
Highlight the iBountyHunter.xcmodeld directory, and select the File Inspector on the Utilities pane. Then in the Versioned Data Model section, select "iBountyHunter 3" as the **Current** version.

③ **Add the new field to the new data model (iBountyHunter3) and generate the new Fugitive class.**
For the image, we'll need a new attribute called "image" that is a binary data type. Then delete the old Fugitive.h and Fugitive.m files and generate new ones via the **New File** menu option.

Check out Chapter 9 if you're still fuzzy on how to do this.

The way to the camera...

...is through the UIImagePickerController. Why? Because our real mission here is to *pick* an image (after one is taken by the camera, or from a stored one). iOS implements image selection through a picker that allows you to get your image from different places, like the camera or the photo library.

The UIImagePickerController class has a lot of built-in functionality, plus it's **modal**, so once you implement it, a lot of things start happening without any additional code in your app:

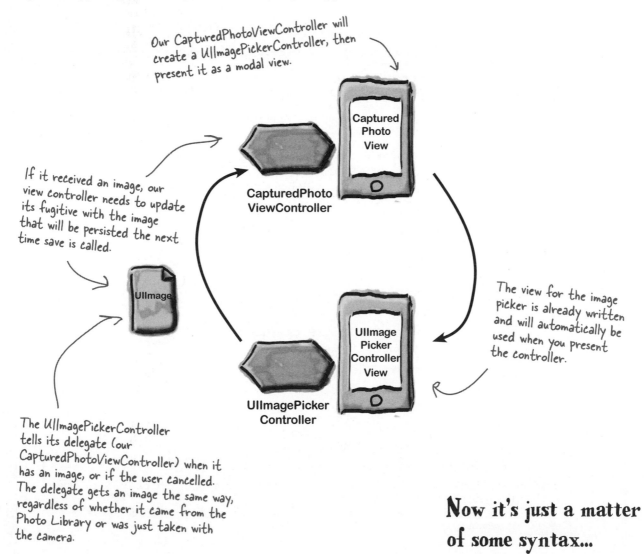

Our CapturedPhotoViewController will create a UIImagePickerController, then present it as a modal view.

If it received an image, our view controller needs to update its fugitive with the image that will be persisted the next time save is called.

The view for the image picker is already written and will automatically be used when you present the controller.

The UIImagePickerController tells its delegate (our CapturedPhotoViewController) when it has an image, or if the user cancelled. The delegate gets an image the same way, regardless of whether it came from the Photo Library or was just taken with the camera.

Now it's just a matter of some syntax...

Ready Bake Code

Here is some code you'll need to tie the image picker together. This code goes in our CapturedPhotoViewController.m as part of the exercise on the next page.

```objc
- (void) viewWillAppear:(BOOL)animated {
    [super viewWillAppear:animated];
    if (fugitive_.image != nil) {
        self.fugitiveImage.image = [UIImage imageWithData:fugitive_.image];
    }
}
```

When the view appears, display the fugitive capture image if there is one.

CapturedPhotoViewController.m

```objc
- (IBAction) takePictureButtonPressed {
    NSLog(@"%@", @"Taking a picture...");
    UIImagePickerController *picker = [[UIImagePickerController alloc]
init];
    picker.sourceType = UIImagePickerControllerSourceTypeCamera |
UIImagePickerControllerSourceTypePhotoLibrary;
    picker.delegate = self;
    picker.allowsEditing = YES;
    [self presentModalViewController:picker animated:YES];
}
```

This allows the users to edit the photo they are choosing.

The picker is displayed asynchronously.

```objc
#pragma mark - UIImagePickerControllerDelegate methods

- (void) imagePickerController:(UIImagePickerController *)picker didFinishPi
ckingMediaWithInfo:(NSDictionary *)info {
    fugitive_.image = UIImagePNGRepresentation([info objectForKey:UIImagePi
ckerControllerEditedImage]);
    [self dismissModalViewControllerAnimated:YES];
    [picker release];
}
```

Remove the picker interface and release the picker object.

```objc
- (void) imagePickerControllerDidCancel:(UIImagePickerController *)picker {
    [self dismissModalViewControllerAnimated:YES];
    [picker release];
}
```

Exercise

Time to get some images! Using the code for the image picker that we gave you, as well as some of your Objective-C skills, let's get the image going.

① **Import the Fugitive header file and declare a property for the fugitive.**
The CapturedPhotoViewController needs to know what fugitive it's working with. Add a Fugitive field and property named "fugitive" to the CapturedPhotoViewController.

② **Store the image when it's selected and update the UIImageView.**
You need to set the image information on the fugitive when the picker gives us an image, then make sure the UIImageView is updated when the view is shown. You'll need an outlet for the UIImageView; then link it in Interface Builder.

③ **Add the code for the UIImagePickerController in the takePictureButtonPressed action.**
Use the code that we gave you to finish up the UIImagePickerController. You'll need to say our CapturedPhotoViewController conforms to the UIImagePickerControllerDelegate and UINavigationControllerDelegate protocols in order to make it the delegate.

④ **Add the "Tap here to add photo" button.**
Using Interface Builder, you'll need to create a button that covers the entire UIImageView and is then set behind it. Don't forget to connect it to your takePictureButton action.

After you create the button, just use the listing of the view elements and put the image view under the "Tap here to add photo" button.

⑤ **Change the FugitiveDetailViewController's showInfoButtonPressed method to set the fugitive.**
You'll need to pass the fugitive information along to the CapturedPhotoViewController when it's created and before it's pushed.

Exercise Solution

Here are all the pieces put together to implement the button.

```
#import "Fugitive.h"                            Import the Fugitive header file and
                                      1         declare a property for the fugitive.
@interface CapturedPhotoViewController : UIViewController
<UIImagePickerControllerDelegate, UINavigationControllerDelegate> {
@private
    UIImageView *fugitiveImage_;
    Fugitive *fugitive_;
                                 We'll need an outlet so we can update the UIImageView
}                                with the selected image.

@property (nonatomic, retain) IBOutlet UIImageView *fugitiveImage;
@property (nonatomic, retain) IBOutlet Fugitive *fugitive;


- (IBAction) doneButtonPressed;
- (IBAction) takePictureButtonPressed;
@end
```

CapturedPhotoViewController.h

```
@implementation CapturedPhotoViewController
                                          2      Store the image when
                                                 it's selected and update
@synthesize fugitiveImage=fugitiveImage_;        the UIImageView.
@synthesize fugitive=fugitive_;


- (void) viewWillAppear:(BOOL)animated {
    [super viewWillAppear:animated];

    if (fugitive_.image != nil) {
self.fugitiveImage.image = [UIImage imageWithData:fugitive_.image];
    }
}
```

CapturedPhotoViewController.m

3   Add the code for the `UIImagePickerController`
         in the `takePictureButtonPressed` action.

```objc
- (IBAction) takePictureButtonPressed {
    NSLog(@"%@", @"Taking a picture...");
    UIImagePickerController *picker = [[UIImagePickerController alloc]
init];
    picker.sourceType = UIImagePickerControllerSourceTypeCamera |
UIImagePickerControllerSourceTypePhotoLibrary;
    picker.delegate = self;
    picker.allowsEditing = YES;
    [self presentModalViewController:picker animated:YES];
}


#pragma mark - UIImagePickerControllerDelegate methods


- (void) imagePickerController:(UIImagePickerController *)picker didFinishP
ickingMediaWithInfo:(NSDictionary *)info {
    fugitive_.image = UIImagePNGRepresentation([info objectForKey:UIImagePi
ckerControllerEditedImage]);
    [self dismissModalViewControllerAnimated:YES];
    [picker release];
}


- (void) imagePickerControllerDidCancel:(UIImagePickerController *)picker {
    [self dismissModalViewControllerAnimated:YES];
    [picker release];
}
```

```objc
- (void)dealloc
{
    [fugitiveImage_ release];
    [fugitive_ release];
    [super dealloc];
}
```

Exercise Solution

Here's all of the pieces put together to implement the button.

④ **Add the "Tap here to add photo" button.**
Drag and drop the button from the Utilities panel. To keep them in the right order in the view, make sure the button is listed above the image view in the listing.

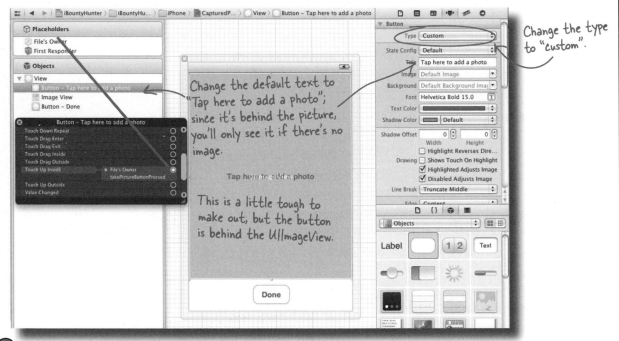

Change the type to "custom".

Change the default text to "Tap here to add a photo"; since it's behind the picture, you'll only see it if there's no image.

This is a little tough to make out, but the button is behind the UIImageView.

⑤ **Change the FugitiveDetailViewController's showInfoButtonPressed method to set the fugitive.**

```objectivec
- (IBAction) showInfoButtonPressed {
    CapturedPhotoViewController *vc = [[CapturedPhotoViewController
alloc] initWithNibName:@"CapturedPhotoViewController" bundle:nil];
    vc.modalTransitionStyle = UIModalTransitionStyleFlipHorizontal;
    vc.fugitive = self.fugitive;
    [self presentModalViewController:vc animated:YES];
    [vc release];
}
```

We just need to set the fugitive on the new property we added to the CapturedPhotoViewController.

FugitiveDetailViewController.m

TEST DRIVE

Build and run to see your new picture view in action.

```
                iBountyHunter  > 🎯 Thread 1 >  👤 11 -[CapturedPhotoViewController takePictureButtonPressed]
 All Output ▾                                                                    ( Clear ) ▢ ▥ ▦
welcome to change it and/or distribute copies of it under certain conditions.
Type "show copying" to see the conditions.
There is absolutely no warranty for GDB.  Type "show warranty" for details.
This GDB was configured as "x86_64-apple-darwin".Attaching to process 10315.
2011-03-27 22:03:14.201 iBountyHunter[10315:207] Taking a picture...
2011-03-27 22:03:14.712 iBountyHunter[10315:207] *** Terminating app due to uncaught exception 'NS
InvalidArgumentException', reason: 'Source type 1 not available'
*** Call stack at first throw:
(
    0    CoreFoundation              0x00fa25a9 __exceptionPreprocess + 185
    1    libobjc.A.dylib             0x010f6313 objc_exception_throw + 44
    2    UIKit                       0x001f3853 -[UIImagePickerController setSourceType:] +
177
    3    iBountyHunter               0x000057c9 -[CapturedPhotoViewController takePictureBu
ttonPressed] + 153
    4    UIKit                       0x0001d4fd -[UIApplication sendAction:to:from:forEvent
:] + 119
    5    UIKit                       0x000ad799 -[UIControl sendAction:to:forEvent:] + 67
    6    UIKit                       0x000afc2b -[UIControl(Internal) _sendActionsForEvents
:withEvent:] + 527
```

— What does this mean?

Argh! It crashed!

What's wrong? Think outside the simulator here...

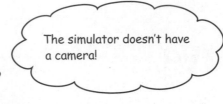

The simulator doesn't have a camera!

Right! And neither do some iPod Touches and iPads.

The simulator is reacting to the fact that you are asking for the camera and it doesn't have one. But more than the simulator not having the camera, some iPod touches and iPads don't either.

Who cares? Apple.

The iPhone isn't the only device using apps

One of the things that Apple requires when you release an app is that it can work on all devices you claim it can, even if a particular device lacks certain hardware capabilities. Part of the approval process for apps is that they are checked for compatibility with the iPod Touch and iPad.

All this means that you need to be aware of when your app may be straying into areas where an iPhone behaves differently than other devices.

How many differences are there, really?

Pool Puzzle

Your **job** is to take items from the pool and place them into the list for the iPhone, iPad, or iPod Touch. You may use the same item more than once. Your **goal** is to make a complete list of the functionality for the iPhone, iPad, and iPod Touch.

<u>iPod Touch</u>   <u>iPhone</u>   <u>iPad</u>

Note: Each thing from the pool can be used more than once!

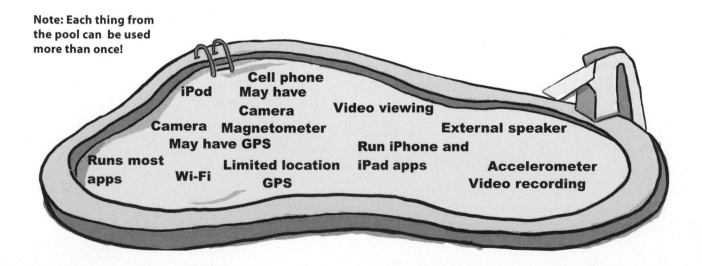

iPod
Cell phone
May have
Camera
Video viewing
Camera
Magnetometer
External speaker
May have GPS
Run iPhone and
iPad apps
Runs most apps
Wi-Fi
Limited location
GPS
Accelerometer
Video recording

Pool Puzzle Solution

Your **job** is to take items from the pool and place them into the list for the iPhone, iPad, or iPod Touch. You may use the same item more than once. Your **goal** is to make a complete list of the functionality for the iPhone, iPad, and iPod Touch.

Watch it!

This list will change.

Apple is always coming out with new devices and updating capabilities. You need to check!

iPod Touch

iPod

Runs most apps

Video viewing

Limited location

Accelerometer

Wi-Fi

May have Camera

You can get some info about location from Wi-Fi.

iPhone

iPod

Runs most apps

Video viewing

GPS

Accelerometer

Wi-Fi

Cell phone

Camera

External speaker

Video recording

Magnetometer

This one can be an issue.

You may have noticed some random stuff on this list— who would've thought about the speaker?

Only on the 3GS and newer

iPad

iPod

Runs iPhone and iPad apps

Video viewing

May have limited location

Accelerometer

Wi-Fi

May have GPS

May have Camera

External speaker

Video recording

Note: Each thing from the pool can be used more than once!

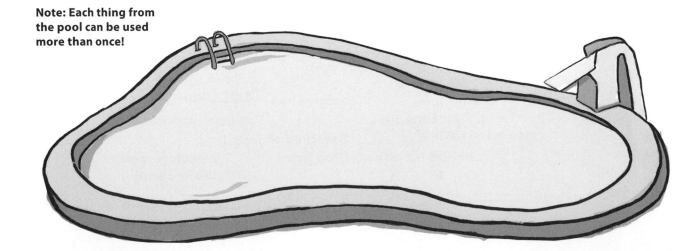

There's a method for checking

With all these little things that can be different between devices, pretty much every time you go to use something from the device, you need to check and see if it's there. For the camera, the UIImagePickerController has a method to check.

You need to be careful to check for specific capabilities for a device, too. For example, we only use still image capture, but if you wanted to do video capture, you need to check that not only does the device have a camera, but also that it's capable of video capture. If you're trying to capture HD video, you need to make sure it can do that, too. For example, the iPhone 3GS can capture video, but not at the same resolution as the iPhone 4.

```
[UIImagePickerController
    isSourceTypeAvailable:UIImagePickerControllerSourceTypeCamera]
```

Since we're getting the info from a source, we need to check and see if the source you want is there.

In our case, we have another option: the photo library. If there's no camera, we can get an image from there instead. If you're writing an application that cannot do something without a camera and the check fails, you need to disable that feature (and potentially hide the controls so the user isn't confused trying to enable that feature). If your application cannot work at all without a camera (or net access or accelerometer, etc.), you can specify device capabilities for your application so users without those capabilities can't even install your application on their device.

⚛ BRAIN POWER

So what happens when the user taps the "Take a photo" button? You check for the camera, then what? What's the user flow?

Prompt the user with action sheets

Action sheets slide up from the bottom of the page and give the user options to proceed. It's similar to a modal view because the user has to address the action sheet before she can move on to anything else. Action sheets are really straightforward to use: they take strings for their buttons and have built-in animations for appearing and disappearing. Our code for the action sheet has some standard stuff included:

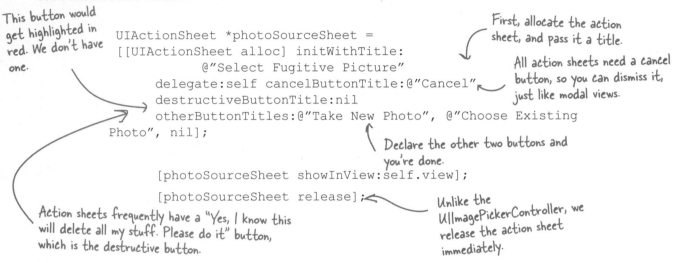

This button would get highlighted in red. We don't have one.

First, allocate the action sheet, and pass it a title.

All action sheets need a cancel button, so you can dismiss it, just like modal views.

```
UIActionSheet *photoSourceSheet =
    [[UIActionSheet alloc] initWithTitle:
            @"Select Fugitive Picture"
        delegate:self cancelButtonTitle:@"Cancel"
    destructiveButtonTitle:nil
    otherButtonTitles:@"Take New Photo", @"Choose Existing
Photo", nil];

    [photoSourceSheet showInView:self.view];

    [photoSourceSheet release];
```

Declare the other two buttons and you're done.

Action sheets frequently have a "Yes, I know this will delete all my stuff. Please do it" button, which is the destructive button.

Unlike the UIImagePickerController, we release the action sheet immediately.

Use action sheets to let the user pick the image source

We know that our options are to use the camera, use the photo library, or cancel, so we'll need to implement the behavior for each option.

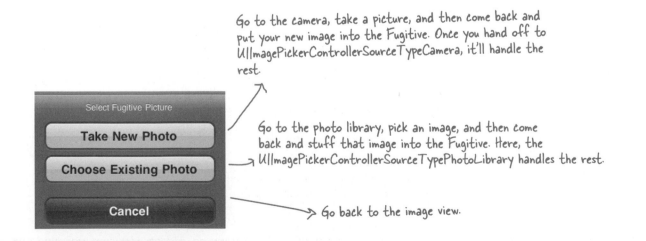

Go to the camera, take a picture, and then come back and put your new image into the Fugitive. Once you hand off to UIImagePickerControllerSourceTypeCamera, it'll handle the rest.

Go to the photo library, pick an image, and then come back and stuff that image into the Fugitive. Here, the UIImagePickerControllerSourceTypePhotoLibrary handles the rest.

Go back to the image view.

Sharpen your pencil

Time to implement the action sheet. There's a lot here to think about since we're changing the flow of the app a bit.

① **Implement the delegate methods for the action sheet.**
Here's enough to get you started. Think about the options for case 1 and the default, and make sure you release the picker and present the view. Also don't forget to declare the UIActionSheetDelegate in the header file.

```objc
- (void) actionSheet:(UIActionSheet *)actionSheet didDismissWithB
uttonIndex:(NSInteger)buttonIndex {
  if (buttonIndex == actionSheet.cancelButtonIndex) {
    NSLog(@"%@", @"The user cancelled adding an image.");
    return;
  }
  UIImagePickerController *picker = [[UIImagePickerController
alloc] init];
  picker.delegate = self;
  picker.allowsEditing = YES;

  switch (buttonIndex) {
    case 0:
      NSLog(@"%@", @"User wants to take a new picture.");
      picker.sourceType =
UIImagePickerControllerSourceTypeCamera;
      break;
```

② **Modify the takePictureButtonPressed action in CapturePhotoViewController.m to include the action sheet.**
iBountyHunter needs to check for the camera, and if there is one, the user gets to pick whether to use the camera or an existing picture. If not, the app should just go straight into the photo library.

This is where the action sheet comes in.

③ **Make your code readable!**
We divvied up the implementation code into three #pragmas: the takePictureButton code, the UIImagePickerController code, and the action sheet delegate methods.

Sharpen your pencil
Solution

The action sheet should be ready to go and
your app has a good user flow now...

1 **Implement the delegate methods for the action sheet.**

CapturedPhotoViewController.h

```objc
@interface CapturedPhotoViewController : UIViewController
<UIImagePickerControllerDelegate, UINavigationControllerDelegate,
UIActionSheetDelegate>
```

```objc
- (void)          actionSheet:(UIActionSheet * ) actionSheet didDismis
sWithButtonIndex:(NSInteger)buttonIndex {
    if (buttonIndex == actionSheet.cancelButtonIndex) {
        NSLog(@"%@", @"The user cancelled adding an image.");
        return;
    }
    UIImagePickerController *picker = [[UIImagePickerController alloc]
init];
    picker.delegate = self;
    picker.allowsEditing = YES;

    switch (buttonIndex) {
        case 0:
            NSLog(@"%@", @"User wants to take a new picture.");
            picker.sourceType =
UIImagePickerControllerSourceTypeCamera;
            break;
t
        case 1:
            NSLog(@"%@", @"User wants to use an existing picture.");
            picker.sourceType =
UIImagePickerControllerSourceTypePhotoLibrary;
            break;
    }
    [self presentModalViewController:picker animated:YES];
}
```

CapturedPhoto
ViewController.m

2 Modify the takePictureButtonPressed action in CapturePhotoViewController.m to include the action sheet.

Change this to SourceTypePhotoLibary if you want to see the action sheet working on the simulator.

```objc
- (IBAction) takePictureButtonPressed {
    NSLog(@"%@", @"Taking a picture...");
    if ([UIImagePickerController isSourceTypeAvailable:UIImagePickerControllerSourceTypeCamera]) {

        NSLog(@"%@", @"This device has a camera.  Asking the user what they want to use.");

        UIActionSheet *photoSourceSheet = [[UIActionSheet alloc] initWithTitle:@"Select Fugitive Picture" delegate:self cancelButtonTitle:@"Cancel" destructiveButtonTitle:nil otherButtonTitles:@"Take New Photo", @"Choose Existing Photo", nil];

        [photoSourceSheet showInView:self.view];

        [photoSourceSheet release];

    }
    else { // No camera, just use the library.
        UIImagePickerController *picker = [[UIImagePickerController alloc] init];

        picker.sourceType = UIImagePickerControllerSourceTypePhotoLibrary;
        picker.delegate = self;
    picker.allowsEditing = YES;
    [self presentModalViewController:picker animated:YES];

    }
}
```

CapturedPhotoViewController.m

Does it work?

Test Drive

Fire up iBountyHunter and drill down through a fugitive to the point of taking a picture. If you've used the SourceTypePhotoLibrary in the takePictureButtonPressed code, you'll get everything to work and see the action sheet.

Your simulator will not have images unless you install them. The easiest way to do that is to drag and drop photos onto the simulator, then click and hold on them in Safari and save the image.

The action sheet pops up, and once you select choose the existing photo...

...you get launched into the photo library and you can select a photo.

Geek Bits

It might be time to register with Apple's Developer Program. If you do, you can install the app on your actual iPhone and test it yourself. Check out the appendix at the end of the book to help you walk through the provisioning process to make it work.

there are no
Dumb Questions

Q: **Don't newer iPhones and iPads support video now? How do I get to that?**

A: It's another media type you can access when you use the UIImagePickerController. By default, it uses still images, which is what we want for iBountyHunter.

Q: **What about the whole augmented reality thing with the camera? Can I do something like that?**

A: Yes. You can give the UIImagePickerController a custom overlay view to use if it invokes the camera. There are still limitations on what you can actually do in the camera view, but you can overlay it with your own information if you want.

Q: **What's with the allowEditing thing we turned on in the UIImagePickerController?**

A: The picker controller has built-in support for cropping and zooming images

if you want to use it. The allowEditing flag controls whether or not the users get a chance to move and resize their image before it's sent to the delegate. If you enable it, and the user tweaks the image, you'll be given editing information in the callback.

Q: **Do we really have to worry about the devices without cameras?**

A: Yes. When you submit your application to Apple for inclusion in the iTunes App Store, you specify the devices your application works with. If you say it works, Apple will test it on both types of devices. They also run tests where your application cannot get network access to ensure you handle that properly as well. Think defensively. Apple is going to test your application in a variety of scenarios.

Q: **Is there any way to test the camera in the simulator?**

A: No. What we've done is about as close as you can get, which is to implement

the code for the camera and test it with the photo library. You've learned a lot so far, and lots of the functionality that you're moving into has outgrown the simulator. GPS functionality, the accelerometer, speaker capabilities, all of these things can't be tested in the simulator, and to really test them, you'll need to install them on your device.

Q: **What's the deal with Apple's Developer Program again?**

A: In order to install an app on your device or to submit an app to the App Store, you need to be a registered iOS developer with Apple. The fee currently is $99. Even if you want to just install an app for your own personal use, you'll need to be registered.

Look at the appendix for more detailed directions on how installing an app on your phone actually works.

Let's show it to Bob...

Bob needs the where, in addition to the when

You've given Bob a way to record the proof he captured someone with a photo, and an easy way to note when it happened, but what about the where?

Cool—I love the pictures—but I need location info about the grab, too.

Bob has a jurisdiction problem.

There are rules about where Bob can nab criminals, so he needs to keep track of where the capture occurred.

The easiest way for Bob to keep track of these things is by recording the latitude and longitude of the capture.

Sharpen your pencil

How are two new fields going to affect the app? Use this space to show where, and on what view, the latitude and longitude info will end up.

Sketch here ⟶

What needs to happen to the data model and the data itself?

....
....
....
....
....
....

Sharpen your pencil
Solution

Here's what we came up with for the new
view and the data changes:

This will just
be a label.

Since we're running low
on space in the view,
we're going to list the
latitude and longitude
together.

What needs to happen to the data model and the data itself?

The database needs to be updated: we're going to be getting a latitude and longitude
value in degrees. To hold them in the database, they'll need to be broken up into two new
attributes for the Fugitive class: latitude and longitude.

LOCATION CONSTRUCTION ▬ ▬ ▬ ▬ ▬ ▬ ▬ ▬ ▬ ▬ ▬ ▬ ▬ ▬

Get into it and get the app ready for the capture coordinates:

☐ Implement the new fields in the view for the location label and the latitude and longitude fields.

☐ Migrate the database again and produce the new Fugitive class with the latitude and longitude fields.

We called them capturedlat and capturedlon and made them type "Double".

LOCATION CONSTRUCTION

Get into it and get the app ready for the capture coordinates:

☑ Implement the new fields in the view for the location label and the latitude and longitude fields.

```objc
 UILabel *capturedLatLon_;

@property (nonatomic, retain) IBOutlet
UILabel *capturedLatLon;
```

FugitiveDetailViewController.h

```objc
@synthesize capturedLatLon=capturedLatLon_;
```

```objc
capturedLatLon.text = [NSString stringWithFormat:
  @"%.3f, %.3f", [fugitive.capturedLat doubleValue],
                 [fugitive.capturedLon doubleValue]];

[capturedLatLon release];
```

Add this to viewWillAppear.

FugitiveDetailViewController.m

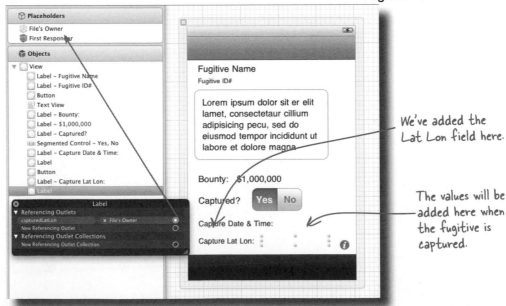

We've added the Lat Lon field here.

The values will be added here when the fugitive is captured.

☑ Migrate the database again and produce the new Fugitive class with the latitude and longitude fields.

We're up to iBountyHunter 4.xcdatamodel.

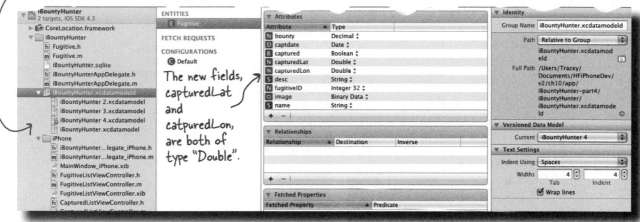

The new fields, capturedLat and catpuredLon, are both of type "Double".

OK, so I'd bet you can get latitude and longitude from the GPS on the iPhone, but didn't you just warn us that iPod Touches and Wi-Fi iPads don't have that?

That's true, but you've got options.

You may remember back in that pool puzzle we said something about the iPod Touch and Wi-Fi iPads being able to handle limited location. iOS has more than one way to get at where you are in the world...

Core Location can find you in a few ways

GPS is often the first thing most people think of for getting location information, but the first generation iPhone didn't have GPS, and neither do iPod Touches or Wi-Fi iPads. That doesn't mean that you're out of options though. There are actually three ways available for iOS to determine your location: GPS, cell tower triangulation, and Wi-Fi Positioning Service.

GPS is the most accurate, followed by cell towers and Wi-Fi. iPhones can use two or three of these, while iPod Touches and Wi-Fi iPads can only use Wi-Fi, but it beats nothing. If your head is starting to spin, don't worry! Core Location actually decides which method to use based on what's available to the device and what kind of accuracy you're after. That means none of that checking for source stuff; the iOS will handle it for you with the **LocationManager**:

```objc
- (CLLocationManager*) locationManager {
  if (locationManager_ == nil) {
    locationManager_ = [[CLLocationManager alloc] init];
    locationManager_.desiredAccuracy = kCLLocationAccuracyNearestTenMeters;
    locationManager_.delegate = self;
  }
  return locationManager_;
}
```

Allocate the CLLocation Manager.

Once the locationManager has the position, it will start sending it back to the delegate.

We set the accuracy to 10 meters for Bob. Higher accuracy can take longer to get a fix, affecting the performance of your app.

Core Location relies on the LocationManager

To use Core Location, you simply need to create a location manager and ask it to start sending updates. It can provide position, altitude, and orientation, depending upon the device's capabilities. In order for it to send you this info, you need to provide it with a delegate as well as your required accuracy. The CLLocationManager will notify you when positions are available or if there's an error. You'll want to make sure you're also properly handling when you don't get a position from the location manager. Even if the device supports it, the users get asked before you collect location information, and can say "No" to having their position recorded (either intentionally or by accident).

BRAIN POWER

Where should we implement this code in our app?

I guess we're going to need a new header file for some Core Location constants?

Yes, and a new framework.

To keep the size of your app small, Apple breaks apart functionality into libraries. As you start adding new functionality, like Core Location, you'll need to start adding frameworks. Since the Core Location framework isn't included by default, we need to add it.

Add a new framework

It's time to add the Core Location framework to the app. Highlight the iBountyHunter target. Click on the **Build Phases** tab and expand the **Link Binary with Libraries** section. Then click the **+** button and choose the CoreLocation framework.

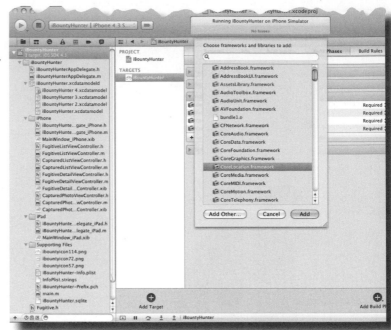

The new framework should be relocated to the /Frameworks folder.

Then update the header file

We still need to declare ourselves as conforming to the CLLocationManagerDelegate protocol and add our property:

```
#import <UIKit/UIKit.h>                          Include the new CoreLocation framework.
#import <CoreLocation/CoreLocation.h>
#import "Fugitive.h"


@interface FugitiveDetailViewController : UIViewController
<CLLocationManagerDelegate> {      We're working through the delegate, so that needs to be there.


    CLLocationManager *locationManager_;
                               Declare the CLLocationManager so we can use it and
                               synthesize it in FugitiveDetailViewController.m.

}

@property (nonatomic, readonly) CLLocationManager *locationManager;
```

FugitiveDetail ViewController.h

BE the developer

Your job is to be the developer and figure out where you're going to implement Core Location into our user flow. Assume that Bob needs the location and date and time to mark a capture.

1 What method will be used to kick off Core Location in the detail view?

....

2 What happens when the location is returned to the view controller?

....

....

3 What happens if Core Location can't get anything or the user disables it?

....

....

4 When will you shut down Core Location?

....

....

5 What about other devices?

....

....

Watch it!

Core Location inhales batteries.

Making frequent calls from your app to find locations will quickly drain batteries, since it turns on the GPS/cellular/Wi-Fi receiver. That'll lead to upset users and cranky iTunes reviews. Keep it to a minimum!

BE the developer solution
Your job is to be the developer and figure out where you're going to implement Core Location into our user flow. Assume that Bob needs the location and date and time to mark a capture.

1 What method will be used to kick off Core Location in the detail view?

The code to initialize Core Location could go into viewWillAppear for the detail view, but we're going to refactor here and create a new method called refreshFugitiveInformation.

2 What happens when the location is returned to the view controller?

We'll know the location manager can get the current position. If the user marks the fugitive as captured, we need to get the current position from the location manager and update the fugitive.

```
- (IBAction) capturedToggleChanged: (id) sender {
  if (self.capturedToggle.selectedSegmentIndex == 0) {
    // The user just marked this fugitive as captured
    fugitive_.captdate = [NSDate date];
    fugitive_.captured = [NSNumber numberWithBool:YES];

    CLLocation *curPos = self.locationManager.location;
        fugitive_.capturedLat = [NSNumber numberWithDouble:curPos.
coordinate.latitude];
        fugitive_.capturedLon = [NSNumber numberWithDouble:curPos.
coordinate.longitude];

  }
  else {
        fugitive_.captdate = nil;
    fugitive_.captured = [NSNumber numberWithBool:NO];
        fugitive_.capturedLat = nil;
        fugitive_.capturedLon = nil;
  }

  [self refreshFugitiveInformation];

}
```

We don't need the continually updating locations, so we'll ask the location manager for its last location when the user toggles the captured control.

This is going to call our new method with all the fugitive information, including updated location information.

FugitiveDetailViewController.m

```
@interface FugitiveDetailViewController ()
  - (void) refreshFugitiveInformation;
@end

- (void) viewWillAppear:(BOOL)animated {
  [super viewWillAppear:animated];

    [self refreshFugitiveInformation];
  // Disable the capture toggle button until we have a location fix
    self.capturedToggle.enabled = NO;
    [self.locationManager startUpdatingLocation];

}


- (void) refreshFugitiveInformation {
    self.nameLabel.text = fugitive_.name;
    self.idLabel.text = [fugitive_.fugitiveID stringValue];
    self.descriptionTextView.text = fugitive_.desc;
    self.bountyLabel.text = [fugitive_.bounty stringValue];
    self.capturedDateLabel.text = [fugitive_.captdate description];
    self.capturedToggle.selectedSegmentIndex = [fugitive_.captured boolValue] ?
0 : 1;
    self.capturedDateLabel.text = [fugitive_.captdate description];
    if (fugitive_.capturedLat != nil) {
        self.capturedLatLon.text = [NSString stringWithFormat:@"%.3f, %.3f",
                                    [fugitive_.capturedLat doubleValue],
                                    [fugitive_.capturedLon doubleValue]];
    }
    else {
        self.capturedLatLon.text = @"";
    }
}
```

To create the new refreshFugitiveInformation, we'll need to pull some information out of the viewWillAppear method and relocate it.

FugitiveDetailViewController.m

BE the developer solution

3 What happens if Core Location can't get anything or the user disables it?

Since Bob needs the location info when he marks a fugitive as captured, we'll
need to disable the captured switch if we can't get anything.

```objc
- (CLLocationManager*) locationManager {
    if (locationManager_ == nil) {
        locationManager_ = [[CLLocationManager alloc] init];
        locationManager_.desiredAccuracy =
kCLLocationAccuracyNearestTenMeters;
        locationManager_.delegate = self;
    }

    return locationManager_;
}
- (void) locationManager:(CLLocationManager *)manager
didUpdateToLocation:(CLLocation *)newLocation fromLocation:(CLLocation
*)oldLocation {
    NSLog(@"%@", @"Core location claims to have a position.");
    self.capturedToggle.enabled = YES;
}

- (void) locationManager:(CLLocationManager *)manager
didFailWithError:(NSError *)error {
    NSLog(@"%@", @"Core location can't get a fix.  Disabling capture
toggle.");
    self.capturedToggle.enabled = NO;
}
```

This is the property getter. If we
haven't configured a location manager
yet, we'll set it up here.

The location manager will
notify the delegate (us) when
it gets a valid position update.

If the location manager can't
get a fix, it will send us error
information.

FugitiveDetailViewController.m

Since the segmented controller really doesn't have a nice
disabled look, you might want to consider using a UIAlertView
to warn the user that they can't mark anyone as captured.

4 When will you shut down Core Location?

We'll shut it down when we leave the detail view.

```
- (void) viewWillDisappear:(BOOL)animated {
    [super viewWillDisappear:animated];

    NSLog(@"%@", @"Shutting down core location.");
    [self.locationManager stopUpdatingLocation];
}
```

Make sure you shut down the location manager when you don't need it to conserve batteries.

FugitiveDetailViewController.m

```
- (void)dealloc
{
    [fugitive_ release];
    [nameLabel_ release];
    [idLabel_ release];
    [descriptionTextView_ release];
    [bountyLabel_ release];
    [capturedToggle_ release];
    [capturedDateLabel_ release];
    [capturedLatLon_ release];
    [locationManager_ release];

    [super dealloc];
}
```

5 What about other devices?

We're good. All we do is tell Core Location the accuracy we want and it deals with the rest. So, the iPod Touch can get just the best data it can, and we'll get that.

Implement all this code and then take it for a spin...

there are no
Dumb Questions

Q: We start and stop Core Location in viewWillAppear and viewWillDisappear. Is that normal?

A: It's normal to start and stop Core Location as you need it. It uses a fair amount of power while it's running, so it's best to shut it down if you don't need it. This gets a little tricky because Core Location can require some time to get its initial position information. To try to make that a little smoother for the user, we enable it as soon as the view appears to give it a head start before the user needs the location.

Q: Is there any way to speed up that initial position?

A: Core Location will try to cache previous position information so it can give you something as quickly as possible. Because of this, if you're really concerned about accuracy, you should check the timestamp sent along with the position information to make sure the position is recent enough for your needs.

Q: Does location accuracy impact things like startup time or battery usage?

A: Absolutely. The more accurate a position you ask for, the more battery Core Location will consume, and it will potentially take longer to figure out. Lower-fidelity information tends to come to you faster. Use whatever accuracy you need for your application, but be aware of the implications of high-resolution information.

Q: Is there a way to just wait for Core Location to have a position rather than having it call back to the delegate like that?

A: No. Core Location, like a lot of other frameworks in iOS, calls back asynchronously as data is available. Network access generally works this way as well. You need to make sure you keep your users informed of what's going on in the application and what they can and can't do at the moment. For example, we disable the Captured button if there's no position information available. Other options display a wait indicator (like a spinning gear) or display position status with a disabled indicator like an icon, button, or label.

Q: Why did we have to move the code around and do all that refactoring?

A: We did it to follow the DRY principle (Don't Repeat Yourself). We cleaned up the code and eliminated duplication by pulling it out into a separate method and calling that from the two places that need it

Q: What's the deal with the private interfaces again?

A: Remember that our header file captures our public interface or API. We don't want this internal method to be part of our API (in other words, we don't want other people to call it). We still want to declare it so the compiler can check that we're calling a valid method, so we add a Private set of methods to our interface in the implementation file. Some people actually put an _ (underscore) before their private method names so that it's obvious that you shouldn't be calling this from anywhere but the class's own implementation. Apple, however, reserves this convention for their private methods.

TEST DRIVE

Implementing Core Location really wasn't that hard, but making it work in the user flow required a bit more work. Now that it's all done, you should be up and running...

To operate the app here, Bob will navigate into the detail view, which will kick off the Core Location manager.

Since we added capturedToggle. enabled = NO; to the viewWillAppear, the user can't engage the control before Core Location starts returning updates.

When the user navigates away from the detail view, Core Location shuts down to save batteries.

It's working! Bob should be psyched...

Just latitude and longitude won't work for Bob

That's great for my forms and everything, but I'm more of a visual person...

It's an iPhone. A map would really be more appropriate.

What's the point of all the network connectivity and fancy graphics if we just show a text field? With just a little bit of code and the iOS Map Kit, we've got something a lot more appealing in the works.

Map Kit comes with iOS

When Apple opened up the API for the Map Kit in iOS 3.0, developers gained access to the maps that come from Google maps, including satellite imagery.

There's lots of customization that you can do with the maps, such as how wide an area they show, what view they start with, and pins and annotations.

Logistically, using Map Kit is a lot like Core Location: you'll need a new framework and will have to #import <MapKit/MapKit.h> in the header file.

MKMapView is a control that pulls map information from Google Maps. You can configure it for the normal road display, satellite imagery, or a hybrid, like you see here.

Depending on the information you want to show on the map, you can create your own views for annotations and show anything you want, like pictures, formatted text, etc.

Map Kit comes with built-in support for pushpins at specified locations, called annotations.

Watch it!

Map Kit requires a network connection.

Since Map Kit pulls imagery information from Google, you'll need to have a network connection for it to be useful. That's not a problem for the simulator (assuming your Mac is online), but it could be an issue for any device with limited connectivity, depending on the location. Map Kit handles this gracefully, but it's something to be aware of.

How can we put this to work?

A little custom setup for the map

Like Core Location, it's not a lot of work to get basic Map Kit support going in iBountyHunter. We're going to create another private method called initializeMapView that we'll call from viewWillAppear in the CapturedPhotoViewController to display the capture location on a hybrid (satellite plus road information) map.

CapturedPhoto ViewController.m

```
- (void) initializeMapView {
    if ([fugitive_.captured boolValue]) {
        CLLocationCoordinate2D mapCenter = CLLocationCoordinate2
DMake([fugitive_.capturedLat doubleValue],

[fugitive_.capturedLon doubleValue]);
        MKCoordinateSpan mapSpan = MKCoordinateSpanMake(0.005,
0.005);
        MKCoordinateRegion mapRegion = MKCoordinateRegionMake(ma
pCenter, mapSpan);

        self.mapView.region = mapRegion;
        self.mapView.mapType = MKMapTypeHybrid;
    }
}
```

Here, we'll pass in the value of the lat and lon where the fugitive was captured.

These values allow us to configure the size of the default map shown.

We pull all this information together to initialize the map.

There are a few map types; hybrid is both satellite and road information.

The size of the map is in degrees. We want the map to be pretty zoomed in.

The mapRegion specifies where the map should be centered and how much should be visible north and south (in degrees). This effectively sets the zoom level of the map.

there are no
Dumb Questions

Q: What's the difference between Core Location and Map Kit?

A: Map Kit is about displaying a map, position-sensitive information, and user interface. Core Location is about getting you information about where **you** are. You can drag and drop a map onto your view in Interface Builder; you pass it some values and it just works.

Core Location, on the other hand, returns values to the delegate, and you need to decide what to do with them. We're going to take that information from Core Location and give it to Map Kit to show us a map of the capture location, for example.

Q: Where do all these frameworks come from? What if I want one that's not on the list?

A: The frameworks are included as part of the SDK. The actual path to the frameworks varies by version and what platform you're developing for. For example, the Map Kit framework we're using is here: /Developer/Platforms/iPhoneOS.platform/Developer/SDKs/iPhoneOS4.3sdk/System/Library/Frameworks/MapKit.framework. In general, you should be able to add frameworks using the method we described in Xcode and not need to worry about a specific location, but if a framework isn't listed or you're adding a custom one, you can point Xcode to the actual path.

Exercise

Implement the map to show the area where the fugitive was captured.

① Add the Map Kit framework and the #import.
Add the framework just like we did with Core Location. While you're at it, make sure that you do the #import in the detail view to include the Map Kit header.

② Configure the photo view to show the map.
Rather than adding a whole new view, go ahead and add the map to the CapturedPhotoView with the image. Resize the image and the button then drag an MKMapView to the bottom half of the view.

③ Add the outlets and code for the MKMapView.
Now that you have all the support stuff in place, go ahead and add the outlets and the actual Map Kit code we gave you to make the map work. Make sure you wire up the outlet in Xcode and call the new initializeMapView method in viewWillAppear.

Resize the image and the button...

...and use the bottom of the view for the MKMapView.

Exercise SoLution

Implement the map to show the area where the fugitive was captured.

1 **Add the Map Kit framework and the #import.**

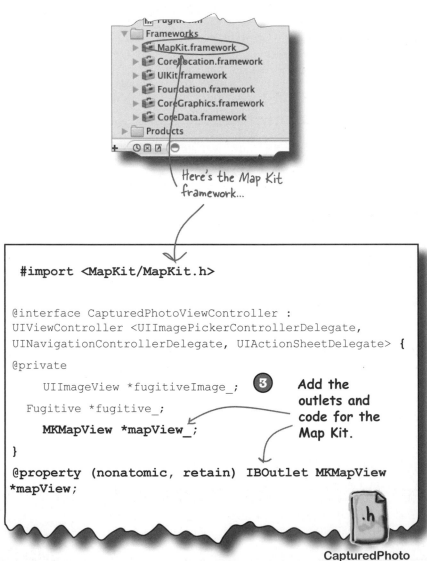

Here's the Map Kit framework...

```
#import <MapKit/MapKit.h>

@interface CapturedPhotoViewController :
UIViewController <UIImagePickerControllerDelegate,
UINavigationControllerDelegate, UIActionSheetDelegate> {
@private
    UIImageView *fugitiveImage_;
  Fugitive *fugitive_;
    MKMapView *mapView_;
}
@property (nonatomic, retain) IBOutlet MKMapView
*mapView;
```

3 **Add the outlets and code for the Map Kit.**

.h

CapturedPhoto
ViewController.h

2 Configure the photo view to show the map.

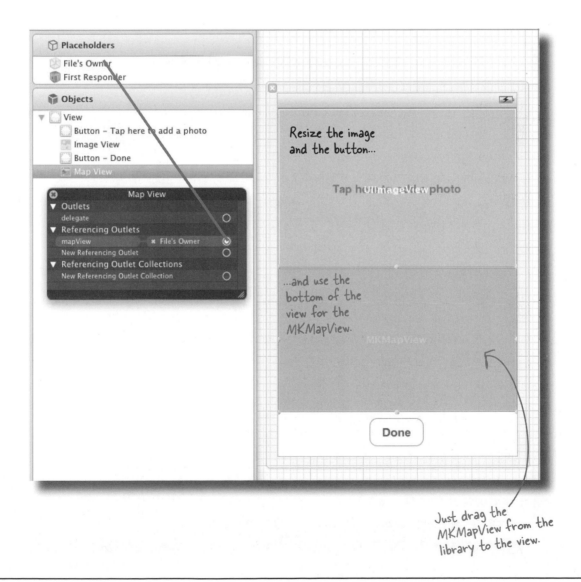

Resize the image and the button...

...and use the bottom of the view for the MKMapView.

Just drag the MKMapView from the library to the view.

③ Add the outlets and code for the MKMapView.

```objc
@interface CapturedPhotoViewController (Private)
- (void) initializeMapView;
@end

@synthesize fugitiveImage=fugitiveImage_;
@synthesize fugitive=fugitive_;
@synthesize mapView=mapView_;
```

```objc
- (void) viewWillAppear:(BOOL)animated {
    [super viewWillAppear:animated];

    if (fugitive_.image != nil) {
        self.fugitiveImage.image = [UIImage
imageWithData:fugitive_.image];
    }

    [self initializeMapView];
}
```

If the fugitive has image data, then we ask UIImage to create an image from it and set it on our image view.

.m

CapturedPhotoViewController.m

```
- (void) initializeMapView {
    if ([fugitive_.captured boolValue]) {
        CLLocationCoordinate2D mapCenter = CLLocationCoordinate2
DMake([fugitive_.capturedLat doubleValue],

[fugitive_.capturedLon doubleValue]);
        MKCoordinateSpan mapSpan = MKCoordinateSpanMake(0.005,
0.005);
        MKCoordinateRegion mapRegion = MKCoordinateRegionMake(ma
pCenter, mapSpan);

        self.mapView.region = mapRegion;
        self.mapView.mapType = MKMapTypeHybrid;
    }
}
```

Like before, we need to configure the mapView. Center on the fugitive location and set the zoom level.

```
- (void)dealloc
{
  [fugitiveImage_ release];
  [fugitive_ release];
    [mapView_ release];
  [super dealloc];
}
```

CapturedPhotoViewController.m

Test Drive

Go ahead and build and run the app. You'll need to make sure that you mark a fugitive as captured, and that the lat/lon field fills in, then flip over the view to look at the map. To try out the zooming on the map, you'd use the "pinching" motion on a real device. In the simulator, hold down option and then click.

TEST DRIVE

To try out the zooming on the map; this is the "pinching" motion in
real life. In the simulator, hold down option and then click.

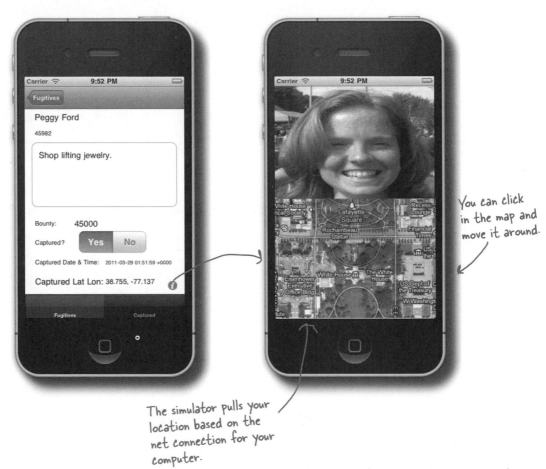

You can click
in the map and
move it around.

The simulator pulls your
location based on the
net connection for your
computer.

**Excellent! Now all we need
is a pin to show where the
capture happened.**

Annotations require a little more ~~work~~ finesse

Annotations are the little flags that come up when you see a point of interest, represented by a pin. The catch? Incorporating annotations means conforming to the Map Kit annotation protocol. Map Kit uses an annotation protocol so that you can use your existing classes and provide them directly to Map Kit. The downside is that means we need to add code to our Fugitive class:

```objc
#import <Foundation/Foundation.h>
#import <CoreData/CoreData.h>

#import <MapKit/MapKit.h>

@interface Fugitive : NSManagedObject <MKAnnotation> {
@private
}
@property (nonatomic, retain) NSDecimalNumber * bounty;
@property (nonatomic, retain) NSNumber * captured;
@property (nonatomic, retain) NSData * image;
@property (nonatomic, retain) NSNumber * fugitiveID;
@property (nonatomic, retain) NSDate * captdate;
@property (nonatomic, retain) NSString * name;
@property (nonatomic, retain) NSString * desc;
@property (nonatomic, retain) NSNumber * capturedLat;
@property (nonatomic, retain) NSNumber * capturedLon;

@property (nonatomic, readonly) CLLocationCoordinate2D
coordinate;

- (NSString *) title;
- (NSString *) subtitle;

@end
```

The MKAnnotation protocol is a little odd in that it defines a property and two getters. These are used by the MapView to position the pin and populate the overlay if a pin is tapped.

Fugitive.h

If you use automatic NSManagedObject file generation again, you'll wipe out these customizations.

Watch it!

Fully implement the annotation protocol

The protocol requires us to have a coordinate property, a title, and a subtitle. Instead of synthesizing that coordinate property, we'll implement it ourselves and just return the fugitive's position, name, etc.

For an application in which you expect to have to do more data migration, you should implement a separate class conforming to the protocol that has a reference to its Fugitive (composition) rather than adding code to the Fugitive class directly.

We conform to the protocol by implementing the property getter and methods. We simply map these to data we already have about the fugitive.

```objc
- (CLLocationCoordinate2D) coordinate {
    return CLLocationCoordinate2DMake([self.capturedLat doubleValue], [self.capturedLon doubleValue]);
}

- (NSString *) title {
    return self.name;
}

- (NSString *) subtitle {
    return self.desc;
}
@end
```

Fugitive.m

Do this!

Go ahead and add the code from
the previous page for the Fugitive.h
and Fugitive.m files. Then add
the bolded code below to your
CapturedPhotoViewController.

If we have a lat / lon for
the fugitive, we add the
fugitive as an annotation
on the map. We can do
this since the fugitive
now conforms to the
MKAnnotation protocol.

```
-(void) viewWillAppear:(BOOL)animated {

   [super viewWillAppear:animated];


   if (fugitive_.image != nil) {

      self.fugitiveImage.image = [UIImage
imageWithData:fugitive_.image];

   }


   if (fugitive_.capturedLat != nil) {

         [self.mapView
addAnnotation:fugitive_];

      }

   [self initializeMapView];

}
```

CapturedPhotoViewController.m

Test Drive

That's it! Everything should be working now. You may not have noticed as you've been working through all this code, but this app is huge and awesome!

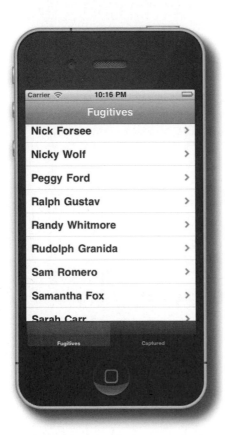

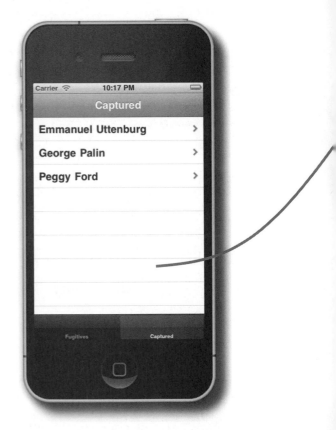

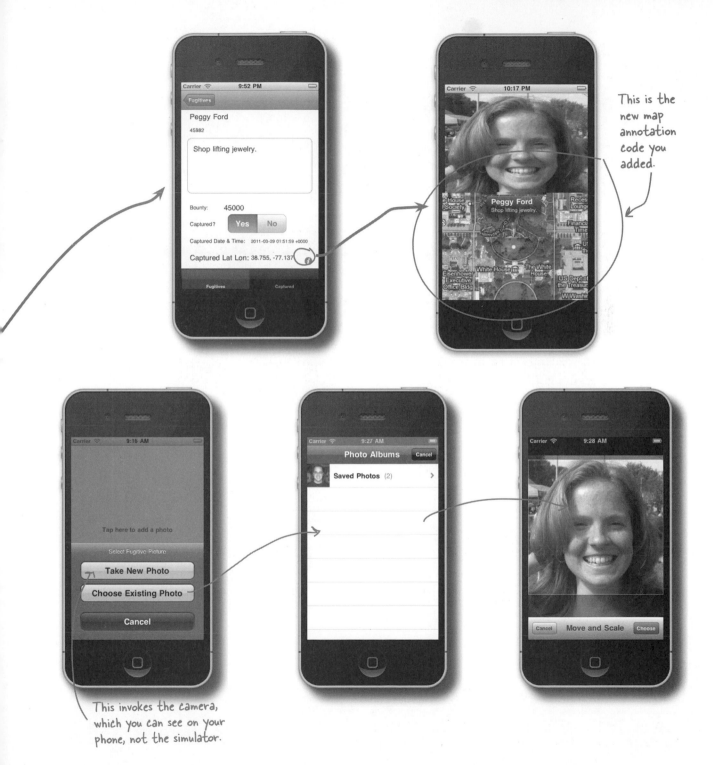

This is the new map annotation code you added.

This invokes the camera, which you can see on your phone, not the simulator.

AddingFunctionality cross

Time to flex the right side of your brain again...

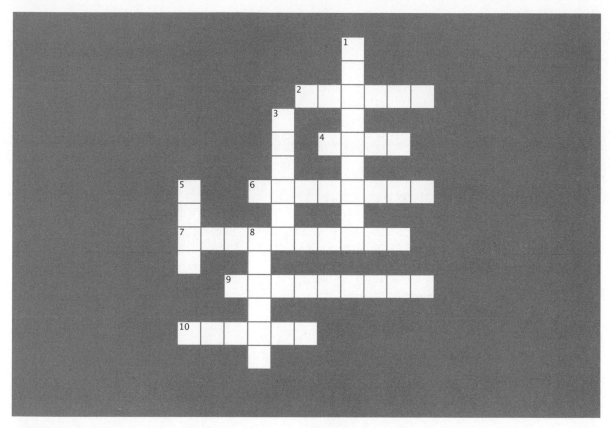

Across

2. UIImagePickerController gets images from the _____ and the library.
4. The _____ animation comes with UIKit.
6. The info circle is just a configured _____.
7. Additional _____ are needed for MapKit and Core Location.
9. Your app must be able to work on the _____ , too.
10. _____ sheets are a good way to get a user to pick an option.

Down

1. The camera cannot be tested in the _____.
3. The iPhone isn't the only _____ that uses apps.
5. Besides GPS and cell towers, _____ can be used to determine location.
8. _____ doesn't work without a Net connection.

AddingFunctionality cross solution

Time to flex the right side of your brain again...

```
                              ¹S
                               I
                          ²C A M E R A
                     ³D    U
                      E  ⁴F L I P
                      V    A
        ⁵W      ⁶U I B U T T O N
         I       C    O
        ⁷F R A ⁸M E W O R K S
         I     A
              ⁹I P O D T O U C H
               K
        ¹⁰A C T I O N
               T
```

Across

2. UIImagePickerController gets images from the _____ and the library. [CAMERA]
4. The _____ animation comes with UIKit. [FLIP]
6. The info circle is just a configured _____. [UIBUTTON]
7. Additional _____ are needed for MapKit and Core Location. [FRAMEWORKS]
9. Your app must be able to work on the _____ , too. [IPODTOUCH]
10. _____ sheets are a good way to get a user to pick an option. [ACTION]

Down

1. The camera cannot be tested in the _____. [SIMULATOR]
3. The iPhone isn't the only _____ that uses apps. [DEVICE]
5. Besides GPS and cell towers, _____ can be used to determine location. [WIFI]
8. _____ doesn't work without a Net connection. [MAPKIT]

Your Location Toolbox

You've got Chapter 10 under your belt and now you've added the camera, Core Location, and Map Kit to your toolbox.

Camera

Is accessed through the UIImagePickerController.

Is not on all devices and you need to handle that.

Allows you to select and edit an image for use in your app directly from your library.

Flip Animation

Comes with UIKit.

Is the typical interface for utility apps on iPhone.

Is usually implemented as a modal view.

Core Location

Can use either GPS, cell tower triangulation, or Wi-Fi positioning service.

Chooses for you which method to use based on the user's device.

MapKit

Comes with iOS.

Requires a new framework.

Can be customized for a variety of views, including pushpin annotations.

11 iPad UI

Natural interfaces

> I think it's important to work with things in nature...

The iPad is all about existing in the real world.

We've built a basic iPad port of an existing app for DrinkMixer a few chapters back, but now it's time to build an interface that works with some real-world knowledge. By mimicking things that people use in the real world, users know what to do with an interface just by opening the app. We're going to use some real-world elements to help Bob catch the bad guys...

Bob needs that iPad app, too...

The iPhone app is up and running and things are great. His on-the-run scenario is handled, but Bob also has some research to do and that isn't going to be comfortable on his iPhone.

> You have to get in the fugitive's mind. It's a painstaking process. Research is key to determining patterns, establishing relationships, and then predicting what they'll do so you can catch them.

This is a different use case.

Bob is going to be sitting down, doing some research, coming up with a plan to track the fugitive.

iPads are used much more frequently for this type of interaction: an extended period of usage time and with broader functionality. Keep this in mind as we work through building the app.

Watch it!

iPhones and iPads are not used the same way.

While there are cases where you're using similar apps on both devices, often the data is going to be consumed differently.

This is the app that you designed earlier...

To show the list of fugitives, we'll have a popover that can appear in this corner with this full list.

iPad App

1. Details on past whereabouts. They'll have a location and details about what the fugitive was doing there.

2. For research, Bob needs the full dossier on each fugitive. Picture and details should all be in the same view.

3. All the information he uses in the iPhone app, too.

We'll add some fun UI touches.

iPad 📶   2:50 PM   100%

Navigation control

Fugitive Name

Image of the Fugitive

Fugitive ID#
Bounty:
This area is for notes and details about the fugitive

The map will show the last known location for the fugitive.

Map of previously known locations

When Bob selects an entry, a TexView describing for the

For the landscape view, we'll have the full list of fugitives displayed, since we have extra space.

More UI goodness—cool page background that looks like a corkboard

iPad 📶   2:58 PM   100%

Navigation control

Fugitive Name

Fugitive ID#
Bounty:
This area is for notes and details about the fugitive

Image of the Fugitive

List of Fugitive Names

Map of previously known locations

When Bob selects an entry, a TextView will display text describing the sightings for the fugitive.

We'll show the fugitive information on index cards.

Why are we wasting all this time on a custom UI? Can't we just use regular controls again?

We could, but it's not ideal.

DrinkMixer worked fine, but it missed out on a lot of what makes iPad apps easy to use. We simply ported our minimalist iPhone UI to a bigger screen. While that was fine for what we wanted to do, it's time to step it up to what the iPad is really good at, which is making interfaces that are closer to the real world.

Natural user interfaces make things more real (and easier)

One of the reasons that the iPad, and tablets in general, have been so successful is due to their ability to take on the form factor of lots of things that we regularly use in the real world. Books, calendars, menus, clipboards, newspapers, magazines, control panels, dials, and displays—they can all be replaced with the right interface in the tablet form factor.

Natural user interfaces (NUIs) is a broad term that means any computer interface that tries to mimic more closely the way we interact with objects in the real world. Beyond multi-touch tablets, Wii uses a gesture recognition in 3D, and Kinect reads body movements to control the system. All these interfaces have exploited the way we already know how to play sports or other games in the real world to allow us to quickly adapt to their apps.

Tablet computing and iPads in particular strive to do the same thing. By leveraging the knowledge that users already have—how to read a book, use a calendar—NUIs make using an app easier and the learning time shorter.

iOS HIG user experience guidelines

The HIG is a great starting point for **user experience** (UX) considerations for the iPad. The iOS Human Interface Guidelines—User Experience Guidelines, and the Case Studies section in particular, are full of pointers about what to do and not do. There is a great example of migrating mail from iPhone to iPad. The main thrust of moving an app from iPhone to iPad? **Realism**.

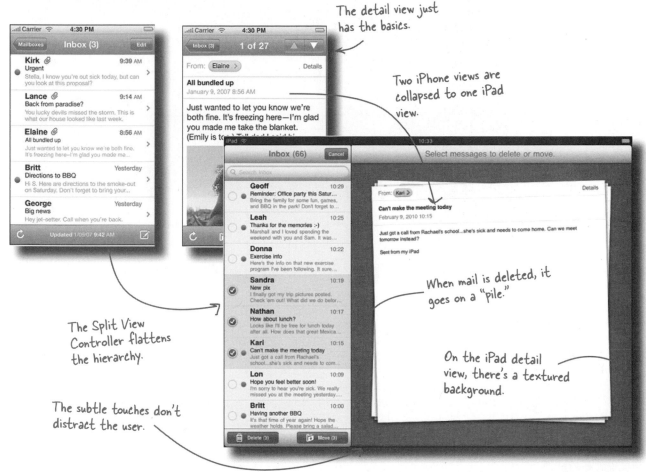

The detail view just has the basics.

Two iPhone views are collapsed to one iPad view.

The Split View Controller flattens the hierarchy.

The subtle touches don't distract the user.

When mail is deleted, it goes on a "pile."

On the iPad detail view, there's a textured background.

It's about realism and details

When you read about iPad design, the HIG is full of references to "stunning graphics" and "adding physicality and realism." As you design your own interfaces, with increased real estate and expected time of interaction with the user, it's important to keep in mind subtle things that you can add that increase the appeal of your app. It's also partly why iPad apps have a greater value to the user, which means you can charge more!

Let's apply this to iBounty-Hunter...

Iterate your interface, too

Most developers are familiar with iterative development for software but for some reason don't apply those same practices to user interfaces. User interfaces, possibly more than any other part of an application, need real user feedback.

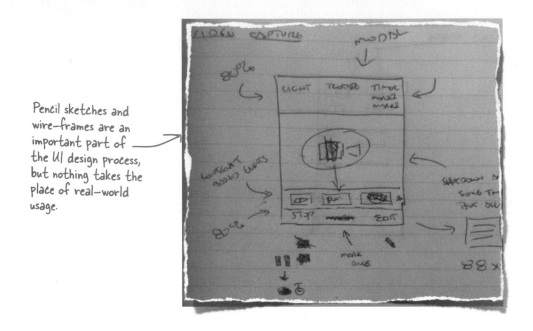

Pencil sketches and wire-frames are an important part of the UI design process, but nothing takes the place of real—world usage.

This iterative approach to user interface design is why taking advantage of natural user interfaces when possible is so important—the designers of those interfaces (and users themselves) have spent a lot of time going back and forth fine-tuning how people interact with them. By incorporating natural UIs into your application, you can take advantage of all that refinement and preloaded user knowledge in your application.

Sketches and wire-frames are a critical part of user interface design, but before you pull out your pencil and start drawing, you need to put thought into **what** exactly is important to your user.

A critical part of user interface design is determining what needs to be **left out**. Some user interface elements only make sense in certain contexts; other elements just confuse things and clutter up the user experience. A good, clean design like iBountyHunter is important.

Frank

Joe

Jim

Jim: I'm confused. Is this a custom UI, or are we using standard controls?

Frank: Really, it's both.

Joe: What?

Frank: When you're working with iOS, most apps are a blend of standard controls and custom interface, and that's what we'll do.

Jim: Oh, so the Split View Controller is still ok?

Frank: Yes. We still have a hierarchical data structure we're working with, so that works for us, but we need to add more detail for Bob to be able to do his research.

Joe: OK, I guess that makes sense.

Jim: So, what's the strategy for building this thing?

Frank: We need to start with the overall app structure. So we'll build the Split View Controller first, then get the views to work properly, and then we'll add the realism.

Joe: What are we adding again to make this realistic?

Frank: We're going to add a corkboard feeling, make the borders on the map and photo thicker, a pushpin, stuff like that.

Jim: OK, I see. So that will make it easier for Bob to digest what's going on.

Frank: Right. Now, for the split view...

BountyHunterHD is based on a Split View Controller

Just like we did with DrinkMixer, we're going to add a Split View Controller, and then modify the basics to add a detail view.

Unlike DrinkMixer, we're not going to be reusing our detail view from the iPhone app. The overall structure of the app means that we'll be working with the same data and some of the same controls between the iPhone and the iPad, but when it comes to the views, we're going to be keeping things separate.

This is pretty typical of real-world apps. Often you start with a given data set that then needs to be applied to different use cases. This is especially true when you're talking about augmenting a website or existing backend framework with an iOS or mobile component.

Your work is really about effectively providing data to the user and setting up the interactivity for each use case. For iBountyHunter on the iPad, Bob needs to do some research.

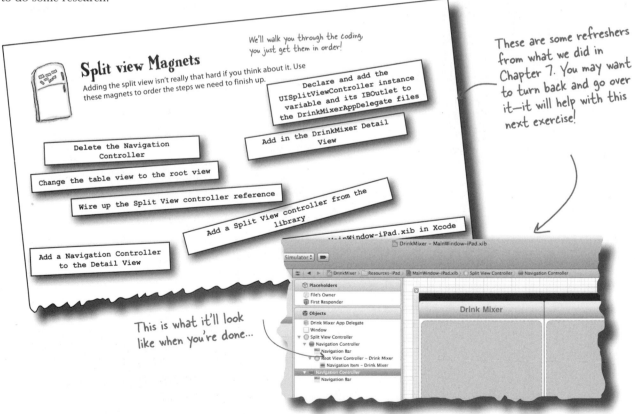

We'll walk you through the coding, you just get them in order!

Split view Magnets

Adding the split view isn't really that hard if you think about it. Use these magnets to order the steps we need to finish up.

Declare and add the UISplitViewController instance variable and its IBOutlet to the DrinkMixerAppDelegate files

Add in the DrinkMixer Detail View

Delete the Navigation Controller

Change the table view to the root view

Wire up the Split View controller reference

Add a Split View controller from the library

Add a Navigation Controller to the Detail View

These are some refreshers from what we did in Chapter 7. You may want to turn back and go over it—it will help with this next exercise!

This is what it'll look like when you're done...

Ready Bake Code

Since you're such a pro at getting split views set up, we think you should skip some steps. Go get the iBountyHunter iPad starter code at *www.headfirstlabs.com/books/iphonedev*. Here's what the new code will contain for you:

Bounty Hunter Starter Code

Contains a new Split View Controller, fully implemented.

Has a stubbed-out detail view for the iPad, called FugitiveDossierViewController.

The code has been updated to handle all the new elements in the detail view.

All the appropriate outlets are wired up so that the view works.

A popover has been implemented for the portrait view.

There's a migrated version of the database with the previously known location information for the fugitives.

If you're rusty on the Core Data stuff, go back to chapter 8 to brush up...

Author's note: If you want to code it up from scratch—go for it, you already know how to do it!

TEST DRIVE

Go ahead and run what we've given you so you know where we are.

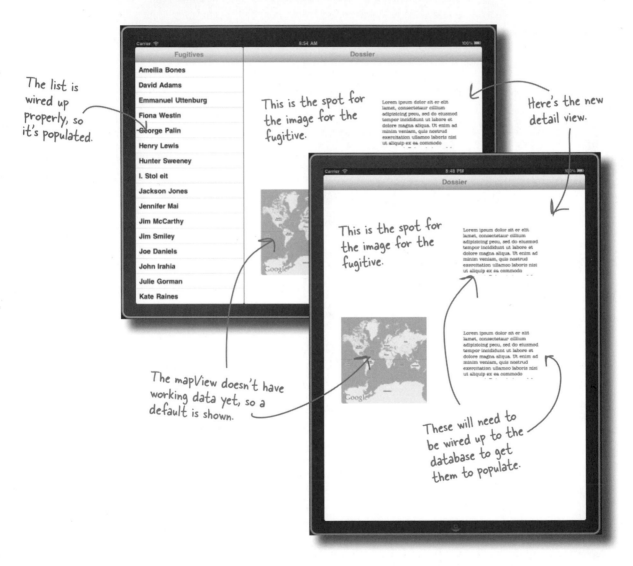

The list is wired up properly, so it's populated.

This is the spot for the image for the fugitive.

Here's the new detail view.

The mapView doesn't have working data yet, so a default is shown.

This is the spot for the image for the fugitive.

These will need to be wired up to the database to get them to populate.

Frank

Joe

Jim

Joe: How are we going to populate this detail view?

Frank: Just like we did in the iPhone version, I'd think, but we should probably break things into a couple of separate methods.

Jim: Why?

Frank: Well, we have a lot to manage here. There's that map view, the image, and the text that all need to be updated.

Joe: Oh right, and that map view needs a decent amount of setup, right?

Frank: Exactly. Plus, remember that with the Split View Controller, we don't re-create the view for each fugitive.

Jim: Right. We need to be able to update the view when a fugitive is selected, not just when viewDidLoad kicks off.

Joe: OK, so what's the plan?

Frank: We need to implement a couple of methods on the detail view to populate the description, the images, etc.

Joe: OK, that makes sense.

Sharpen your pencil

Implement four new methods in FugitiveDetailViewController.m.

☐ Create a private method called prepareFugitiveDescription that returns a string containing all the vital stats for our Fugitive: name, bounty, and description.

☐ Create a private method called prepareMapDescription that returns a string containing all the information for the fugitive's last known locations.

☐ Create a private method called updateDossier that uses our prepareFugitiveDescription and prepareMapDescription and sets up the image, description, map, and popover.

☐ Finally, we need one method to pull everything together: the public showFugitiveDossier method. This sets the current fugitive and then calls the updateDossier method and dismisses the popover if it's visible.

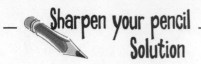

Sharpen your pencil
Solution

Implement three methods to update
FugtiveDetailViewController.m.

```objc
@interface FugitiveDossierViewController ()

    - (void) updateDossier;

    - (NSString *) prepareFugitiveDescription;

    - (NSString *) prepareMapDescription;

@end
```

```objc
#pragma mark - Helper Methods                    FugitiveDossierViewController.m


- (NSString *) prepareFugitiveDescription {
    return [NSString stringWithFormat: @"Name: %@\r\nID: %@\r\
nBounty: %@\r\nDescription: %@",

      fugitive_.name,

      [fugitive_.fugitiveID stringValue],

      [fugitive_.bounty stringValue],

      fugitive_.desc];

}


- (NSString *) prepareMapDescription {
    return [NSString stringWithFormat: @"Last Seen: %6.3f,%6.3f\r\
nDescription: %@",

            [fugitive_.lastSeenLat doubleValue],

            [fugitive_.lastSeenLon doubleValue],

            fugitive_.lastSeenDesc];

}


- (void) updateDossier {
    if (fugitive_.image != nil) {
        self.fugitiveImageView.image = [UIImage
imageWithData:fugitive_.image];

    }
```

Keep going into the code on the next page...

```
    fugitiveDescription_.text = [self prepareFugitiveDescription];
    mapDescription_.text = [self prepareMapDescription];


    CLLocationCoordinate2D mapCenter = CLLocationCoordinate2DMake([fugiti
ve_.lastSeenLat doubleValue],
    [fugitive_.lastSeenLon doubleValue]);
    MKCoordinateSpan mapSpan = MKCoordinateSpanMake(0.005, 0.005);
MKCoordinateRegion mapRegion = MKCoordinateRegionMake(mapCenter, mapSpan);


    self.mapView.region = mapRegion;
    self.mapView.mapType = MKMapTypeHybrid;


    if (popOver_ != nil) {
        [popOver_ dismissPopoverAnimated:YES];
    }
}

- (void) showFugitiveDossier: (Fugitive *)someFugitive {
    self.fugitive = someFugitive;
    [self updateDossier];
}
```

FugitiveDossierViewController.m

Do this! Now you just need to call showFugitiveDossier when the device is an iPad, and the user taps a row. Here's the code:

```
-               (void)
        tableView:(UITableView *)tableView didSelectRowAtIndexPath:(NSIndexPa
th *)indexPath
{
    if (UI_USER_INTERFACE_IDIOM() == UIUserInterfaceIdiomPad) {
        [self.dossierView showFugitiveDossier:[items_
objectAtIndex:indexPath.row]];
    }
    else {
        FugitiveDetailViewController *detailViewController =
[[FugitiveDetailViewController alloc] initWithNibName:@"FugitiveDetailViewControll
er" bundle:nil];

        detailViewController.fugitive = [items_ objectAtIndex:indexPath.row];
        [self.navigationController pushViewController:detailViewController
animated:YES];
        [detailViewController release];
    }
}
```

FugitiveListViewController.m

Test Drive

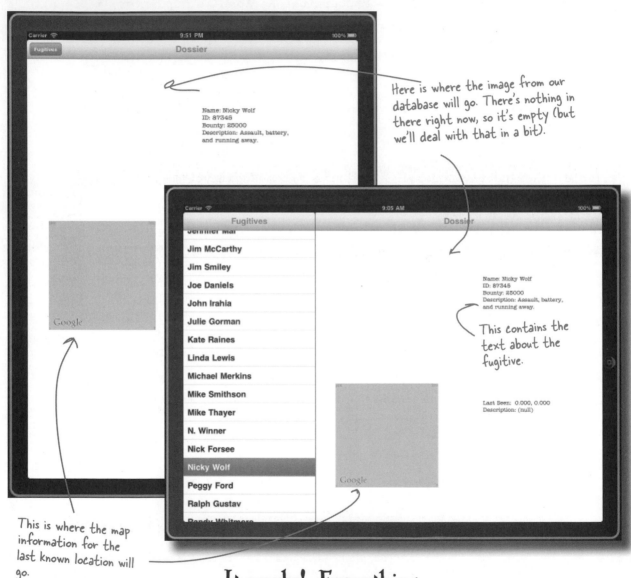

Here is where the image from our database will go. There's nothing in there right now, so it's empty (but we'll deal with that in a bit).

This contains the text about the fugitive.

This is where the map information for the last known location will go.

It works! Everything is updated, but now we need some polish...

BRAIN
BARBELL

Here is the sketch we came up with for the UI before. What do we need to work on next?

For the landscape view, we'll have the full list of fugitives displayed, since we have extra space.

More UI goodness—cool page background that looks like a corkboard.

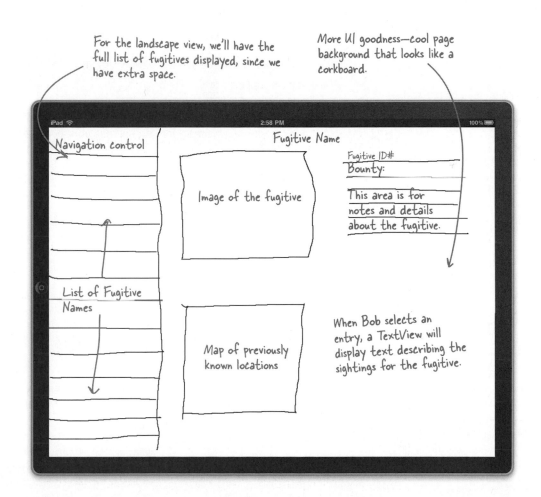

Navigation control

Fugitive Name

Fugitive ID#
Bounty:

Image of the fugitive

This area is for notes and details about the fugitive.

List of Fugitive Names

Map of previously known locations

When Bob selects an entry, a TextView will display text describing the sightings for the fugitive.

there are no Dumb Questions

Q: We still have a few issues in the code; for instance, picking a fugitive without a last known location shows "null." Are we going to fix those things?

A: Yes, we'll definitely fix some of them as we clean up the UI, but some we'll leave for you to either put on some finishing touches or add new functionality.

Q: You called a method private earlier. Is it really private?

A: Sort of. By putting it as a class extension at the top of the implementation file, we aren't declaring the method to be part of the public interface, meaning people who might look at our class's header file won't see the method there. However, there's nothing preventing someone from actually trying to invoke the method if they knew it existed. So, from that perspective, it's not really private as much as "unlisted."

Q: Isn't all this "Natural User Interface" stuff just a new way of saying "eye candy"?

A: No, most definitely not. Sure, by moving to more natural user interfaces, you generally improve the look and feel of an application, but that's almost a side effect. You make assumptions about how to interact with things in the real world all the time. For example, you generally want to *pull* on a handle but *push* on a touch plate on a swinging door. You probably assume that turning a dial to the right will increase whatever it is you're adjusting while turning it to the left will decrease it, etc. With the larger and high-quality display on the iPad,

you can incorporate these concepts into your application and bring an immediate familiarity to it. If you're writing a calendar application, don't assume that you should (or even can) reinvent how people want to view their calendar. Take advantage of established "user interfaces" in day planners and wall calendars—they've been around a lot longer and have had lots of time to ~~get it wrong~~ evolve.

Q: Wait—so if I'm supposed to incorporate things people are used to, doesn't this depend on who the people are?

A: Absolutely! That's a really subtle but important point. By incorporating familiar interfaces and real-world analogs, you can take advantage of existing user knowledge, but you're relying on the user having *that knowledge* to some extent. If you target an international audience, you need to keep each audience in mind when you localize your application. For example, if one group of users' paper calendars always start on Monday (versus Sunday) and you're trying to mirror the paper calendar look, getting the starting day wrong can be pretty jarring (and break the very familiarity you're trying to achieve).

Q: I've meant to ask this for a while, but is stuffing images in the database really a good idea?

A: For our application it's OK because it simplifies things, but in general you might want to go with something a little more scalable. One option is to have the image wrapped in its own Core Data entity that's lazy-fetched rather than part of our main

Fugitive entity. An even better option is to store the image on the file system and just keep a URL (path) to it in the Core Data entity. Neither of these approaches would be major changes to what we've done so far but would give you better scalability as the number (and size) of the images grow.

Q: Is it normal to come back and do the UI after you've implemented functionality?

A: It's normal to come back and theme the UI after you have functionality in place, but you definitely shouldn't leave the rough UI work until the end. Things that seem like neat UI "innovations" turn out to be really difficult to use or annoying after the first few minutes. It's also very common to realize that you really want Functionality X to be "right here" while you're using Functionality Y. Something that was just two taps away now seems very distracting to constantly move in and out of views to reach. These are the kinds of things that are difficult to find without working prototypes of the UI and really can't be put off until later. Styling a navigation bar with a leather texture can wait— figuring out the basic UI flow through critical use cases can't.

Q: How come we aren't using any detail indicators in the table view?

A: Good question! Since pushing the detail view doesn't involve changing views in the iPad, we aren't going to have a disclosure indicator. Remember, disclosure indicators mean that there is another view that will displace the current one. Since the table view list isn't going anywhere, it isn't appropriate.

The app works great! Now we need to add the custom stuff, right?

Yes!

The app works, everything updates, and now it's time to add the UI on top. This is going to add that touch of realism that makes the app easier to use and takes advantage of the iPad's capabilities.

We also need to do something about what happens when there isn't any data—empty map views and image views don't look very good.

Pull it all together

When we first sketched up a view, we said that we needed some "UI goodness" and had a couple of ideas about what that would mean, like a corkboard background, for instance.

One important thing to realize is that a lot of what we'll do here is *styling*. That's important, and will make a difference, but on more complicated applications, you need to think not just about how things look, but how users will interact with your application. We're giving our UI a natural *look*, but for bigger applications, you need to think about a natural *feel* too.

To make this app really look good, all those added elements need to work together, and they'll work to create a **theme**.

More UI goodness—cool page background that looks like a corkboard

Unifying the custom stuff

More than just adding some touches of realism, like we talked about with NUIs, we're going to put together a unified look, or **theme**, for the app. A UI theme consists of fonts, images, colors, and backgrounds that all work together to create a consistent look for an app.

Look and feel goes beyond just images and colors, though. Smooth animations, transitions, etc., all play a role and need to be consistent with the look and feel you're trying to achieve. For example, using a page curl transition when you've styled everything to look like brushed metal with steel rivets isn't going to look cool or seem intuitive. It's going to look *and feel* wrong (most likely, the developer just figured out how to do page curls and wanted to throw them in somewhere!).

Creating a consistent look and feel is also where you're likely going to start to need help. App development can be a profession, and while you can work with some small apps on your own, adding final polish may require some design help. For our purposes here though, using the real-world analog of pushpins on a corkboard and an appropriate font will be enough for iBountyHunter.

Authors' note:

We are not designers. We have design help!

Pushpin

Notebook paper feeling

A **dossier**-type font

Our spy-looking font. Looks like a typewriter with bolded text for each item.

Our background

Name: Nick Forsee
ID: 23594
Bounty: 32000
Description: Mean left hook, wanted for drug running.

Placeholder images for missing people and places...

Do this! Download the four images you'll need for the theme. Go to *www.headfirstlabs.com/books/hfiphonedev* and download *corkboard.png*, *RedPushPin.png*, *question_mark.png*, and *silhouette.png*.

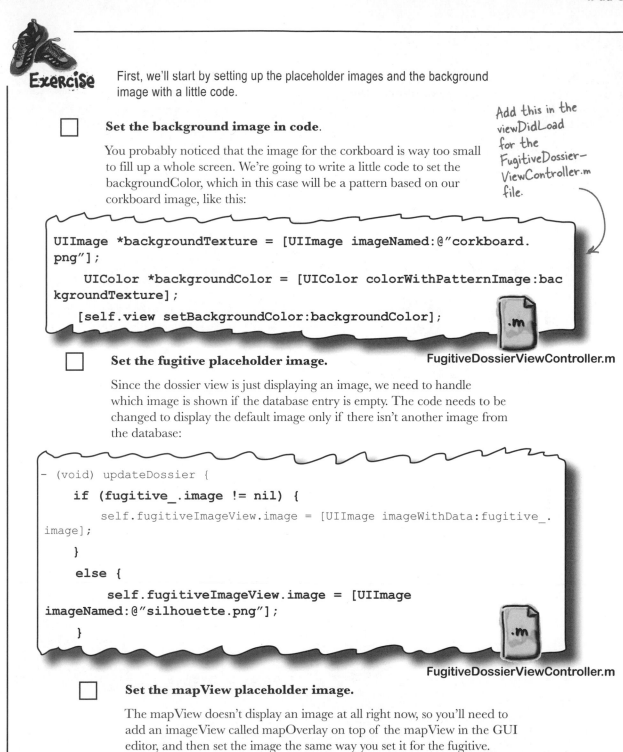

Exercise

First, we'll start by setting up the placeholder images and the background image with a little code.

☐ **Set the background image in code**.

Add this in the viewDidLoad for the FugitiveDossier-ViewController.m file.

You probably noticed that the image for the corkboard is way too small to fill up a whole screen. We're going to write a little code to set the backgroundColor, which in this case will be a pattern based on our corkboard image, like this:

```
UIImage *backgroundTexture = [UIImage imageNamed:@"corkboard.
png"];

    UIColor *backgroundColor = [UIColor colorWithPatternImage:bac
kgroundTexture];

    [self.view setBackgroundColor:backgroundColor];
```

FugitiveDossierViewController.m

☐ **Set the fugitive placeholder image.**

Since the dossier view is just displaying an image, we need to handle which image is shown if the database entry is empty. The code needs to be changed to display the default image only if there isn't another image from the database:

```
- (void) updateDossier {
    if (fugitive_.image != nil) {
        self.fugitiveImageView.image = [UIImage imageWithData:fugitive_.
image];
    }
    else {
        self.fugitiveImageView.image = [UIImage
imageNamed:@"silhouette.png"];
    }
```

FugitiveDossierViewController.m

☐ **Set the mapView placeholder image.**

The mapView doesn't display an image at all right now, so you'll need to add an imageView called mapOverlay on top of the mapView in the GUI editor, and then set the image the same way you set it for the fugitive.

Exercise Solution

First, we'll start by setting up the placeholder images and the background image with a little code.

 Set the mapView placeholder image.

The mapView doesn't display an image at all right now, so you'll need to add an imageView called mapOverlay on top of the mapView in the GUI editor, and then set the image the same way you set it for the fugitive.

Set the background color to white for the image view and set the default image to question_mark.png.

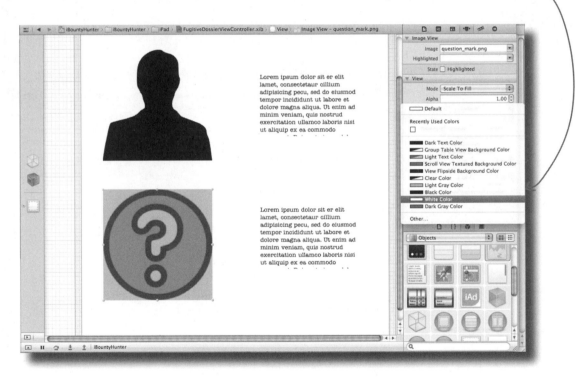

BRAIN BARBELL

If you create a new fugitive without an image or map information, does your new code work? What about for old fugitives?

What, where did the map go? Now it only shows the question mark, no matter what.

In Xcode, these two edges line up.

MKMapView

The question mark image is always on top.

When we created the new imageView in Xcode, we put it on top of the mapView. But we only want the imageView to be the top visible layer if there *isn't any map information*. If you're not used to working with graphics programs for layout (including those to build GUIs), there is a concept at work here that we need to point out.

Graphics programs work with the concept of **layers**. That means you can lay images on top of each other, and they can be completely hidden, partially hidden, or partially shown. Views work the same way. Each view can have multiple subviews stacked (layered) in a specific order.

In iBountyHunter, when there is map information, we need to hide the imageView. We can do this in code.

TEST DRIVE

Add the bolded code to FugitiveDossierViewController.m inside the updateDossier method to get the imageView out of the way depending on whether we have map information.

Put this code inside the updateDossier code to fix the overlay issues.

```
    self.mapView.region = mapRegion;
    self.mapView.mapType = MKMapTypeHybrid;
    self.mapOverlay.hidden = YES;
}
else {
    self.mapOverlay.hidden = NO;
```

FugitiveDossierViewController.m

Test Drive

Add the bolded code to FugitiveDossierViewController.m inside the
updateDossier method to get the imageView out of the way depending on
whether we have map information.

*Go ahead and
click around. If
you have data for
a fugitive, the
images will switch.*

*Once you select
a fugitive, this
text should be
populated...*

This is
looking good, but
what about formatting
the text and the notebook
paper with the push pin?

Remember this?

A **dossier**-type font

It seems we have a problem...

UITextView has some limits. Go into Xcode and highlight one of the UITextViews, then you can see what changes you can make. Among other things, you can change the font type:

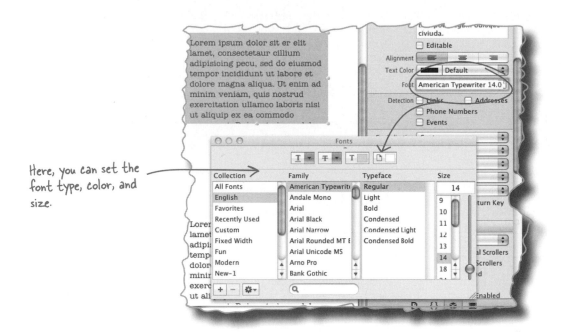

Here, you can set the font type, color, and size.

...you can only change things for the entire field!

Although the text view has served our purposes so far, introducing the requirement to be able to bold just one word means that we need to change our view. UITextViews can be formatted through a recent addition to iOS called NSAttributedString, but these are not for the faint of heart. If you want to start treating any of the text differently (color, bold, underlining, etc.), you need to amp things up a little. Rather than going the NSAttributeString route, we can take advantage of everyone's favorite markup language, HTML, with some styling through CSS.

There's another control for this kind of thing...

UIWebview has lots of options

Although inserting a web view might not be your first thought, it's often one of the best ways to handle complex text formatting. Web views not only allow you to embed material on the web directly into your app without leaving and going into Safari, but you can also load from HTML/CSS files that you ship (or generate) as part of your application.

UIWebViews are basically Safari in a box—not only can they render HTML, they can also be used to embed lots of document types, including Microsoft Office and Apple's iWork office suite (Pages, Numbers, and Keynote), PDFs, and RTF documents.

In short, anything Safari can render, a WebView can render too, inside your application. More than just a developer convenience, this can also be really important for user flow.

Fireside Chats

Tonight's talk: **We need more options!**

UIWebView:

Well UITextView, I guess you've outlived your usefulness.

That's true, you're really good at what you do, it's just...well, you're so limited.

All true, but it really starts to fall apart when you need to get fancy. Developers who use me get HTML5 and CSS3 support, not to mention the ability to show PDF, Word, Excel, Keynote, Numbers, and PowerPoint files.

UITextView:

What? I've been performing great.

That's not true. Without any code at all, you can cut and paste, scroll through text, select text, and search it.

That's true, but I'm a whole lot simpler. And if you really want fancy colors and whatnot, you can get there if you try hard enough.

UIWebView:

But I'm much more than just fancy colors. With CSS, you get all the styling and layout support you get with normal web development—and you can use the same tool. Not only that, but you can use JavaScript for interactivity.

Actually, you can give me a string, too— it just has to be an HTML string. I also support loading local resources like embedded CSS files, images, JavaScript, or even full HTML files.

Hmm.. not really. I can show HTML forms and things like that, but no, I guess I really don't fit for text editing or things like that.

Oh yeah. Like I said, basically anything you can do with a web page you can do with me in terms of interacting with the user. As for interacting with the rest of the application, that's a little tricker. I have a couple of delegate methods that get called when I need to know if I can follow a link that the application can use to move information out, and I can evaluate any JavaScript the application sends me and return the results. But, admittedly, it's not quite as simple as just manipulating a string.

I can live with that. I'm like a browser in a box, you're more of a...souped-up Text Field.

UITextView:

But we're talking about jamming a web browser into the application. You can just hand me a string and I'm good to go, you don't need to go and load a website or anything.

Interesting. OK, can you edit the text?

Can you interact with the user or the rest of the application at all?

Here's what I think. I think I'm more about straightforward text editing, you're more about style.

I liked how I put it better.

HTML, CSS, and Objective-C

Using a UIWebView is like a cross between a website with basic HTML/CSS and Objective-C. All three of these things work together to create the view that the user is going to see.

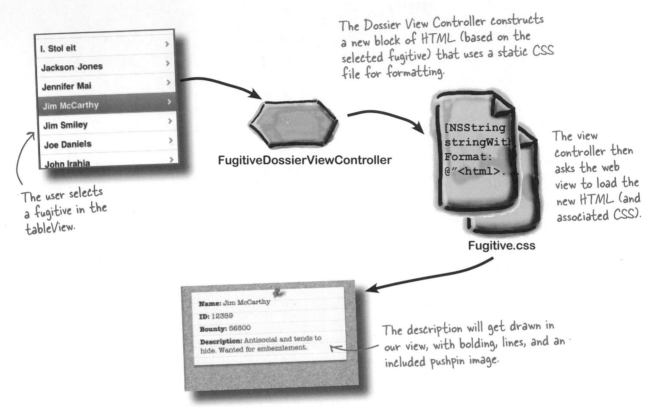

The Dossier View Controller constructs a new block of HTML (based on the selected fugitive) that uses a static CSS file for formatting.

FugitiveDossierViewController

The view controller then asks the web view to load the new HTML (and associated CSS).

Fugitive.css

The user selects a fugitive in the tableView.

The description will get drawn in our view, with bolding, lines, and an included pushpin image.

Using UIWebView

For our purposes, we're going to need to generate an HTML version of our fugitive description and last known location. We can then apply some basic CSS to get it to look however we want. We're going to be working with CSS to actually draw the notebook paper area within the view, so it won't be an image. We're also going to set up the pushpin image directly from the CSS so it will stay within the WebView and move and scale as needed for the view.

To do this we're going to need to make a couple of changes. First, we need to swap out our text views for UIWebViews. That's pretty straightforward.

Next, we need to generate the HTML. We can use NSString's stringWithFormat to do that. Normally it's a lot easier to write the HTML and CSS you want and get things set up using a Web Browser or any other HTML editing tool, and then move it into code. We came up with HTML that looks like what you see on the opposite page:

You don't need to be an HTML and CSS genius to follow along here. But our friendly editor would be remiss if she didn't use this moment to shamelessly plug "Head First HTML with CSS and XHTML" for those who'd like to learn more...

We'll get into more detail about the CSS in a minute...

```
<html>
  <link rel="stylesheet" type="text/css" href="fugitive.css"/>
  <body>

    <dl class="dossier">
      <dt>Name:</dt><dd>%@</dd>
      <dt>ID:</dt><dd>%@</dd>
      <dt>Bounty:</dt><dd>%@</dd>
      <dt>Description:</dt><dd>%@</dd>
    </dl>
  </body>
</html>
```

Here we load our fugitive style sheet. We'll bundle that with our application and load it right from the app bundle.

We'll use an HTML definition list with a custom class. The web view handles the rest.

Finally, we'll need to tell the new WebViews to load our dynamic HTML by using loadHTMLString. We want to use our local CSS file, so we need to give the WebView a code format baseURL that points to our application bundle. After that, the WebView handles the rest. Let's get that going...

Exercise

First we'll get the HTML and webViews working to replace the textViews. Leave out the CSS link code for now, we'll get to that in a minute.

① Delete the two text views and replace them with UIWebViews.
Turn off "User Interaction Enabled" and uncheck "opaque" in the Utilities pane for both UI WebView. Don't forget to handle the IBOutlets to these views as well. You'll need to change their types in the header and then reconnect them in Interface Builder. Finally, set their background color to clear in viewDidLoad.

② Refactor the code for the prepareFugitiveDescription.
We'll need to prepare the fugitive description with HTML and then we'll #define a constant to handle the case when we don't have a fugitive.

For now, leave out the CSS link while we get the view working.

③ Refactor the code for the prepareMapDescription.
We'll need to prepare the fugitive description with HTML and then we'll #define a constant to handle the case when we don't have a fugitive's position.

④ Load the HTML text in updateDossier and viewDidLoad.
Now that we can create HTML versions of our descriptions, we need to update our updateDossier method and viewDidLoad to tell the WebView to load its content from an HTML string rather than just setting a simple string on the text view like before.

Exercise Solution

First, we'll get the HTML and webViews working to replace the textViews. Leave out the CSS link code for now, we'll get to that in a minute.

1 **Delete the two text views and replace them with UIWebViews.**
Turn off "User Interaction Enabled" and uncheck "opaque" in the Utilities pane for both UI WebViews. Don't forget to handle the IBOutlets to these views as well! You'll need to change their types in the header, then reconnect them in Interface Builder. Finally, set their background color to clear in viewDidLoad:

```
[fugitiveDescription_ setBackgroundColor:[UIColor clearColor]];
[mapDescription_ setBackgroundColor:[UIColor clearColor]];
```

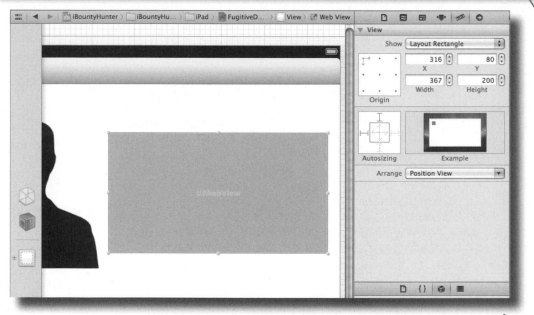

We could set this in Interface Builder too, but where's the fun in that?

Refactor the code for the prepareFugitiveDescription.
We'll need to prepare the fugitive description with HTML and then we'll
#define a constant to handle the case when we don't have a fugitive.

```objc
- (NSString *) prepareFugitiveDescription {
    NSString *response = nil;

    if (self.fugitive) {
        response = [NSString stringWithFormat: @"<html><body><dl
class=\"dossier\"><dt>Name:</dt><dd>%@</dd><dt>ID:</dt><dd>%@</
dd><dt>Bounty:</dt><dd>%@</dd><dt>Description:</dt><dd>%@</dd></dl></
body></html>",

                        fugitive_.name,
                        [fugitive_.fugitiveID stringValue],
                        [fugitive_.bounty stringValue],
                        fugitive_.desc];
    }
    else {
        response = NO_FUGITIVE_SELECTED_HTML;
    }
    return response;
}
```

We use stringWithFormat to populate our generic HTML template with real fugitive data. We could also extract this HTML into a constant to clean this method up even further.

```objc
#define NO_FUGITIVE_SELECTED_HTML @"<html><body><dl
class=\"dossier\"><dt>No fugitive selected.</dt><dd></dd></dl></
body></html>";
```

FugitiveDossierViewController.m

If we don't have a fugitive selected, we just use static HTML.

First, we'll get the HTML and webViews working to replace the textViews. Leave out the CSS link code for now, we'll get to that in a minute.

Exercise Solution

③ Refactor the code for the prepareMapDescription.

We'll need to prepare the fugitive description with HTML and then we'll #define a constant to handle the case when we don't have a fugitive's position.

```
- (NSString *) prepareMapDescription {
    NSString *response = nil;
    if (self.fugitive && self.fugitive.lastSeenDesc) {
        response = [NSString stringWithFormat: @"<html><body><dl
class=\"dossier\"><dt>Last Seen:</dt><dd>%6.3f, %6.3f</
dd><dt>Description:</dt><dd>%@</dd></dl></body></html>",
                    [fugitive_.lastSeenLat doubleValue],
                    [fugitive_.lastSeenLon doubleValue],
                    fugitive_.lastSeenDesc];
    }
    else if (self.fugitive) {
        response = NO_KNOWN_LOCATION_HTML;
    }
    else {
        response = NO_FUGITIVE_SELECTED_HTML;
    }

    return response;
}
```

Just like in prepareFugitiveDescription, we just use a static HTML template and populate it with real fugitive data.

```
#define NO_KNOWN_LOCATION_HTML @"<html><body><dl
class=\"dossier\"><dt>No last known location.</dt><dd></dd></dl></
body></html>";
```

This constant is for when we have a fugitive selected, but don't have a last known location.

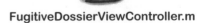

FugitiveDossierViewController.m

4 **Load the HTML text in updateDossier and viewDidLoad.**
Now that we can create HTML versions of our descriptions, we need to update our updateDossier method and viewDidLoad to tell the WebView to load its content from an HTML string rather than just setting a simple string on the text view like before.

Here, we get a URL to our application bundle so the WebView can find the fugitive.css file we reference in our HTML.

```
NSString *path = [[NSBundle mainBundle] bundlePath];

    NSURL *baseURL = [NSURL fileURLWithPath:path];

    [fugitiveDescription_ loadHTMLString:[self
prepareFugitiveDescription] baseURL:baseURL];

    [mapDescription_ loadHTMLString:[self prepareMapDescription]
baseURL:baseURL];
```

Once we have the baseURL, we simply ask the WebView to load the generated HTML string with the fugitive information.

FugitiveDossierViewController.m

Test Drive

The refactoring should be complete. The formatting isn't done yet (that will happen with the CSS), but for now, the webViews should be in place and functioning...

We set the background to clear, but other than that, it still looks pretty much the same...

Use CSS for the remaining formatting

Now we're ready to get into the CSS. We have a bunch of things we need to accomplish with the formatting, and all of it's going to happen inside this CSS file:

- Bolding for each of the line items in the fugitive description

- A paper-like note card with background lines

- The typewriter-looking font

- Adding a pushpin on top of the note card paper

Formatting Text Up Close

Here's our stylesheet that we'll use for formatting the text in our webview.

```css
dl.dossier
{
    min-width: 300px;
    min-height: 150px;
    -webkit-box-shadow: rgba(0, 0, 0, 0.5) 0 0.3em 0.3em 0;
    background-image: -webkit-gradient(linear, 0% 0%, 0% 100%, color-
stop(95%, #FAFAFA), color-stop(95%, #FAFAFA), color-stop(100%, #DDF));
    background-size: 1.6em 1.6em;
        margin: 0;
        padding: .5em;
    font-family: "AmericanTypewriter";
}

.dossier dt
{
    padding-right: .2em;
    display: run-in;
    font-weight: bold;
}

.dossier dd
{
    margin-top: .5em;
    margin-left: .5em;
    margin-right: .5em;
    padding-right: .5em;
}


.dossier:after
{
    display:block;
    content:"";
    position:absolute;
    width: 50px;
    height: 35px;
    background: transparent url(pushpin.png);
    top: -.05em;
    left: 50%;
}
```

At the top level, we have a definition list with a dossier class. We do a little fancy CSS to get a notebook-looking background without needing an image.

Here's where we set the typewriter font that we want for all of our text.

The remainder of our styles are pretty simple—a bold font and some padding and layout information.

And here we drop in the pushpin. Again, we do this in CSS so that the WebView handles everything. We could have laid another UIImageView on top, but then we would have had to coordinate the two in code.

.CSS

Fugitive.css

Test Drive

This is it! Go to *www.headfirstlabs.com/books/hfiphonedev* and get the fugitive.css file and add it to the /SupportingFiles directory. Then add the following HTML right after the <html> tag in the four locations in FugitiveDossierViewController where you generate the map and fugitive descriptions:

```
<link rel=\"stylesheet\" type=\"text/css\" href=\"fugitive.css\" />
```

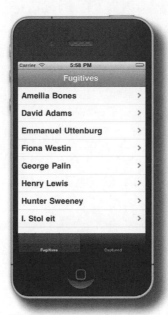

> I love it! Now I can use all this information to track down my fugitives and catch them faster!

Justice is served!

Bob is really happy, and this is a great universal app. Two completely different use cases have been handled: catching the fugitive and reporting it, as well as researching the fugitive in detail.

There's only one database to maintain, but two totally different views, and the code is shared, so making updates should be a breeze.

Congrats!

NUI Cross

This is it! Exercise your vocab skills and make sure
you learned some new lingo...

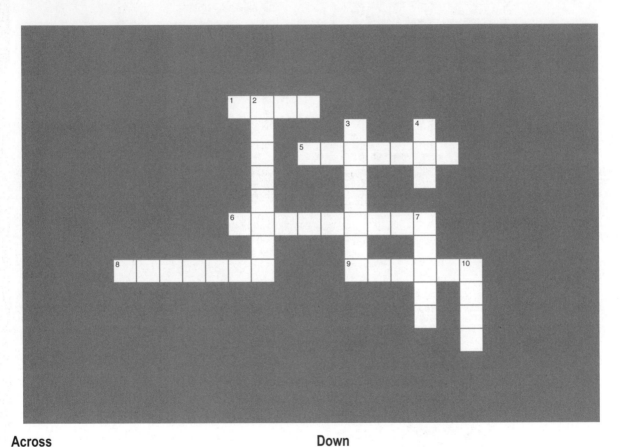

Across

1. WebViews can be laid out with _____.
5. _____ in UI helps users figure out how to work with the app.
6. iPhones and iPads have _____ use cases.
8. This type of view displays text with lots of formatting options.
9. Views are constructed with _____.

Down

2. This displays text, but has limited formatting options.
3. This kind of interface is preferable for iPad.
4. Webviews are formatted with ___.
7. The unifying design for an app is sometimes called a _____.
10. Text in TextViews must be formatted the _____.

Your NUI Toolbox

You've got Chapter 11 under your belt and now you've added iPad user interface skills to your toolbox.

NUIs

Leverage users' knowledge of the real world to make learning apps easier.

Use realism and details to make an app feel more familiar.

Custom UIs

Try to be consistent by using a theme.

Fonts, images, and textures all work together to create a theme.

UIWebView

Can talk to local material in the app or the web.

Uses HTML/CSS to format content.

Much more flexible than UITextView for UI touches.

NUI Cross Solution

This is it! Exercise your vocab skills and make sure
you learned some new lingo...

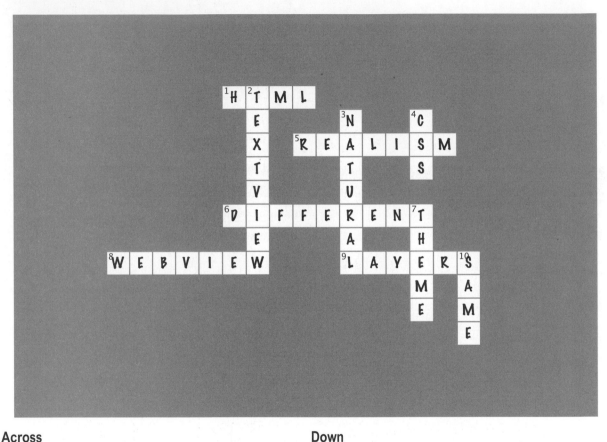

Across

1. WebViews can be laid out with _____. [HTML]
5. _____ in UI helps users figure out how to work with the app. [REALISM]
6. iPhones and iPads have _____ use cases. [DIFFERENT]
8. This type of view displays text with lots of formatting options. [WEBVIEW]
9. Views are constructed with _____. [LAYERS]

Down

2. This displays text, but has limited formatting options. [TEXTVIEW]
3. This kind of interface is preferable for iPad. [NATURAL]
4. Webviews are formatted with ___. [CSS]
7. The unifying design for an app is sometimes called a _____. [THEME]
10. Text in TextViews must be formatted the _____. [SAME]

i leftovers

The top 4 things
(we didn't cover)

Ever feel like something's missing? We know what you mean...

Just when you thought you were done, there's more. We couldn't leave you without a few

extra details, things we just couldn't fit into the rest of the book. At least, not if you want to

be able to carry this book around without a metallic case with castor wheels on the bottom.

So take a peek and see what you (still) might be missing out on.

#1. Internationalization and Localization

iOS devices are sold in over 80 countries and support 30 languages out of the box. Depending on your application, you should consider supporting multiple languages and cultures. Internationalization is the process of identifying the parts of your application that are culture or language-specific and building your app in a way that supports multiple locales. Some of the things you should look at are:

- Nib files (views, labels, button text, etc.)

- Location or culture-specific icons and images such as flags or text

- Included or online help and documentation

- Static text in your application

Once you've identified the culture or language-specific parts of your application, the next step is to localize them. iOS has strong support for localizing resources and separates the localizable resources from the rest of the application so you can easily use a localization team or outsource the effort all together.

Up until now, our resources have been included in our application in the .app directory. Once you start localizing resources, Xcode creates an lproj directory for each localization (locale) you add and moves the locale-specific resources there. For example, if you provide both English and French translations of your nibs, then you will have an en.lproj (or English.lproj) and fr.lproj directories in your application.

You can change your language and locale on iPhone by going into Settings→General→ International.

Localizing nibs

Xcode has built-in support for localizing nibs. Before you start translating anything, you need to ask Xcode to create the locale-specific directories.

Select a nib and pull up the Utilities panel.

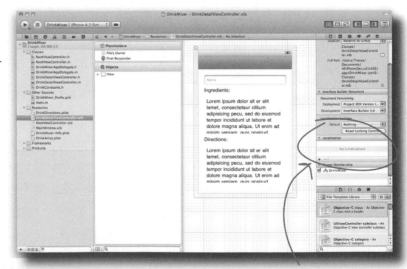

Localization info is here.

Next, click on the + button under the Locialization group. Xcode will turn your nib entry in the project list into a group with each localization listed beneath it. Xcode copies your original nib into your default localization.

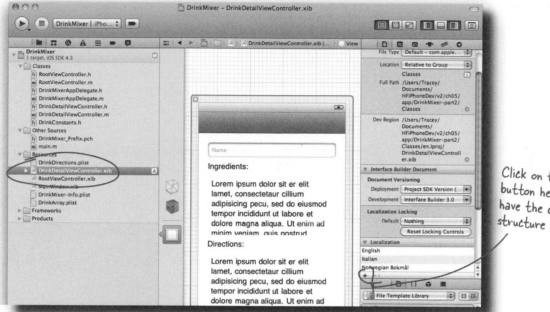

Click on the "+" button here to have the directory structure created.

The next time you click the + button, a drop-down box will appear and you can select any language you want to use. There will be a new nib created for each language.

Just select every country you want here.

Now all you need to do to localize the nib is double-click the language you want to localize and translate any text. Remember that depending on the language, you may need to adjust layout as well.

For large projects, there is a command-line tool called ibtool that you can use to extract all string values from a nib into an external file, then merge translations back into the nib later. This allows for bulk extraction and translation, but you need to be particularly careful about layout issues since you're not visually inspecting each nib. Once a nib has been translated, you can have Interface Builder mark it as locked to prevent any accidental changes to the text or layout that could impact your translations. See Apple's documentation on bundles and nib localization for more information.

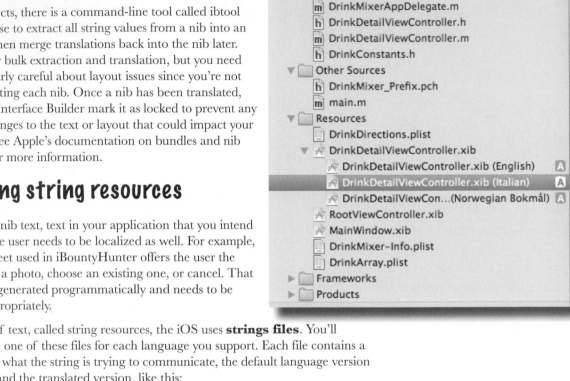

Localizing string resources

In addition to nib text, text in your application that you intend on showing the user needs to be localized as well. For example, the Action Sheet used in iBountyHunter offers the user the option to take a photo, choose an existing one, or cancel. That button text is generated programmatically and needs to be translated appropriately.

For this type of text, called string resources, the iOS uses **strings files**. You'll generally have one of these files for each language you support. Each file contains a description of what the string is trying to communicate, the default language version of the string, and the translated version, like this:

```
/* Confirms a really bad decision. */
"All In" = "All In";

/* Cancels the dialog */
"Cancel" = "Cancel";

/* Title for the important alert view */
"This is important!" = "This is important!";

/* Warns the user about impending badness. */
"This will empty your bank account. Are you sure?" = "This will empty
your bank account. Are you sure?";
```

Each string resource can have a description that helps the translators understand the context of the string.

Then each string has the original string and its translation.

Generating your strings file

You could create your strings file by hand, but a much simpler way is to have Xcode generate it for you. Xcode does this by looking for the localization macros that load the translated text. To support localized strings, you should use one of the NSLocalizedString macros, like this:

The first argument to NSLocalizedString is used as a key into the translations file. This is usually the default language for the string.

The second argument is the comment to be shown with the string in the strings file.

```
- (IBAction) pushMePressed: (id) sender {
    UIAlertView *alertView = [[UIAlertView alloc]
      initWithTitle:NSLocalizedString(@"This is important!",
                              @"Title for the important alert view")
      message:NSLocalizedString(@"This will empty your bank account.  Are you sure?",
                              @"Warns the user about impending badness.")
      delegate:nil
      cancelButtonTitle:NSLocalizedString(@"Cancel", @"Cancels the dialog")
      otherButtonTitles:NSLocalizedString(@"All In",
                              @"Confirms a really bad decision."),
      nil];
    [alertView show];
}
```

If you've used the NSLocalizedString macros in your code, you can generate your strings file simply by running the genstrings command at the command line, like this:

```
genstrings -o English.lproj *.m */*.m
```

You'll want to run this for each translation you support. This will create a file named Localized.strings in the specified locale directory that you can give out to translators. You'll need to add that strings file to your Xcode project like any other resource, but once it's there, the iOS will look in the appropriate strings file at runtime based on the language the users select for their device.

The iOS provides robust localization capabilities, including currency, time, and date presentation support; we've just scratched the surface. Apple provides several documents on internationalization and localization, including the **"Introduction to Internationalization Programming Topics"** document in the Xcode documentation, to help you with more complex scenarios.

Watch it!

iOS caches resources!

If you've installed your app before doing translations, it's likely that the iOS has cached resources so that even after adding translations, you won't see them until you uninstall and reinstall your app!

#2. View animations

If you've spent any time with an iOS device, you know that smooth transitions and graceful animations define the user experience. In the applications we've built so far, we've only touched on a few basic animations (like the flip animation used in iBountyHunter). However, everything from adding and removing table rows to sliding controls around the screen can be animated.

Animating table view updates

If you're going to add or remove multiple rows in a table view, you can ask it to provide a smooth animation (as well as a more efficient handling of updating the table view itself) by sending it the beginUpdates message before you start manipulating the data, then an endUpdates when you're finished, like this:

```
[self.tableView beginUpdates];
[self.tableView insertRowsAtIndexPaths:insertIndexPaths
    withRowAnimation:UITableViewRowAnimationRight];

[self.tableView deleteRowsAtIndexPaths:deleteIndexPaths
    withRowAnimation:UITableViewRowAnimationFade];

[self.tableView endUpdates];
```

When inserting multiple rows, you can use the insertRowsAtIndexPaths to tell the tableView the new indexPaths you want to add. The tableView will immediately ask the datasource and delegate for cell information for those new rows and, if you specify the animation information, they'll smoothly slide into the table.

The beginUpdates and endUpdates tell the tableView that you're about to make multiple changes so it won't actually animate anything until it gets the endUpdates call; then everything (the insertions and deletions) will be animated at once.

Animating view and control changes

Similar to table views, UIViews have built-in support for smoothly animating changes to several of their properties. You simply need to tell the view that you want it to animate a change by sending it the beginAnimations message, describing the end point of the change, and then asking it to start the transition by sending it the commitAnimations message. The following UIView properties can be animated automatically:

UIView property	Description
frame	The physical rectangle that describes the view—the view's origin and size—in the superview's coordinate system
bounds	The origin and size of the view in local coordinates
centerpoint	The center of the view in the superview's coordinates
transform	Any transformations (rotations, translations, etc.) applied to the view
alpha	The transparency of the view

#3. Accelerometer

One of the most versatile pieces of hardware in iOS devices is the accelerometer. The accelerometer allows the device to detect acceleration and the pull of gravity along three axes. With just a few lines of code, you can tell whether the device is right-side up, upside down, laying flat on a table, etc. You can even detect how quickly the device is changing direction.

All you need is the UIAccelerometer

Getting orientation information from your device is straightforward. There's a shared UIAccelerometer instance you can access. Like many other iOS classes, the UAccelerometer has a delegate protocol, UIAccelerometerDelegate, that declares a single method for receiving acceleration information. The class you want to receive that acceleration information should conform to the UIAccelerometerDelegate protocol and implement didAccelerate: method.

```
- (void)accelerometer:(UIAccelerometer *)accelerometer
didAccelerate:(UIAcceleration *)acceleration;
```

You'll receive a reference to the accelerometer along with an instance of a UIAcceleration class, which contains the actual acceleration information.

To receive acceleration information, you simply need to tell the accelerometer about the delegate and how frequently to send acceleration information, like this:

```
self.accelerometer = [UIAccelerometer sharedAccelerometer];
self.accelerometer.delegate = self;
self.accelerometer.updateInterval = 0.5f;
```

Get the shared accelerometer...

...then configure the delegate and an update rate in seconds. We're asking for two updates a second.

Each UIAcceleration object contains acceleration information along the x, y, and z axes and a timestamp indicating when the data was collected. In a simple example, you can update labels with the acceleration information, like this:

```
- (void)accelerometer:(UIAccelerometer *)accelerometer
didAccelerate:(UIAcceleration *)acceleration {
    self.xOutput.text = [NSString stringWithFormat:@"%.4f", acceleration.x];
    self.yOutput.text = [NSString stringWithFormat:@"%.4f", acceleration.y];
    self.zOutput.text = [NSString stringWithFormat:@"%.4f", acceleration.z];
}
```

Understanding device acceleration

First, the bad news. The simulator doesn't simulate the accelerometer at all. You'll get no information back, regardless of how much you shake your Mac. You need to install the application on a real device to get actual accelerometer information back. But once you do...

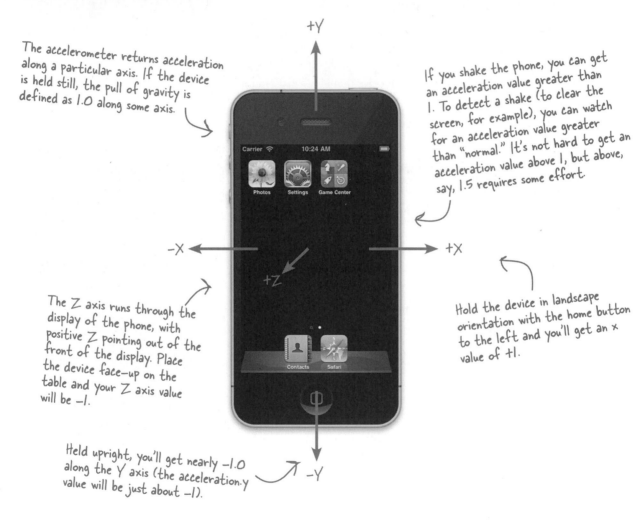

The accelerometer returns acceleration along a particular axis. If the device is held still, the pull of gravity is defined as 1.0 along some axis.

If you shake the phone, you can get an acceleration value greater than 1. To detect a shake (to clear the screen, for example), you can watch for an acceleration value greater than "normal." It's not hard to get an acceleration value above 1, but above, say, 1.5 requires some effort.

The Z axis runs through the display of the phone, with positive Z pointing out of the front of the display. Place the device face-up on the table and your Z axis value will be −1.

Hold the device in landscape orientation with the home button to the left and you'll get an x value of +1.

Held upright, you'll get nearly −1.0 along the Y axis (the acceleration.y value will be just about −1).

If you're building a typical view-based application, UIKit hides a lot of the need for the accelerometer by letting you know about orientation changes and automatically providing undo/redo when the user shakes the phone. The accelerometer is most useful for custom-drawn applications like games (steering or balance) and utility applications (for example, levels).

#4. A word or two about gaming...

iOS games are a huge market and get played a lot, but they're also pretty advanced applications. It's outside of the scope of our book to get into those applications—which can use multi-touch interactions, Quartz and OpenGL graphics, and peer-to-peer networking—but here, we'll give you a quick pass at the technologies that you can use and where to find more information about them.

Multi-touch

You probably noticed that we only used one of the possible events that can be triggered for a button in our apps, the **touch up inside** event. iOS is capable of detecting up to five finger touches at a time and can interpret how each of those fingers is interacting with the screen with several different types of events.

In addition to touches, iOS can detect swipes and gestures that can be configured as well. By defining the length and direction of a swipe, you can create lots of different ways to interact with your application.

Pinching is a custom gesture that Apple uses in many of its default applications, most notably Safari, to zoom in and out of a view. It is just registering for a two-finger touch and keeping track of the change in the distance between them: If it increases, zoom out, if it decreases, zoom in.

Using these events means you can create custom interfaces—not just touching buttons—for your user. Working with multi-touch means that your view needs to be configured to be a multi-touch view, and then you need code to work with each different type of event you're interested in leveraging.

Working with these events requires working with the responder chain (see the UIResponder class reference) and the UIEvents class reference.

These are all the button events than can be triggered.

Button
▼ Sent Events
Did End On Exit
Editing Changed
Editing Did Begin
Editing Did End
Touch Cancel
Touch Down
Touch Down Repeat
Touch Drag Enter
Touch Drag Exit
Touch Drag Inside
Touch Drag Outside
Touch Up Inside
Touch Up Outside
Value Changed
▼ Referencing Outlets
New Referencing Outlet
▼ Referencing Outlet Collections
New Referencing Outlet Collection

Quartz and OpenGL

Quartz and OpenGL are the two ways to create graphics on iOS, and they're both big enough to be books on their own. Here's a small sample of what you'd be dealing with:

Quartz

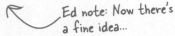

Ed note: Now there's a fine idea...

Quartz is the simpler of the two, allowing you to draw in two dimensions directly into the view. The drawing code uses the Core Graphics Framework and renders directly into the view. It follows a **painter's model**, which means that the order of commands is important. The first thing drawn will be covered up with a subsequent drawing in the same location. Quartz can handle shading, color, and interfacing with other image and video types.

The **Quartz 2D Programming Guide** in the developer documentation has a lot of information to help get you started.

OpenGL

OpenGL can work in two or three-dimensional graphics and is significantly more complex, but that means that you have more flexibility to work with. It is a well-established, cross-platform library that has been implemented for mobile devices with OpenGL ES, and it's used through the OpenGL ES Framework.

You can use it to draw lines, polygons, and objects, and animate them as well. A good place to get started is with the **OpenGL ES Programming Guide for iOS** in the developer documentation.

Game Kit

New with the iOS 3, the Game Kit framework allows you to use both peer-to-peer networking and voiceover bluetooth to facilitate interaction with other devices within game play. This functionality does not exist for the first generation iPhone, iPod Touch, or the simulator alone.

Similar to the image picker, there is a GKPeerPickerController that provides a standard interface for finding other devices running your application and establishing a connection. After that connection is established, you can transmit data or voice between devices.

A good place to get started is with the **Game Kit Programming Guide** to leverage this new functionality in your app.

ii preparing an app for distribution

Get ready for the App Store

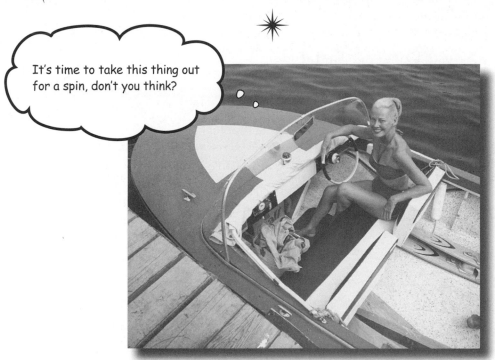

It's time to take this thing out for a spin, don't you think?

You want to get your app in the App Store, right?

So far, we've basically worked with apps in the simulator, which is fine. But to get things to the next level, you'll need to install an app on an actual iPhone, iPad, or iPod Touch before applying to get it in the App Store. And the only way to do that is to register with Apple as a developer. Even then, it's not just a matter of clicking a button in Xcode to get an app you wrote on your personal device. To do that, it's time to talk with Apple.

Apple has rules

We've talked about the HIG and how stringent Apple can be throughout the approval process—they're protecting their platform. Part of that requires keeping track of what goes on your own device, even when it's stuff you've written yourself.

Here, we're going to give you an overview of how you can get an app onto your device, and then, in turn, ready for submission. We can't get into the nitty gritty of the full process—for that, you need to be a member of the iOS Development Program and pay the $99 fee.

> The iOS Development Guide in the Xcode documentation has some more good information that you can look at before you join the Development Program.

Start at the Apple Developer Portal

The Developer Portal, where you first downloaded the SDK, is also your hub for managing all the parts of electronic signatures that you'll need to get an app up and running on your iOS device.

First, get your Development Certificate

Getting through the process to go from having your app in Xcode to installing it on an iPhone, iPad, or iPod Touch for testing requires a Development Certificate and a Provisioning Profile. This certificate is signed by you and Apple to register you as a developer. It creates a public and a private key, and the private key is stored on the keychain app on your Mac. Here's how getting that certificate works.

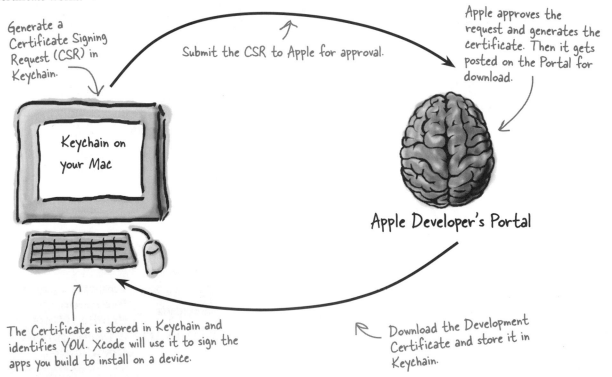

Generate a Certificate Signing Request (CSR) in Keychain.

Submit the CSR to Apple for approval.

Apple approves the request and generates the certificate. Then it gets posted on the Portal for download.

Keychain on your Mac

Apple Developer's Portal

The Certificate is stored in Keychain and identifies YOU. Xcode will use it to sign the apps you build to install on a device.

Download the Development Certificate and store it in Keychain.

The Provisioning Profile pulls it all together

Now that you have a Development Certificate in place, to complete the process, you need a Provisioning Profile. That electronic document ties the app (through a UDID), the developer, and the certificate together for installation onto the device.

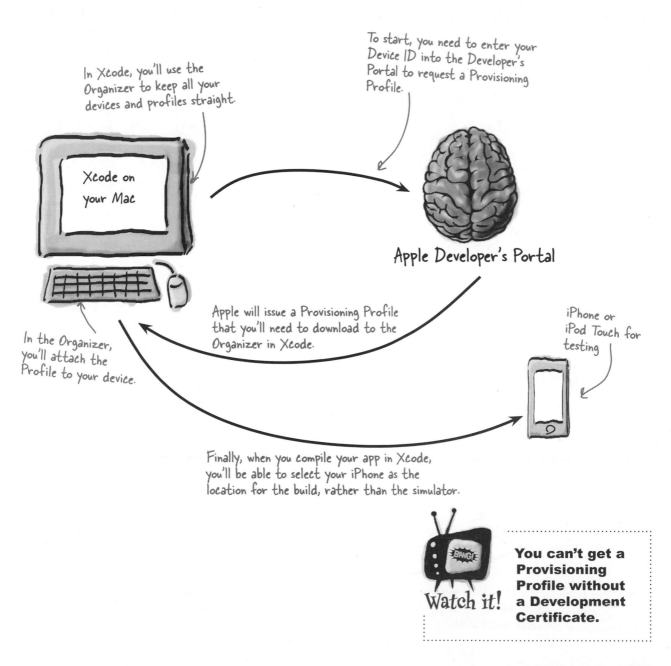

In Xcode, you'll use the Organizer to keep all your devices and profiles straight.

To start, you need to enter your Device ID into the Developer's Portal to request a Provisioning Profile.

Xcode on your Mac

Apple Developer's Portal

In the Organizer, you'll attach the Profile to your device.

Apple will issue a Provisioning Profile that you'll need to download to the Organizer in Xcode.

iPhone or iPod Touch for testing

Finally, when you compile your app in Xcode, you'll be able to select your iPhone as the location for the build, rather than the simulator.

BANG!

Watch it!

You can't get a Provisioning Profile without a Development Certificate.

Keep track in the Organizer

The Organizer is a tool that comes with Xcode that we haven't been able to talk much about, but it's key for keeping all this electronic paperwork straight. In Xcode, go to the **Window→Organizer** menu option.

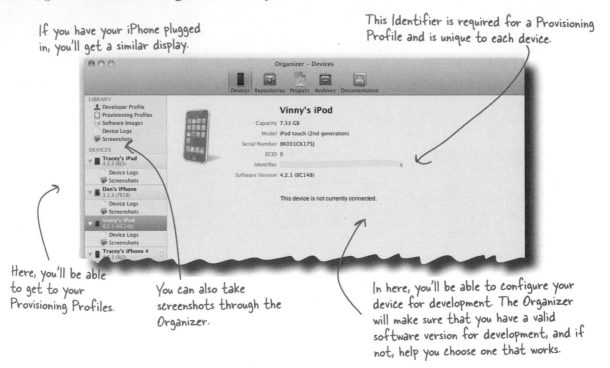

If you have your iPhone plugged in, you'll get a similar display.

This Identifier is required for a Provisioning Profile and is unique to each device.

Here, you'll be able to get to your Provisioning Profiles.

You can also take screenshots through the Organizer.

In here, you'll be able to configure your device for development. The Organizer will make sure that you have a valid software version for development, and if not, help you choose one that works.

A few final tips...

This quick overview gives you an idea of how the process works, but you need to get into the Developer Program to learn all the details. Our goal here was just to help you see the big picture of the process.

There are a couple of things to be aware of. First, when you're developing as part of a team, the team admin has to be involved in many of these steps. Second, you need to go through this process to install *anything* on your device, regardless of whether you plan to release it to the world or not.

And finally, what about the app store? Once you've joined the Developer Program and the application has been tested, then you can submit it for approval.

> **More Information**
>
> After you've joined the Developer Program, get into the Developer's Portal and look for the iPhone Development Program User Guide.
>
> It has a lot of good information to get you through the process.

Index

Symbols

A

N

T

U

Get even more for your money.

Join the O'Reilly Community, and register the O'Reilly books you own.It's free, and you'll get:

- 40% upgrade offer on O'Reilly books
- Membership discounts on books and events
- Free lifetime updates to electronic formats of books
- Multiple ebook formats, DRM FREE
- Participation in the O'Reilly community
- Newsletters
- Account management
- 100% Satisfaction Guarantee

Signing up is easy:

1. **Go to: oreilly.com/go/register**
2. **Create an O'Reilly login.**
3. **Provide your address.**
4. **Register your books.**

Note: English-language books only

To order books online:

oreilly.com/order_new

For questions about products or an order:

orders@oreilly.com

To sign up to get topic-specific email announcements and/or news about upcoming books, conferences, special offers, and new technologies:

elists@oreilly.com

For technical questions about book content:

booktech@oreilly.com

To submit new book proposals to our editors:

proposals@oreilly.com

Many O'Reilly books are available in PDF and several ebook formats. For more information:

oreilly.com/ebooks

O'REILLY®

Spreading the knowledge of innovators   www.oreilly.com

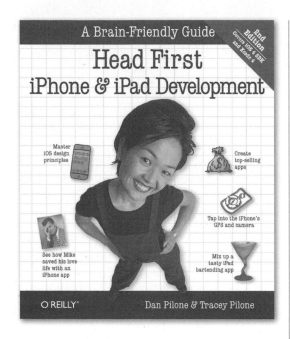